# THE
# TREASURES OF LANCASHIRE

*Norman B. Borough*

North West Civic Trust

© North West Civic Trust 1989

Published by the North West Civic Trust
        Environmental Institute
        Greaves School
        Bolton Road
        Swinton
        Manchester M27 2UX
        England

ISBN 0 901347 49 X

Text and photographs by Norman Bilsborough

Line drawings by Stephen Essex

Other titles by NWCT:
        *The Treasures of Cheshire*
        *Guide Across Manchester*

Printed by Shanley Printers Limited, Bolton

*Front Cover:*   *The Ashton Memorial, Lancaster*

*Back Cover:*   *Rufford Old Hall, West Lancashire*

# CONTENTS

Eaton Hall · Chester

# FOREWORD

Lancashire is surely a very special county, rich in people and places, and endowed with a distinct and powerful character. Although its name came relatively late onto the historical scene, it more than made up for that by its unparalleled contribution to our country's industrial and economic growth in the 18th and 19th centuries and to the widespread and far-reaching social reforms born of that revolution. The position of pre-eminence which it established then has, in fact, never been wholly lost, for within the boundaries of the 'old' Lancashire we can see again the sign of native resourcefulness adapting to meet the challenges of a new age.

It is heartening to see a new confidence emerging and I believe it is no accident that this stems from a growing appreciation of the county's heritage, and of how best to use it. We simply cannot afford to ignore what has been handed down to us, and when therefore the opportunity arose for me to help the North West Civic Trust give birth to this book, I was delighted to do so. It was not only to do with my family's past and growing associations with Lancashire, it was also the conviction that the Trust would do for Lancashire what it has already done so well for Cheshire — entertain and instruct a wide audience on the treasures which the county contains and, in so doing, help to raise its profile.

I believe that this book is a timely reminder of the value and importance of what our forefathers created. I commend it to you, the reader, unequivocally.

**THE DUKE OF WESTMINSTER**

# PREFACE

The Treasures of Lancashire is the product of a team effort, and the team has had many members. Parish clerks, officers of civic societies, local historians, school-teachers, landowners and farmers — these and others willingly opened their doors, shared their knowledge, acted as guides and mentors and otherwise helped us understand and piece together the making of the County and its rich resources. It is not possible to name them here, but we are most grateful for all their contributions to the shaping of the book, as we are to all those involved in its production.

The team has done well, but without financial backing and effective leadership it simply would not have functioned, nor would the book have come about. That it has happened at all is a tribute to the generosity of the Duke of Westminster, whose enlightened sponsorship enabled the Trust to embark on this enterprise — we are deeply indebted to him for seeing the 'common ground' and enabling us to turn our ideas into action. That it has taken such pleasing shape is a tribute to the author, Norman Bilsborough, whose considerable talents have been committed tirelessly to the task of researching, writing and designing this book. The Trust is indebted to him too, and I'm sure that his skill and diligence will be rewarded by a sense of genuine achievement and by the knowledge that the book will give pleasure to many.

To Norman we owe thanks for the photography also. Stephen Essex has again served the Trust well with his illustrative work, and Maureen Nugent's word-processing and proof-reading have been an important part of the production process.

The Treasures of Lancashire is not a specialist work. It is a book designed for everyone, a celebration of a great county, and one which deals not only with its familiar riches but also with the hidden or forgotten. I hope that it will be enjoyed and treasured by many.

**Alan Edwards**
Director, North West Civic Trust

*Croxteth Hall, Merseyside*

# CHAPTER 1 : LANCASHIRE — THE LAND OF PLENTY

The truly fascinating thing about **Lancashire** is its tremendous diversity, and the fact that it has something to offer for everyone. It has of course a wide range of physical environments, from the isolated moorlands of East Lancashire to the cultivated lowlands of the Fylde, and from the enclosed intimacy of its river valleys to the wide open spaces of the coastal plain. It has too some marvellous variations of architectural expression, from the humble weavers' cottages of its traditional textile areas to the historic mansions of its towns and cities. Then also it has a remarkable tale to tell in terms of its social and economic experience — the subjugation of the land, the development of industry, and the growth of trade, all of which are represented by its many-faceted heritage. In brief, Lancashire 'has the lot', something for everyone, whether they be the long-term resident or the passing visitor.

## A Brief History

Whilst Lancashire is certainly an attractive area to settle in now this has not always been the case, and centuries ago it was physically a rather inhospitable part of the country with many of its lowland areas covered by forest and natural scrub and bordered by meres and extensive peat mosses. These presented a formidable barrier to early potential settlers, who preferred the drier ground of the hills and moors along the eastern edge of what was to become Lancashire. The sparse population to be found in the area thus tended to be concentrated on the more elevated uplands, and evidence of Bronze Age settlement has been found on Winter Hill near Bolton and on the Bleasdale Fells just to the south of the Forest of Bowland, while Warton Crag near Carnforth displays the remains of occupation during the Iron Age period.

Then the Romans appeared on the scene, although their contribution to the area was mainly in terms of the roads which their occupying forces constructed rather than any permanent civilian settlements which were established here. Although the Romans had begun the conquest of Britain in AD 43 it was not until AD 78 that Agricola brought the Twentieth Legion (Valeria Victrix) to what is now Chester with a view to conquering the North West. The following summer saw the start of this campaign, Agricola leading his soldiers northwards across the Mersey and on towards the Ribble and the eastern Pennines. Fortifications were soon built to protect the small garrisons at Ribchester and Manchester, with basic roads being constructed to link these forts with those at Lancaster and Carlisle further north. By the time Hadrian's Wall was completed in AD 128 the permanent road network initiated by Agricola was also essentially in place, although in many respects the Lancashire area played second fiddle to what was to become Yorkshire — the principal roads were to the east of the Pennines and tended to focus on York as the 'capital' of northern Britain.

In the first half of the second century the roads through Lancashire were improved and increased while the forts were made bigger and stronger, although to the Romans this does not seem to have made the area any more attractive. To them Lancashire was rather depressing because of its climate and its distance from Europe, so consequently no Roman villas were built here and very few civilians put down roots. Some Roman traders probably did live for short times in and around the bigger forts, but their occupation was probably no more permanent than that of the soldiers themselves who departed when their tour of duty was finished.

Perhaps of rather more significance is the fact that the Roman forts did often influence the development of later settlements, as is evident at Ribchester, although this was not always the case. Manchester is just one example of a mediaeval town which grew up at some distance from the Roman remains. Despite their apparent lack of interest the Romans still managed to leave behind them some interesting remains, including inscribed altar-stones and tombstones, various coins and pieces of jewellery, and an elaborately carved bronze helmet found at Ribchester as well as a bronze statue of Jupiter from Manchester.

The departure of the Romans may well have raised hopes in the minds of the original British or Celtic inhabitants that they would be able to return to a peaceful existence of their own, but this was not to be. The following centuries saw successive waves of Anglian, Danish and Norse raiders, many of whom settled in the area and left us with distinctive place names which reveal the extent of their relative occupation. The struggle against these invaders culminated in the Battle of Brunanburgh (or Brunaberg) in AD 937, in which Athelstan (grandson of Alfred the Great) defeated a coalition of his enemies and was acknowledged as king of the English. As a consequence the land between the Ribble and the Mersey passed into the hands of the king, remaining as a royal domain until after the Norman Conquest.

Twenty years after the Conquest came the Domesday Survey, providing us with the earliest surviving 'gazetteer' of the Lancashire area. However, of the 1,700 pages in the two volumes of Domesday Book the area between the Ribble and the Mersey only merited one and a half pages of description, and even then this constituted an appendix to the account of Cheshire! This poor coverage was due partly to the fact that 'Lancashire' did not then exist as an administrative unit and partly to its being comparatively poor and sparsely populated.

At the time of the Survey the royal estate between the Ribble and the Mersey was divided into six unequal divisions called 'wapentakes' or hundreds (Newton, Warrington, West Derby, Salford, Leyland and Blackburn), with much of the area being woodland or mossland and only relatively small patches of land being cleared and cultivated. There were no towns at all, with the ten thousand or so inhabitants living in scattered farmhouses or groups of cottages. To the north of the Ribble the land was divided into two extensive wapentakes — Amounderness, centred upon the manor of Preston, and the 'King's land in Yorkshire', which included the Lonsdale area. Much of the land here was 'waste', with only sixteen of the sixty-two berewicks in Amounderness being inhabited. In terms of its ownership the land on both sides of the Ribble was given to Roger of Poitou for his help in the Norman

*Shireburn Almshouses, Ribchester*

1

Conquest, and he in turn rewarded his own supporters with baronies in exchange for their military service.

The predominant occupation of the inhabitants of lowland Lancashire was agriculture, with what cleared land was available being commonly used to grow oats under a field system which opened up the opportunity for tenants and small owners to exist side by side in an early 'enclosure' arrangement. Sheep and cattle farming tended to predominate on the upland areas, with a much more scattered settlement pattern being characteristic. However, much of the countryside remained in an uncultivated condition even into the middle of the 12th century, when the systematic clearance of wood and scrubland began in earnest. An important contribution to this process was made by the monastic orders such as the Cistercians, who founded Whalley Abbey with its extensive sheep farming interests, and the Premonstratensians, who built a small priory at Hornby as well as a larger abbey at Cockersand.

As the countryside was gradually brought under control, and farming and agriculture improved and extended, so markets and fairs began to be established in an increasing number of towns and villages. These institutions were generally created by royal

*St. Peter's Church, Heysham*

charter, often in conjunction with the designation of a town as a borough. InLancashire four boroughs were created by royal charter in the 12th and 13th centuries — Preston in 1179, Lancaster in 1193, Liverpool in 1207 and Wigan in 1246. These four boroughs ruled themselves through mayors, aldermen and burgesses, and they held their own courts as well as regular markets and fairs from which they drew considerable rents.

Fairs and markets were not just limited to boroughs, however, and by the early part of the 14th century most sizeable settlements could boast of the right to hold these events, with several of the markets being held twice

weekly. The growth in farming and commerce throughout Lancashire during mediaeval times, together with the growth in population, was also accompanied by an increase in the building of churches — by the end of the 13th century the number of churches in Lancashire had more than doubled when compared with the number in existence at the time of the Domesday Survey.

Agriculture continued to be the basis of the Lancashire economy well into the 17th century, but within this were the seeds of the county's future industrial prosperity — particularly the early textile industry, which was based upon the production of wool from the sheep flocks of the Lancashire moorlands. Here the relatively unfavourable conditions for agriculture turned the attention of the inhabitants increasingly to the spinning and weaving of woollens, encouraged by the availability of soft water. Whereas wool was primarily a product of the eastern uplands, flax and hemp were grown on the West Lancashire plain providing the basis for a linen industry which was well established by Tudor times.

Initially the majority of woollen producers were yeomen who worked at home with their families, making use of their own wool and being free to sell their cloth to the highest bidder. Then gradually these people came to be employed by clothiers who supplied the raw material and expected to receive the woven cloth in return. Towards the end of the 16th century a few well organised producers became established, particularly in the Manchester and Salford locality, each employing up to a dozen or so people in a textile workshop. This tendency towards specialisation in employment also began to be increasingly commonplace in the dyeing and fulling of cloth, while certain market towns such as Bolton, Bury and Rochdale began to take on a specialist role in the storage and sale of textiles.

Then too, some parts of the county became particularly well known for one type of product rather than another. Southern

*Deane Church, Bolton*

*An early weaving hamlet on the Lancashire fringes*

Lancashire began to specialise in smallwares such as ribbons, garters and haberdashery, while in central and eastern Lancashire fustians came to be particularly prominent. The manufacture of textiles was still primarily a rural occupation even up to the 17th century, but the merchants increasingly congregated in the towns, with Manchester and Salford proving to be particularly important locations. These, then, were some of the tell-tale signs of the future industrial growth which was to hit Lancashire in the 18th and 19th centuries.

In the midst of this came the English Civil War, which must have had a significant disruptive effect on the continuing development of the economy and society in Lancashire even though the majority of the population probably supported neither of the two sides. Traditionally the towns in the south east of the county held out for Parliament while the country gentry were for the King, although soon after fighting started in September 1642 a number of towns on the important north-south route were held firstly by one side and then by the other — among them being Lancaster, Preston, Wigan and Warrington. The eventual capture of Lathom House near Ormskirk by the Parliamentarians in December 1645 put an end to the first phase of the Civil War, but a second campaign was to follow in 1648 when

Charles I gained the support of the Scots. His ultimate defeat was made certain, however, by the Battle of Preston in 1648 when Cromwell routed the Scottish forces firstly at Ribchester and then in a running battle on the road down to Warrington. The Scots again invaded Lancashire three years later, this time in support of Charles II, but again they suffered defeat at Warrington. The Earl of Derby, who had supported the Royalist cause, was captured and then beheaded in October 1651.

Less than a century later Lancashire was again the scene of further troubles in the form of the Jacobite rebellions, provoked by the supporters of James II who felt that the claim of his son James Edward to the throne should have been acknowledged on the death of Queen Anne in 1714. In 1715 an initial attempt was made in Scotland to replace George I by 'James III', as a result of which the Lancashire Jacobites invited the Scottish Jacobites to invade England by way of Lancashire. This invitation was accepted and on the 7th of November James Edward was proclaimed king at Lancaster. The rebellion was short-lived, however, and in less than a week the Jacobite forces had surrendered in the face of two government armies. Thirty years later saw another Jacobite uprising, this time in support of 'Bonny Prince Charlie', or Charles Edward, the son of James III.

Heading south from Scotland he was able to muster support in Lancaster, Preston and Manchester, but this evaporated soon after he turned back at Derby and retreated northwards.

The intermittent hostilities of the Jacobite revolts probably disturbed Lancashire less than the Civil War, and the 18th century was marked by a considerable increase in population sustained by 'imported' food which was paid for out of the growth of local industry and consequent expansion of trade. Much of this early 'industrial' growth was still contained within rural areas, but increasingly the towns came to be important centres for trade and distribution with Liverpool and Manchester going from strength to strength. Manchester in particular was a focus for the other smaller textile towns around it, and by 1800 the main roads to it from Bury, Bolton, Wigan, Warrington, Oldham and Ashton had all been turnpiked.

Improved communications were of course an important factor in Lancashire's continuing growth, and initially most turnpikes had a specific purpose such as the easier carriage of yarn and cloth into and out of Manchester or the all-weather transport of coal to Liverpool from mines in Prescot and St. Helens. Later the network of turnpike roads was extended to make travelling generally easier for everyone. Regular stagecoach services between Lancashire and London were introduced from 1760 onwards, and by the end of the 18th century daily coach services linked all the main towns in Lancashire with one another.

The need to move bulky materials which were difficult and uneconomic to transport by road led firstly to the dredging and widening of rivers for this purpose and then to the excavation of canals or 'cuts'. The Sankey Canal was opened in 1757 as England's first man-made waterway, followed quickly by a number of others often with the financial backing of the Duke of Bridgewater and the technical expertise of James Brindley. Then in the 19th century came the railways, able to carry similar loads to the canals but much more quickly. In the early 1820s plans were discussed for a line connecting Manchester to Liverpool, but it was only in 1830 that this became a reality. However, the great commercial success of this line proved that railways were here to stay, and by the middle of the 19th century an extensive and growing network of lines had already been established. Another important link between Manchester and Liverpool was the Manchester Ship Canal, opened to traffic in 1894 and establishing Manchester as the sixth busiest port in Great Britain.

Alongside the innovations in its communications Lancashire also became noted for important inventions in the textile

3

*The Leeds-Liverpool Canal: one of Lancashire's early trade arteries*

industry, which changed the nature of production from a home-based activity to a factory-oriented one. The introduction of the 'flying shuttle' by John Kay in Bury was the first major improvement, making the handloom more efficient, followed by the invention of the 'spinning jenny' by James Hargreaves of Stanhill in 1764. This latter machine simulated a row of hand-spinners, and as it was too large for the room of a cottage it tended to be operated within small workshops and factories. There still existed, however, the problem of producing a strong enough thread or warp yarn, but this was overcome firstly by Richard Arkwright's water-frame spinning machine (so called because it could be driven by water power in a factory) and then by Samuel Crompton's spinning 'mule' which enabled a very fine warp yarn to be produced. Crompton's home town of Bolton thus became the centre of fine yarn spinning, although initially the mule was operated as a hand powered machine.

The power preferred for spinning machines was water power supplied by fast flowing Pennine streams, but the invention of Watt's steam engine offered a more reliable source of power which was eventually adopted firstly for spinning and then more gradually for weaving. By the beginning of the 19th century cotton had almost entirely replaced wool and linen as the basis of the Lancashire textile industry, with carding and spinning being the first processes transferred to the factory. Weaving proved rather more resistant to change, however, with considerable opposition being expressed against the new

machines, and even by the 1820s and 1830s handloom weavers were still in a majority in Lancashire. In fact by 1830 there were an estimated 100,000 weavers in Lancashire alone, with up to one sixth of the population dependent on handloom weaving. Yet in the case of weaving too the development of the more efficient powerloom was to prove decisive, leading to the incorporation of this process within the factory system.

Concomitant with the increasing concentration of textile production within factories was the development of Lancashire's industrial towns. The 19th century not only witnessed a rapid expansion of population, with many of the older settlements expanding until they were five times as big, but also a distinct concentration of people into industrial centres in the lower, wider valleys. The Lancashire textile industry had initially been a rural activity scattered over numerous townships, but with the development of the factory system and the steam engine production was moved from the inconvenient upper river valleys to places where there was space for building and where communications were much easier.

The advent of the powerloom was particularly significant in weaving towns like Blackburn - in 1801 its population was 11,980 but by the turn of the century this had reached 108,865. This pattern was also true of non-textile areas, as seen in the growth of the glass and copper industries on the south east Lancashire coalfield during the 19th century which transformed what had been just a small hamlet into the extensive town of St. Helens. Then of course there was the continuing growth of the boom towns of Liverpool and Manchester, with the development of the cotton trade bringing Manchester's

*Hall i'th Wood, Bolton — where Samuel Crompton invented his spinning mule*

population up to the half-million mark by the end of the 19th century.

The importance of the cotton trade in Lancashire can be gauged from the fact that by the middle of the 19th century there were over half-a- million cotton workers in Great Britain, two thirds of whom lived in Lancashire, while in money terms the export of cotton goods accounted for between 30 and 40 per cent of all the exports from the United Kingdom. Even up to 1850 much of this export business had been produced on handlooms, but in the following thirty years the number of powerlooms increased fourfold. In addition there was the growth of specialist weaving sheds and factories as well as the development of some regional variations in production, so that the Preston and Chorley district concentrated on fine light fabrics while towns like Blackburn and Accrington were known for dhooties, shirts and other goods shipped exclusively to India. In terms of cotton spinning Bolton and Manchester developed a reputation for fine spun yarns while Oldham produced coarser weaving yarns.

Whilst the spinning and weaving of cotton was pre-eminent in Lancashire, it was not of course the sole activity. The dyeing and bleaching of finished cloth were related industries which were also important in their own right, while the production of textile machinery was of major significance in a county which based its livelihood primarily on textiles. Then there was the extraction of coal in south west Lancashire, which was of vital importance to the chemical industry of Widnes and glass making in St. Helens as well as to the iron foundries of Wigan. Paper making was prevalent along rivers such as the Irwell and the Darwen, while watch making remained the main source of employment in Prescot throughout the 19th century.

Agriculture in Lancashire was not slow to respond to the opportunities which the 19th century brought with it, and the expansion of Liverpool led to the development of market gardening close by while the Fylde became a major granary for the county. The market opportunities presented by the growing towns also paved the way for the drainage and reclamation of large areas of mossland, adding considerably to the acreage under cultivation. There was also a growing emphasis on livestock, with roughly half of Lancashire's farms being concerned with dairying.

Rapid industrialisation and urbanisation of course brought its problems, particularly with regard to housing and the overcrowding which developed because of the need for people to live near their workplace. Health measures had to be introduced to tackle the worst excesses, and in 1844 Manchester council forbade the building of any more

*Avenham Park, Preston*

back-to-back houses while two years later Liverpool appointed the country's first medical officer of health. Better water supplies obtained from upland areas inside and outside the county helped further, followed by the passing of the first truly effective Public Health Act in 1875. The quality of life in towns also began to improve as numerous public parks were laid out and as increasing opportunities for leisure, recreation and entertainment became available. The extension of the railway network also allowed increasing numbers of workers to get away to the Lancashire coastal resorts on cheap day excursions and for their annual holidays. Southport was one of the most popular places to visit, and as early as 1855 40,000 day visitors were arriving by rail from Manchester and the other cotton towns.

If the 19th century in Lancashire witnessed the evolution of a completely new physical character as a result of rapid economic growth and urbanisation, then the 20th century has seen some equally dramatic changes as the county has attempted to come to terms with the decline of its traditional industries. The transformation which has been achieved has been really quite remarkable, although in some respects this could be seen as a continuation of trends from the previous centuries — the industrial basis of the county

is now characterised by diversification rather than concentration, older housing areas have been upgraded, new residential environments have been created in places like the Warrington and Central Lancashire New Towns, and town centres have been enhanced to provide better facilities for the businessman and shopper alike. Then too the improvement in communications has continued through the development of the motorway network, while better provision has been made available for the enjoyment of Lancashire's marvellous coastline and countryside. All in all, the 21st century beckons with the county in better heart than ever before.

*The Old Fire Station, Salford*

5

*Glasson Dock, near Lancaster*

times. Stretched out between these are evidences of Lancaster's commercial prosperity during the Georgian period, the result of its development as a major port.

To the north east of Lancaster is the Lune Valley, lined by some quite delightful villages situated at the foot of the wooded escarpments on both sides of the river. Many of these villages are built around the sites of earlier motte and bailey fortifications, with attractive groups of stone cottages clustered together in the shadow of ancient parish churches which often date back to the Norman period. These villages are now as peaceful as one would wish to find them, but surprisingly many have a varied industrial background — Wray, for example, discovered that the water power from the fast flowing waters of the River Roeburn was a magnet to spinners, weavers, millers and coopers.

Another river valley, the Conder, runs to the south east of Lancaster and displays a gentle pastoral character as it heads down to Galgate, an important point on the Lancaster Canal. A branch of this canal connects Galgate with Glasson Dock on the Lune estuary, a relatively 'recent' settlement which features some of this area's maritime heritage. Across the Lune estuary from here is the village of Sunderland, Lancaster's earliest port and the place at which cotton is reputed to have been first brought into Lancashire. Then further northwards along the coast is the

## A Broad Panorama

There is probably no better place from which to begin a broad perspective on Lancashire in all its splendour than Lancaster, a strategic defensive and administrative centre from the very earliest days. It was here that the county found its genesis, for it was in this spot that Roger of Poitou chose to build the castle from which he could watch over his lands to the north and south of the Ribble. These had been granted by William the Conqueror for Roger's part in the Norman Conquest, and they included Furness and Cartmel beyond Morecambe Bay. Nowadays these are incorporated within the county of Cumbria (and as such have been excluded from consideration in this book), but in Roger of Poitou's time they were linked to the rest of what is now Lancashire by the route across the sands of the Kent and Keer estuaries.

Lancaster itself is a marvellous expression of the diversity which is to be found in the county as a whole — on the one hand the Priory and Castle on Castle Hill underline the administrative power exercised by church and state during the mediaeval period, while on the other hand the Ashton Memorial in Williamson Park emphasises the influence and patronage exerted by the city's industrialists in Victorian and Edwardian

*A homely cottage in Silverdale*

resort of Morecambe, very largely a creation of the railway era and at one time known as 'Bradford-by-the-Sea' because of its attraction to Yorkshire textile workers.

To the north of Lancaster the villages are just as attractive as in the other parts of Lonsdale, but in some respects they take on a rather different character since this is limestone country and an area where quarrying and lime burning have frequently been significant local industries. Here too are located some of the county's most important wildlife habitats, including Warton Crag and Leighton Moss.

The Fylde Coast of Lancashire is principally known for its golden sands and busy holiday resorts, with Fleetwood and St. Annes being largely planned 'creations' of the Victorian era taking advantage of the new opportunities for travel which the railways provided. In between these of course is Blackpool, which itself only really developed as a popular resort when a branch railway line enabled people from the Lancashire and Yorkshire textile towns to travel here relatively easily. Inland from the coast are the lovely rural villages of the productive Fylde plain, their tranquility contrasting markedly with the bustle of the seaside. Some of the larger and more important villages and market towns are situated along the Wyre as it makes its way through the heart of the Fylde plain, its tributaries finding their source in the western flank of the Bowland Fells. The fast flowing waters of the Wyre's feeder streams were

*Evening shadows along Chipping's main street*

*Cobbles and cottages in Slaidburn*

instrumental in encouraging the growth of industrial settlements in these upland areas, with a concentration on textiles and paper making.

Textiles were also an important factor in the development of Preston further south, although its position guarding a crossing point of the River Ribble assured it of a prominent place in the country's history from the very earliest times. The lower reaches of the Ribble just to the north east of Preston are watched over by some impressive historic houses, while upstream the Ribble valley is the location of some intimate villages and farming hamlets as well as the larger settlement of Clitheroe. Running northwards from the Ribble is the River Hodder which leads to the pretty villages of the Bowland Forest, set in the midst of an area of such landscape beauty that it is often described as 'Little Switzerland', while to the south is the more sombre bulk of Pendle Hill with its tales of witches and evil doings. Then lying at the western extremity of Pendle is Whalley, completely different in character by virtue of its long religious history and the abbey ruins which can still be found here.

To the south of Whalley Lancashire takes on a more obviously urban and industrialised character in the form of a belt of traditional

*Carr House, Bretherton*

East Lancashire Uplands, this part of the county provides a full and fascinating view of Lancashire's industrial heritage. During the second half of the 19th century, for example, the industrial prosperity of Rossendale was such that it was known as the Golden Valley, and today a cotton mill in Helmshore near Haslingden is home to the Museum of the Lancashire Textile Industry. Still, if it's beautiful scenery which you are looking for then you could do little better than to take some time to discover Lancashire's 'Lakeland' — the series of reservoirs constructed on the fringes of open moorland between Blackburn and Bolton to supply the needs of Lancashire's growing industry and population during the 19th century.

The physical and economic diversity in Lancashire is particularly evident as we move from the East Lancashire Uplands to the West Lancashire Plain, from remote moorlands to cultivated lowlands, from the predominance of textiles to the pre-eminence of agriculture. There is a link, however, and that link is the Leeds and Liverpool Canal — not only did it play a vital role in advancing the growth of the East Lancashire textile towns, it also boosted farming production in West Lancashire since it provided transport for fertilisers, grain, manure and coal. Nowadays the Leeds and Liverpool Canal is no longer a major artery of trade, but it is still a very attractive feature of the West Lancashire Plain as it makes its peaceful journey through a large part of this area. West Lancashire is not only the location of some lovely villages and market towns whose 'roots' are in the fertile soil, it is also the home of the largely Victorian seaside resort of Southport. With the coming of the railway Southport developed as a holiday centre and as a 'dormitory' for middle class city workers.

Southport was in fact just one of several residential districts along the West Lancashire coastline which grew up in response to the demand for out-of-town accommodation from Liverpool's wealthier merchant class. Liverpool's prosperity was of course the result of its remarkable growth as a port during the

*Gatehouse at Lathom Park, West Lancashire*

textile towns extending eastwards from Blackburn and Accrington to Burnley, Nelson and Colne. Whilst open moorland is never far away, in an area which we have termed the

*Smithills Hall, Bolton*

*The Corn Exchange, Manchester*

18th and 19th centuries, and as well as its majestic maritime architecture of warehouses and docks the city boasts some of the grandest civic buildings in the North West as well as some quite delightful public parks and residential areas. The outer ring of Liverpool's suburbs consists of a number of attractive and historic villages, among them West Derby, Childwall, Gateacre and Woolton, whose origins pre-date even those of Liverpool itself, while further eastwards are a group of towns with quite distinctive industrial backgrounds — watch making in Prescot, glass in St. Helens, chemicals in Widnes and copper smelting in Warrington.

If Liverpool developed as a great maritime metropolis, then Manchester grew up as an even greater manufacturing one — particularly during the Victorian period, when it was a city of countless spinning mills, silk and cotton manufacturers, textile finishers and rich merchants. Its splendid Victorian architecture is an enduring testimony to its wealth and prosperity at the time when King Cotton ruled. Many of the towns around it — Salford, Ashton, Oldham, Wigan, Bolton, Bury and Rochdale — were drawn into its commercial orbit by the market place facilities which Manchester offered, being linked physically firstly by turnpiked roads and then later by the radiating lines of an ever-growing rail network. Yet each of these towns has its own story to tell, with more than enough of their own heritage and landscape. Here too, on the fringes of the Pennines, can be found the upland villages which grew up around the domestic woollen industry, which in some measure was to prepare the way for the even greater success of the later cotton trade.

*Skerton Bridge, Lancaster*

*Capernwray Hall, near Carnforth*

# Chapter 2: LANCASTER AND LONSDALE

**Lancaster** is a splendid and fascinating place which proudly boasts a long history. It is a city of great charm and character far in excess of its comparatively small size, offering marvellous views up and down its intimate narrow streets and around its quaint corners. Surprisingly, Lancaster has only been a 'city' since the 14th May 1937, when it was granted the honour by royal charter on the morning of King George VI's coronation. This was given not only as a mark of special favour but also because of the close links between the Duchy of Lancaster and the Crown since the time of Henry IV. Prior to this, however, it had been a significant town in its own right for many centuries, having been granted its first charter declaring it to be a borough in 1193.

Lancaster has been an important and strategic centre from the very earliest days, as is fitting given its prominent physical position on a hilltop overlooking the Lune estuary and guarding the entrance to the river valley. It was initially the site of a Roman fort, then an Anglo-Saxon monastery, and later a Royal castle, and for a long time afterwards it was the county town of Lancashire. It was also the location of the infamous Lancaster Assizes, at which more people were sentenced to death than anywhere outside London. During the 18th century Lancaster's prosperity grew apace through its development as a port trading with the West Indies, this prosperity being extended into the 19th century by virtue of the town's industrial growth. More recently Lancaster has developed as an educational centre, with the University of Lancaster being founded in 1964, as well as a popular tourist location drawing upon its centuries of history.

In physical terms the city is dominated by the elevated site of the Castle and Priory Church to the west and by Williamson Park with its awe-inspiring Ashton Memorial to the east. In many respects these prominent features also represent the major social and cultural influences which have moulded Lancaster as we now see it, through the powerful alliance of State and Church on the one hand and the patronage of commercial prosperity on the other.

Between these impressive landmarks lies what is essentially a Georgian town, with very little remaining from the period between the Norman Conquest and the 18th century. This situation has resulted largely from Lancaster's earlier role as a fortification against invaders from the north, and the tendency for such marauders to leave their mark by burning large parts of the town as it then existed. Consequently there is very little left of Lancaster's heritage prior to 1700, apart from the Castle and St. Mary's Priory Church. It is also interesting to note that there is not one church in Lancaster, apart from St. Mary's and the Friends' Meeting House built in 1708, which dates from before 1772. Even so, much of the present city centre is built upon the original mediaeval street pattern that existed here prior to the Georgian period, as is evident from the many narrow alleyways that are still retained between the main thoroughfares.

The fine Georgian buildings that are such a feature of Lancaster resulted from the city's prosperous development as one of the main west coast ports, trading with America and the West Indies. St. George's Quay on the Lune was constructed between 1750 and 1755 to handle this great influx of trade, and a range of 18th century warehouses was built to accommodate the tobacco, sugar, rum, cotton and dyestuffs being brought here.

Attractive new residential areas were also being developed at this time for the wealthy merchants and shipowners who had a share in Lancaster's thriving prosperity, especially around Castle Hill and Dalton Square as well as Queen's Square and Queen Street. It appears that Dalton Square in particular was intended to resemble the new and elegant squares of London. Church Street was also the scene of new construction during this period, with some of its substantial properties being built as town houses for local county families. Thomas West's account of Lancaster in 1793 is an apt summary of the quality of life which must have prevailed here during Georgian times:

> "The new houses are peculiarly neat and handsome, the streets are well paved, and thronged with inhabitants, busied in a prosperous trade to the West Indies, and other places. Along a quay noble warehouses are built".

Although there was probably human occupation on the site of Lancaster thousands of years ago, it was really the Romans who started a recognised settlement here. In fact the name 'Lancaster' is derived from the Roman 'castrum' or camp which was situated by the Lune or Loyne, constructed on an easily defended hill site in a bend of the navigable river where it was still tidal and yet fordable at low water. The name of the

*Lancaster's historic skyline*

11

Roman military station which was established here on Castle Hill is unknown, although it appears that it accommodated a garrison of five hundred horsemen and prompted the growth of a small town of shops, inns, private houses and temples on the slopes below. Of the Roman fort itself only a small part known as the Wery Wall now survives, on the north east side of Castle Hill, although alongside are the more substantial remains of a Roman bath house which might well have been attached to an inn for official travellers.

In Anglo-Saxon times a church or monastery was built within the area previously occupied by the Roman fort, although the only remnant of this structure is a part of one wall which was incorporated into the west end of the Priory Church. The most important Anglo-Saxon discoveries were made in 1902-3, when ten fragments of pre-Norman crosses were found during the construction of the King's Own Memorial Chapel within St. Mary's.

However, it was really during the Norman period that the more substantial structures which we now see on Castle Hill began to take shape. It all began in 1070 when William I bestowed the Halton manor (in which Lancaster was situated) upon Roger of Poitou, who erected a 'motte and bailey' fortress as his headquarters. By 1102 he had replaced the rather simple wooden tower with a more impressive quadrangular stone keep, which ultimately became the massive Lungess Tower still to be seen today. Earlier still, Roger of Poitou had founded and endowed in 1094 the Priory church, and by establishing Lancaster as the religious and administrative centre in the manor of Halton he had greatly increased the town's importance.

A turning point in Lancaster's development came in 1193, when it was given the status of a borough by the Foundation Charter of John, Earl of Mortain, who granted to the burgesses of Lancaster all the liberties given to the burgesses of Bristol. During the early part of the 13th century considerable work was carried out on the castle itself during the reign of King John to produce the mediaeval castle of Lancaster, although apart from the Keep, Hadrian's Tower and the lower parts of the Gateway and the Well Tower very little remains of this structure.

Soon after 1400 further work was undertaken in adding the Gatehouse, an imposing fortification which was built to improve the castle's defences against the raiding Scots. Named after John O' Gaunt, the second Duke of Lancaster, the Gatehouse was actually built by his son who had seized the throne in 1399 and been crowned as Henry IV. Ever since that time the reigning king or queen of England has owned the estates belonging to the Duchy of Lancaster.

*The Gatehouse, Lancaster Castle*

In 1415 the alien Priory Church was suppressed because it was held by the Abbey of St. Martin of Sées in Normandy, and handed over to the nuns of the Convent of Syon and Isleworth in 1424. Just a few years later it was made a parish church for the area, and around this period much of the present church was built.

During mediaeval times Lancaster grew fairly substantially throughout a period of relative stability, with the basic layout of the borough remaining much the same into the early 19th century. However, the peace was disturbed during the Civil War when Parliamentary troops seized and garrisoned the Castle in February 1643, whilst a month later a Royalist army plundered the town and burned Penny Street. Further trouble developed in the late 17th and early 18th centuries when Lancaster became the scene of failed aspirations to the throne of England — in 1651 Prince Charles was proclaimed king here, prior to marching south to his defeat at the Battle of Worcester, while in 1715 the Scottish Jacobites marched into the town and proclaimed James III at the market cross.

Settled times returned, however, and Lancaster's trade flourished as the navigation of the Lune was improved and impressive stone warehouses were built along its banks. One of the results of this growth in trade was the development of Lancaster's famous furniture industry, probably utilising the mahogany timber which was being shipped to Britain at that time as ballast in vessels returning from the Indies. Furniture making was really started by Robert Gillow, who had moved to Lancaster from Great Singleton, and his business was so successful that by the early 19th century the name Gillow had become a household word.

Another local industry which achieved national prominence, particularly during the latter part of the 19th century, was the manufacture of oilcloth and linoleum. The leaders in this industry were James Williamson and Sir Thomas Storey, both of whom proved to be important and generous benefactors in Lancaster. It was James Williamson who proposed the laying out of Williamson Park on an area of old quarries to the east of the town, although it was his son,

Lord Ashton, who completed the work in 1881 and went on to donate not only the new town hall in Dalton Square but also the monument to Queen Victoria which faces it. Sir Thomas Storey for his part presented the Storey Institute to the town, built on the site of the old Mechanics Institute and equipped at a cost of about £20,000. In it were housed a Public Free Library, a School of Art and a Technical School.

The most appropriate starting place for an itinerary of Lancaster's important buildings is undoubtedly Castle Hill, for it is on this elevated site that the city had its genesis. The Castle itself, with its battlemented walls and towers, presents a rather sombre and forbidding appearance particularly appropriate to its earliest function as a fortified stronghold. The Gatehouse is especially reminiscent of this, a solid stone built structure with twin towers which is one of the finest examples of its kind in Britain. Over the gateway are the arms of Henry IV, who was responsible for the construction of the Gatehouse, together with a full-length figure of his father John O'Gaunt which was introduced in 1826.

For centuries Lancaster Castle has been a place not only for sanctuary and defence but also for the dispensation of justice and punishment, and today it remains in use as a prison. County assizes were established here as early as 1166, and were held three times a year until 1972, whilst the earliest mention of the castle being in use as a prison was in 1196. After the English Civil War the building was in regular use as a gaol up to 1916, and although there was then a break in occupation the Castle was returned to prison service in 1955. It was here, in the Well Tower on the north side of the Gatehouse, that the famous Lancashire Witches were imprisoned prior to their trial and execution in 1612, whilst many other executions also took place in the area known as Hanging Corner (just outside the Castle) up to 1865.

The oldest part of the Castle is Lungess Tower, a massively constructed fortification dating from the 13th century with walls which are several feet thick. This can be seen most easily from the area between the Castle and the Priory Church, together with the Shire Hall and County Courthouse which were part of the improvements made at the start of the 19th century to designs by Thomas Harrison and William Blackburn. Joseph Michael Gandy, a celebrated artist and architect, was responsible for the tower to the north of the Well Tower which was built to house convicts about to give 'King's Evidence'.

The splendid setting which Lancaster Castle enjoys on Castle Hill is shared by the Priory Church of St. Mary, which can be admired from miles around. Although the site was first established as a monastery in 1094, its lands were later confiscated early in the 15th century by Henry V and the monks replaced by a vicar and six assistant priests in 1430. Much of the present church dates from around this time, its considerable size reflecting the large areas of Lunesdale and Wyresdale which were encompassed within its very extensive parish. The tower, however, was rebuilt in 1755 and is the first example of the Gothic revival in Lancashire. The church's fine exterior is matched by an equally impressive interior, and of particular interest are the 14th century choir stalls with their carved misericord seats which may have found their way here from Cockersand Abbey after the dissolution of the monasteries.

From the top of the steps at the east end of the church, close to what is now the wall of the prison, one can enjoy the excellent views of the city which are afforded by Castle Hill's elevated position. These views stretch out over the roofs of Lancaster's historic buildings and reach right across to Williamson Park on the far hillside, which is dominated by the Ashton Memorial.

From the west end of the Parish Church one can follow Vicarage Lane down to the river on the north side of Castle Hill, passing the remains of a Roman bathhouse across the field on the right hand side as well as the last vestige of Lancaster's Roman fort. The Lune was the basis of the town's growing prosperity during the course of the 18th century, and walking along St. George's Quay one cannot help but be impressed by the splendid variety of old stone warehouses and inns which are tightly packed together here in a long line close to the water's edge. Several of the buildings were constructed on unstable ground along the riverside and have consequently settled at rather 'drunken' angles, but happily this is not true of the former Custom House which is very much the focal point of the quay.

This attractive stone building with its Palladian-style front elevation featuring a colonnaded portico was built in 1764 and designed by Richard Gillow, one of the famous furniture making family who also turned his hand to architecture. It appears that he intended the Custom House to be a symbol of Lancaster's new wealth, with each of the columns of the portico being rather grandly fashioned from a single block of local sandstone, and there is no doubt that he succeeded in his purpose. As well as acting as a Custom House the building also served as the offices of the Port Commission, the body which was responsible more than any other for Lancaster's growing prosperity in the 18th century, and it is quite appropriate that it

*Lungess Tower and the Shire Hall*

*The Priory Church of St. Mary on Castle Hill*

*Riverside warehouses along St. George's Quay*

should have been recently restored to house the city's Maritime Museum as a continuing witness to this important aspect of Lancaster's heritage.

The earliest reference to Lancaster as a port was in 1297, although it was not until the start of the 18th century that it attained any real significance as local merchants began to trade around the Baltic and then across the Atlantic. By 1749 the merchants and ship owners had persuaded Parliament to pass an Act authorising the foundation of a Port Commission, with the specific purpose of improving navigation up the Lune as well as building a stone quay and charging tolls to cover the expense of this. The following years saw the warehouses being built and the arrival of a wide range of 'exotic' products such as sugar, cotton, rum and mahogany. In return Lancaster exported its locally-made furniture and the general merchandise emanating from its growing hinterland. It was therefore hardly surprising that John Crofts could write such a glowing account of Lancaster as he did in 1759:

'You will be pleased with your approach to Lancaster. Ships of 300 tons burthen are navigable up the Lun, about seven miles to that town. A complete quay wall of 200 yards length, built within these seven years...The Castle, which is pretty

intire, is their county gaol. A delightful prospect from the Church Yard which is on the same hill'.

Yet by the end of the 18th century a decline had already set in, with the port suffering badly from the adverse effects of the Napoleonic Wars and from the growth in importance of Liverpool's docks and warehousing facilities. Although coastal trade continued to prosper in Lancaster even this was diminished as a result of the development of the railways, and the end of the port's life eventually came with the construction of Preston Docks in 1892 and Heysham Harbour just up the coast in 1904. Thankfully, however, St. George's Quay has remained largely intact with most of its former warehouses now being very attractively converted to residential use.

Upstream from St. George's Quay the river is spanned by two road bridges, Greyhound Bridge taking traffic northwards out of the city and Skerton Bridge bringing traffic into Lancaster. Skerton Bridge is a particularly graceful stone structure which was opened in 1788 to replace the mediaeval bridge then in use and also provide a grander and more dignified entrance to the town. The bridge was designed by Thomas Harrison and its five shallow arches made possible for the first time the construction of a flat (rather than 'humped') carriageway. Along with the bridge

Thomas Harrison designed a group of three lodges on Parliament Street to enhance the approach over the river, together with a connecting screen wall.

Nine years later the Lune was spanned by another fine piece of architecture, this being the splendid aqueduct built by John Rennie and Alexander Stevens to carry the Lancaster Canal across the river further upstream. It

*Another part of St. George's Quay*

appears that this imposing structure with its partly balustraded walls became a tourist attraction as soon as it was opened, but unfortunately the cost was so great that the canal company could not complete the link to the Leeds and Liverpool Canal over the River Ribble which would have made the whole venture profitable. Both the aqueduct and Skerton Bridge did, however, lead to the further development of Lancaster on both the north and east sides.

Walking back up into the centre of the city from the river provides an opportunity to discover more of Lancaster's important buildings, beginning with the Judges' Lodgings just below Castle Hill at the junction of Church Street and China Street. This thoroughly imposing house is reputed to be the oldest now standing in Lancaster, being built during the second half of the 17th century on the site of an even older house which was known as the Old Hall. This had been the residence of Thomas Covell, a prominent Lancaster citizen and governor of the Castle at the time of the Pendle Witches' trial in 1612; the cross which stands in front of the present building was erected in commemoration of him.

The New Hall which was built in place of Thomas Covell's house was completed in 1662 by the Cole family, and although extensions were added to the rear in the 19th century it appears externally very much as it would have done when first constructed. Inside, the oak panelled room on the ground floor with its fine wall cupboard and the fire surround in the entrance hall are amongst the few original internal features of interest which still survive. During the early 19th century the property was purchased to provide suitable accommodation for visiting judges sitting at

*The Judges' Lodgings, just below Castle Hill*

the Lancaster Assizes, and hence its present name, but it is now a museum of furniture and dolls.

Not far away from the Judges' Lodgings, towards the top end of Church Street, can be seen a fine Georgian house which is now the Conservative Club. This property was originally built in about 1740 for the Dukes of Hamilton, who lived at Ashton Hall just three miles to the south of Lancaster. The doorway of this house is particularly attractive, with its columns and pedimented porch, whilst adjacent to it are early wrought-iron railings with a conical snuffer which would have been used by the household servants to extinguish their burning torches. The equally impressive town house adjoining the Conservative Club was built in 1775 for the Wilson family of Dallam Tower, its main features of interest being a fine ceiling in the hall and a series of wooden screens on the ground floor which hinge back to form a large suite for entertaining.

More terraces of Georgian town houses can be found around the southern edge of Castle Hill in Castle Park, which is part of an esplanade running up to the crest of the hill and offering attractive views over the west side of Lancaster. Castle Park House bears a 1720 datestone and is one of the more important properties here, many of which were the town houses of the local gentry who would have moved into the town at the time of the Assizes and Quarter Sessions. At the top end of the terrace on Castle Park is a house which now forms part of the George Fox School, named after the founder of the Quakers who preached here in 1652 and was

twice imprisoned in the Castle during the 1660s for his religious beliefs. Another interesting building worth noting is the former Dispensary, built from local sandstone and facing the Castle at the foot of Castle Park; this dates from 1785, when it was established to provide free medicines and other medical help for poor people.

Not far away from here is Market Street which leads into Market Square and the Old Town Hall. This is yet another substantial and important Georgian building, first built in 1783 and then considerably enhanced by Thomas Harrison through the addition of a rotunda and cupola. Since 1923 it has housed the City Museum, but originally its ground floor was open and unglazed and

*Doorway of the Conservative Club*

*The Old Town Hall*

*The Music Room*

used as a corn exchange. This continued the market function of the site, since a tollbooth had once stood here from the time when Lancaster's citizens had been given the right to hold a weekly market on Saturdays. It was the granting of this market charter in 1193 which paved the way for Lancaster's later commercial prosperity.

Just along Market Street and around the corner in Sun Street is one of the city's most unusual buildings, a delightful structure known as the Music Room. This dates from about 1730 and appears to have been built as a pavilion or summerhouse at the end of a private garden, which was later developed as Sun Street. The Music Room is hemmed in by other buildings close by, although this hardly detracts from its wonderfully detailed Baroque facade with an Ionic triumphal arch in the centre. In the first floor room there is some exceptionally fine plasterwork typical of the Baroque period which is reputed to have been cast by Italian craftsmen, although it has since been restored with great care by the Landmark Trust. On the walls are to be seen the Muses of eloquence, history, music, astronomy, tragedy, rhetoric, dancing, comedy and amorous poetry, whilst on the ceiling is a goddess with a torch. It seems likely that the name Music Room is a corruption of 'Muses Room', reflecting the importance of the fine plasterwork to be found here.

In sharp contrast to the elaborately detailed decoration both internally and externally of the Music Room is the much plainer architectural style of the Friends' Meeting House in Meeting House Lane, the continuation westwards of Market Street. This building was put up in 1708 by the Quakers themselves, reflecting their considerable importance and early growth in Lancaster even though many of their members had been imprisoned in the castle dungeons during the 17th century.

Returning back towards the city centre and into King Street one is delighted to discover on the right hand side an intimate enclave of ancient almshouses known as Penny's Hospital. These tiny cottages, situated around a central courtyard with a chapel at one end, were built in 1720 under the will of Alderman William Penny to provide accommodation for twelve poor men of the district. More recently they were modernised to form six rather more spacious dwellings, but without any alteration to their external appearance. Further along King Street one can turn right into Middle Street and then into High Street, another prime residential area during the Georgian period. One of the houses built here during the prosperous late 18th century, for the lawyer John Rawlinson, has a particularly fine facade with elaborate window frames and an impressive doorway.

Passing eastwards across the city centre

through Common Garden Street and Brook Street one arrives in Dalton Square, another of Lancaster's impressive focal points. This was originally the site of a Dominican friary established around 1260, but after the dissolution of the monasteries the land was bought by the Daltons of Thurnham Hall. By the late 18th century Dalton Square was being laid out as a high class residential area, although Palatine Hall on the northern edge was originally built as Lancaster's first Roman Catholic Chapel in 1798.

Towards the end of the 19th century and at the start of the 20th the Square began to take on a rather grander civic significance, and at the very centre of the formal gardens (an area previously known as The Oval) is a memorial statue to Queen Victoria which was given to Lancaster by Lord Ashton. The figure of the Queen is of bronze on a stone plinth surmounted by four lions, whilst carved in relief on the sides of the plinth are the great scientists, writers, artists, philanthropists and politicians of the day — including Benjamin Franklin, Isaac Pitman, General Gordon, Rowland Hill, Florence Nightingale, Lord Macaulay and Charles Dickens, along with many others. Also included are Lord Ashton's father, James Williamson, and his son-in-law, Viscount Peel, as well as the figures of Truth and Justice.

On the south side of Dalton Square is the Town Hall, another imposing building and again a gift of Lord Ashton to Lancaster. This was opened by him in 1909, having been designed by E.W. Mountford in a rather grand neo-Georgian style with a suitably rich interior of marble and elegantly carved wood panelling. At the top of the front steps is a giant portico with a richly decorated pediment which features a statue of Edward VII flanked by the figures of Loyalty and Justice. This leads on to a tunnel-vaulted

*Dalton Square*

*Lancaster's imposing Town Hall*

staircase hall with a dome in the centre, and from the staircase landing there is entry to the horseshoe-shaped Council Chamber as well as the state suite (which includes the Mayor's Parlour) and other meeting rooms and offices. A separate entrance at the back of the building leads up to the grandiose Ashton Hall with its own organ, balconies and portraits of past mayors. The whole edifice is watched over by a very substantial four-dial clock tower. The memorial to Queen Victoria and the then new Town Hall together cost Lord Ashton over £155,000, an indication not only of his expansive generosity but also of the wealth which his factories in Lancaster had brought him.

This wealth was largely the result of the Williamson family's great success in the manufacture of oilcloth and linoleum, although these products relied quite substantially upon the textile industry which had become established in Lancaster with the coming of the canal. The canal runs to the

east of the city centre, and from Dalton Square one can make a brief detour up Nelson Street and along St. Peter's Road to discover some of Lancaster's impressive canalside cotton mills. Opened in 1797, the canal brought with it a reduction in the cost of transporting coal to Lancaster with the consequent growth of the textile mills and other industry. This particular canal also had the benefit of being built to follow the contours, so that very few locks were required, and for some years travellers were provided with a fast packet boat service on which they could travel at the unusually high speed of 10 miles per hour, in comfort, between Kendal and Preston.

St. Peter's Road leads on to Moor Lane, which runs back into the lower part of the City following the slope down towards the Lune. It brings us first to the Duke's Playhouse, converted to a theatre from what was formerly a Georgian church built of stone in a rather modest architectural style. Of much greater interest is St. John's Church, situated a little further down the hill on the corner of Chapel Street and North Road. As well as being rather more decorative generally this particular church displays a delightful rotunda and spire on top of its more substantial square tower. The building dates originally from 1754-55, although Thomas Harrison again had a hand in things with some later alterations which included the addition of both the tower and the spire. As well as an apsidal-ended chancel the church features a west door which is decorated by a moulded architrave together with a convex frieze and cornice, whilst over it is a panel which records the erection of the tower by a benefactor in 1784. Inside the church the galleries are supported by square piers with Ionic columns above them.

Retracing our steps up Moor Lane and along St. Peter's Road brings us to the Roman Catholic Cathedral, the third of three churches in this part of the City. The most dramatic feature of this building, erected in 1859 to a design by Edward Paley as a replacement for the earlier Catholic chapel in Dalton Square, is its marvellously tall spire which is one of the best in Lancashire. It also has one of the finest interiors of any church in the county, by virtue of its high nave and vaulted chancel as well as its decorative stained glass.

From here East Road takes us straight up a steep hill to what must surely be Lancaster's crowning glory - Williamson Park and the recently restored Ashton Memorial, both of which were donated to the town by the Williamson family. This part of Lancaster had originally been rough moorland interspersed with old quarries, from which the town's building stone had been extracted, but in the 1860s it was decided to lay out a carriage drive, seats and viewpoints here utilising the labour of local cotton workers who were forced into unemployment as a result of the 'cotton famine' caused by the American Civil War.

Then in 1877 James Williamson bought the quarry rights and began to create a public park at his own expense. In addition to the rich and varied planting which was introduced throughout the park, encompassing an area of nearly forty acres, special rock gardens were established at the foot of each quarry face. James Williamson, and his sons who carried on the work after his death, also provided an ornamental lake, a bridge and an 80-foot cascade, as well as a Palmhouse which now accommodates an exotic collection of butterflies.

Close by is the magnificent Ashton Memorial, or 'The Structure' as it is sometimes known locally, once described by the architectural historian Nikolaus Pevsner as "the greatest monument in England". This inspiring piece

*The Ashton Memorial in Williamson Park*

of architecture is externally clad in white Portland stone, being designed by John Belcher R.A. and built between 1907 and 1909 by Waring and Gillow of Lancaster at a cost of £87,000. The building was erected by Lord Ashton as a memorial to his family, although local tradition suggests that it was built particularly in memory of his second wife. The interior of the monument consists mainly of two domed chambers, one above the other, whilst the exterior has five outside balconies of varying character at different heights.

It is from these balconies that one can enjoy some breathtaking views, not only of the rich architectural heritage of Lancaster laid out in the valley below but also of the great expanse of coastland and moorland with which this delightful city is so admirably surrounded. Robert Southey's comments from 1807 are a fair summary of what Lancaster has to offer:

"Another easy stage brought us to Lancaster, one of the best built cities in the Kingdom. The view as we left it after dinner was truly fine; two stone bridges over the river Lon, the town on the opposite bank, and on the highest part of the hill a castle, which has been newly built or repaired as a prison — Lancaster could scarcely have appeared more beautiful in the days of the shield and the lance."

An ideal place from which to commence a survey of the Lune Valley is the village of **Halton,** just a few miles to the north east of Lancaster, as it was the gift of the manor of Halton to Roger of Poitou in the 11th century which paved the way for Lancaster's own development as a strategic administrative and judicial centre. Halton, like Lancaster, enjoys an elevated position above the Lune and also has its own Castle Hill, a high mound above the rest of the village which was the site first of a Roman camp and then later of a Saxon castle.

The parish church of St. Wilfrid is also of great antiquity, having been founded in the 7th century, and although much of the church has been rebuilt on more than one occasion the ancient tower is an impressive pointer towards it historic origins. Both inside the church and in the churchyard are several very old crosses, some of which are understood to date from the 9th century and the earliest days of Christianity, which had spread across the North of England from about AD 563. Many of these crosses have been 'restored', but one appears to carry both Pagan and Christian symbols and is the only such relic known to do so. The churchyard of St. Wilfrid's was also the scene of an important archaeological discovery in 1794, when a Roman votive altar (at which offerings were made when a military expedition was undertaken) was found here.

Close to the church and leading up to the main village crossroads are several attractive terraces of stone cottages as well as some unusual larger houses with mock battlements, perhaps reflecting in retrospect Halton's early origins as a fortified castle site. The village is now a pleasant and peaceful blend of old and new properties, something of a residential suburb for Lancaster, but life has not always been so quiet - at one time industry thrived here, and in the 18th century several mills and a foundry were established in Halton. Yet these days there is little to disturb the comparative tranquility which now prevails and which attracts not only numerous passing visitors but also the many fishermen who frequent this part of the Lune

Valley just below the rushing waters of a nearby weir.

From Halton the road runs eastwards for two miles before it crosses the river at the **Crook o'Lune,** a well known beauty spot which now has the benefit of a car park and access to the long distance Lune Valley footpath following the line of a former railway track. For centuries people have come here to savour the delights of this classic country scene, with the river winding slowly but gracefully through a wooded gorge. Queen Elizabeth I is reputed to have visited the spot, as did Turner the painter and Wordsworth the poet. Thomas Gray was so taken up with its beauties that in 1769 he wrote of it in these glowing terms: "On each side rise two sloping hills, clothed with thick woods, variegated rock and herbiage: between them in the richest of valleys the Lune serpentises for many a mile and comes forth ample and clear......a perfect landscape". Happily the scene is much the same today as it was then, and although the river has since been crossed by both road and rail bridges these merely serve to provide a better view of this matchless scene.

Over the river one arrives quickly at the villages of **Caton** and **Brookhouse,** part of the larger parish of Caton-with-Littledale. It appears likely that there was a settlement here in Saxon times, and whilst it is known that there was a corn mill and a fulling mill as long ago as 1266 the area was predominantly an agricultural one until the end of the 17th century. With the coming of the Industrial Revolution and the use of water power on a large scale all this changed, particularly in Caton where the fast flowing Artle Beck provided sufficient power for as many as four mills to be driven from the same mill race. One of the mills, Low Mill, is reputed to have been the oldest cotton mill in England and was in use until 1970. The early owners

obviously took a particularly philanthropic view of their business because records show that they provided their own shoemakers, tailor's shops and smallholdings to cater for the needs of their apprentices, many of whom were brought from Liverpool.

Several of the mills had a variety of different uses during their existence, and would have handled corn, cotton, flax, silk, bobbins and brushes. Sailcloth was also made in Caton, and this would have been supplied to all the shipyards and docks on the North West coast. Caton also possessed an important market in earlier times, and the 'fish stones' which can still be seen at the base of an ancient hollow tree near the main road to Lancaster are said to have been the place where local monks displayed their fish catches for sale.

These monks may have come from Gresgarth Hall to the south of Caton, since it is thought that this substantial house in its own landscaped grounds was originally built at the end of the 12th century as a monks' rest house, for use by the Abbott of Furness when visiting the Abbey estates in Yorkshire. Parts of the original building still exist, but it has been considerably added to at various times. The last addition took place in 1805 with the introduction of the neo-Gothic south west wing.

The parish church of St. Paul is to be found at Brookhouse rather than Caton, approached by a narrow road which runs between rows of pretty white painted terraced cottages and the local public house. It is believed that a church existed here as early as 1230, although the present building dates from about 1865 and incorporates an earlier tower built in the 16th century. A particularly interesting feature is the old doorway which has been built into the west wall of the church, this being a remnant of the original 13th century structure which

*The Crook o' Lune's verdant landscape*

first occupied the site. The sculptured arch of the doorway depicts the Temptation of Eden, and the top of a tree and the heads of Adam and Eve together with the serpent and the figure of an animal are still just discernible. Also worth noting are the fine windows, especially the transoms which form the lower part of the tracery. In each window these have been cut from a single block of stone, instead of being cut from several pieces and fixed separately as is usually the case.

Next door to the parish of Caton-with-Littledale is **Claughton** (pronounced 'Clafton'), which at just 2½ miles by 1½ miles is the smallest parish in Lancashire. Yet despite its diminutive size it lays claim to having several features of great historical interest, particularly within its parish church which existed here in 1200. One such feature is the east window, dating from around 1300, but of much greater importance is the larger of the two bells in the bellcote - this has an inscription dating it to 1296, which makes it the oldest bell in England. Claughton Hall also has an ancient foundation, with its oldest parts believed to date from 1216, but the real interest lies in the fact that it was dismantled stone by stone during the early part of the present century and moved from its original position down in the village to a spot higher on the hillside, where it was re-erected.

Travelling north-eastwards from Claughton to the village of Hornby one becomes increasingly aware of the splendid pastoral beauty of the Lune Valley, the lush green fields of the flood plain hemmed in by undulating wooded escarpments to the north and the south. On the way to Hornby can be seen the Old Toll House, the oldest in Britain and the first to take a penny toll. Rather appropriately the windows were arranged so that the road could be seen for a quarter of a mile in both directions. The Old Toll House Garage also has an interesting claim to fame, in that it was here that white lines were painted on a road for the very first time. It appears that the proprietor of the garage during the 1920s took the initiative to paint white lines along the sides and down the centre of the road in order to reduce the many accidents at this particular corner. The authorities were unhappy with this development, but the garage proprietor obtained the support of King George V himself for what he had done and white lines soon became accepted and used all over the world.

Like many of the villages in the Lune Valley, **Hornby** has a wealth of ancient history behind it in addition to the castle, church and attractive stone cottages which are clustered together on both sides of the River Wenning before it joins the River Lune a mile downstream. The village straddles an ancient north-south trackway that was used for centuries by salters and packhorses, heading

*Hornby Castle*

southwards to Slaidburn by a high level route which went over the fells and through the royal hunting area of the Bowland Forest. Evidence for an even earlier history of the village is found at the Castle Stede fortified site on a bluff overlooking the Lune, just to the north of Hornby. This is said to be the finest example of a moated motte and bailey castle in Lancashire, and the suggested site of the original castle of Hornby erected by Horn and his Danish followers.

It is the current Hornby Castle which is the dominant feature of the village, standing on a high mound above the River Wenning and rather more closely related to the village than the earlier Castle Stede site. The castle as it appears now dates largely from the middle of the 19th century, when a new building was erected in a Gothic style prior to the Tudor keep being restored and the watch tower rebuilt with an embattled parapet. Other additions to the north and south sides and improvements to the keep were also made in the late 1800s. It is the keep or pele tower which is the oldest surviving feature of the castle, dating from the 13th century but restored by Sir Edward Stanley some three centuries later.

It was Sir Edward Stanley who was also responsible for the building of the unusual octagonal tower possessed by the parish church of St. Margaret of Antioch, which dates from about 1300 when it was built as a

chapel of ease to the parish church at Melling. It is reputed that Sir Edward Stanley ordered the erection of the tower after the victory at Flodden Field in 1513, as an expression of thanks for his safe return. Sir Edward, who was given the title of Lord Monteagle by Henry VIII after the Battle of Flodden, also ordered the building of a new chancel to house his tomb, but he died in 1524 before its completion. One of the most important features of the church is the fragment of an ancient cross seen under the tower and depicting Christ at the feeding of the five thousand; known as the 'Loaves and Fishes Cross', there is no other like this in England.

On both sides of the broad main street in Hornby are attractive rows of quaint cottages built of buff-coloured sandstone under stone flagged roofs, but there are also things to discover along both banks of the River Wenning. Here can be seen dippers and pied wagtails searching the rocks at the water's edge, together with the occasional kingfisher, while during the spring and summer the calls of curlews and lapwings are to be heard everywhere. Not far away, the shingle beds of the Lune itself are the frequent haunt of oystercatchers, plovers and sandpipers, whilst in winter flocks of fieldfares and redwings commonly search the fields for food. The hedgerows around Hornby, some of which may be several centuries old, are also rich in a variety of plant life — oak, ash, elm, sycamore, willow, holly and hazel are all to be found, and in June and July the hedges are white with the heads of elder flowers.

To the north of Hornby, at the point where the earliest castle site kept a watchful eye on the Lune Valley, the mediaeval Loyn Bridge with its three stone arches provides a crossing to the other river bank. The road then heads westwards to **Gressingham,** a delightful settlement of lovely stone cottages shaded by leafy trees and within a stone's throw of a bubbling stream. The most impressive house in the village is the old Hall, mentioned in the Domesday Book when the manor of 'Ghersinctune' belonged to Tosti before coming into the ownership of the Gersingham family, whose crest the Hall still bears. Commanding an excellent view across the river to Hornby Castle, the Hall features a three-flight Jacobean staircase as well as an unusual kitchen table made from a huge slab of blue slate. This passes through the kitchen wall into the pantry, where it is supported by stone buttresses. Close to the Hall is the parish church, situated on a mound above the nearby stream and built of stone in the 13th century. Prior to this parishioners had faced the weekly peril of fording the river in order to worship at Melling. Although the church was rebuilt in 1734 and then restored in 1862 it still retains a late Norman doorway in good condition.

Before continuing up the Lune Valley from Gressingham it is worthwhile making a note of **Aughton** to the south west, situated on the wooded slopes across the river from Claughton and sharing in a similar linguistic peculiarity which requires its name to be pronounced 'Afton'. This small village consists of only a few cottages and a number of 17th century farmsteads, but it nevertheless achieved at least some fame for itself through the tradition of the Aughton Pudding. In earlier times local basket makers introduced the practice of boiling willows so that they could be peeled throughout the year rather than just at sap-time, and on the occasion of

every twenty first year the villagers would boil an enormous plum pudding once the boiler was set up. People from a large area would join in the festivities, but by 1887 the custom had sadly been allowed to die out.

Basket making was also an important activity in the village of **Arkholme,** just a few miles further up the Lune Valley. This is a particularly beautiful place to come across, a classic rural village of lovely houses, carefully-tended gardens and an intimate community atmosphere arising from every resident being acquainted with everyone else. From the village crossroads, where the welcoming and historic Bay Horse Inn stands, a narrow road makes its way down to the 16th century parish church which overlooks the river from the site of a Norman bailey. On either side of the road are clusters of splendid houses and cottages, built of warm grey stone hemmed in behind ancient walls which are edged by uneven cobbled footpaths. Their well maintained but completely natural gardens are exquisite, as is the churchyard and the shady walks down to the river bank. From here riverside walks go down towards Hornby and up towards the next village of Newton. It was from here too that the willows used for basket making were obtained, and several families in the village would be engaged in this craft at any one time. One of these was the Ireland family, who made baskets in Arkholme over the course of four generations.

Local trade was always quite important here, in what was traditionally a farming village. A grant of a weekly market at 'Erghum' for hemp and flax and an annual fair was approved in 1280 during the reign of Edward I, although all that now remains of the old

market cross is a small part in the churchyard. The church itself lacks a tower, but it nevertheless has a bell which is one of the oldest in Britain. It also features two horns carved in stone, reminders of the days when the Warden of Cawood Forest blew his horn daily out over the wilds.

Passing on from Arkholme through the hamlet of Newton one arrives at the village of **Whittington,** a more extensive settlement of terraced cottages and old stone farmhouses featuring mullioned windows. The parish church of St. Michael the Archangel enjoys an elevated position on higher ground above the rest of the village, having been built in 1291 on the site of an earlier fortification. In the midst of this quiet and verdant setting it is interesting to learn that coal workings were present here in the 17th century, as they were in a number of the other villages of the Lune Valley. Whittington's main claim to fame seems to be through William Sturgeon, the inventor of the electromagnet, who was born here in 1783. Nowadays there seems little to disturb the settled tranquility of what is yet another delightful spot on the wooded slopes of the Lune Valley.

To travel back across the River Lune from here first requires a brief journey northwards over the county boundary into Kirkby Lonsdale and Cumbria, but in less than a mile to the south east we are welcomed back into Lancashire at the point where the unusually named township of Burrow-with-Burrow begins. The main road down to Settle brings us firstly to **Cowan Bridge** in the parish of Ireby and Leck, a small settlement in which the Bronte sisters went to school before moving on to Casterton. A tablet erected on

*A cottage in Arkholme . . .*

*and another along the village's main street*

one of the houses known as Bronte Cottage indicates that Maria, Elizabeth, Charlotte and Emily Bronte lived here as pupils of the Clergy Daughters' School in 1824-25. Founded by the vicar of Tunstall the school was later moved to larger premises at Casterton, and the original school building became a bobbin mill.

A narrow country lane leading off the main road takes us up to **Leck** itself, a comparatively isolated backwater of farms and cottages with its own church and school where life seems to be lived out at a rather more leisurely pace than elsewhere. Local people regard this area as the last outpost in Lancashire because it is sandwiched between Cumbria to the north and North Yorkshire to the south, and this must surely be the day-to-day experience of the family at Leck Fell House. At 1300 feet above sea level this remote sheep station is said to be the highest farm in the county, often being under a covering of snow when places lower down are not and equipped necessarily with its own electricity generator.

From Leck another narrow lane, hemmed in by drystone walls and green verges full of wild blue geraniums during the summer months, crosses the fields south-eastwards and comes out at **Ireby.** This is another delightfully peaceful little hamlet off the beaten track, a very attractive blend of cottages and farms situated on both sides of a small stream which is crossed by an ancient stone slab footbridge. One of the oldest properties here is Over Hall, a farmhouse with a datestone of 1687 but which is thought to have been built in about 1634 by a Robert Tatham. The later datestone may relate to the marriage of Sir David Fleming's daughter to John Tatham in 1687, when 100 horses and their riders were said to have been entertained at Over Hall for four days. Perhaps the festivities took place in the large open room which is still to be found inside, with its great big fireplace and old gallery as well as seats around the edge.

The narrow lane from Leck to Ireby continues down to the main road, and from there it is just a couple of miles back to Cowan Bridge where another country lane off to the left follows the line of Leck Beck down towards the Lune. On the north side of Leck Beck is **Over Burrow,** where Agricola built and garrisoned a large military station as he marched from Manchester to Scotland in AD 79; and it appears that the Lunesdale Highway connected Low Burrow Bridge with the camp here before continuing on to Ribchester. Then in 1740 Burrow Hall was built almost on the elevated site of the fortress.

Southwards from here the present Kirkby Lonsdale to Lancaster road passes on into Tunstall, where the 15th century parish church is built on the site of an earlier building from the 13th century. Inside the church can

be found some Flemish glass in the east window as well as a lovely Georgian font with a marble bowl. Not far away is the moated Thurland Castle, originally the home of the Tunstall family. The house has been renovated several times, once after being besieged by Roundheads in 1643 and then after being destroyed by fire in the early 18th century.

The next village down the Lune Valley is **Melling,** and one would be hard-pressed to find a more attractive range of stone cottages and 17th century houses anywhere. The parish church of St. Wilfrid is also of interest, standing as it does in the bailey of yet another fortified site above the valley pasturelands. The church appears to have been in existence at the time of the Norman Conquest, and even though it has been restored and altered since then, it still retains its Norman doorway. A cobbled area just off the main road provides some form of protection from passing traffic as visitors mount the stone steps and pass through a delicate wrought-iron gateway into the quiet courtyard.

*St. Wilfrid's Church, Melling*

The main road follows the course of the River Lune down into Hornby, but the minor road which leaves Melling on the northern side of the churchyard passes through fields and woodlands to Wennington and then on to the delightful and yet surprising village of **Wray.** The delight comes from the lovely rows of old stone farmhouses and cottages which line the long main street through the village, whilst the surprise emanates from the fact that for centuries Wray was a thriving industrial community. The fast flowing River Roeburn which drops down into the village from its wooded gorge to the south provided the all-important water power, and from early times there were millers, tanners, coopers and malters among the inhabitants of Wray.

Growing prosperity brought about substantial development in the village, which now features an unusually large number of good yeoman houses with dated doorheads and plaques of the 17th and 18th centuries. There appear to be at least ten on the main street, with that dated 1656 being one of the earliest; this was the house of Captain Richard Pooley, who in 1684 founded what is now one of the oldest endowed schools in the country with an initial endowment of £200. By virtue of its industrial character Wray had become crowded and rough by the 19th century, and although its physical extent then was smaller than now its population was three times as large. As the trades operating in the village diversified so Wray became crammed with sailmakers, hatters, cordwainers, weavers, coalminers and quarrymen.

Nowadays there is very little remaining of this industrial heritage, although one of the hatters, William Wainman, did leave his initials and the date of 1820 laid out in the cobbles outside his house at the bottom end of the main street. What was Wray's main 'industrial' building, a mill on the far side of the Roeburn to the south of the village, is also still in existence. This had a long and varied history of wool carding, cotton spinning, silk throwing and bobbin turning before it was more recently converted to residential use. In stark contrast to the present day, Wray had an unsavoury reputation during the 19th century for being rowdy and boisterous, and in 1833 the Lancaster newspaper reported that it was "absolutely dangerous for respectable persons to venture out after dark, especially females; there exists such a set of unruly persons, whose conduct ought to be put a stop to by enforcing the law".

Wray has also had a long association with nonconformist religion, particularly with the Quakers or the Society of Friends, and the old Quaker Meeting House which can be seen at the northern end of the village dates from 1704. This was built after the 1689 Act of Toleration had allowed greater religious freedom to the Quakers, although prior to that time the Quaker community in Wray had experienced fairly regular harrassment as well as periods of confinement in Lancaster Castle for the non-payment of tithes. The Meeting House which they were allowed to build at the start of the 18th century has since become a Methodist schoolroom, but it has probably stood longer and changed less than any other building in Wray. It was built to a fairly standard pattern, with the present size and shape of the roof and the walls as well as the mullioned windows being much as they were originally. The graveyard is also much the same, having been enlarged in 1727, but since Quakers were not allowed to mark their graves at first the earliest of the ten neat headstones is dated 1838. However, there are likely to be more than 250 people buried here in unmarked graves.

To the south of Wray is **Botton,** an upland area of scattered hill farms which is included within the parish. Several of the houses here are more imposing than those within the village of Wray itself, largely because they had the benefit of extensive woods at a time when the timber trades (tanning, coopering, charcoal burning and house building) were flourishing. Cragg Hall is one such example, having been built by Henry Bateson who owned the mills in the tiny hamlet of Millhouses on the River Hindburn nearby. This very substantial stone property bears a date of 1693, although it seems likely that it incorporates parts which are very much older.

The whole of the parish of Wray-with-Botton is a comparatively unknown area which is well worth exploring, not only to discover the beautifully wooded river gorges of the Roeburn and the Hindburn but also to enjoy the remote and lovely moorlands as well as the isolated farms which are to be found here. One particularly interesting farmstead is Outhwaite, situated on the fells above the River Roeburn — at one time this was a Quaker penal colony, and within the complex of farm buildings are still to be seen an old jail as well as the stocks and a whipping post!

*Interesting doorway at Outhwaite*

Just a few miles to the south west of Wray is yet another isolated and little-visited beauty spot. This is the area of **Littledale,** part of the parish of Caton-with-Littledale and reached by road from the village of Brookhouse. At the heart of Littledale is the

Artle Beck, running through an attractively wooded gorge to Caton where it joins up with the Lune. Centuries ago the Artle Beck and its tributaries would have provided the power to run a fulling mill, corn mill and bobbin mill which were located in the valley, but now the tranquility of this delightful spot is disturbed only by the occasional motor car. Until fairly recently the parishioners here were served by St. Anne's Church (a daughter church of St. Paul's in Brookhouse) which was built in 1752 and which also acted as a school for the people of Littledale, who in those days found the two mile journey down to Brookhouse very difficult to negotiate in winter time; now the building is occupied as a private house.

From Crossgill in Littledale the narrow country road climbs up from the wooded gorge below and on to open fells, passing several scattered farms before dropping down into **Quernmore** at the head of the Conder Valley. The impression here is of a rather more settled and gentle pastoral landscape, the valley sides being undulating rather than steep and the fields being more open than wooded. Yet here again one can sense the same peace and seclusion which is to be experienced in many of the river valleys running into the Lune. Although Quernmore's history has been relatively unspectacular by the standards of other settlements further up the Lune Valley, it would still seem that its ancient highways have been trodden by Roman legions, soldiers, rebels, monks and smugglers. Then at a later date came judges and witches, for along these tracks the demdikes were brought for trial to Lancaster Castle. The name 'Gallows Field' also bears witness to the fate of many local wrongdoers.

To the uninitiated, both the spelling and pronunciation of the name Quernmore provides some difficulty. Old records have shown it as Quarlemore, Queremore, Wharlemore, Whernmore and Quarmoor, with the latter being the closest to the accepted way of saying the name now. It appears that the name is derived from the time when 'querns', a particularly ancient form of hand mill, were hewn from the rocks found on the extensive moors in the area. Pottery was one of the industries carried out here, as was slate quarrying in the 17th century and the smelting of ironstone (for which the abundance of wood for charcoal was an obvious asset). Coal seams were also discovered in Quernmore during the 18th century, and the undulating nature of some fields is a continuing reminder of this. As the land was gradually cleared of the woods which predominated here smallscale industry gradually gave way to farming, although at one point the two were successfully combined in the form of corn milling. The local quarrying of large millstones required for the water powered mills was an obvious advantage for this. Milling continued in the

*Cragg Hall, Wray-with-Botton*

*Quernmore's tranquil pastures*

area until the Second World War, and the farms now concentrate on dairying.

The development of farming in the area was also strongly influenced by the creation of a fine agricultural estate around Quernmore Hall, commencing from the late 18th century when the property was bought by a landowner interested in rural conservation. A splendid new hall was built at the same time using locally quarried stone, and this is now St. Paul's Priory. The other main building of importance in the area is St. Paul's Church, built in 1860 after Quernmore was constituted as a separate parish. The east window of this 14th century-style church was salvaged from the wreck of 'The Fairy Vision' after it was lost in fog off the mouth of the River Rhone, and its fine colouring depicts the nativity, crucifixion and resurrection of Christ.

Narrow country roads follow the line of the River Conder down the valley from Quernmore to **Galgate,** a pleasant village of robustly built stone cottages which grew up chiefly on silk spinning. A number of the original mills can still be seen, although since the start of this century these have been converted to other uses, and many of the terraced houses in the northern part of the village were built by local mill owners in order to provide not only accommodation for their workers but also extra voting power at election times. It appears that there used to be a yearly fair held in Galgate on Low Sunday, but that it was moved to Low Monday after objections from the churchwardens in 1808. As part of the celebrations there was a ceremony called 'Mayor Choosing', whereby the first man found drunk and asleep

anywhere in the village on the morning after the fair was chosen as 'mayor' for the following year. The proceedings were generally characterised by rough behaviour and excessive drinking, with the chosen person being blackened with soot and covered with flour, so it is not surprising that this unofficial custom eventually lapsed.

Galgate is already well known to many people since the main railway line and the A6 trunk road pass through the village, as does the Lancaster Canal. This waterway, covering a distance of 41 miles between Preston to the south and Tewitfield to the north, was first opened in 1797, and by virtue of a carefully chosen route along the contours is the longest lock-free stretch of canal in the country. Another section of canal was built from Wigan to within a few miles of Preston, and although several proposals were made to link the two canal ends by crossing the River Ribble only a horsedrawn tramroad was ever built. More success was achieved further

northwards, however, and in 1819 the canal finally reached Kendal. This length included a flight of eight locks at Tewitfield and a tunnel at Hincaster. Several years later the Glasson Branch was opened, linking the main stretch of the canal just half a mile south of Galgate to the port of Glasson and the sea.

One can also get to Glasson Dock (as it is more usually known) by a narrow country lane heading westwards from Galgate. This follows a rather twisting route, between tall hedges and the green fields with their contented grazing cattle, down to the hamlet of **Conder Green.** On the way one is suddenly faced by the wide expanse of the Lune estuary stretching out in front, with the flat river plain in the near distance. Conder Green itself is situated at the head of the tiny Conder estuary, with the waving marshland grasses providing an air of remoteness and untrammelled mystery. Nearby are a few scattered farms and beyond them distant views back towards the Bowland hills, while

*The Stork Pub, Conder Green*

the first hint of the nearby shore is given by a cluster of white painted cottages and The Stork pub. Refreshment has been served from this ancient hostelry since the very earliest days, and Tyldesley the diarist referred to it in 1712 when he dropped in here for a drink.

Unlike most places in the Lune Valley, **Glasson Dock** is a relatively 'recent' settlement. Only 200 years ago it was nothing but fields and marshland, apart from a few thatched cottages and farm buildings situated in what is now known as Old Glasson. Then in 1787 a wet dock was built by the Lancaster Port Commission in order to overcome navigation problems on the Lune, with the consequent birth of a whole new community here at Glasson. The dock covers an area of just under three acres and was once variously described as being able to accommodate '25 large merchantmen' and 'merchant vessels of 200 tons burthen', but today is likely to contain up to five tramp ships unloading animal feed imported via Holland or West Germany. There is also usually the Lancaster Port Commission launch, perhaps a fishing trawler and a variety of private yachts and cruisers.

Further development took place in 1826 when the canal spur linking the Lancaster Canal with Glasson Dock was completed, and although the additional traffic generated by this did not lead to much demand for local labour it did require the building of dwellings for the canal lock keeper and for the keeper of a warehouse built where the canal branch entered the basin. This basin covers an area of just under 17 acres and was built to replace a smaller reservoir whose water could be released through sluices to clear out the dock. Nowadays the basin offers moorings and piers for pleasure craft and also provides opportunities for windsurfing, while close to the northern corner can be seen the original Lock Cottage (built by the canal company in 1825) which is still used to accommodate the lock-keeper working here.

The canal company also acquired land to build a row of nine cottages at the bottom of Tithebarn Hill, now the main street in the village, although it appears that only one of the cottages was ever occupied by a canal employee. Close by is Ten Row, laid out by the Port Commission to provide an access to the foreshore without having to pass along the west side of the dock; its name derives from the row of ten cottages which were built here during the late 1830s to provide accommodation for the skilled labour which was moving into Glasson Dock at that time to work in the shipyard. This had been opened in the mid-1830s by James Penny Nicholson and Daniel Simpson on Port Commission land adjacent to the dock, and although the building of ships was relatively unprofitable their repair proved to be a much more

*Glasson Dock and its busy marina*

successful venture which led to the longer-term growth of Glasson Dock.

Ten Row stands on land which had been given by John Dalton, the Lord of Thurnham Manor, to his elderly unmarried daughter Elizabeth, and the terrace forms one side of a square. The other three sides consist of the next row of cottages on Tithebarn Hill, the four cottages of West View and the six cottages of River View. The cottages around this square were not, however, the only houses constructed for shipyard workers, and Victoria Terrace and Railway Place were both built at about the same time. In little more than 15 years these developments had taken Glasson Dock from a hamlet of around 30 to a village of 300.

This growth had been largely due to the success of the shipyard rather than the coming of the canal, for even by the late 1840s the canal was beginning to lose out to the speed and convenience which the railways could offer. Although there was no direct competition until 1883, when the rail link from Glasson Dock to Lancaster was

established, the financial pressures were making themselves felt well before that time. The 5-storey canal warehouse which stood by the basin became less and less used as commercial traffic was switched to other routes, with the result that it had to be demolished in 1939.

Since that time, however, the tide has turned again in favour of the waterway. The railway line was uprooted in the 1960s, after the freight service had been terminated in the previous decade and the passenger service had been brought to a halt some 20 years earlier, but by contrast the canal is now thronged with pleasure craft while the canal basin operates as a busy marina. Glasson Dock continues to receive merchant trade, although the shipyard eventually closed in 1969, and it is also a popular place for visitors who can enjoy a stroll along the dockside or around the canal basin where the glinting waters lap against the multitude of boats and yachts which are moored there.

Much of the land upon which Glasson Dock was built had been in the ownership of the

*Thurnham Hall in the late evening sunshine*

*The Chapterhouse, Cockersand Abbey*

Dalton family, who had been lords of the manor of Thurnham since 1556. The family seat was **Thurnham Hall,** just under a couple of miles to the south east of Glasson Dock, although this impressive building has since been converted into a country club. The Hall originally displayed an older front with mullioned windows and massive bays as well as a large tower-flanked courtyard, but in 1823 John Dalton took down this front and erected in its place a facade of attractive ashlar stone with a castellated parapet and a large projecting castellated porch. The Daltons were well known Catholics, so it is not surprising that a priest's hiding place was discovered within the Hall.

By 1785, however, greater religious freedom prevailed and a chapel was built near at hand, although in 1847-48 this was replaced on the same site by a much larger and more substantial church building with a spire. Its isolated setting on the edge of mature

woodland is really quite superb, and it is well worth making the effort to track down this particular church.

Another ecclesiastical building well worth discovering is the chapterhouse of **Cockersand Abbey,** a burial place for the Dalton family. This stands on a fairly bleak and lonely site in the midst of open fields on the coastline overlooking the Lune estuary and Cockerham Sands, and it is all that remains of the large abbey which grew up out of a hermitage established here in the 12th century. In 1190 the place was transformed into a monastery or abbey of the Premon-

stratensian Order and evidently received considerable gifts of land. The abbey buildings covered nearly an acre of ground and tradition says that they stood within an enclosure of seven acres. In 1539, however, the abbey was dissolved and the land eventually came into the ownership of the Dalton family. Interestingly, the last person to be interred in the chapterhouse was Miss Elizabeth Dalton, who died in 1861 and who had been responsible for building some of the houses in Glasson Dock.

Looking northwards across the Lune estuary from Cockersand Abbey and Glasson Dock one can pick out the settlements of Sunderland and Overton, reached by going back into Lancaster and crossing over the Greyhound Bridge before turning left to follow the line of the river southwards. On the way into Lancaster the road passes Ashton Hall, the very impressive and stately house which became a residence of James Williamson the industrialist in 1895, and from which he took the title of Lord Ashton when he was made a peer of the realm in the same year. The castellated appearance of Ashton Hall is a reminder of the history and antiquity of this site, for there was a building here in 1527 when John Laurence owned the property.

*Mausoleum at Thurnham Church*

*The stately grandeur of Ashton Hall*

*Arkholme in the Lune Valley*

*The North Pier on Blackpool Promenade*

Closer in towards the centre of Lancaster one passes another superb piece of architecture, the Royal Albert Hospital, which was originally built as an asylum between 1868 and 1873. The architects were Paley and Austin, who utilised a 'domestic Gothic' style of design for the building. The asylum catered for the treatment of mentally handicapped children from Lancashire, Yorkshire, Westmorland, Cumberland, Northumberland, Durham and Cheshire, and by the end of the 19th century had developed a reputation for being the finest institution of its kind.

Over on the other side of the Lune the road down to **Overton** crosses low-lying areas of the estuary which are frequently cut off by the advancing high tides. Overton itself is a very pleasant village consisting of one narrow main street hemmed in by terraces of white painted cottages dating from the early 18th century, many of which were built with stone from the ruined Cockersand Abbey. There is also an ancient church at the southern end of the village, probably built during the 12th century and incorporating a Norman doorway. Four river pilots are buried within the churchyard walls, two of them, James Spencer and his son Thomas, piloted vessels up and down the Lune estuary for a total of 94 years.

The road through Overton continues out along the estuarine sands and marshlands to the little settlement of **Sunderland,** with frequent roadside warnings about the dangers of being cut off by high tides — making you glance nervously back over your shoulder as you go! It is the way that the high tides come up to make this little peninsula virtually an island 'sundered' from the mainland which has given it its name. Out here on this isolated headland overlooking the Lune estuary you really do feel as if you have arrived at one of Lancashire's furthest extremities — and that getting back may not be very easy!

Sunderland was the original port for Lancaster before either St. George's Quay was developed in the 1750s or Glasson Dock was constructed in the late 18th century, and most of the properties here were built by Robert Lawson, a merchant from Lancaster, during the period 1715 to 1720. Trade with both the West Indies and Africa was carried on from Sunderland, with the goods then being carted by road or river lighters to Lancaster itself. Other local trades such as rope making and joinery also thrived here, but they eventually withered away as the facilities just across the Lune grew in importance. Nowadays salmon fishing and mussel gathering are the main activities undertaken from this one time port, which is also said to have been the place at which cotton was first brought into Lancashire.

*The village of Sunderland, at one time Lancaster's port*

There are several terraces of old cottages and former warehouses which line the once bustling quayside, as well as some rather more substantial properties. One of these is the Old Hall, to be found at the southernmost point of the little lane running through Sunderland and said to have had the river rushing in through the front door and out at the back when the tides were particularly high. The two-feet thick walls and ancient roof flags which can be seen here have withstood the storms and fury of the sea for probably three centuries now, while the mahogany of the staircase could well have been part of the first such cargo to be imported into England and unloaded at Sunderland's mooring stumps.

Sunderland also had some passing connections with the slave trade, and although slaves as such were taken only to the West Indies to work in the plantations some African people would have arrived in the Lancaster area as household servants. In Sunderland there is the grave of one such person, named Sambo, who came here in 1736 but died just a few days after his arrival. Local legend suggests that he died of a broken heart when his master left him, but it is more likely that a fever was the real cause. His grave became something of a tourist feature in those times, and it can still be found close to the seashore with a memorial which records the last few verses of an elegy which was written about him.

The road back to Overton from Sunderland can be followed north westwards through Middleton and then on into **Heysham,** a village situated in the lee of a headland whose origins go back a very long way indeed. Heysham, or Hessam as it was called, is recorded in the Domesday Survey of 1086, but evidence for a fairly important Saxon settlement here is to be found in the presence of both St. Patrick's Chapel and St. Peter's Church.

*St. Patrick's Chapel, Heysham*

St. Patrick's Chapel is now just a ruin, although what remains on the rocky outcrop on which it is situated presents a dramatic scene. The chapel probably dates from the 8th century, measures 27 feet long by 9 feet wide, and is thought to be an enlargement of a slightly earlier building. Nearby are six graves cut into solid rock, with another two on the lower side of the site, each of which would have had stone lids to protect the bodies. Similar graves have been found at Hexham in Northumbria as well as in Ireland, and they would probably have been used for the burial of eminent persons (whether priests or kings) for whom special treatment seemed appropriate. Other graves have been found elsewhere on the site, there being about 80 burials altogether, and the evidence suggests that it was in use as a cemetery during the 10th and 11th centuries.

*Ancient graves at St. Patrick's Chapel*

*St. Peter's Church, Heysham*

Just a short distance down the slope of the headland from St. Patrick's Chapel is St. Peter's Church, said to have been founded in about AD 967 and therefore one of the oldest churches in continuous use in western Europe. Occupying a sheltered site which looks out towards Morecambe Bay, the building has been altered and added to over the years so that it presents an attractive amalgam of many styles and dates, and amongst its interesting features are an east window in the chancel of about 1330.

It is thought that St. Peter's may have been used as the parish church with St. Patrick's being a separate chapel for specialist uses, although the exact relationship between the two buildings has not yet been finally determined. Like St. Patrick's, however, St. Peter's does have some interesting gravestones and relics. One of these is an Anglo-Norman hogback tombstone which intermingles Norse mythology with Christian symbols, whilst another is the 13th century slab on the west wall, decorated by a foliated cross alongside a sword, which is likely to

have been placed over a Crusader's tomb.

Another important historic building in Heysham is the Old Hall at the southern end of the village, built in 1598 but substantially altered in a restoration which took place in 1888. Originally this three storey building had a large central hall with a long window divided by five mullions, a hearth almost seven feet wide and a porch which reached the full height of the house. The Old Rectory close to St. Peter's Church is also of interest — it has a date of 1680 on the lintel over the front door and has been known as Greese House, from the Old French word for the flight of steps which leads from the road to the main entrance. Back along Main Street in the village itself can be seen more stone built houses which date from the same period as the Old Rectory.

Farming has been the traditional occupation in Heysham, particularly dairying, although fishing and mussel gathering used to be another way of earning a living, as did brewing and the sale of nettle beer to visitors

in the area. By the latter part of the 19th century special attractions were being developed for tourists, with the Strawberry and Recreation Gardens being laid out in around 1869. At about this time there was a brief flurry of industrial activity, and by the turn of the century the Midland Railway had built Heysham Dock at a cost of £3 million. In its early days the harbour admitted trawlers and boats carrying imported raw materials such as iron ore, timber and cork, and even now the port is still busy with general cargo and also offers a regular ferry service to the Isle of Man.

Just up the coast is the well known holiday resort of **Morecambe,** which claims to be exceeded in importance by Blackpool alone. In comparison with Heysham Morecambe is of relatively recent origin, having been officially named as such only since the last quarter of the 19th century. Before that time it was known as Poulton-le-Sands and consisted of the three small villages of Bare, Poulton and Torrisholme. It was the coming of the railway in 1847-48 which really prompted the area's growth as a holiday resort, in conjunction with the development of the harbour through its increasing steamer traffic and iron ore imports as well as the the Irish cattle trade.

With the extension of the railway network and the increase in leisure time as a result of improving social conditions people began to flock to Morecambe in their hundreds. It was especially popular with the textile workers of Yorkshire in general and of Bradford in particular, so much so that the town was for years known as 'Bradford-by-the-Sea' or 'Little Bradford'. Commuting was a feature of life even in those early days, and it became fashionable to live in Morecambe and travel by rail to work in Bradford.

Numerous private hotels and boarding houses grew up to accommodate the influx of holidaymakers to the town, and by 1870 Morecambe had become an important and relatively prosperous community. The original Winter Gardens was opened in 1878 as a 'People's Palace of Varieties and Aquarium', and with its ornate architecture it represented more than anything else the grand ambitions of the town. In the following years more and more buildings appeared and new services were introduced, so that by the early 1920s Morecambe had become largely what it is today. One of the most significant events at this time was the passing of the Morecambe Corporation Act of 1924, which gave the Council powers to build its town hall, promenades, bathing pools, sea walls and parks.

The attractions on offer in Morecambe probably reached their peak of popularity during the war years, when thousands of servicemen and civil servants were sent to the town. After the war the new affluence of the 1950s and 1960s prompted considerable improvements as the resort adapted to the changing tastes of its holidaymakers. The Superdome is just one of many recent new attractions, although both the long established Pleasure Park and the Illuminations continue to prove as popular as ever.

Fishing has been the other important industry in Morecambe, and again it was the coming of the railway which transformed the earlier small-scale fishing activities into an important business of significance to the whole town. The railway made possible the quick transport of perishable fish and shellfish to the markets, and so opened up the way for hundreds of people and scores of boats to be employed in the mussel industry alone. The fishing industry probably reached its height in the 1920s, at about the time when the fishermen formed themselves into the Morecambe Trawlers' Co-operative Society. This helped to raise the financial rewards and standard of living of the fishing families and also provided a better opportunity to purchase more modern equipment.

In addition to the harvesting of mussels from mussel beds, cockling has been an important part of the fishing industry, with the shellfish being gathered from the sands by the use of special tools known as jumbos and craams. The jumbo was employed during winter months to beat the sands, attracting cockles to the surface, while the craam was a fork-like tool used to scoop them up from two or three inches below the top of the sand. Probably the best known of all the local fishing products are Morecambe shrimps, which are caught from special trawlers known as 'nobbies'. It is said that a Morecambe 'nobby' sailor was so skilled because of the uncertain nature of the local tides and currents that he could sail just about anywhere.

The main road from Morecambe through to Carnforth hugs the coastline for several miles before arriving at **Hest Bank,** part of the larger parish of Slyne-with-Hest. As with Galgate to the south of Lancaster, this is a place where road, rail and canal come together, and it is also famous as the starting point for the 'Crossing of the Sands'. This route over to Kents Bank and the Grange Peninsula was the first leg of what was for many years the preferred way of journeying up to Scotland, rather than risking the more hazardous route over the Cumbrian hills. The southern end of this track across the shifting sands is marked still by the Hest Bank Hotel, which acted then as a lighthouse to guide the travelling parties.

The coming of the canal helped to sustain the importance of Hest Bank by increasing the volume of goods which could be brought here for transhipment on the journey across Morecambe Bay. The coming of the railway in 1854, however, meant that the crossing of the sands was no longer necessary for those people and goods travelling further north, and by 1856 it had been effectively discontinued as a regularly-used route. Yet the railway also brought increasing numbers of visitors to the area, and a number of Victorian boarding houses sprang up on Station Road in response to the demand for holiday accommodation. Nowadays Hest Bank is much more of a pleasant residential suburb for Lancaster than a holiday resort on the coast, but it is still an attractive stopping-off place for visitors who pass through here on canal barges.

Further northwards is **Bolton-le-Sands,** originally a fishing village and the mother parish for Slyne-with-Hest. The busy A6 road rather fortunately by-passes the old village centre, which lies on higher ground to the east, with the Lancaster Canal taking a pleasant but inconspicuous route round the backs of the houses on the main street. Along this narrow thoroughfare are to be found a very agreeable assortment of old stone cottages, with some rather more substantial houses dating from the 17th and 18th centuries located along a quieter lane called The Nook. At the southern end of the village is the parish church of Holy Trinity, which dates from 1094 and enjoys a delightful setting within its shady and tranquil churchyard.

From the north side of Bolton-le-Sands the

*One of the houses to be found along The Nook in Bolton-le-Sands*

Lancaster Canal passes on into **Carnforth,** a small town which developed not because of the coming of the waterway but rather through the advent of the railway. Carnforth did, however, get a mention in the Domesday Book under the name 'Cliseneford', although by 1212 this had changed to 'Carneforth' and by the 16th century it had taken on its present form. In mediaeval times Carnforth consisted of only 105 acres of land and 12 small cottages, and the area had to wait until the development of communications in the 19th century before a sizeable town became established here.

The coming of the Lancaster Canal in 1797, in the form of the section between Tewitfield and Preston, brought no canal settlement but did stimulate the workings of large glacial deposits of sand and gravel in the area. By 1845 three quarries had been established near the waterway. Then in 1846 the London and Carlisle Railway Line was opened to passenger traffic, followed by a link to Ulverston which was opened in 1857 and which provided a connection to the iron-mining district of the Furness area. In conjunction with these developments, and in order to handle the anticipated increase in rail traffic, a new station was then built in Carnforth.

Things really began to develop after 1864, following the decision to promote a company to smelt Furness hematite at Carnforth. This iron ore was readily accessible from the Furness area due to the development of the railway system, and with the completion of the South Durham and Lancashire Railway it was possible to obtain supplies of coke for the furnaces direct from the Durham coalfields. The construction of a further railway link with the West Riding of Yorkshire was then undertaken to provide direct access to the iron and steel centres of Yorkshire. Since it was estimated that the works would employ between 200 and 500 men it was decided to build housing for the workers close to the plant, and in 1864 a row of twenty cottages was erected along Warton Road. This was followed by a much more extensive settlement of brick and stone cottages at Millhead just to the north of the railway line, and although the ironworks were demolished in 1931 the cottages still stand as a testimony to Carnforth's early industrial heritage. All this development could not fail to attract interest, and in 1866 a local paper reported that 'from a small if not insignificant village Carnforth is now rising into importance'.

Nowadays the interest in Carnforth focuses predominantly upon 'Steamtown', one of the area's major tourist attractions and the largest mainline steam locomotive depot in the British Isles. Here are to be seen some of the most impressive and most famous steam engines ever built — including the 'Flying Scotsman' in its original LNER apple-green livery, the 'Sir Nigel Gresley' (sister engine to 'Mallard', the world steam record holder), and the LMS Class 5 'Leander' (one of a number of Steamtown's motive units which are still regularly involved in mainline service). Steamtown started in 1968 with only a handful of steam preservationists, but now it employs over 30 people who are permanently involved in rebuilding, refurbishing or simply maintaining locomotives and rolling stock.

A narrow swaithe of open countryside separates Carnforth from the pretty village of **Warton** which nestles at the foot of Warton Crag. This natural fortification has been of importance to man for a very long time, and objects from the Neolithic and Romano-British ages have been found in caves on its north west side. On the summit there are remains of ramparts forming part of the defences of a hill fort built by the Brigantes, who probably lived in stone huts on the dry, south-facing slopes when not under attack. During the 9th and 10th centuries Vikings from Ireland and the Isle of Man raided all along the coast, and although they settled in many places in Cumbria they do not appear to have come to live in Warton. Christianity did reach these parts, however, and the first church here was built on higher ground in the locality and dedicated to St. Oswald.

Following the Norman Conquest the feudal system was established, with Warton coming to be regarded as part of the Barony of Kendal. By 1199 the village had been granted a market charter, and during the 13th century it grew in importance. The beginning of the 14th century saw the construction of the first stone church here and also the Old Rectory, the home of the de Thweng family who were the patrons of the church at that time. By the 15th century the Washington family (who had come to the area from County Durham in the middle of the 13th century) had also risen to prominence among the wealthy landlords in the north of England, and at the same time the Kitsons were living at Warton Hall.

During the next hundred and fifty years village life revolved around the church, the Rectory, the Hall and the market place, although by the 17th century the standard of living for the farmers, yeomen and tradesmen had improved so markedly that stone built houses began to take the place of less substantial living quarters. Over the course of the following hundred years or so Main Street assumed much of its present appearance, with many of the properties being built of local rubble stone which was then waterproofed by the application of a lime and sand render.

At the southern end of Main Street is the

*Part of Warton Crag*

parish church, dedicated to St. Oswald. The oldest part of the present building is the south aisle wall, which dates from the 14th century and incorporates two windows from that period. The tower, however, dates from the 15th century when the whole church took on more or less its present shape, except for the north aisle which was built in the 16th century. It is the tower which was constructed by Robert Washington, and it is from here that the American flag flies on Independence Day as a reminder that George Washington, the first President of the United States of America, was a descendant of the Washington family of Warton. On one of the inside walls of the tower can be seen the Washington coat of arms, which is said to have inspired the design of the 'stars and stripes' of the American flag.

Opposite the church are the ruins of the Old Rectory, a particularly important historic house. Built in the early years of the 14th century it consists in plan of a ground floor service area over which was a large hall where the lord and his family and distinguished guests dined. It is a remarkably complete example of an 'end-hall house', which was to be the ancestor of the great houses of mediaeval and Tudor times.

Closer to the centre of the village along Main Street is Washington House, another historic building of some significance in Warton. Whilst it is not possible to say which branch of the Washington family first came to live on this site, the present house was rebuilt in the late 18th century and there was probably a house here well before the date of 1612 indicated by a stone incorporated into the front of the property. The great corbelled chimney stack still to be seen was probably part of the earlier dwelling. An interesting reminder of the housekeeping of previous times is the bread oven built into the wall with an outlet into the chimney, a facility which was introduced in the 16th century.

Many of the other buildings on Main Street also offer fascinating glimpses into Warton's history. The Shovel Inn, for example, originally housed the meetings of the Manor Court or Court Leet after the decay of the Old Rectory. Nearby is the school building erected in 1902 to house pupils from the old Grammar School, and the inscription stone from this earlier building still tells visitors that Matthew Hutton, Bishop of Durham, had the school endowed in 1594 'For God and good education'. Matthew Hutton eventually became Archbishop of York. Then across the road is School House, at which Grammar School boys who could not return home each day were boarded; with its porch and lower mullioned windows it is obviously one of Warton's many 17th century buildings, and its roomy interior features a curved oak staircase and oak floors.

*One of the cottages at The Green, Silverdale*

The narrow country lane from the centre of Warton can be followed around the base of the Crag, over the low-lying Leighton Moss and then on into **Silverdale** in the most north-western corner of the county. The locals are proud of their village's setting against a backcloth of great beauty, in the form of the Lakeland hills and the open sea of Morecambe Bay, but they are also eager to emphasise Silverdale's own charm and peacefulness. This part of the county is really a microcosm of Lancashire's special qualities, for here can be found miniature crags and limestone scars as well as small but densely wooded areas, a delightful shoreline and open fields. There is also evidence of a long period of human settlement in the vicinity, with a marvellous variety of old cottages, houses, farms, drystone walls, wells and watering places.

The derivation of the name 'Silverdale' is not from its attractive natural setting or even the silver birch trees and limestone rocks to be found in the area; it comes rather from the name of a Viking family which settled here, signifying that the valley belonged to Sigward or Soevers. During mediaeval times this name went through such variations as Soeversdal, Swierdelage, Selredal, Celverdale, Sellerdal, Siluerdal and Silurdale to Silverdale. Little is known of Silverdale in this period, probably then only a small crofting village, although documents of 1246 refer to a fortified manor possessed by Adam d'Avranches which would appear to have occupied the present site of Leighton Hall. The oldest properties in Silverdale are those at The Green, with one dating from 1550, and Gibraltar Farm, which was built about the same time.

As well as being engaged in small-scale farming the inhabitants of Silverdale were also involved in fishing, and there was a considerable cockle and fluke trade from the village. Then in the late 18th century a copper smelting works was built here, although all that remains of this now is the chimney near Jenny Brown's Point. The ore treated at the works was obtained from quarries at Crag Foot and at the Cove, with the former having been used since Tudor times. Silverdale also became more widely known through the travellers who used to take the short journey across the sands of Morecambe Bay to and from the north west parts of England and beyond, and as early as 1836 the Silverdale Hotel was opened to provide food and accommodation for those people arriving by stagecoach.

Just over twenty years later the railway line between Lancaster and Ulverston was constructed, bringing an increasing number of seasonal visitors to the area, and by the latter half of the 19th century Silverdale had become a quiet seaside resort where medicinal baths of fresh sea water could be taken in one of the small villas by the shore. Silverdale also became a popular place for wealthy people to retire to, along with their servants, and it was this trend which led to the building of the larger houses and ensured the continuing growth of the village. Elizabeth Gaskell was a frequent visitor here, along with her young family and nurse, and parts of nearly all her books were written while she stayed at Gibraltar Tower in Silverdale.

In addition to its social history the village has a great deal to offer from the point of view of its natural habitats. Down by the shore the salt marshes extend to the shallow waters of the bay, which retreat on the ebb tide to leave uncovered large expanses of golden sands. The wide stretches of 'sea-washed' turf are given a pink sheen when the sea thrift is in bloom, while the edges of the many channels through the turf are the home of plants such as the sea aster, white goosefoot and sea purslane. The low limestone cliffs edging the shore provide a different environment for other types of plants, while a little distance inland from the coast are to be found the limestone hills and shady woods which provide a shelter for many varieties of fern.

Further to the east of Silverdale is **Leighton Moss,** the largest area of reed bed in north west England and now a significant nature reserve owned and managed by the Royal Society for the Protection of Birds. The reed beds are the most important part of the reserve because they have become the northern stronghold of the rare bearded-tit and are also the major British breeding centre for the bittern. For most of the year visitors to the Leighton Moss reserve are able to see the

*Jenny Brown's Point, Silverdale*

resident population of black-headed gulls, coots and waterhens, while on certain occasions there is the chance to see ospreys and marsh harriers in passage. On the nearby salt marshes, now under the care of the RSPB, it is also possible to observe large numbers of wigeon and mallard in the autumn months as well as curlews and oystercatchers.

Almost next door to Leighton Moss is **Leighton Hall,** a delightful stately home situated at the far end of a broad expanse of open parkland bounded by mature trees. The approach is rather grand but so too is the background, for beyond the house can be seen the wooded hills of southern Cumbria

and then the Lakeland fells. Leighton Hall itself has a very impressive appearance, with its dramatic neo-Gothic facade of white limestone style being added in the early 19th century by Thomas Harrison. This new frontage was introduced to replace that of an earlier Adam-style house which had itself been erected on the site of an older building in 1763. It was at about this time that the woods were replanted and the park laid out. By 1822 the property had passed into the hands of Richard Gillow (the grandson of Robert Gillow, the founder of the famous furniture firm of Gillow and Co. in Lancaster) and it is now owned by the Gillow-Reynolds family.

Inside the house visitors can see many rooms created to a neo-Gothic design as well as some fine pieces of original Gillow furniture. The hall, for example, is an exceptionally good example of the early Gothic Revival style, with long delicate pillars supporting a landing and framing a beautifully curved stone staircase, and among the various items of furniture is an interesting eight-winged table by Gillow known as a 'Daisy Table'. Then through the library is the dining room, in which can be found more examples of early Gillow furniture; of particular interest here is the large expanding table, thought to be the prototype of all leafed tables.

The library also gives access to the drawing room, in which can be found an early 18th century games table by Gillow as well as a satinwood writing table which typifies the best of English furniture design. At the top of the staircase is the 'Portico Room', decorated in a typically mid-Victorian style, and also the principal bedroom, a good example of the late Victorian period and furnished with a magnificent suite in bird's-eye maple. Outside

*Leighton Hall and its parkland setting*

*Leighton Hall*

in the grounds of Leighton Hall visitors can enjoy the extensive herbaceous border which lines a long narrow lawn originally designed for archery, as well as the shrubbery walk which was an inseparable part of all early 19th century gardens.

East of Leighton Hall and directly north of Warton are the two very pretty villages of **Yealand Conyers** and **Yealand Redmayne,** partly hidden from passing traffic on the nearby A6 road by the woodland which clothes the lower slopes of Warton Crag on which these villages are situated. The name 'Yealand' apparently means 'High Land', while the other appendages originated

during the 13th century when the Yealand estate passed to two daughters who were then married to men with the surnames of Conyers and Redmayne — hence the distinction between the two settlements. By and large farming has been the predominant occupation here over the centuries, although quarrying has also been of some significance. Lime burning was another local activity, and a ruined kiln can still be seen in the fields near to Yealand Conyers, close to the road which goes down to Leighton Hall. Back in the 15th century flax weaving was also established as an important industry in the area, and in Yealand Conyers one can still find a building once known as a 'heckling shop' where the

flax was carded and combed. Adjoining this building on the main street through the village are some former weavers' cottages.

Like many villages in this part of Lancashire, Yealand Redmayne and Yealand Conyers were important centres for nonconformist religion and in particular for the Quakers. Yealand Conyers is especially significant because it has the oldest and probably most attractive Friends' Meeting House in the area, a humble building dating from 1692 which sits in peaceful seclusion a little distance from the main village street. Screened by ancient yew trees and what was at one time a Quaker day school, the Meeting House is largely undisturbed by modern comings and goings, and the panelled assembly room inside remains very much as it always has been.

*The Friends' Meeting House, Yealand Conyers*

The next village to be discovered after Yealand Conyers is **Borwick,** a really delightful place which is very much off the beaten track even though both the M6 motorway and the Lancaster Canal run close by. At its heart is a lovely village green bounded by attractive old cottages and

presided over by Borwick Hall, the traditional home of the lords of the manor. The oldest part of the Hall is its pele tower, an early stone dwelling house built with defence in mind, probably constructed shortly after the Great Raid in 1322 when the marauding Scots on their way to Lancaster may well have destroyed an earlier wooden home of the Lords of Borwick. If their house was burned to the ground, a new one would have been erected as soon as possible and local stone used rather than wood. To all intents and purposes they obviously did a good job of the rebuilding, as the walls at the base of the tower average six feet in thickness.

The north wing was the next part of the Hall to be built, probably by George Redmayne between 1532 and 1548. Then Robert Bindloss, a wealthy cloth merchant from Kendal, acquired the property in 1567 and immediately built the narrow east wing. He also erected the west wing, the most important part of the house, finishing it in 1595 (the year of his death). On the ground floor is the Great Hall, used as a parlour on formal occasions, with some early oak panelling and an old fireplace, while above is another long room originally used as a library and at one time decorated with a beautiful plaster ceiling.

These two floors are linked by a stone staircase, which rises in its own tower at the back of the house and displays the inscription 'Alixander Brinsmead Mason 1595' on a stone slab supported on pillars. It is thought that he was the person responsible for the construction of this wing. Outside the Hall there are attractive terraced gardens on the south side as well as an impressive Gatehouse which guards the way into the property. This was built by the third Robert Bindloss in 1650, and he and his wife's initials can be seen inscribed on a panel over the gateway.

Borwick has traditionally been an agricultural area, with the land being held by the owners of Borwick Hall, although some quarrying has also taken place here as well as the spinning and weaving of flax for local consumption. It was this overriding control exercised by the lords of the manor which ensured that change happened very slowly,

*Borwick Hall*

and for many years farming in Borwick seemed to be a long way behind what was happening elsewhere. The same has been true of church matters, as the Dean and Chapter of Worcester Cathedral have remained rectors here (as part of the larger parish of Warton) since 1547, when it was passed on to them by the monarch of the time. In many respects this atmosphere of continuity and changelessness still prevails within the village to a large degree, even though the Hall is now run as a residential training centre by the Lancashire Youth Clubs Association and the Lancashire Education Committee.

The neighbouring village of **Priest Hutton** displays many similar characteristics to Borwick, although there has been no dominant family and industrial activities such as cinder burning and quarrying attained rather greater importance. Nevertheless its old cottages, limestone walls and narrow lanes give the same appealing sense of mellow immutability.

From Borwick the road crosses the valley of the River Keer to the east and then runs alongside tree-lined fields towards **Capernwray Hall,** a very impressive 'battlemented' house in extensive grounds built by the Marton family in the 1830s and now occupied as an international Bible school. Capernwray Old Hall, some distance away on the road to the village of Over Kellet, seems to date from the 12th century when Adam de Capernwray lived here, and recent restoration work has revealed ancient walls

some six feet in thickness. Nearby, the River Keer is crossed by a venerable packhorse bridge dating from the Saxon period which is on an early route from Borwick to Over Kellett, while just a hundred yards upstream is a former corn mill (with its waterwheel largely intact) latterly converted into a house.

Like Borwick, **Over Kellet** has an attractive village green as a focal point, although this one is considerably larger and is marked by four roads into it from the north, south, east and west. Around the green are an attractive range of old farmhouses and cottages, with many dating from the 17th and 18th centuries. The main house here is Hall Garth, standing in its own grounds, although what is seen now was built in the 1820s to replace a much older building on the same site. One of the cottages across the village green from Hall Garth has an orchard which was an early Quaker burial ground, and the cottage itself is likely to have been a Friends' Meeting House.

The mainstay of the village economy over the centuries has been farming, and even now working farms still exist close to the centre of Over Kellet. The parish church of St. Cuthbert's, situated some distance to the south of the village on an elevated site above the road, dates from the 12th century and was probably built as a place of worship for monks from Cockersand Abbey who appear to have run a hospice on the site of nearby Kirk House Farm. Less than half a mile away is Birkland Barrow, a recently restored historic farmhouse which also had monastic links and

*The village green in Borwick*

*Capernwray Hall*

offered the facility of a fish pond used by the monks to retain the fish which they caught in the Lune.

To the south of Over Kellet is the village of **Nether Kellet,** similar not only in name but also in character. In many respects it remains very much a farming community, although quarrying has taken place here for centuries

*Birkland Barrow, Over Kellet*

and is still carried out in the nearby hills — as is evident from the constant stream of heavy lorries heading down towards the motorway. Lime burning has also been an important local industry, with the remains of former lime kilns to be seen around the village as well as a pub named 'The Limeburners' for good measure. Like Borwick, Nether Kellet was marked by a considerable degree of control exercised by the main landowners well into the 20th century, and very few houses were in owner-occupation until the Second World War when the different estates were gradually being sold off.

As in Over Kellet, several working farms still operate from within the village itself, characteristic of the unchanging nature of many places on the fringes of the Lune Valley. Here again is to be found a traditional village green, around which the village is focused, as well as the added features of several old wells and pumps which are a further reminder that the rate of change has

been a relatively slow one. From the village green the road runs south for a mile or so to a point overlooking the village of Halton and the River Lune, from where our journey through the Lonsdale area first began.

*Little Marton Windmill, Blackpool*

# CHAPTER 3: THE FYLDE AND THE WYRE

This part of the county is one which encompasses within it some of the most dramatic contrasts in Lancashire, not only in physical and geographic terms but also in social and economic ones too. The **Fylde** — a name derived from an Old English word meaning 'plain' — can be defined somewhat loosely as the area to the west of the A6 between the Lune and Ribble estuaries, a predominantly flat and relatively treeless expanse of lowland interrupted by the occasional eminence of higher ground. The fact that it is now a fertile agricultural area displaying a settled pastoral beauty is largely the result of man's unstinting endeavour to drain and subdue what was formerly a rather hostile marshland. Of a rather different character are the many tributaries feeding the Wyre which flow from the foothills of the Bowland fells through pleasantly wooded gorges, having commenced their journey from the harsher and more exposed moorland escarpments to the east.

This physical contrast is matched by some marked social and economic differences. For example, the main economic activity on the Fylde has traditionally been farming and market gardening (and more latterly tourism), but the fast flowing streams which supplied the Wyre further downstream provided the necessary water power to encourage textile mills and early industrial activity in places such as Dolphinholme, Oakenclough and Calder Vale. The better ground here in the east paved the way for settlements to be more widely spread, while on the Fylde human occupation was primarily concentrated in a smaller number of distinct villages because travel over the mosses and marshes was initially very difficult.

This does not appear to have hindered the Romans too much, though, in their determination to construct a road through the area from Ribchester, crossing the Fylde along a route which passed through the middle of Kirkham on its way up to a fording point on the River Wyre somewhere to the east of Fleetwood. It is quite possible that this was the site of the Roman port of 'Portus Stetenorium', although its precise location is rather vague and no positive traces have so far been identified. Some suggest that it was situated two miles north of Fleetwood at the point where the River Wyre discharges into the Lune Deeps.

Our 'gateway' into the area of the Fylde and the Wyre is **Ellel Grange,** close to the Hampson Green junction of the M6 motorway and just a mile to the south of Galgate. The stately house which now occupies the site, together with its impressive tower which can be seen above the tops of the encircling trees, was largely the work of William Preston during the 19th century, although it seems that there was a 'grange' here at Ellel centuries before in the ownership of Cockersand Abbey. Members of the famous Gillow family lived here during the 18th and 19th centuries, and then the property ultimately returned to the Preston family who had been the original owners.

Apparently William Preston was born on a farm which was the last remnant of the property formerly owned by the Prestons, his ancestors being the old Prestons of the original Ellel Grange, and as a youth he determined to buy back the land which had belonged to his forefathers. With this in mind he went to the office of his uncle, Robert Preston, a Liverpool merchant, and by virtue of hard work and perseverance he eventually achieved his goal. For good measure he also became the Mayor of Liverpool and High Sheriff of Lancashire.

Some years after the building of his mansion at Ellel Grange William Preston arranged to have a church erected close by, this being completed in 1873. The result was a very impressive piece of Victorian church architecture, designed to a 13th century French Gothic style and incorporating an

*Ellel Grange near Hampson Green*

exceptionally graceful and colourful interior. The upper part of the nave walls and the entire roof of the church were covered with highly accomplished paintings in a Byzantine style, featuring evangelists and apostles as well as gilded pictures of angels, stars and flowers. The work undertaken on the interior of this church, which is known as St. Mary's, represented a high point in the art of ecclesiastical decoration.

Travelling southwards along the A6 there are picturesque glimpses through the trees of another substantial house, Hay Carr, just beyond the Lancaster Canal. This stone built property was a comparatively small building until it was enlarged at the south end in 1835 and then further extended on the north east side with some rather later additions. Not far from here a narrow lane off to the right directs us away from the busy A6 across undulating fields and over the canal to **Cockerham,** a quiet little village which enjoys an elevated position above the flat coastal plain to the west. The old terraced cottages on either side of the main street running through the village give an unspoken hint of its antiquity, and it seems that it was mentioned in the Domesday Book under the name Cocreham — which is not far removed from the present spelling. The manor was given to the canons of Leicester in the latter half of the 12th century, but after a period with the Abbot of Cockersand in the 14th century it eventually passed to four joint 'Lords of Cockerham' in the 1700s.

The oldest building in the village is Cockerham Hall, a substantial farmhouse situated in the fields below the rest of Cockerham on the west side. Although fairly

unassuming from the outside, this property is of considerable architectural and historical significance, as it is a rare North Lancashire example of a late mediaeval timber-framed hall dating from about the 1470s. Much of the original structure has survived, including the main hall which measures 25 feet long by 21 feet wide, although added to this at a later date (perhaps at a time of increasing security and prosperity) was the stone cross-wing.

Next in importance to the Hall is the Parish Church of St. Michael standing in splendid isolation to the south west of the village, a solid stone structure which seems to have turned its back on Cockerham itself and instead directs its attention to the considerable expanse of Cockerham Moss below it. St. Michael's was originally founded in about 1160, although it was rebuilt in the first half of the 17th century. Apart from the tower, this 17th century church was then superseded by a later one occupying the same site and completed in 1814. Perhaps it was the separation of the village from the church's watchful gaze which led to Cockerham becoming the 'lively' place that it was in the early 19th century — horse races, bowling, cock fighting and coursing are said to have taken place here at that time.

Small wonder, then, that a legend which has persisted in the village has to do with the antics of the devil, who is said to have wrought havoc here before being finally vanquished by the local schoolmaster. The story does that the devil agreed to being set three tasks by the schoolmaster, on the basis that if he failed in any one he would leave Cockerham forever - but if he succeeded the schoolmaster would forfeit his own soul. The

schoolmaster told the devil to first of all count the dewdrops on a nearby hedge, and then to count the ears of corn in a nearby field. Both of these tasks were accomplished with relative ease, but then Old Nick was asked to spin a rope of sand that would bear washing in the River Cocker. Luckily for the local schoolmaster this proved impossible, and the devil had to admit defeat. The end of the affair is recorded in this way by a local rhyme:

'The devil was foiled, wrath, and gave
him a shaking;
Up he flew to the steeple — his frame
all a-quaking.
With one horrid frig — his mind very
unwilling
He strode to the brig o'er Broadfleet at
Pilling'.

A tradition which has rather more substance to it than the legend of the devil's antics at Cockerham is that of fluke fishing, an activity in which a number of the local families would have been engaged even up to relatively recent times. Fluke or sand fishing is a method of catching fish which has been practised in the Morecambe Bay area for many generations and which probably dates back to before the time of the monks at Cockersand Abbey. Generally the fishermen made their own nets of cotton string, this being knitted into a diamond-shaped mesh some forty yards in length and up to three feet deep. The maximum length of a complete net when set was three hundred yards, tapering from a depth of three feet at the centre to two and a half feet at each end.

The net was then fixed in place using stakes and spars of hazel or ash, in such a way as to allow the base of the net to move with the incoming tide and to return to the correct position for netting the fish when the tide turned. The deepest part of the net was usually in the centre of a semi-circle in the drain channel of the water, with the ends of the net being turned inwards to prevent the fish escaping. There was no 'closed season' for this type of fishing, although the weather usually dictated that it took place between April and October.

For transporting the catch, which might average around twenty stone, the fishermen used fairly simple horse-drawn carts of a type which were generally found on local farms, and these could be seen on the sands until just a few years ago. During the course of a day the fishermen would cover considerable distances, especially in the Cockerham and Pilling area where they could travel up to five miles across the sands just to collect one catch. Nowadays, however, there is little call for this type of fishing as modern methods have effectively ousted it as a way of catching fish except in the more remote areas.

The giant stride which the devil is reputed to

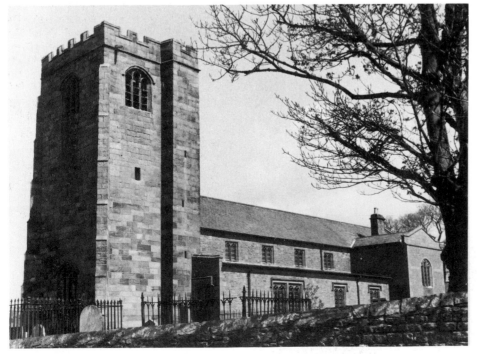

*St. Michael's Parish Church, Cockerham*

*A Fylde farmhouse on the road to Pilling*

have taken from Cockerham Parish Church to Pilling Bridge actually covers a distance of four miles, and disbelieving visitors are often shown the dent in the parapet of the bridge made by his hoof when he came down! For ordinary mortals restricted to rather slower means of getting around the journey to Pilling will no doubt take a little longer, even though the road is predominantly straight and very flat. However, this does enable you to enjoy some far-reaching views across the former marshlands, now largely drained to provide pasture for herds of Friesian cattle, and to anticipate your arrival in Pilling where the spire of the parish church acts as a marker in guiding visitors across the great green expanse from Cockerham. Along the way are to be seen some old farms and cottages which must have existed here long before the modern methods of flood protection were introduced, since they are elevated a little above the surrounding fields and protected from a watery siege by their own encircling mounds.

**Pilling** itself is a very historic settlement, founded on what was essentially an 'island' with the sea on one side and marsh on the others, and there is evidence of occupation in the area as far back as the Bronze Age period. Towards the end of the 11th century the land here was passed to the monks of Cockersand Abbey, who held it until the dissolution of the monasteries in the 16th century, and even now there are several fields in the locality which have the same names as they did when the Abbey held the manor. Across these fields is an ancient moated site (dating from the pre-Christian era) which was probably the first place of worship in Pilling and where a service is still held once every year to commemorate the village's early Christian origins.

The chapel which existed here is first mentioned indirectly in official records dated 1272, but a petition to the Bishop of Chester in 1716 mentions an ancient tradition that the chapel was built around 1209. During those early days it was served and maintained by

the canons of Cockersand Abbey, until dissolution in 1539. By 1717 it was decided to build a new and larger church about one and a quarter miles to the west, and the old chapel and graveyard were left to fall into decay. The new Georgian church that was built is tucked away in a secluded setting down a narrow track to the side of The Ship Inn, and over the main entrance is a sundial to the memory of Rev. G. Holden. This one-time village curate who was in Pilling from 1758 to 1767 is particularly famous for his tide estimation tables, still used as the basis of tide calculations today, and in many respects he is the main claim to fame for a village which by and large has kept itself to itself. The present parish church enjoys a rather more prominent setting than its earlier Georgian counterpart and was built in 1887 to a design by Paley and Austin.

Pilling has always been a classic rural village, with its economy based largely upon agriculture and horticulture together with some mixed animal husbandry, and at one time its rows of traditionally-built thatched cottages would have presented a 'picture postcard' appearance for visitors to enjoy. Now, however, these cottages have been largely demolished and replaced by newer dwellings, but despite this the village atmosphere has been retained and at various points throughout Pilling one can still see older and largely unchanged properties. Carr House, for example, occupies its own moated site, while Fluke Hall was built in the 1830s on the edge of the marsh. The village also has a former windmill which apparently functioned as a water mill at the same time, although it is now in residential use and the sails have long since disappeared.

Windmills are something of a feature of the Fylde landscape even though many have been demolished over the years, and in the village of **Preesall** to the west of Pilling another of these interesting structures is to be seen. Preesall itself is a pretty collection of old cottages which huddle together just below the

crest of a prominent hill dominating the surrounding low countryside. As one might guess from its elevated site there is evidence of occupation in the Preesall area from the earliest times, and a prehistoric canoe and flint implements have been found in the nearby mosses as well as a hoard of Roman coins at Hackensall Hall. Place names show subsequent occupation by Celts, Anglo-Saxons and Norsemen, while Hakon's Hough (the site of the present Hackensall Hall) was presumably occupied by a Viking named Hakon; the Mount, an ancient mound upon which now sits the War Memorial, is locally believed to be Hakon's burial mound.

As one might expect, Preesall is mentioned in the Domesday Book, under the name of Pressoude, and it appears that the name could have originated either from there being a Priest's Hall here or from a combination of words meaning 'a salt farm near the sea'. In the 12th century the farmland, fisheries, and wreck-gathering rights were divided between two main families; one of these was headed by Geoffrey, the bowman of King John, who received his land as a grant and in return had to perform guard duties at Lancaster Castle. By the 13th century the Abbot of Cockersand Abbey had appeared on the scene, with the Abbey being given 900 acres of farmland and some fisheries in return for providing a monk to sing masses at the chapel at Hackensall Hall.

When the estate was eventually split in the latter part of the 16th century about three-quarters of the land came into the possession of Edmund Fleetwood of Roshall in 1596, and it was his descendants who built the present Hackensall Hall which dates from 1656 and is one of the oldest buildings in the area. Another historic property is Parrox Hall, which became the centre of the remaining quarter of the estate; owned initially by the Butler family it then passed by marriage to the Elletsons, who have held it for the last two

*The village of Preesall*

and a half centuries. The present building was probably constructed during the latter part of the 16th century, and although it has been extended and re-ordered over the years the basic layout has remained largely intact.

Preesall established itself early on as an important market centre for the surrounding district, as witnessed by the presence of its own corn mill and two public houses as well as by the founding of a Charity School by Richard Fleetwood in 1695. Then in 1872 rock salt deposits were discovered beneath the village and for about 30 years Preesall became a centre of salt mining. In 1883 the Fleetwood Salt Company was established to expose and develop the saltfield and by 1891 the Fleetwood Chronicle was reporting that the salt works were continually being extended and that cottages were being built to accommodate the workers in the industry. By the end of 1891 a reliable pipeline was in operation under the River Wyre and salt was being shipped out of Fleetwood.

The bulk of the salt appears to have been extracted in the form of brine, but this brought about considerable subsidence problems. One of the most noticeable episodes occurred in 1923, when subsidence in the ground to the west of the village led to the opening up of a huge pit known as 'Bottomless'. This enormous hole was over 100 yards in diameter and between 200 feet and 400 feet deep, and the Fleetwood Chronicle recorded that '...intermittently, as you look at the great cavity...there come sounds as of the rushing of a subterranean cataract, then a rumble rising to the roar of thunder...The roar has been heard at Pilling, four miles away...This great hole, which is daily visited by hundreds of people from far and near, including many geologists...is of such a depth that it could swallow the Blackpool Tower and leave no trace of it'.

The crater was still expanding in January 1924, as the Fleetwood Chronicle was again quick to note:

"Last weekend there were alarming extensions to the great yawning crater...Many persons were wakened in the small hours of Sunday morning by bedsteads quivering beneath them...At night, brilliantly illuminated by huge white and red arc-lamps the scene of the subsidence is an eerie spectacle. Coloured lights make the shiny sides crimson in appearance and the terrifying sounds of titanic earth combats which ascend from indeterminable depths cause even the most hardy to step back hurriedly".

These cataclysmal events are a far cry form the transcending peace and quiet which prevails in Preesall nowadays, but physical evidence of the salt industry which operated in this area is still to be seen in the many 'flashes' and brine pits to the west of the village.

To the north west of Preesall at the mouth of the River Wyre is Knott End-on-Sea, a small coastal resort with a pleasant main street which curves down towards a quiet promenade with excellent views across to Fleetwood on the other side of the river. The first buildings here were groups of fishermen's cottages along the east bank of the Wyre and at the 'knott' of hard land which forms a point on the estuary. It seems that the word 'knott' is of Danish origin and indicates rounded rocky ground. This fishing settlement grew substantially during the 17th and 18th centuries as a pilot base for the upstream ports of Wardleys and Skippool and then later as a ferry point in conjunction with the development of Fleetwood. More recently the bracing sea air and the broad, flat sands stretching out into Morecambe Bay have led to Knott End's growth as a small holiday resort and a place for retirement.

Just a short distance from here, further along the coast, is the hamlet of **Pilling Lane,** which developed as a farming, fishing and cockling settlement famous for its early potatoes. It was farming rather than fishing, however, which was the great strength of the area, and in the mid-19th century the farmers of Pilling Lane dominated the markets of Garstang, Lancaster and Preston.

From Preesall the road running southwards passes through the village of Stalmine before reaching **Hambleton,** where a local salt industry was in evidence from the 15th century to the early 1700s. Here the tides played an all-important role in the making of salt, as two or three days after a high tide the shallow hollows where salt water had evaporated were raked and the slitch (or sandy mud) shovelled into heaps for further drying. This slitch was then washed to produce brine, which in turn was boiled in large shallow pans to produce the salt particles. This boiling (or 'welling' as it was known) over a turf fire had to be carried out undercover so as to prevent heat loss and dilution of the brine by rainwater, and the long low buildings where the welling was done were known as 'saltcoats'. People working the saltcoats were known as 'saltwellers', and in Hambleton the saltwellers were all farmers who looked upon the making of salt as an additional source of income. The salt industry here appears to have gone into decline at the beginning of the 18th century when cheap salt was being produced all year round in Cheshire, and practically all traces of the saltcoats were washed away by a great storm in 1720.

Less than half a mile to the south of Hambleton the River Wyre is crossed by the Shard Bridge, and from here the road runs first south and then west to bring us into **Skippool.** This was once a small port which served the ancient market town of Poulton-le-Fylde, and even now the many sailing boats tied up at Skippool Creek are reminiscent of how busy the riverside would have been when ship building was carried out here and flax and cotton were being received and stored in the wharfside warehouses. With the advantage of its own port **Poulton-le-Fylde** (its name means 'the town by the pool', with 'le Fylde' being added in 1842 to distinguish it from the village near Lancaster) developed as a commercial centre for the many hamlets and villages around it,

*Poulton-le-Fylde's parish church*

*The Market Place, Poulton-le-Fylde*

supplying goods and services to the local farming communities. During the 18th and 19th centuries there were quarterly cattle and cloth fairs held here as well as weekly corn markets, and as Blackpool grew in popularity as a seaside town so the owners of its lodging houses and hotels travelled to Poulton to buy goods and produce for the visitors.

Poulton-le-Fylde's history goes back a very long way indeed, and it is one of the oldest towns in the ancient area known as Amounderness. The Romans were in the district until AD 420, and an ancient trackway or causeway known as the Danes Pad is said to have been constructed by them. About a mile and a half of such a causeway has been traced across Pilling Moss, several feet below the surface — it is solidly formed of sections of large oak trees laid upon sleepers and fastened into the ground by wooden pegs, but being less than two feet in width. After the Romans left the locality was inhabited by the Saxons, who built a chapel on the site of the present church building, and by the Vikings, who gave place-names such as Poulton, Thornton, Norbreck and Warbreck. In the

Domesday Survey the settlement here is listed as 'Poltun', and its lands were granted by William the Conqueror to Roger of Poitou. He in turn granted the church to the monastery of Lancaster in 1094, two years after it had been rebuilt.

During the mediaeval period the town seems to have been relatively peaceful, and as a market centre for the surrounding area life would have focused largely upon the Market Place. This is still very much the hub of activity in Poulton-le-Fylde, with one end being dominated by the very attractive Parish Church set in the middle of a shady churchyard and the other end featuring some fascinating relics of commerce and local justice. These include a fish slab on which the market prices were fixed, a restored market cross with its original steps, a whipping post (now, thankfully, without its manacles), and the stocks. Records show that two vagabonds and offenders, Jonathan Bell and John Smith, were publicly whipped for 'divers notorious misdemeanors' in 1648, while Elizabeth Johnson and Jane Clark had earlier been set in the stocks in 1629 as 'wandering

persons' accused of stealing linen clothes. Both these instruments of correction appear to have been in use up to the early part of the 19th century.

The relative stability and peacefulness that existed in Poulton-le-Fylde is also evident from church records, which show that a minister named Peter White held the living of the parish church from the time of the Spanish Armada until the Civil War, a record period of sixty-three years. Even in 1641, when Parliament enforced a declaration in favour of the Protestant faith, little trouble was given despite the district being predominantly a Roman Catholic one. Yet it was not only its market and its tendency towards law and order which made Poulton the 'metropolis of the Fylde' during this period, because for at least five centuries a Court of Petty Sessions was held here and in addition it had the benefit of its own port at Skippool.

During the 18th and 19th centuries Poulton further developed its importance as the centre of the farming community in this part of the Fylde, and there were many traders, craftsmen and retailers who supplied goods and services to the farmers and their families. In addition coffee and cloth fairs were held in Poulton market place three times a year, together with a weekly corn market. Poulton also had an air of busyness because the seasonal nature of farm work combined with the comings and goings of seafarers meant that there were always itinerant workers in the area. As a result ale houses flourished here to provide both refreshment and accommodation, with one of the oldest and most important being the Golden Ball Hotel. Besides offering the usual facilities of a public house it also served as Poulton's reading room, where newspapers could be read in the atmosphere of a gentlemen's club, and it was here that the news of the Battle of Waterloo in 1815 was first received.

At least some tranquility in Poulton-le-Fylde is still preserved within the hallowed confines of the Parish Church of St. Chad, a building which dates largely from the 18th century. Although not named in the Domesday Survey of 1086, the church's dedication to a 7th century Bishop of Lichfield suggests that there has been a place of worship on this site for well over a thousand years. Whilst there is now no trace of the building created by Roger of Poitou in the 11th century, it is thought that this was initially a narrow structure of red sandstone to which an aisle was later added on the north side. In 1751 this church either collapsed or was pulled down, and it was rebuilt to transform what had been a mediaeval building into the largely Georgian one to be seen today. The tower was in better condition, however, and it survived the rebuilding so that this is now the oldest part of the church. It has been suggested that the carved stone in the choir vestry bearing the date 1638 and six sets of initials commemorates the building of the tower and the church-wardens in office at the time of its erection.

Up to 1868 the inside of the church was perfectly rectangular, but in that year a semi-circular apse was added in order to provide more worthy surroundings for the altar. Most of the interior of the church has remained unaltered since the rebuilding of 1751, particularly the box pews of the north and south galleries where one can still see the brass plates indicating their former owners. On one of these is the name of Christopher Albin, who was the original purchaser of the pew when it was put up for sale in 1752. This system of the private ownership of pews continued until 1914, when after much opposition all pews in the church were declared 'free and open'.

Most of the properties in the Market Place were also rebuilt just twenty years prior to the re-building of the church, as a result of some wayward sparks from a torchlight funeral procession in 1732 which burned all the surrounding thatched cottages to the ground. The damage was so extensive that a national appeal was launched to help meet the costs of the rebuilding, with a plea for help being made from every pulpit in the land. It is interesting to note that the Parochial Church Council of St. Chad's received a letter just a few years ago from a church in Bedfordshire saying that in 1732 they had donated 6d. to Poulton's disaster fund, and as their church roof now needed repairing would St. Chad's like to return the favour!

At the bottom end of the Market Place can be seen the houses of two of Poulton's more important merchants, who were very influential in the district. Sir Alexander Rigby built his town house in 1693 on the site of what is now the National Westminster Bank, after becoming a successful trader in the 1690s. Unfortunately his business began to fail and although he sold most of his land he was eventually imprisoned in London's Fleet prison for debtors where he died in 1717. His neighbour James Baines met with rather more long-term success in his woollen drapery business, and by the time of his death in 1717 he had founded three schools as well as bequeathing money for maintenance and schoolmasters' wages. Money was also left to develop a fund for poor apprentices within the area, to enable them to learn their crafts.

Perhaps James Baines had been rather more fortunate in the local custom of Teanlay Night, which involved the lighting of bonfires on Hallowe'en. As part of this old tradition the bonfire would be circled with white-coloured stones which were then thrown into the fire by the participants and left overnight. Successful retrieval of one's own stone the following day was considered a good omen for personal prosperity, although presumably many people must have learnt that the trick was to choose one with a distinctive shape!

Travelling northwards from Poulton-le-Fylde to Fleetwood the road follows the line of the

*Marsh Mill, Thornton*

42

*Lytham Hall on the Fylde*

*Terraced cottages in Calder Vale*

River Wyre, passing through **Thornton** en route. The most notable building here is Marsh Mill, now the last complete windmill in the North West. Built in 1794 by Ralph Slater, a Fylde millwright who also built mills at Pilling and Clifton, it was initially used to grind various grades of flour but was later used for grinding meal for farm use until it finally stopped work in 1922. As is the case with other mills in the region the five storey brick tower is broad in proportion to its height, enabling it to accommodate the exceptionally large machinery.

The ground and first floors of the mill are designed as storage rooms with drying rooms attached, while the second floor contains the machinery for dressing the corn after grinding; it is at this level that the tower is encircled by the gallery or stage which provides access to the sails. The millstones themselves are on the third floor, while the top floor (known as the dust floor) separates the milling operations from the sail mechanism housed in the revolving cap. This physical layout within the building meant that the grain, lifted by sack hoist to the top of the mill, would work its way down through the processes of milling and dressing arranged in a vertical sequence. The power required for these operations was transmitted from the sails via a horizontal shaft to a vertical one running down the centre of the mill, this in turn driving the millstones and the auxiliary machinery below.

Originally Marsh Mill would have been fitted with common sails which were of a lattice like framework rigged with cloth, but these were replaced with the type invented in 1807 by Sir William Cubitt. As on most mills in this part of the country the sails are double, that is with working surfaces on both sides of the whip or back, and they are tapered so that all the shutters are of a different length. It is also interesting to note that the outer three shutters of the trailing edges are tipped forward to act as an air brake and keep the sails down to the required speed of between 12 and 16 revolutions per minute. In the earliest days of windmill engineering the sails, or sometimes even the whole mill, had to be pushed round

to face into the wind, but Marsh Mill incorporates fantail machinery which is set at right angles to the sails so that they are automatically re-aligned as the wind veers. The boat-shaped cap on top of the mill, made up of rafters and tarred boarding, is a characteristic feature which was shared by many of the Fylde windmills.

The miller's aim was to grind the corn to a consistent degree of fineness, this depending not only on the speed of the stones but also on the rate of grain feed as well as the gap between the stone faces. Regulation of this gap was known as 'tentering', and the gear for this operation was located immediately below the stones on the floor below. Tentering was originally all done by hand, but in 1787 governors were introduced which automatically made the correct adjustment in relation to sail speed. The second floor was also the level at which the auxiliary machinery for the final dressing was housed, such as the boulter for separating flour from bran and the wire machine for dressing the flour. These machines worked on the sieve principle and were driven by a horizontal countershaft which in turn took its drive from the great spur wheel on the floor above.

From Marsh Mill the road carries on northwards, over what must have been low-lying marshland before drainage was undertaken, into **Fleetwood** at the very top of what is generally recognised as the Fylde coast. The contrast between Poulton-le-Fylde and Fleetwood could not be more marked — Poulton is an ancient market centre which has evolved gradually over the centuries and has grown in a natural way around the parish church and the market place, while Fleetwood is very much a 'planned' town of the early 19th century based on a formal street pattern radiating from The Mount. The whole development was the 'brainchild' of Sir Peter Hesketh-Fleetwood, whose family had owned land here for centuries and who envisaged the creation of a new holiday town for working-class people from the industrial mill settlements of the North West. Unfortunately the cost of this ambitious scheme proved to be far greater than had been anticipated,

and Sir Peter ended up auctioning all his possessions as well as his home at Rossall in order to pay his creditors. Although he then went to live in the south of England in poverty the new town which he had created continued to grow both as a port and as a holiday town.

The land on which Fleetwood stands belonged to the 'wapentake' or Hundred of Amounderness, mentioned in the Domesday Book. At that time the area was sparsely populated, mostly laid waste and granted to Roger of Poitou by William the Conqueror as a reward for his support at the Battle of Hastings. The land passed through various hands over the centuries and was sold by Henry VIII during his dissolution of the monasteries, with Edmund Fleetwood being the first of that family name to reside at Rossall Grange. By the 1830s the Fleetwood family owned more than a third of the coast from Lancaster to Southport, and although the Rossall estate was still as desolate as it always had been Sir Peter Hesketh-Fleetwood was excited by a vision to establish a holiday town at this point on the coast.

There is little doubt that his enthusiasm was fuelled by the opening of the Liverpool to Manchester passenger railway line in 1830, an event which was one of the most spectacular in the county's history and which he attended as High Sheriff of Lancaster. For the first time people were able to travel long distances comparatively quickly, and Sir Peter realised that his dream of a holiday town was a distinct possibility. However, he had first to persuade the railway company to run the train to his part of the coast, and after much deliberation they agreed to this on condition that he would personally underwrite the project if insufficient capital was raised from the sale of shares. Motivated by his own idealism as well as his optimism that others would support the venture he accepted this condition and a start was made.

The area chosen for the new town of Fleetwood was really only a wild and windswept rabbit warren which occupied the northern part of the Fylde peninsula and

*Queen's Terrace, Fleetwood*

*The lower lighthouse in Fleetwood*

which had been valued at just £50 in 1824. When work began in the summer of 1836 the only human settlement here was a cluster of fishermen's cottages, and the development of the town began by the extension of the railway from Preston to Fleetwood. Following the formation of the Preston and Wyre Railway, Harbour and Dock Company a single-line railway was opened on the 15th July, 1840 amidst great celebrations, although in the meantime houses, hotels and a wharf had already been built.

From the very beginning Fleetwood was a 'planned' town, and Sir Peter Hesketh-Fleetwood engaged a top London architect, Decimus Burton, to draw up the overall layout and also design the major buildings. Burton had already attained a considerable reputation for his work on the Wellington Arch and the Athenaeum in London, and several of Fleetwood's buildings have that sense of grandeur to be found in properties in the capital. The plan adopted by Burton provided for wide, airy streets to radiate outwards from the focal point of Tup Hill, the last in a chain of sandhills which was renamed The Mount. These streets were then marked out by plough and laid with a shingle hardcore obtained from the nearby beach.

The advantage of the newly-created rail link was a key selling point in attracting people to come to Fleetwood, as is obvious from the original prospectus which declared that the site 'is admirably adapted for combining the advantages of a commercial port with those of a watering place. The Preston and Wyre Railway, being part of a continuous line to

London, will afford cheap and ready access to Fleetwood from Manchester and other manufacturing towns of Lancashire. The residents of Preston, Blackburn, Bolton, Chorley and Wigan will reach it in little more than an hour'.

It is hardly surprising that one of Fleetwood's most impressive buildings is the North Euston Hotel, designed by Decimus Burton and opened in 1841. At that time Fleetwood was on the shortest route from London to Glasgow, via rail and sea, and it was hoped that the hotel would attract numerous visitors travelling between the two cities. The name reflects the close link with Euston railway station in London, while the style also has 'metropolitan' connotations by virtue of its imposing curved facade and the entrance portico supported by Ionic columns. This enabled ladies and gentlemen to alight from their carriages without being too exposed to the elements. The third floor with its mansard windows was not part of the original design but was added around the turn of the century with the intention of enhancing the appearance of the building.

By the time the North Euston Hotel had been opened the town was already flourishing and houses, shops, churches, schools and boarding houses were springing up to fill in the skeletal street pattern designed by Decimus Burton. The railway was also bringing in increasing numbers of visitors, and in 1846 Fleetwood received its largest ever Sunday School trip — two engines and fifty-six carriages were required to convey the 4,200 adults and children who arrived on that occasion! Wealthier visitors took up residence in Lower Queen's Terrace, a long row of large and impressive Regency-style stone houses completed by Burton with his usual architectural flair in 1844. Close by stands the group of brick built houses known originally as Upper Queen's Terrace and which included the Customs House, dating from 1836; this has since become the offices of the District Council.

The 1840s were very much the boom years for Fleetwood in terms of visitors, and the period was crowned by the visit of Queen Victoria in September 1847, the first occasion that she had come to Lancashire. By this time, however, the cost of all the development which Sir Peter Hesketh-Fleetwood had undertaken was proving too great to bear, and he had to sell off his estates in Blackpool, Preston, Churchtown and Southport. He even had to dispose of his own home and auction all his possessions in order to meet his creditors' demands. Matters were made worse by the fact that a branch railway line provided better access to Blackpool and the number of visitors to Fleetwood fell sharply.

Despite the reverses in its fortunes Fleetwood continued to grow, particularly as a port, although this too declined at the turn of the century with the opening of Preston Docks and the Manchester Ship Canal. The fishing industry went from strength to strength, however, and the town grew to become the third largest fishing port in the country. Unfortunately the fishing trade also suffered a decline as a result of the recession of the 1970s, and Fleetwood now has only a small inshore fleet. The Isle of Man steamer service which began in 1840 was also severely curtailed in more recent years, with the result that just a few sailings are undertaken in the summer season. Even the railway line, the town's 'raison d'etre', was eventually closed, but this has not stopped thousands of visitors coming to Fleetwood every year to enjoy the bracing sea air and the many foreshore amenities, as well as the magnificent views of Morecambe Bay and the Lakeland hills from the top of The Mount Pavilion. These must have particularly excited Decimus Burton and Sir Peter Hesketh-Fleetwood when they first contemplated the laying out of their holiday town.

*The Mount Pavilion, Fleetwood*

The Mount is very much a focal point in Fleetwood, not only because of its height but also because the early street pattern was built around it. The Pavilion which now sits on top of The Mount was built in 1902, to replace the earlier 'Chinese pavilion' designed by Decimus Burton, and its four-faced clock was presented to the town in 1919 as a memorial to the men killed in the First World War. Fleetwood's two land-based lighthouses also figure prominently in the town's landscape, being designed again by Burton and completed in 1840. They formed part of the plan for the navigation of the Wyre Channel and were originally gas-lit before being converted to fully automatic electric operation.

In order to navigate the channel the lights are aligned one above the other to enable a straight course to be steered until a sharp turn is made at the approaches to the port. The lower lighthouse is situated on the seafront at a height of 30 feet above the high water level, and is constructed of Stourton Hill white stone in a Classical style, while the upper lighthouse, some distance behind it, is an imposing column of red sandstone which stands 90 feet above the high water level. This latter structure is also known as the Pharos Lighthouse because Burton designed it as a replica of the Pharos Lighthouse in Alexandria, one of the Seven Wonders of the World.

Burton was also responsible for the design of the port which was to play such a significant role in the town's growth, and his 1841 Building Plan of Fleetwood shows landing stages, a harbour-master's office, timber yards and other port facilities on the riverside opposite Queen's Terrace and Dock Street. These facilities were extended in the 1870s with the introduction of further buildings, and then in the early 1900s the timber pond was converted to a fish dock with warehouses and adjacent railway lines to allow the fast loading of the catch. By 1922 four thousand men and boys were employed here in the fishing industry.

Decimus Burton also had a hand in the design of a number of other civic projects in Fleetwood, including the Parish Church of St. Peter which stands on a raised plot of land at the junction of Lord Street and North Albert Street. This building is constructed of a dark brown sandstone in a Gothic style, and its tower originally carried a spire which eventually became unsafe and had to be demolished in 1904. Burton was equally at home with the design of rather more humble buildings, and in Mount Street (one of the roads radiating from The Mount itself) there are some good examples of terraced houses built for the working-class people of Fleetwood. The quality of this housing and the public amenities provided by Sir Peter Hesketh-Fleetwood, as well as his desire that

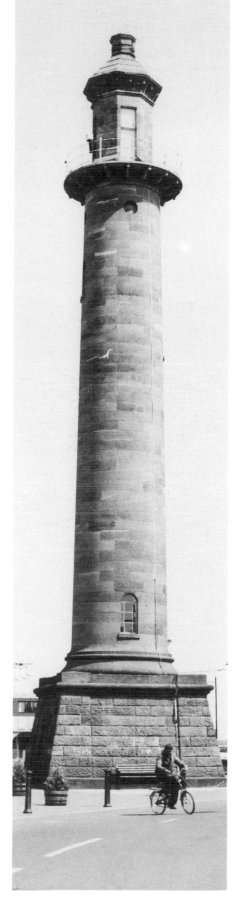

*The Pharos Lighthouse, Fleetwood*

every ratepayer should have a say in the running of the town, indicates the philanthropic attitude which he adopted in pursuing his vision for Fleetwood.

Mention should also be made of two of Fleetwood's better known transport facilities — the ferry and the trams. The Fleetwood to Knott End Ferry has operated from the very earliest days of the town's development, and was run initially as a family business. Then in 1893 the Fleetwood Improvement Act of that year authorised the local council to establish a regular service over the Wyre, and by 1894 the Council had taken over the responsibility for this. At the height of its operations, towards the end of the Second World War, nearly a million and a half passengers were using the ferry annually. Since that time the numbers making use of the service have dwindled considerably, and it is now operated once more by a private firm.

Just as Fleetwood achieved a notable 'first' in having a railway link from an inland town, so it was one of the first places in the world to have a tramway running through its streets. The line was officially opened in 1898 with power for the trams being carried on overhead cables suspended from iron pillars, some of which were decorated with ornamental scrolls and described as being 'undoubtedly most pretty'. In 1920 the tram company operating the line was taken over by the Blackpool Corporation, which had been running a service in its own area, and one of its first acts was to join the two lines together so that it was possible to travel right from Starr Hills at the southern end of Blackpool to the Pharos Lighthouse in Fleetwood. In this way the 'competing' holiday resorts of Fleetwood and Blackpool became inextricably linked, with the more modern town of Cleveleys acting as something of a buffer between them.

The history of **Blackpool** is similar in many respects to that of Fleetwood in that the town developed rapidly during the 19th and 20th centuries, although it was already a recognised resort by the end of the 18th century. Its early boundaries were within the township of Layton-with-Warbreck, part of the ancient parish of Bispham recorded in the Domesday Book. During the 14th century the Butler family were granted manorial rights over much of the Fylde coast area including "Le pull", a stream which drained the mile-square Marton Mere into the sea. The peat lands through which this stream ran had the effect of discolouring the water, and as a result the name Black Poole originated.

In 1602 entries in the Bispham parish register mention 'de blackpoole' as a collection of cobble and clay huts spread along the coast, but by the end of the century a number of the landed gentry had settled in the area. By 1735 the first accommodation specially reserved for visitors was made available, and by 1780 the 'resort' could boast four substantial hotels as well as a number of other guest houses. Even so, the historian William Hutton was recording in 1788 that 'although about fifty houses grace the sea-bank, it does not merit the name of a village, because they are scattered to the extent of a mile'.

At the turn of the 19th century the development of the resort came close to stagnation through the inaction of the principal landowners, but the situation was transformed by Henry Banks (often considered to be the 'Father of Blackpool') who in 1810 bought the Lane Ends estate. He soon built the first holiday cottages, and then in 1837 built Blackpool's first assembly rooms in Victoria Terrace. The introduction of the railway from Preston to Fleetwood enabled many people to visit Blackpool by means of horsebus or wagonette transport from Poulton station, although by 1846 a proper branch line was brought into Blackpool itself enabling thousands of visitors from Lancashire and Yorkshire to reach the town with comparative ease.

The first place of amusement to be opened in Blackpool was Uncle Tom's Cabin, perched on the crumbling cliffs to the north of the town, followed by the North Pier which was built of cast-iron and opened in 1863. In 1867 the Prince of Wales Arcade opened (now the site of the tower) and the following year saw the Theatre Royal and the South Jetty (now the Central Pier) added to the list of attractions. Then in 1870 a Promenade was completed from South Shore to Claremont Park, immediately to the north of the Metropole Hotel. At this point in time the resort seemed to be lacking in indoor facilities so the Winter Gardens Company was formed to build an indoor Promenade and Pavilion, the construction of which forced the rival North Pier company to build its Indian Pavilion at the seaward end of the pier.

As a result of the rapidly increasing number of attractions and consequent growth in the number of trippers wishing to visit Blackpool the single-line coastal railway between Lytham and Blackpool Central was re-built as double-track and linked with the Kirkham to Lytham line. The increasing popularity of the resort also forced the local council to look at its own transport provision, and to supplement the town's horsebuses and landaus Blackpool became the site of the world's first permanent electric street tramway in 1885.

In the 1890s it was estimated that Blackpool's 7,000 dwellings could accommodate 250,000 holidaymakers as well as the permanent resident population of 35,000. These visitors required entertaining, and the decade saw the development of many of the resort's most famous attractions. The original

Opera House was built in the Winter Gardens complex, Blackpool Tower (built to a height of 518 feet as an imitation of the Eiffel Tower) was opened in 1894 and a permanent circus, ballroom and aquarium incorporated into the buildings beneath it. Then in 1897 the Golden Mile was created when the Corporation banned stalls from the beach and traders moved into the gardens of houses on the Promenade.

During the early part of the 1900s the tram network was extended, and in later years took over the Fleetwood Tramroad and also built the line to Starr Gate in the south. The years 1902 to 1905 saw the building of the present Promenade between the North and South Piers, a project which involved reclaiming some 22 acres from the sea, and about the same time the foundations of the Pleasure Beach were laid with the erection of the first features in the sand dunes beyond South Shore. Since that time many additional attractions have been introduced to create the present 40-acre fun park.

The first static 'illuminations' in Blackpool were erected on 2nd May, 1912 when Princess Louise opened the Princess Parade, and because they were so well received they were revived in late summer. A more ambitious display was produced in the following year, but the First World War interrupted 'the Lights and they were not seen again until 1925. After another break for the Second World War they were revived again in 1949 and are now one of Blackpool's greatest attractions. The period between the two wars was largely a time of consolidation, with many civic developments being introduced such as the Promenade extensions at Bispham, Norbreck and South Shore, the Open Air Baths, Stanley Park and its nearby aerodrome, and the Derby Baths.

*Blackpool Tower during the Illuminations*

*Blackpool Tower, Promenade and beach during the day*

The town has remained conscious of the need to continually improve the facilities and attractions which are on offer to its visitors, and recent years have seen a considerable increase in shopping opportunities with the development of the Hounds Hill Shopping Centre based on the Victorian architecture of the nearby Winter Gardens, which themselves have recently undergone a multi-million pound refurbishment to ensure that they retain their role as a key conference venue. The changing tastes of holidaymakers have also been catered for with the development of the new climate-controlled Sandcastle Centre.

So what is it that continues to make Blackpool such a popular place for young and old alike? Probably its greatest natural asset is its beach, the golden sands stretching for seven miles along the Fylde coast and backed up by a host of attractions within a few hundred yards of the shore. On the one hand there is the bustling area between the North and Central Piers with its donkeys, ice cream and seafood stalls, and on the other there are the quieter stretches around Bispham and Squires Gate. Across the busy Promenade on the south side of the Tower is the brash and breezy Golden Mile, not to everyone's liking of course but certainly a place where those who want to indulge their fancy for chips, hamburgers, candy floss and rock can do so with every few steps — to say nothing of the opportunities to cross the palm of clairvoyants with silver or try one's luck in the greatest array of slot machine arcades in Britain. The Golden Mile is also the home of the Louis Tussaud's Waxworks as well as a host of other exhibitions, discos and cabaret spots.

Just a mile further down the Promenade is Blackpool Pleasure Beach, probably Britain's most popular tourist attraction. In this 40-acre amazement and amusement park there are said to be more spectacular thrill rides than anywhere else in Europe — with its roller coasters, big wheels, water rides and scores of other well known features it is a must for most of Blackpool's visitors, or at least for those with stronger stomachs! Then of course there are the resort's three famous piers with their theatres, amusement arcades, shops, restaurants and bars — North Pier is a favourite sunbathing spot, Central Pier has children's amusements and the panoramic Cinema USA, whilst the South Pier has an Astroslide and has recently taken on the appearance of a circus marquee.

Linking all that Blackpool offers on its seafront are the Illuminations, extending the summer season well into the autumn and providing 'the greatest free show on earth'. The display stretches along the seafront for more than five miles, transforming the Promenade into an extravaganza of colour. More than 75 miles of wiring carries the power to 375,000 lamps of 100 types and

*Stanley Park, Blackpool*

sizes, 50 miles of festoon strip, 1,500 floodlights and spotlights, 500 pylons, 500 designs and features, and 60 major tableaux. It is hardly surprising that the Illuminations attract around eight million visitors to Blackpool in the eight weeks that they are switched on.

For those who prefer a rather less hectic holiday Blackpool offers the beautiful Stanley Park, a 256-acre informal recreation area which is ideal for more leisurely holiday pursuits. Situated less than two miles from the seafront the park contains six bowling greens, two 18-hole putting greens and several tennis courts as well as a 26-acre lake which is the perfect setting for a cruise by motor-boat, rowing-boat or pedal-boat. The land for Stanley Park was purchased in the 1920s when there was growing concern over the need to provide some recreational open space in the town, and the Corporation commissioned Thomas Mawson and Sons of London and Lancaster to prepare a comprehensive park, recreational centre and planning scheme on the land.

There was a particular emphasis upon providing a more spacious home and leisure environment, and so the park and its surrounding boulevards of housing were designed together, bearing in mind the importance of easy access from all parts of the expanding town. The houses around Stanley Park are similar in scale and share many common details and materials, while the park itself is a combination of formal areas such as the Italian Garden and the Rose Garden and informal areas such as the golf course. The recreation facilities were provided as part of the original layout, as were the many buildings throughout the park designed to be complementary to its character. At the time of its opening in 1926 by Lord Derby (Edward George Villiers Stanley, from whom the park takes its name) it was acknowledged to be "one of the most comprehensive park schemes carried out in these islands".

The comparative peace and quiet which characterises Stanley Park is the predominant feature of **Lytham St. Annes,** the southernmost resort on the Fylde coast and one with a rather different reputation to that of neighbouring Blackpool. Lytham St. Annes is really two places not one, although it now forms a continuous development around the coast from the sand dunes at Starr Hills to the mud-flats at the mouth of the Ribble estuary. The township of **St. Annes,** the first place you come to after Blackpool, was established in much the same way as Fleetwood had been, as a completely new planned resort developed on virgin land, although St. Annes appeared on the scene nearly fifty years later than its northern predecessor. A leading role in the genesis of St. Annes was played by Mr. James Fair, the agent for the Clifton family living at Lytham Hall who were the major landowners in the area. It was his vision initially that Lytham Common, between Lytham and Blackpool, should be the site for a new resort, and the land was then surveyed and a plan produced which incorporated wide and impressive streets.

Yet it was left to his son, Thomas Fair, to implement this vision with the help of the Clifton family in conjunction with a group of Lancashire industrialists. The prime mover now became Elijah Hargreaves from Rawtenstall, who visited Blackpool on holiday in 1874 and saw the potential which this part of the coast had for creating a town

of fine houses, wide streets, good hotels and pleasant parks, particularly as new road and rail links had recently been established between Lytham and Blackpool. His businessman's mind also recognised the possibilities which existed here for the development of an attractive residential area to which people could escape from the Lancashire mill towns. Hargreaves met Fair at the Clifton estate office in Lytham, learned that his dream was shared by Thomas Fair and his father, and began to lay a foundation which would turn their dream into a reality.

The outcome of all this was the formation of the St. Annes-on-the-Sea Land and Building Company Limited, which Hargreaves and his business acquaintances set up to carry out the development of the town. The company's earliest meetings were held at the Queen's Hotel in Rawtenstall, but in 1876 its offices were moved to St. Annes itself. In return for leases of 999 years on an extensive area of land this company agreed to make roads, lay sewers, build houses, hotels and shops and construct a public market and a town hall as well as public baths, wash-houses, a pier and a landing stage. All this was to be undertaken in line with the high standard of development which the Clifton family insisted upon, and Messrs. Maxwell and Tuke, the architects of Blackpool Tower, became architects to the new company.

The company quickly made a start on the construction of a promenade as well as on the

building of the St. Annes Hotel, which commenced in February 1875. Shortly after the laying of the foundation stone for the hotel the St. Annes Land and Building Company not only began to promote the new town's interests through advertisements in the newspapers but also persuaded the railway companies to provide improved services to the town. In 1878 the St. Annes-on-Sea Local Board was set up in recognition of the rapid growth of the town, with responsibilities for paving, street lighting and sewage disposal, the result being that by the end of the century St. Annes had made secure its position as a popular seaside resort.

The new town began to be described as 'The Opal of the West', and the properties of its air and sea-water were boasted of as an elixir of life. Consequently people flocked to live in St. Annes and benefit from its atmosphere and environment. Perhaps the most impressive indicator of the town's success was its Pier, which was opened in 1885 by Lord Derby. Its original length was 315 yards, and it featured a Moorish Pavilion with domes decorated in gold leaf as well as an enchanting Floral Hall for vaudeville artists and orchestras to entertain the vast crowds that descended upon the town. Although serious fires have taken their toll of the Pier, with part of it having to be demolished, it has recently been restored so that it is still an excellent example of Victorian pier design.

**Lytham** has a longer history than St. Annes,

*St. Annes' Pier*

*Part of 'leafy Lytham'*

dating back to Domesday Book, and in many respects its leafy streets and graceful avenues are characterised by a greater maturity and pervading charm which could only develop through the passage of time. Even so, for centuries the only settlement here was a small fishing village perched at the end of an unbroken range of sandhills that ran northwards to Blackpool. Yet, as with all the towns on the Fylde coast, it was the coming of the railway in 1846 which began to change all this. Lytham then became easily accessible from Preston and the rapidly expanding industrial towns of Lancashire, and the way to its development as a holiday resort and residential area was opened up.

The issue of season tickets on the railways had also cut travelling costs and enabled rail commuters to work in Preston and live in Lytham, a situation which was not discouraged by the Clifton family who had been here since purchasing the manor in 1606. As major landowners and lords of the manor the Cliftons and their agents chose to keep a close control over the general development of the town and were instrumental in encouraging the extension of the railway from Lytham round the coast to Blackpool. The agent for the Clifton family believed that this line 'would open out the most beautiful sites for marine villas that can be found in the North of England', perhaps building upon the popularity which Lytham had gained as a place for sea bathing even before the railway came.

Many of the buildings in Lytham itself are indicative of the considerable influence and patronage which the Clifton family exercised in the area, with most of their properties being constructed of reddish brown bricks in a Classical style. At the heart of the town is the Market Square, a pleasant tree-lined area

which was landscaped by the Cliftons in 1850. This was the former village green which contained the stocks and the fish stones, but then in 1848 the Market House was built on the west side at a cost of £1,000. In 1872 a tower and lantern were added to the building in order to accommodate a clock which was donated by Lady Eleanor Cecily Clifton. Not far away is the former Estate Office of the Clifton family which was built in about 1860, and above the main doorway can be seen a Venetian window over which are the Clifton family arms.

Just across the road from the Estate Office is a fine curved terrace of brick built houses with attractive doors, windows and tiled canopies. This is Hastings Place built in 1854 by a brother of John Talbot Clifton. At the back of Hastings Place and not far from the former railway station, now a restaurant and public house, is Sparrow Park and the site of a memorial to Col. John Talbot Clifton, who died in 1882. The memorial consists of a stone drinking fountain and horse trough contained within a rectangular shelter; carved scrolls and sea creatures are used for decoration and the tiled roof is supported by carved wooden pillars. The original site of the memorial was the village green, since it was an important water supply for the community.

Immediately to the north of here is the main entrance to Lytham Hall, consisting of an impressive brick and stone archway with small gatehouses on either side as well as wrought-iron gates. Above the archway is the emblem of the Cliftons, a hand and dagger. Lytham Hall itself, the home of the Clifton family, is a quite breathtaking building which was erected in 1757-64 by John Carr of York. Situated within very extensive grounds it is a marvellous piece of Georgian architecture displaying a Roman doric doorcase above which are four Ionic columns supporting a

projecting pediment. The grandeur of this stately mansion is a fitting reminder of the wealth and influence which the Clifton family held. Something of their role in the commercial development of Lytham can also be seen among the substantial properties facing out over Lytham Green to the Ribble estuary — the Queen's Hotel situated on Central Beach was built by John Talbot Clifton in 1854, starting life as the Neptune, while the Clifton Arms Hotel on West Beach is an earlier example of Clifton family enterprise (dating from 1840) which was later leased to a private company.

Yet the architectural heritage left by the Cliftons did not always take such a grand form, and on Henry Street just off Clifton Square are to be found some comparatively humble estate cottages. Commonly recurring architectural features on these dwellings include the gable ends with their barge boards

*Lytham Hall*

*The main entrance to Lytham Hall*

*Some of Lytham's humbler heritage*

and wooden finials as well as the dripstone mouldings over the windows and the cobblestone patterns of the garden walls. Most of the buildings in Lytham date from the Victorian era, but several properties on Dicconson Terrace at the top of Henry Street were built in the Georgian period. Lytham has a host of other interesting buildings which are attractively framed by their leafy surroundings, but in certain parts of the town it is the pavements which are of particular importance. Along streets such as Bath Street and Queen Street the terraces are fronted by paving executed entirely in small evenly-sized grey pebbles, with a pattern in white pebbles in front of each doorway. The intricate designs include a ship, a windmill, an anchor, a star, birds and other symbols connected to Lytham's early role as a fishing village.

No survey of Lytham could be complete without mention being made of its well known Green and the windmill which stands upon it. The Green was originally an area of sand-dunes, which were gradually tamed following a serious flood in 1729 by the construction of a sea wall which still forms part of the sea defences of the town. The Green was given to the people of Lytham by the Clifton family in 1923. The windmill situated on the Green dates from about 1805, when Richard Cookson obtained a lease from the Squire of Lytham to erect a 'windy milne' here, although records show that there has always been at least one mill in Lytham since 1190. Like Marsh Mill at Thornton, Lytham windmill incorporates a fantail to keep the mainsails facing directly into the wind, and in many respects its method of operation in grinding corn to produce flour was much the same. Next to the windmill is the old lifeboat

house, constructed largely of cobblestones. This building was paid for by the Clifton family and is another reminder of their benevolent involvement in the life of Lytham.

From Lytham itself the main road heads eastwards towards Warton, crossing a creek between the two places which was the site of a thriving but rather short-lived port which once served Lytham. The port handled livestock, coal, timber and other commodities, but with the growth in importance of the docks at Preston business at Lytham Dock faded away almost as soon as it had begun. All this took place during the early part of the 19th century, when Lytham proved too remote and too small to serve Lancashire's cotton manufacturing industry.

Yet towards the end of the same century Lytham Dock was given a new lease of life as a shipbuilding yard. During the sixty years or so of its operation from this yard the Lytham Shipbuilding and Engineering Company produced a wide range of small ships, including vessels for wartime use by the Admiralty as well as cargo boats, tugs, ferries and shallow-draught stern wheelers for service on African waterways. Unfortunately the silting up of the channel leading to the shipyard brought about the closure of the yard in 1955, with a ferry for Lake Windermere being the last vessel to be built here.

**Warton** itself, within the parish of Bryning-with-Warton, is situated on low-lying ground looking out over the Ribble estuary to the south. Warton was mentioned in the Domesday Survey as being held by the manorial lord of Wood Plumpton, whilst the earliest mention of Bryning and Kellamergh

is in 1200 when they are referred to a Briscath Brunn and Kelgmersberg. These two tiny hamlets have largely retained their agricultural character, but Warton has changed considerably and has taken on much more of a suburban nature, although there are still some older farmhouses and cottages to be seen in the village along Preston Old Road. The present Parish Church of St. Paul was consecrated in 1886, but within the churchyard can be found evidence of an earlier church dating back to the 17th century.

Neighbouring **Freckleton** is rather larger than Warton, although its history also goes back at least to the Domesday Survey when it was mentioned as comprising four carucates of 'arable soil'. By the late 19th century, however, its agricultural economy was being supplemented by employment at a local cotton weaving mill, which was reported to hold 320 looms and was producing sacking, sailcloth and ropes. Freckleton's inhabitants appear to have had a long history of religious observance, with a Quaker Meeting House being built here in 1668 as well as Wesleyan and Primitive Methodist Chapels in 1814 and 1862 respectively. Holy Trinity Parish Church dates from 1839 and contains a fine old oak pulpit.

Situated just a couple of miles to the north of Warton is the village of **Wrea Green,** within the parish of Ribby with-Wrea. This is probably one of the best known and most beautiful villages on the Fylde, its lovely green at the centre of the village acting as a delightful focal point for the many activities which go on here. With a church, school, pub, farm and cottages gathered around the fringes of the Green, together with a traditional duck pond on the Green itself, it presents an idyllic and typically English village scene — particularly when the local cricket team has a match here during the summer months or when the schoolchildren are brought out for their games lessons. It is no wonder then that Wrea Green has won Lancashire's Best Kept Village competition at least five times. Very little seems to have changed in the village's appearance since mid-Victorian days, when a writer described it as having 'cottages, some thatched and some slated, planted round a Town's Common, a pleasantly elevated patch of green broadsward occupied with geese, ducks and horses'.

Farming has traditionally been the main source of employment for the inhabitants of Wrea Green, although some were forced to find work at the flax mill in nearby Kirkham. It was to Kirkham that all the people in the village were required to go for the purpose of church worship during mediaeval times, but by the early part of the 18th century Wrea Green had the benefit of a combined school and chapel. This was largely the result of

*Wrea Green's village pump*

money being left by a certain Nicholas Sharples in his will, to improve upon the village school which had been built in 1693 from a legacy of £180 provided by a local tailor. The chapel was dedicated to St. Nicholas, the patron saint of children, which was a good choice as the building was both a school and a chapel, but it may also have been intended as a gesture of gratitude to Nicholas Sharples.

By the middle of the 19th century the school and chapel had been replaced by a new stone built parish church, again dedicated to St. Nicholas, with a new boys' school being erected next to the girls' school nearby. Several of the present cottages on Church Row were built with handmade bricks salvaged from the demolition of the school and chapel, although the oldest property in the village would appear to be Cookson's Farm on the edge of the Green. This has a datestone of 1613 over the front door, even though the house has been rebuilt a number of times since then. Other features which complete Wrea Green's classic village appearance are the cast-iron village pump and a former windmill which has been converted into a house.

From Wrea Green the road runs eastwards and passes close to Ribby Hall, an impressive Georgian house, before crossing the main Blackpool road on its way down into the centre of **Kirkham.** In many respects Kirkham has fulfilled a comparable function to the similar-sized settlement of Poulton-le-Fylde, acting as a market centre serving the surrounding farming communities, and during the course of its long history it has seen many changes. Its central position has enabled it to develop over the centuries as the 'hub' of the Fylde, helped by the fact that the Romans built a small fort on Carr Hill to guard the road which they had constructed between Ribchester and the mouth of the Wyre.

After the Romans departed the Fylde area was settled by Angles from the other side of the Pennines and by Vikings arriving from Ireland and the Isle of Man. Kirkham's name, suggesting a settlement with a church, was given by these early inhabitants and first recorded as such in the Domesday Survey of 1086. The church in Kirkham later became the mother church for a very large parish stretching from the Ribble to the Wyre and containing fifteen townships. To assist the vicar in the administration of such a large area each township was required to make two representatives available to him, and the resulting council known as The Thirty Men of Kirkham continued to function until the 19th century.

Kirkham's role as a market centre for the surrounding district really began in 1296 when it was granted a charter constituting it as a borough and permitting it to hold a weekly market and fair. At that time the lordship of the town was in the hands of Vale Royal Abbey in Cheshire, but upon the dissolution of the monasteries Kirkham was given to Christ Church in Oxford, which leased most of its rights to the local Clifton family. The Court Leet governing the town was consequently presided over by the Clifton's agent. By the middle of the 18th century Kirkham began to develop as an early industrial centre, through the establishment of flax spinning mills and the manufacture of sailcloth. This was followed in the 19th century by the building of several cotton mills and the coming of the railway in 1840, which brought further employment. Nowadays most of the town's mills have disappeared and it is a largely residential area, although some light industry remains to provide a degree of local employment.

The focal point of present-day Kirkham is still very much its historic market place, at the

*Some of Wrea Green's older cottages*

*Kirkham's 'fishstones'*

junction of the earlier main routes into the town and the top end of Church Street. Although the market cross and the stocks have long since disappeared, the cobbles have been retained together with the old 'fishstones'. These consist of flat slabs of stone set on stone uprights in the form of two semi-circular counters, from which fish was sold on market days. Nearby are some of the impressive Georgian properties, such as Hillside and Ash Tree House, which were built by Kirkham's chief flax merchants during the late 18th and early 19th centuries when the town was experiencing a period of particular prosperity.

From the Market Place Church Street runs appropriately down to the Parish Church of St. Michael, occupying the site of a church dating from the 16th century which in turn had replaced an even older place of worship. The present building dates from 1822 with its tower, spire and peal of bells being added in 1844. Other features of particular interest include a medieval font, a 14th century nave recess within a traceried arch, an ancient coffin under the tower and a handsome 18th century candelabrum. The church also boasts parish registers dating from 1539, just one year after the keeping of such records was decreed by Thomas Cromwell (the Vicar-General to Henry VIII), as well as the records of The Thirty Men of Kirkham from 1570.

Closely associated with the Parish Church was the original Grammar School, founded in 1550 on a site nearby and made a free school in Stuart times. In the early part of the present century the school was moved into new buildings on Ribby Road to the west of the town centre. Not far away from the school is the Roman Catholic church of St. John, built in 1845 and said to be the first Catholic church since the Reformation to have a peal of bells.

Following the main street back down towards the Market Place from here brings us to Town End, another focal point and originally the end of the built-up area. The names of the streets which diverge from here are reminiscent of Kirkham's past history - Moor Street preserves the memory of the town moor which was enclosed in 1550, Mill Street is a reminder of Birley's flax mill demolished some years ago, while Orders Lane was originally called Old Earth Lane and led to the

townfields of Kirkham. At the opposite end of Kirkham the early extent of the town is marked by a former windmill, now converted into a house, and in between these two extremities can be seen some attractive Georgian terraced houses lining the main street.

From Town End, Kirkham merges almost imperceptibly into **Wesham,** part of the parish of Medlar-with-Wesham. Medlar lies to the north of Wesham, beyond the M6 motorway, and is still a predominantly rural area, whereas Wesham itself grew considerably during the 19th century with the advent of the railway and the influx of cotton spinning. The manor was originally in the hands of the Abbot of Cockersand Abbey, until the dissolution of the monasteries when it passed to the Westbys of Mowbreck Hall. It remained their property until 1893, when it was purchased by the Earl of Derby; since then Mowbreck Hall has been demolished, although the coachhouse remains as the tangible evidence of what must have been an impressive estate.

Before the cotton mills came to Wesham it was primarily an area of small farms, although the weaving of flax was carried out as a cottage industry during the 18th century. In fact it was flax weaving which acted as a foundation for the cotton spinning introduced by the local landowning families in the 19th century. One of the cotton mills built in the

village, now converted to a biscuit factory, had 1250 looms in it and provided employment for people from a wide area. The population explosion which Wesham experienced during the Victorian period is apparent from the fact that the Parish Church, the Roman Catholic church and the Methodist church were all established here between 1884 and 1896. An associated feature of industrialisation was the development of a workhouse, now Wesham Park Hospital.

To the north of the hospital an ancient track passes through what was 'Old Wesham' and alongside the Mowbreck Hall estate before coming out at the village of **Treales,** the first of a number of delightful rural settlements around Kirkham and part of the large parish which also encompasses the villages of Wharles and Roseacre. This is an unspoilt rural area characterised by scattered farmsteads, quiet country lanes, small woods and thatched cottages, with Treales being the main centre of population. The Parish Church was erected in 1853 and endowed five years later by the Dean and Chapter of Christ Church in Oxford, while Treales School was acquired in 1876. To the north is the village of **Wharles,** with its thatched pub (the 'Eagle and Child') and an interesting old brick built thatched cottage dating from 1650.

A narrow country lane on the south side of Treales brings us to the parish of Newton-

*A 17th century thatched cottage at Wharles*

with-Clifton, which consists of the villages of **Newton-with-Scales** and **Clifton-with-Salwick.** The parish church for the area is situated at Lund-in-Salwick, and although the present building only dates from 1824 there is evidence of a church on the site as early as 1349. It is recorded that in 1688 a man by the name of Matthew Hall 'set up a scandalous trough for a font at Lund Chapel'. This 'scandalous trough' measures eighteen inches long and a foot wide, and it appears to be of Roman origin. Across the road from the church is another piece of history, one of the Fylde's surviving windmills, while in the opposite direction is a thoroughly modern development — the Springfields Works of British Nuclear Fuels Limited, providing a rather dramatic contrast to its more traditional 'neighbours'.

The main road from Preston to Blackpool skirts round the edges of both Clifton and Newton before bypassing Kirkham and coming out at the parish of **Westby-with-Plumptons.** This is one of the largest parishes in the Fylde and is primarily an agricultural area, with higher land to the north which offers an attractive prospect of the coast as well as the first glimpse of Blackpool Tower for travellers heading westwards. A windmill which once occupied a site on this elevated ground stood out so prominently that it was used as a navigational aid by sailors. Much of the parish's history has revolved round the Clifton family, who held the manor as early as 1280. It then passed to the Fleetwood family, but by 1876 John Talbot Clifton of Lytham Hall was lord of the manor by right of inheritance. Westby Hall had been the seat of the Cliftons, and in 1849 a school free to all denominations was established near the Hall by Thomas Clifton of Lytham. The Roman Catholic Church of St. Anne at Westby was

*The former village 'fire station' in Singleton*

designed by Pugin and built in 1860, whilst a Church of England School was erected at Higher Ballam in 1890.

To the north of Westby, beyond the M55 motorway, is the parish of **Weeton-with-Preese,** notable chiefly for its attractive village green at the centre of Weeton itself. On one side of the green is an old thatched house dating from the 17th century, while on the other side is the Eagle and Child public house built during the same period. The local C of E church came onto the village scene rather later, being established in 1842.

Further northwards again is the delightful village of **Singleton,** sheltering beneath a canopy of tall trees which adds to its sense of intimacy. Here one can see some lovely terraced cottages, constructed of warm red brick with intriguing front porches, as well as the former village fire station which has a 'black and white' design perhaps more characteristic of Cheshire than Lancashire. Most of the properties seem to have been built during the Victorian period to provide accommodation for workers on the local estate; other needs were met by the construction of the present church in 1859, on the site of earlier buildings, and by the opening of a church school in 1863.

Singleton is reputed to have been the residence of one of the more famous Lancashire witches, Meg Shelton, who is said to have milked the cows of her neighbours and carried the milk away in a pitcher which walked in front of her in the shape of a goose. A suspecting neighbour put an end to her game by striking the 'goose' so that the pitcher was broken and the milk flowed out. Not surprisingly the villagers in Singleton were keen to get rid of her, and Meg's grave can be seen in Woodplumpton churchyard beneath a large boulder to ensure that she cannot escape from her tomb.

Just two miles to the east of Singleton is the equally delightful village of **Thistleton,** a cluster of vernacular houses and working farm buildings which are similarly sheltered by mature trees to provide a tranquil and unspoilt setting. Although the properties here range in date from the late 17th century to the early part of the 20th the varying styles and materials used in their construction have blended together well to present a unified and coherent whole, knit together by the carefully-tended hedges which are a distinctive feature of the village. As one approaches Thistleton from Singleton the first properties to be noticed at the entrance to the village are Lane

*Weeton village green*

End Cottage, a thatched brick house dating from the 1670s, and Town Head Farm, a red brick house dating from the second quarter of the 19th century with its barn and shippons which are probably a hundred years older. Next door is Ivy Farm, a red brick house dating from about 1740 which was probably thatched when first built, and then four pairs of estate cottages built during the mid 19th century.

Across the road from here can be seen the Old Post Office, a comparatively plain house dating from the early part of the 19th century and built of handmade brick with stone lintels and sills. The neighbouring properties are typical semi-detached estate cottages built in the middle of the 19th century, to a design readily found in estate improvement books of that period and with red tiled roofs, while Thistleton House next door dates from the same period but probably incorporates an earlier building. To the rear is Maltkiln Farm, a largely 18th century brick house which probably had a thatch roof originally. Following the bend in the road one can see firstly Lodge Farm, a red brick house dating from the late 18th century, and then a little further on Plane Tree Farm. This is a much older house, dating from about 1700-1720, which like several other properties was originally covered by a thatch roof. In many respects this variety of properties to be found in Thistleton is typical of other traditional villages on the Fylde, ranging from brick built thatched cottages to the more substantial estate houses sharing a common design.

The road continues eastwards from Thistleton to **Elswick,** just a mile further on. This is another old village which is first mentioned in the Domesday Book, where it is referred to as Edelsuic; some time later it is recorded with the name Ethelyswick, meaning the dwelling place of someone called Ethel. During the 13th century the land was cultivated by Cistercian monks, whose monasteries were situated at Sawley and Whalley. Less peaceful times, however, were experienced during the English Civil War of the 17th century, and some evidence of Cromwell's march (in the form of cannon balls and earthworks) have been discovered from time to time.

It was at this point that Elswick Congregational church was founded in 1649, perhaps by local farmers who had taken up arms on the side of Cromwell in their fight for a free Bible, a free church and freedom to worship according to their consciences. They contributed their share to Puritan England by resisting the doctrines of the divine right of kings and the overriding of civil law by ecclesiastical law, with the result that this little village of Elswick is looked upon as the cradle of nonconformity in Lancashire. Persecution was common, however, and for many years nonconformity of every type was suspect and susceptible to fines, imprisonment, exile and even death.

The first chapel was built on a common called Lees, to the south of the village, although the only relic of that building is a chained Geneva Bible now preserved in a glass case in the present church. The chapel at Elswick Lees was replaced by another, still standing to the east of the present church, which was built in 1753 and enlarged in 1838. This rather humble building was in turn replaced by a grander Gothic style church which was opened in 1874, although the earlier chapel still acts as a 'home' for the Elswick Church Anniversary. This has been an established feature of church life on the Fylde for many years now, and is always held on the Thursday following Whit Sunday. Some idea of its status can be gauged from the fact that in 1933 over 1500 people descended on Elswick Church and its grounds, and in 1936 the preacher for Anniversary Day that year wrote '… I was assured by responsible officials that this was their 287th Anniversary…After this I shall not be so easily impressed by the supposed honour of being asked to officiate at a church's jubilee or even centenary; for as compared with the little Elswick Church are not things only of yesterday?'

**Great Eccleston** can be found just over a mile to the north of Elswick and just a few hundred yards from the banks of the River Wyre, although the tollbridge across the Wyre is actually in the nearby village of Little Eccleston. The earliest reference to Great Eccleston is in the Domesday Book, being one of two places called 'Eglestun' which belonged to the fee of Garstang or Wyresdale. Later references to the village are few and far between, perhaps a reflection of the fact that people have gone quietly about their business in what has always been a predominantly agricultural community. The farmers here have traditionally been involved in dairying and the growing of wheat, oats, barley, beans and rushes, with the latter providing the basis for a local 'industry' in times gone by of rush light-making. Rushes were also used as a floor covering in the local church, and a rush-bearing ceremony held each year was the opportunity for these rushes to be renewed. Whilst the character and layout of Great Eccleston has remained relatively unchanged over the years, a quiet place bypassed by the main road to Blackpool, back in the 17th and 18th centuries it was known as 'Little London' because it was such a social centre for the surrounding area. This probably resulted from the fact that the village seems to have had more than its fair share of inns and public houses. Two of these, the White Bull and the Black Bull, still face one another across the village square, which acts as the main focal point for the village.

Just off the village square is Leckonby House, originally the stables to the home of the Leckonby family who were great landowners in Great Eccleston for five generations up to the 18th century. The original Leckonby House was destroyed by fire in 1766 after Richard Leckonby had been imprisoned in Lancaster Castle for debt. In the field behind the present Leckonby House is a small square stone building, probably erected in the 17th century and used as a dovecote. In mediaeval times all cattle, except a few required for breeding, were killed at the start of winter, with doves being killed during the course of the following months for fresh meat. Inside the dovecote the bricks are set at different angles to provide roosting places for the birds, which would have gained access by way of the wooden slats in the lantern top.

The parish church for Great Eccleston is actually situated just to the south west of the village in the tiny hamlet of Copp, this name being derived from the old Saxon word 'kopff' meaning the head or top of anything (indicative of the fact that this spot occupies the top of a small hill). The site at Copp was chosen because it was at the edge of St. Michael's-on-Wyre Parish where it bordered Kirkham Parish, being conveniently located between the two existing churches. When it was originally built in 1723 the church took the form of a small chapel with a floor of puddled clay, the building being whitewashed annually with the help of money raised by an assessment on the pew owners. Then in 1884 the building was completely restored and enlarged to create the present St. Anne's Parish Church as it now stands.

The next crossing of the Wyre upstream from Great Eccleston is in the picturesque village of **St. Michael's-on-Wyre,** which as one might have thought takes its name from the Parish Church. This ancient place of worship proudly stands close to the river on a spot which was probably first chosen by 6th century Irish missionaries, although the

*St. Michael's Parish Church*

building itself dates originally from the Norman period, and its squat stone tower seems to be the epitome of unchanging stability. It seems likely that St. Michael's was one of the three churches of Amounderness mentioned in the Domesday Survey, together with the churches at Kirkham and Poulton, and therefore was the centre of one of three big parishes which covered nearly all of the Fylde.

The parish of St. Michael's, together with all its 'fruits, hay, tithe of lambs, calves, foals, poultry, geese, eggs, milk, flax, hemp, apples, garlic, onions, pigeons, etc., etc.,' was later given by Henry IV as an endowment for Battlefield Collegiate Church after his victory outside Shrewsbury, so it has obviously been a rich and productive area for many centuries. Nowadays dairying seems to be the predominant activity here, making the best use of the verdant pasture lands situated alongside the raised banks of the river.

The church tower, a focal point in the area generally, actually dates from a rebuilding of 1611 and bears the badge of the family of Theobald Walter, the king's cupbearer. At this time, and up to the Jacobite rebellion, the Butler family were lords of the manor, but their place was taken by the Ffrances who bought their forfeited estates. As sole landlords the Ffrances became the local 'squires', claiming the manor house and also St. Catharine's chantry chapel in the parish church. In return they completed the drainage of the mosses in the area and brought about widespread prosperity. The sense of peace and prosperity which still prevails here, together with a sense of history, is reinforced by the presence of rows of old stone cottages which line the main road through the village.

That road takes us on from St. Michael's to **Churchtown,** another historic place nicely tucked away and hidden from view, and one which is well worthwhile taking the time and trouble to discover. A century ago it was reported that Churchtown was 'a clean tidy village, hidden amid trees, sweetly isolated, and as quiet all day through...as if people had either left it or locked themselves up in their houses'. Since that time very little seems to have changed — evident particularly from the old-fashioned village shops and the cobbled footpaths which still border the narrow main street, as well as from the general stillness. The village is home to St. Helen's Church, the ancient parish church of Garstang, and because of this link it used to be known as Garstang Church Town while the settlement two miles to the north was known as Garstang Market Town. Nowadays of course the names of Churchtown and Garstang are sufficient on their own to distinguish the two places, although Garstang has obviously outgrown its early spiritual centre.

The church takes its own name from the mother of the Roman emperor Constantine, as this was a favourite dedication for churches founded by Celtic missionaries. Known sometimes as 'the Cathedral of the Fylde', St. Helen's is the mother church for nine neighbouring parishes and contains examples of almost every style of architecture since the Norman Conquest. The oldest parts of the building are the pillars to the north of the nave, dating from 1200, although there is evidence that a pre-Conquest nave was enlarged by adding first a north and then a south aisle. At the west end of the south aisle is a 13th century window in a Decorated style, whilst the chancel arch is of the same period and was built to replace a small round-headed Norman arch leading to an apsidal chancel.

The Lady Chapel on the south side of the nave was founded by Margaret Rigmaiden of Wedacre, who died in 1516, while the south chancel aisle was formerly a chantry founded in 1499 by Roger de Brockholes. The chancel itself is particularly fine, with restored flanking screens as well as mediaeval choir stalls with carved misericords. The north chancel aisle has a pillar in the arcade which is an extremely good example of Early English work, whilst beneath the east window of the aisle is the so-called 'lepers' window'. The vestry, dating from the late 16th century, features some delightful Tudor windows and is built mainly of dressed stone in contrast to the stone rubble of the rest of the church. Local tradition suggests that this may have been brought from Cockersand Abbey and re-used here. All these architectural features are sheltered beneath the church's fine original Tudor roof.

Surrounding the church is an almost circular churchyard, suggesting that this was a religious site well before Christianity was introduced here. The churchyard has apparently witnessed something in the region of 50,000 burials since 1657 when the parish registers were first kept, although prior to the 17th century bones would have been removed at intervals to a charnel house on site. As well as some interesting old gravestones the churchyard now contains parts of a mediaeval cross, a Georgian sundial and an early 19th century brick built Sunday school.

The gates on the north side of the churchyard give access onto Church Street, which leads up to the centre of the village marked by a 'village cross'. On either side of this attractive narrow thoroughfare are some interesting historic properties which reflect the antiquity of the village generally. Among the first to be seen 'en route' from St. Helen's are Churchgate Cottage and Churchgate House, which were originally one property. The present Churchgate House was the first vicarage in Churchtown, dating from 1698 when it was rebuilt by the Reverend Henry Richmond, although there is evidence of an earlier building on the same site dating back to 1190. Churchgate Cottage is probably a late 18th century replacement of a 17th century single storey building which was a service wing when the present Churchgate House was built. Further along is the Punch Bowl Inn, an ancient hostelry which was originally known as 'The Covered Cup' after the communion chalice which formed the principal element in the arms of the Butler family, one-time occupants of nearby Kirkland Hall.

*St. Helen's Church, Churchtown*

On the opposite side of Church Street can be found a pair of old brick cottages dating from the early 19th century and featuring small horizontally-sliding sash windows which could well be original. One of these cottages is the village shop, largely unchanged inside after decades of service and still retaining many early advertising signs on its front elevation. The oldest dwellings in this quite remarkable village, Manor House and Manor Cottage, are to be seen on the same side of Church Street by the 'village cross'. This unusual structure is in fact an 18th century dialpost, effectively the village clock of its time, and its south-facing sundial is mounted on top of a Tuscan column. As in other parts of the village the pavement in front of these cottages is made up of ancient cobbles, although at one time the whole street would have been cobbled on either side of a central open drain. In between the cobbles a unique variety of clover, known locally as the Keys of Heaven and marked by orange flowers, has taken root here despite the winter frosts and the threat of re-surfacing.

*Churchtown's 'village cross'*

To the north of the village cross, Church Street gives way to Ainspool Lane, along which can be found the Post Office together with three white painted cottages which were originally thatched and which still retain their cruck frames within the gable walls. Eastwards from the cross Garstang Road leads to the top of Vicarage Lane, at the end of which is the Old Vicarage dating from the 18th century. The second of Churchtown's three vicarages, this attractive two storey building is constructed of mellow red brick and features a traceried fanlight surrounded by a semi-circular porch as well as a double flight of stairs with iron railings.

The north-eastern corner of the village is

marked by two buildings dating from the late 18th century — the Horns Inn public house and the old School House, the latter being given by Elizabeth Butler in 1790 as a schoolmaster's residence. This is a two storey stone building with dressed stone quoins which until comparatively recently was always occupied by the headteacher at the school. The current Church of England school is nearby, having been built in 1876 to replace an earlier school on the same site dating from 1812. This itself had been the successor to the original parish school which had been founded for free education as early as 1602.

Churchtown's most substantial building is Kirkland Hall, some distance to the north of the village and separated from it not only by a long driveway but also by the busy Garstang to Blackpool road. Although the Hall itself

was designed in 1760 by the architect John Carr, who also built Lytham Hall, there are parts of some earlier 17th century buildings which have been incorporated on the site. It was in the previous century that the property had come into the ownership of the Butler family, who held the Kirkland estate in succeeding generations until the latter half of the 19th century. At the entrance to the Hall can be seen some attractive ornamental gates with square stone piers surmounted by cornices and animal heads; these originally occupied a site in the village itself, but were moved to their present position when the A586 was built to bypass the village in 1935.

This road links up with the A6, which in just over a mile takes us northwards to the old-established market town of **Garstang.** A rather more direct route between the two places is offered by a footpath across the

*The Town Hall and market office in Garstang*

fields, and it was probably this which was used by Garstang worshippers years ago as they regularly made their way to St. Helen's Parish Church in Churchtown. This footpath would probably have been one of several used by funeral bearers as they too negotiated their journey to Churchtown over poor terrain and considerable distances, so it is not surprising to discover that there are remains of stone crosses marking their frequent resting places at various points between Garstang and St. Helens. Things were made considerably easier by the designation of St. Thomas' on Church Street in Garstang as a parish church in 1880, this having been first licensed as a chapel of ease as early as 1437 before being rebuilt, restored and enlarged at various times during the 17th, 18th and 19th centuries.

The name 'Garstang' appears to have originated in Saxon times, either in the form of Gayrstang after a Saxon baron called Garri who settled here during the 6th century or in the form of Gaerstung from a Saxon word meaning common land or meadow land. We can say with rather more certainty that by Norman times it was known as Cherestanc, being mentioned in the Domesday Book under this name, although the earliest reference to a lord of the manor of Garstang was in 1226 when William de Lancastre gave land in the Vill de Gayrestange to the Abbot of Cockersand 'to hold as of their Church of St. Helen'. At about the same time he gave to Robert le Botiller 'the mill of Gayrestange with its site and pool'. The manor was passed on to many other families during the course of the centuries until it was sold off in lots in 1919, mostly to the existing tenants.

The right to hold a market on Thursday each week at Garstang and in addition a fair of two days' duration on the vigil and Day of the Feast of St. Peter and St. Paul was granted by Edward II to the abbots of Cockersand, but the dissolution of the abbey led to the lapse of this privilege. Then in 1597 a weekly market and two fairs each year were granted to the town by Queen Elizabeth I to assist with the relief of the poor, although it was only in 1679 that Garstang received its first Charter of Incorporation from Charles II. This made the town into a free borough, providing for the appointment of eight local men to act as a governing body which eventually became known as the Mayor and Corporation. This body was then dissolved under the Municipal Corporation Act of 1886, and since 1889 the town's property has been vested in the Garstang Town Trust.

The town experienced particular growth during the coaching era, when the stage and mail coaches made stops at many of the seven hotels and inns to be found on the main street. Garstang's prosperity increased further with the opening of the Lancaster Canal in 1797, although this was somewhat short-lived because of the competition from the

*The Old Grammar School, Garstang*

railway line which effectively bypassed the town from the 1840s onwards.

Today the main A6 road also bypasses Garstang, ensuring that this fascinating historic town can be enjoyed in comparative peace by those who want to take the time to study its old buildings or amble along its riverside walks. The focal point of Garstang is its Market Place, at the centre of which is a market cross first erected in 1754 and later restored in 1897 to commemorate Queen Victoria's jubilee. Garstang's market cross resembles that of neighbouring Churchtown, although its Tuscan column is topped by a ball rather than a sundial and the cobbled pavements around it were the site of the town's stocks and fish stones.

It was the charter granted during Elizabeth I's reign which established the separate identities of Garstang Church Town and Garstang Market Town, and the map-maker Blome noted that 'Garstang hath a great market for corn, cattle, yarn and fish'. It was also well known for cheese, and the steps of the market cross were used for laying out wares. Close by is the Royal Oak Hotel, a one-time coaching inn during the Georgian era, while across the Market Place stands the Town Hall and market office; this is the third Town Hall to occupy the site since 1680. On the north side the Market Place gives way to the High Street, the main thoroughfare through the town marked not only by some delightful old cottages but also by the entrances to narrow weinds. In certain cases these ancient passageways open out into shopping areas at the rear of the High Street, while in others they provide quiet pedestrian routes down

towards the banks of the River Wyre.

At the end of the High Street, marking the northern boundary of Garstang's historic centre, is the rather attractive Old Grammar School which was built in 1756. Although its use as a school ended in 1928 it has recently been restored as the town's Arts Centre. At the opposite end of the town, Church Street takes us on past the Georgian parish church of St. Thomas and a range of impressive Victorian houses before coming out at the canal basin. This is one of Garstang's prettiest spots, with the rippling waters of the basin being hemmed in on three sides by attractive cottages and an old tithe barn dating from 1710 which has been converted into a

*The Royal Oak Hotel in Garstang*

*The Old Tithe Barn, Garstang*

restaurant and agricultural museum. Just a short distance to the south of the basin the canal is carried across the River Wyre by a splendid aqueduct which was designed by the noted architect and engineer Rennie in about 1793.

Garstang's oldest remaining building is Greenhalgh Castle, situated at the end of Castle Lane on a hillside to the east of the town on the other side of the Wyre. Built by Thomas Stanley (the first Earl of Derby) in 1490 it was one of the last Royalist strongholds north of the Trent to hold out against Cromwell's forces. However, it capitulated after the siege of 1645-46 and a few years later was largely dismantled, with what was left being further reduced by time and weather as well as by local people plundering the stone for their own use.

From Garstang the River Wyre can be followed northwards upstream to the picturesque village of **Scorton,** a lovely settlement of cottages and terraced houses nestling in the midst of woods at the foot of the Grizedale fells. The name 'Scorton' is probably Anglo-Saxon in origin, signifying an enclosure at or near a long incision or mark - perhaps referring to the long slanting gorge at the rear of the village. Yet although it bears an Anglo-Saxon name Scorton is not a particularly old place and does not feature in the Domesday Survey. The earliest reference to the village goes back to 1587, but most of its development seems to have taken place during the 18th and 19th centuries as a result

of the patronage of its landed owners. Up to the middle of the 19th century the Duke of Hamilton was in possession of Scorton, and it was he who gave land for a school on the east side of the village as well as a site for a Wesleyan Methodist Chapel.

In 1853, however, the village and other parts

of the Duke's estate were purchased by Mr. Peter Ormrod of Bolton, who then built for his own occupation the substantial residence known as Wyresdale Park to the north east of Scorton. His family was also responsible for the erection in 1878-79 of the church at the southern end of the village, the spire of which can be seen from some considerable distance.

*Some of Scorton's attractive old cottages*

The Ormrods furthermore played a part in providing employment for people in Scorton through their ownership of a cotton mill situated at the north end of the village, which had been erected during the early part of the 19th century. The Ormrods spent significant sums of money improving the district generally, and the 'lakes' on either side of the Wyre to the north of the village are the result of the development of a fish hatchery business by the family during the 1890s.

Situated a little above the valley of the River Wyre at this point, enjoying a panoramic view of the extensive fells over to the east, is the rather isolated parish church of St. Paul, known also as **Shireshead Old Church** to distinguish it from the 'new' church of St. James which was consecrated in September 1889 to more adequately serve the village of Forton. The present St. Paul's Church was built in 1805, although an earlier building for worship had occupied the same site at least since 1520. This was probably erected by a lord of Wyresdale for his own use as well as for his tenants, saving them all a journey of about four miles to the parish church at Cockerham.

Shortly after the Norman Conquest the whole of this area would have been served by priests from Cockersand Abbey, but in about 1430 the parish of Cockerham was established together with a vicar and several curates to look after the outlying chapels; even to this day the vicar of Cockerham is the patron of the living of Shireshead. Among the interesting features of St. Paul's Church are its traceried windows, which are unusual in that the tracery is all formed of iron and probably one of the oldest examples of its type in the country. The building as a whole is rather simply built of stone, although its relative plainness is relieved by an appealing twin belfy at the west end.

Just a short distance from St. Paul's Church is the quiet hamlet of **Hollins Lane,** probably a rather busier place during the latter part of the 18th century when coaches and other vehicles going north and south ran through here. Then in the early 1820s the main road from Preston to Lancaster, which had gone through Hollins Lane, was completely realigned and improved to provide a better route for the fast mail coaches which were enjoying their heyday. This meant that Hollins Lane became a comparative backwater, with the new toll road following approximately the line of the present A6.

It is to the west of the A6 that one finds the rather more substantial village of **Forton,** a very pleasant place which was recorded in the Domesday Book under the name of 'Fortune'. Close to the junction of the two roads passing through the village is a humble little village shop, some interesting old stone

*An early independent chapel, to be found in Forton*

built farms and cottages, and an early independent chapel founded in 1706 under the Five Mile Act. This determined that 'dissenting teachers' who refused to conform to the rules of the Established Church were barred from teaching their religious doctrines within five miles of any Corporate town. As a result chapels for preaching their doctrines beyond the prescribed boundary were built in different places throughout the country, with Forton being one of them.

Crossing back over the busy A6 and the even busier M6 motorway, our travels up the Wyre valley bring us into **Dolphinholme,** with the oldest part of the village being clustered along both sides of the river at the bottom of a wooded gorge. Dolphinholme appears to have come into existence as a settlement of some size through the establishment of a worsted factory here at the end of the 18th century, and so it is not surprising to find two long rows of terraced cottages in the upper part of the village which were built to accommodate the local millworkers. The mill itself was situated in a hollow by the Wyre, together with a number of cottages which are still there. The waterwheel in operation here was the biggest in England and second only to that at Laxey in the Isle of Man. At one point there were about 1400 people employed at the mill, out of a total population of nearly 3,000.

In those heady days of the early Industrial Revolution it must have been a hectic place indeed, in dramatic contrast to the peace and quiet which has prevailed since the works closed during the 1860s. Dolphinholme's importance as an industrial centre is underlined by the fact that it is said to have been one of the first places in the United Kingdom to be lit by gas. This was originally made here in about 1801, and stored in a

holder on the east side of the works before being used in the factory and in some of the village shops. Very little of Dolphinholme's industrial heritage is to be seen now, apart from the rows of millworkers' cottages in the upper village and a substantial stone built warehouse on the banks of the river in Lower Dolphinholme, and the passage of time has allowed nature to gently cover over the scars of a forgotten era.

From Dolphinholme the road runs eastwards to **Abbeystead,** following the wooded gorge of the Wyre upstream to the point where its two main feeder streams converge. Just below here is a reservoir built by Lancaster Corporation, although it has been blended into the landscape so well that it now looks like a beautiful lake and as such forms a very attractive feature in this idyllic little spot, Abbeystead itself is a small hamlet consisting of some impressive farmhouses and farm buildings, many of which date from the Victorian period when they were built in conjunction with the Earl of Sefton's estate here. It was he who erected a rather splendid mansion close to the Wyre between 1885 and 1887, which he then used as a 'shooting box'. On the north side of the road passing through the village is a school which was founded and endowed in 1674, while just a hundred yards or so to the south is the supposed site of an abbey founded by Cistercian monks in the 12th century. No physical remains of this exist now, and the only evidence left is the name of the village itself - Abbeystead means 'an abbey place'.

Before heading south from Abbeystead to the Trough of Bowland, one of Lancashire's most popular scenic routes, it is well worthwhile making a detour along the single-track road which follows the course of the Tarnbrook Wyre. At the end of this rather tortuous

*Abbeystead*

journey one is rewarded by the delightful sight of the hamlet of **Tarnbrook,** a completely unspoilt collection of cottages and farm buildings where time seems to have stood still. Out in the fields by the riverside during the summer months one can still see the local farmers turning their hay by pitchfork rather than by mechanical means — one secretly imagines that this is because modernisation

has yet to reach this rather isolated corner of the county, although at the same time commonsense suggests that it may just be that the fields are too small for tractors to operate efficiently. Then again, the hanging out of washing on bushes in the garden might be another pointer to the belief here that the old ways really are the best. As well as still being a very traditional farming community,

Tarnbrook has the unusual distinction of having a Mountain Rescue Post — indicative of the fact that this is a good place from which to explore the vast expanse of the surrounding fells.

From Tarnbrook our route takes us southwards towards Marshaw before turning back in the direction of Scorton again, but this

*Tarnbrook*

*An isolated farmhouse in the Forest of Bowland*

*Jubilee Tower, just above Abbeystead*

*Mill managers' houses in Calder Vale*

time following the Trough of Bowland road over the fells. The road runs along the foot of Hawthornthwaite and Catshaw Fells before taking a left turn over Harrisend Fell on the way to Oakenclough and Calder Vale. The comparatively stark landscape of these fells is a dramatic contrast to the pastoral beauty of the Wyre valley, but it is certainly no less enticing and it offers the added bonus of some superb views of the Lune estuary when Harrisend Fell is reached.

**Oakenclough** is a small and scattered community which appears to have developed largely as a result of a paper mill being sited here to make use of the water power available from the swiftly flowing River Calder. One of the oldest paper mills in the country, it was bought by John Jackson in 1827 from Richard Curtis, a paper manufacturer and farmer who had gone bankrupt. John Jackson built and lived at the adjacent house known as Calder Bank, now a restaurant, and his descendants continued to live there for well over a hundred years.

About a mile and a half downstream from Oakenclough is the delightful 'model' industrial village of **Calder Vale,** which was largely created by the Jackson family with the intention of improving the already existing industrial potential at Oakenclough. In 1835 Calder Vale Mill was erected by the Jacksons for the purpose of cotton spinning, to be closely followed by the provision of some neat stone built terraced houses for the workforce because of the isolated position of the mill site in relation to local centres of population. Then in 1848 Low Mill was built for the weaving of cotton, as well as some additional housing, with the waste from both mills being carted up the valley to the mill at Oakenclough where it was used in the paper making process there. All three mills were owned by the Jackson family and were originally worked by water power from the River Calder, although Low Mill (since demolished) was equipped with steam power from an early stage in its life.

The two villages were connected not only in terms of their economies but also in terms of their communities, in that many people resident in one place might be employed in the other. Research into census records has revealed that most of the people in Calder Vale in the mid-19th century came from the Lancashire Plain, and in particular from the Over Wyre area of the Fylde. The people here were not from industrial families but came instead from an agricultural background, perhaps evident from the care with which they have traditionally tended their gardens. Yet at the same time the folk in Calder Vale have developed their own identity, partly as a result of the village's geographical isolation but also as a result of the high level of inter-marriage which took place at an early stage.

It should come as no surprise to the visitor, therefore, that Calder Vale has a unique character and atmosphere all of its own, as well as being something of a 'picture postcard' village with its pleasing rows of stone cottages and its verdant surroundings. One might initially be taken aback, though, by the comparative isolation of the local church and primary school nearly a mile to the north east of the village itself, until one realises that this picturesque position on the slopes above the river enables the church and school to serve both Calder Vale and Oakenclough. The church was built by public subscription and consecrated in 1863.

From Oakenclough and Calder Vale the road runs southwards to **Claughton,** passing en route the higher ground of Sullom where wild deer once roamed; it now offers the prospect of some far-reaching views towards Preston and the Fylde on clearer days. Claughton itself, pronounced 'Clighton' to distinguish it from other similarly named places, was mentioned in the Domesday Book as the Old Norse settlement of 'Clactune' — a hamlet near the small hillock. Nowadays it is still very much a hamlet in size, encompassing a hall, church, school and a few cottages and farmsteads, some of which are cruck framed buildings with steeply pitched thatch roofs.

From Claughton a pretty country lane follows the course of the River Brock upstream towards the settlement of **Bleasdale,** passing on the way a well-known beauty spot at Brock Mill. This was originally the site of a water powered corn mill, and some of the old millstones are still to be seen in the gardens of nearby houses. Nowadays the old mill marks the starting point of a nature trail, and a landscaped car park has been created close by. Another corn mill, known as Higher Brock Mill, was located further upstream together with a blacksmith's forge, which has since been converted into a Post Office and cafe.

From this point a long driveway heads directly northwards up into Bleasdale itself, bringing us out onto an extensive plain of pasture land set against a backcloth of encircling fells. A little beyond the school here is the rather austere-looking and unusually named Parish Church of St. Eadmer of Admarsh in Bleasdale. The present building dates from 1835 when it was erected by John Dewhurst, although mention is made of 'Eadmor's Chapel' on a map of 1598. The original church on the site may have been even older, since St. Eadmer was a religious writer of the 12th century.

Settlement in the Bleasdale area actually appears to date from the Bronze Age period,

*Brock Bottoms, near to Brock Mill*

evident from the discovery here of a post-and-stake circle monument at the end of the 19th century. The circle can be found less than half a mile to the north east of the church within a wooded copse, which itself is an early Bronze Age circular village site with an off-centre communal hut. This hut was surrounded by a ditch, beyond which would have been several living huts, with the whole settlement being enclosed by a palisade of oak pole construction. At the centre of the mound upon which the communal hut was built was found a stone-lined cist containing two cremation urns, and it seems likely that these are amongst the earliest collared urns to be found in Britain. Another recently identified site to the east of Chipping, as well as other Bronze Age activity in the area, points to the settled nature of society during this very early period of Lancashire's history.

Heading back towards Higher Brock Mill, with Fair Snape Fell behind and Parlick to the side, one's attention is caught by **Beacon Fell** in the distance — since the coniferous plantation on top of this smaller but more clearly defined summit is in sharp contrast to the unadorned slopes of the fells to the rear. Opened in 1969 as Lancashire's first Country Park, Beacon Fell covers an area of 550 acres and is steeped in history. It lies along the route of a branch road which the Roman forces built between Ribchester and their camp on the Lune at Lancaster, probably towards the middle of the 3rd century, but in later centuries it became one of a chain of hills which were selected to provide important signalling facilities in times of danger.

However, it was not always the highest hills which were the most suitable for the siting of signalling stations, since a low hill standing by itself could be widely seen and more easily recognised. Beacon Fell was therefore ideally suited for signalling and was also readily accessible for horses and carts and the transportation of fuel. In addition it was conveniently located between the beacons of Clough Pike near Lancaster and Rivington Pike near Bolton, playing its part in enabling a message to be sent sixty miles across Lancashire and Cheshire in only eleven minutes.

Beacons were used regularly as a form of communication from the very earliest times, and a tax named 'beconagium' was levied in the 12th century to pay for the costs involved. As late as 1830 Clarke's 'New Lancashire Gazetteer' described the beacons on the hills of northern England as having been of durable construction and consisting of a small circular enclosure of unhewn stone, narrowing into a cylinder, on top of which was a hearth of flat stones to contain the fuel. In later years Beacon Fell became an extensive gathering ground for water, which was fed into the nearby Barnsfold Reservoir just to the south east of the fell, and it was in connection with this that a substantial programme of afforestation was undertaken during the early part of this century. This has given Beacon Fell its distinctive green 'cap' of conifer trees.

Beacon Fell is located within the parish of **Whitechapel,** the original place name of which was 'Threlfall', and in earlier times Beacon Fell was called 'Threlfall Beacon'. Whitechapel has a considerable history, and large parts of the parish were owned by the Order of the Knights of St. John of Jerusalem, also known as the Knights Hospitallers and established towards the end of the 11th century. These monastic knights had military as well as religious purposes, and they upheld an oath to defend the cause of the Cross and lead a life of poverty, chastity and obedience. A number of the older houses in the Whitechapel area also have religious connections, since many were occupied by Roman Catholic families. Ashes Farm, for example, one of the oldest dwellings in the district and featuring a unique winged figure

*The conifer-capped crest of Beacon Fell*

carved in stone over the front door, was the home of the influential Roman Catholic Threlfall family, while Whitehill Farm occupies the site of a monastery which belonged to the Franciscan order. The Hesketh family who lived here were also influential Roman Catholics, establishing a small chapel nearby.

The Parish Church of St. James in Whitechapel is a fairly humble country church built of local stone during the 18th and 19th centuries, although it dates back to pre-Reformation times when it was a private oratory and just 27 feet by 13 feet in size. During the 18th century the church also provided accommodation for the village school, although a new school building was eventually erected in 1810 just a short distance away. To complete the facilities on offer to local residents a village hall was erected close to the school just after the First World War, although this was replaced by a more modern building in 1964. Also nearby is the Cross Keys Inn, a 16th century coaching house which is run in conjunction with a working farm. The Cross Keys has thankfully avoided modernisation and is still a good example of a more traditional and unspoilt public house with a real country flavour, relating very well to the rural character of this part of Lancashire.

A mile to the south of Whitechapel is the picturesque village of **Inglewhite**, with its triangular green and old market cross. The Green is surrounded by groups of 17th century houses, a smithy and the Green Man Inn, whilst the market cross consists of a stone column about 10 feet tall mounted on a circular base of five stone steps. Cut into the shaft is the date 1675 and the initials H.C.I.W., which refer to Justice Warren who was then lord of the manor. At one time Inglewhite was an important venue for local agricultural fairs, and on those occasions the Green was the main area on which trading took place. No doubt this was helped by the fact that the Green was the point at which several lanes from the outlying districts converged. The

Green was also the spot where bull-baiting once took place.

Inglewhite also has something of an industrial past, as is evident from the names of Button Street, Silk Mill Lane and Factory Bridge. As well as a button mill there was a small bone mill and a silk mill, the latter being operated by water and hand power before ultimately being closed down at the beginning of the 19th century. Prior to this the village had achieved some fame between the 17th and 19th centuries because of the great healing properties of the drinking water from the Holy Well of St. Anne, which was said to have 'a sulphureous smell, as strong as that near Harrigate in Yorkshire'.

Inglewhite and Whitechapel are both within the parish of **Goosnargh**, which covers over 9,000 acres and is believed to be the second largest parish in England. The village of Goosnargh is a rather pretty place in which the 11th century church of St. Mary the Virgin acts as a focal point, drawing towards it the

*St. James' Parish Church, Whitechapel*

*Inglewhite Cross*

*Another part of Inglewhite village green*

village school and a couple of public houses as well as a number of older cottages. The name 'Goosnargh' could well mean 'cultivated land', since the Domesday Book mentions that the village (at that time recorded under the name Gusanarghe) had about 160 acres of cultivated land. By the reign of Edward III in the 14th century Goosnargh had developed into a prosperous parish and high taxes were being levied on corn, wool and lambs.

At that time St. Mary's was a chapel of ease for the mother church in Kirkham, and it remained part of the parish of Kirkham until 1846. During the course of the preceding centuries, however, various improvements and extensions were made to St. Mary's so that its outward appearance now bears the marks of the passage of time — the chancel and Lady Chapel date from the 16th century, the porch from the 17th century and an ornately designed brass chandelier from the 18th century. The tower of the church is a substantial structure which has walls sixty feet high and six feet thick at the base; incorporated within one of these walls is a circular stone said to represent either a spinning wheel or a charm against witches, since the practise of witchcraft was prevalent here in earlier days.

From mediaeval times onwards Goosnargh had '24 Sworn Men' whose duty was to guard against injustice and maintain the church services. In 1673 these Sworn Men were required to establish a school close to the church, and by the early 18th century children were being taught reading free of charge but had to pay five shillings for the privilege of learning writing and accounts. In 1839 the school was re-built, and the present Goosnargh C of E school incorporates this building as well as a more recent extension. Also close to the church is the very substantial Bushell House, a beautiful Georgian building

set in elegant gardens which almost seems too big for the village. This was originally the residence of William Bushell, who in the earlier part of the 18th century directed that the house should be used as a hospital for elderly Protestant gentlemen and gentlewomen.

Nearby Mill Lane leads firstly to Church House, occupying the site of an ancient monastery, and then down towards the spot where Goosnargh corn mill was located. Although the Goosnargh area was largely agricultural in nature, the village itself saw the development of a flourishing business in the

*Bushell House, Goosnargh*

cottage industries of spinning and weaving cotton, linen and woollen materials. The village also became well-known for its locally-produced Goosnargh cakes, which used some of the surplus butter available from dairy farming in the area.

Neighbouring **Whittingham** is famous chiefly for Chingle Hall, reputedly the most haunted house in the country and said to have been built in the 13th century. The Hall was constructed in the form of a crucifix and was surrounded at one time by a moat, part of which still remains. Chingle Hall was an important house for Roman Catholics during the 17th century persecutions, and it incorporated 'hiding holes' for priests as well as places where religious articles could be concealed. Whittingham is also known for its almost self-contained psychiatric hospital, which at one time had a patient population exceeding 3,000 as well as its own railway system. The main purpose of the railway was to carry the 12,000 tons of coal which the hospital consumed annually, but a passenger service also operated twelve times a day.

From Goosnargh a narrow country lane takes us westwards between green fields and over the M6 motorway before bringing us into the village of **Barton,** a linear settlement which straggles along both sides of the A6 road. St. Lawrence's Church is situated alongside the A6 and was founded in about 1577 as a chapel for the use of the lord of the manor, but by 1723 it had become a semi-public building. After being extended in 1845 the chapel was consecrated as a parish church in 1850 and was then rebuilt at the end of the 19th century. Nearby a small village school with accommodation for 90 children had been built in 1848, superseding a simple Dame's school with seven scholars which had been in existence previously. A Roman Catholic school was opened on Station Lane in 1863, close to the Newhouse Roman Catholic Chapel which had been built in 1741. Leading off the busy A6, Station Lane presents the more peaceful side of Barton's nature, running down towards the Lancaster Canal which offers a pleasant walk along its easy-going towpath.

To the north of Barton is the village of **Bilsborrow,** again dissected by the A6. Apart from the noise of passing traffic the village is a relatively tranquil place, offering good views of both Beacon Fell and the Forest of Bowland to the east as well as quiet walks along the Lancaster Canal to the west. From here country lanes can be followed southwards to the villages of **Catforth** and **Woodplumpton,** which lie on the edge of the Fylde and are largely agricultural in nature. There are numerous old cottages to be seen throughout the area, many of which were originally thatched, whilst the Lancaster Canal could be considered as one long beauty spot between the two villages. Many of the canal bridges are of particular interest, whilst the canal banks are a haven for flora and fauna.

One of the oldest buildings in Woodplumpton is St. Anne's Parish Church, which probably started life as a manor chapel during the early part of the 13th century. By the year 1552 the first known curate had been appointed by the vicar of St. Michael's-on-Wyre. At that time the church probably consisted of just the north aisle, but over the course of the next hundred years both the nave and the south aisle were added to produce the building largely as it stands at present. By 1747 an

*Woodplumpton Parish Church*

appeal was made by the parishioners for financial help to restore their ageing church since the timber in the roof was 'greatly decayed and the walls of the said Chappell very much crackt, shattered and in danger of falling'.

Restoration work was obviously undertaken at that time, although the well-known church architects Austin and Paley were brought in at the start of the present century to raise the roof, insert dormer windows and prop up seven of the stone piers. The small bell tower, in the form of an octagonal lantern, probably dates from the 18th century restoration — although the church boasts a bell which bears the date of 1596 and was in operation until 1946. Interesting features outside the church include the stocks, a 17th century sundial and a witch's grave. The 'witch' was found crushed between a barrel and a wall and was buried by torchlight. Her body reportedly rose to the surface after several attempts at burial, so she was finally laid face downwards and the spot exorcised by a priest before a large boulder was placed there to prevent further 'resurrection'.

In the centre of Woodplumpton village is to be found Cuckstool Farm, a substantial brick cottage which at one time had a thatched roof. The building is a typical example of the two-tier thatched cottages of the 17th century, with their beamed rooms and 'dormer' window, although this particular one has some additional interest in that the one-time entrance to a weaving or spinning room can still be seen outlined in the east wall. Presumably the cottage was also close to the site of the village 'cuckstool', an instrument of

punishment used for ducking not only garrulous or offending women but also insolvent burgesses who could not pay their bills.

Those with an interest in the macabre might wish to pay a visit to the 19th century Roman Catholic Church of St. Robert's in Catforth. Among several religious relics preserved here is a skull, which for a long time was thought to be that of a priest martyred during the 16th century. This explanation has apparently been disproved by recent scientific examinations.

The village of **Broughton** marks the end of our tour around the Fylde and Wyre area, and this large settlement is to be found just two miles to the east of Woodplumpton. In earlier days the village essentially consisted of a concentration of cottages at the crossroads where the A6 and the Woodplumpton to Goosnargh road met, but in recent years there has been a substantial amount of new residential development to create what is now largely a dormitory suburb of Preston. However, Broughton's early origins can still be discovered from the older properties around Four Lane Ends. One of the pubs located at this junction used to be known as the Shuttleworth Arms, taking its name from the Shuttleworth family who were lords of the manor of neighbouring Barton. Then close by was the village smithy as well as the local corn mill, the latter building remaining in its original form despite being converted to a variety of different uses in more recent years.

Alongside the A6 is Toll Bar Cottage, which functioned as its name suggests and still

*Broughton Parish Church*

projects out into the road. The actual turnpike was a moveable barrier made of wood near the toll-house; this was turned when the toll was paid and allowed the use of the road as far as the next toll-bar. The turnpike system was ended in 1875 as a result of the general demand for better highways, but even so things must have improved considerably since 1770, when it was reported that the Preston to Lancaster road had 'ruts four feet deep, floating with mud, and able to accommodate a sheep'.

Broughton Parish Church, dedicated to St. John the Baptist, is situated about half a mile to the south of the main village centre and is now within earshot of the M55 motorway. Some authorities think that there was a church here even before any were built in Preston, and the date of the foundation is believed to have been about 1110. The early church was probably of wooden construction, and there were two successive wooden churches on the site before the reign of Henry VIII. The present stone tower dates from 1533, whilst the rest of the church was rebuilt in 1826. A visitor in 1872 described the general architecture of the building as being 'strong and simple — quite devoid of ornament, homely, substantial'. Inside the church there is an old stone font which probably dates from the Saxon period, as well as a set of bells dating from pre Reformation times which are among the oldest in the county. Externally the church is hemmed in by a low stone wall, and close to the tower there are some well-worn stocks as well as a mounting block, while to the rear is an old cottage which is all that remains of the Church Inn which stood there. In earlier times, when families rode or drove to church, the Inn was used for the 'baiting' of horses and for the refreshment of worshippers after the service.

*Cuckstool Farm, Woodplumpton*

*The 'Hark to Bounty' Inn, Slaidburn*

# Chapter 4: PRESTON AND THE RIBBLE VALLEY

**Preston** occupies an important position at the very heart of Lancashire and as such has traditionally been the administrative centre of the county, with the headquarters of the county council, the crown courts and a wide range of regional and sub-regional offices being situated here. The town is also conveniently located between the capitals of England and Scotland, on one of the major routes between the two countries, and during the course of its history it has been visited by a number of distinguished people on their journeys north and south. Among them was Edward I, who passed through Preston on his way to Scotland in 1306 and issued two proclamations from here; Robert the Bruce, however, was rather more destructive when he came to Preston from the opposite direction in 1323, and his visit was marked by his decision to set fire to the town. Then in August 1617 James I stopped off at the Market Place on his way from Scotland to London, while some 30 years afterwards Preston was to become the scene of fierce fighting during the Civil War period.

In later years Preston became a great centre for the Jacobite cause, and in 1715 the Market Place saw the Old Pretender being proclaimed by a body of James' supporters. After a skirmish the 1,600 soldiers who had occupied the town were forced to surrender, and their leaders were summarily dealt with in London soon after. In 1745 the Young Pretender also visited Preston, and although

he too was proclaimed in the Market Place he attracted only half-hearted support — so not long after marching out of the town he was in full retreat northwards with his bedraggled followers.

Preston's history as a centre of commerce goes back to at least the reign of Henry II, when the town received the right to hold a 'Guild Merchant', although there is evidence to suggest that an even earlier charter was granted by Henry I in 1100. Since the middle of the 16th century the famous Preston Guild has been held every 20 years, always with great celebration and civic pride even though the considerable privileges which were bestowed upon the Guild Burgesses have now virtually disappeared. For a full week the town enjoys itself in festivity and hospitality, and the Guild brings together people from across the world. Preston also has a long parliamentary history, in that it was represented in Parliament as long ago as 1295 and is preceded in this by only one other English town.

Preston's continuing importance over the centuries is apparent from an account given by Daniel Defoe, who noted that 'though there is no manufacture, the town, being honoured with a Court of Chancery and the officers and justices for Lancaster, is full of gentlemen, attorneys, proctors and notaries, the process of law being here of a different nature from that of other places...To this town

the gentry resort in the winter from many miles round, and there are, during the season, assemblies and balls in the same manner as at York'.

The lack of manufacture which Defoe noted was remedied towards the end of the 18th century, by which time Preston had begun to develop as an important textile centre. A leading event in the town's industrial growth had been the invention by Richard Arkwright in 1768 of his famous water-frame cotton spinning machine, at his house on Stoneygate close to the parish church. A few years later Samuel Horrocks built his first mill, to be rapidly followed by a host of other mills engaged in the spinning of cotton, and by the middle of the Victorian period the town had grown substantially by virtue of its increasing industrialisation. The first census, undertaken in 1801, recorded a population of 14,300 living in the borough, but by 1841 this had increased to 53,482 and then to 98,793 in 1881. By the end of the Victorian era Preston's population had grown to 115,483.

It seems that the inventiveness demonstrated by some of Preston's inhabitants extended not only to the town's industry but also to its inebriates, for it was here that the teetotal movement was first founded. The rallying call for total abstinence which was heard in Preston soon spread throughout the country, and to support the movement the first temperance newspaper saw the light of day

*The Harris Library, Museum and Art Gallery in Preston*

*The Parish Church*

*Winckley Square*

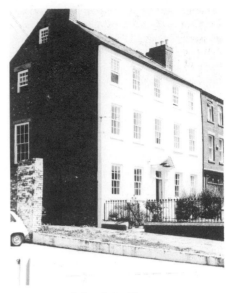

*Arkwright House*

*Perspectives on Preston*

here as did the first temperance hotel. Perhaps all this sobering activity also provided the opportunity for Preston people to think more clearly than their provincial counterparts, since Preston was the first town outside London to illuminate its streets with gas.

There are really very few 'ancient' buildings still to be seen in Preston, and its mediaeval heritage is now represented only by the street pattern and by historic street names such as Fishergate, Friargate, Stoneygate and Cheapside. Even the parish church is very largely a mid-Victorian building, although it stands on a site which was the centre of a Norman parish and which had been used for Christian worship as early as the 7th century. The original building had been dedicated to St. Wilfred, but at the time of the Reformation it was re-dedicated to St. John.

Thankfully much more of Preston's Georgian architecture is still around to be enjoyed, particularly on the south side of the town centre between Fishergate and Avenham Park. The imposing town houses around Winckley Square are now largely in use as offices, but their delightfully stylish architecture still conveys something of the atmosphere of a prosperous and perhaps more leisurely era. From the comparatively sheltered seclusion of Winckley Square, with its small central green crossed by several footpaths, one can follow Ribblesdale Place or Starkie Street down towards the larger public open spaces of Avenham Park and Miller Park. Situated alongside the River Ribble these two parks offer the varied delights of tree-lined walks and formal gardens as well as their great green 'carpets' for informal recreation.

The civic pride generated in the town during the Victorian period is to be seen most

dramatically in the buildings around the Market Square. The most notable of these is the Harris Public Library, Museum and Art Gallery on the east side, built between 1882 and 1893. Nearby is the imposing County

Sessions House, completed in 1903 and designed to an English Renaissance style with a graceful tower rising to a height of 179 feet. Adjoining the County Sessions House is the Town Hall, a somewhat later building which

*Some of Preston's grand civic architecture*

dates from 1933 but whose architectural style blends in very successfully with that of its neighbour, whilst over the other side of Lancaster Road is to be found the thoroughly modern Guild Hall. This impressive building was completed in 1972 as a multi-purpose entertainments complex.

In the Market Square itself there are two structures of particular interest. The first of these is the War Memorial, standing on the northern side of the Square just in front of the Head Post Office. This Memorial was designed by Sir Giles Gilbert Scott, the architect of the Whitehall Cenotaph, and erected in 1926. Then at the other end of the Market Square is the Obelisk, re-erected in 1979 to celebrate Preston's Octocentenary. The Obelisk had been introduced originally in 1782 to replace several previous market crosses, and in 1816 gas pipes were inserted into the shaft and a 22-inch diameter glass vase placed on top to create a 33-foot high 'beacon' which shed light over a space of 4,000 square yards. In 1853, however, it was dismantled and taken to Hollowforth Hall in Woodplumpton, where it stayed until it was restored to the Market Square in 1979.

Preston's most dramatic landmark is one which represents perhaps better than any other the town's aspiring ambitions during the Victorian period. This is the 303-foot high spire of St. Walburghe's Church, raised to its lofty heights above the surrounding terraced houses by the architect John Hansom (after whom the hansom-cab was named). Built of white limestone with a slim tower it is very reminiscent of Salisbury Cathedral and is a well known feature of Preston's remarkably varied skyline; it is particularly attractive on a sunny day when the white spire can be seen from miles around.

Our travels into the Ribble Valley start first of all at **Grimsargh,** about five miles to the north east of Preston. The main feature of interest in this village seems to be the opportunity for recreation — the village green is one of the largest in Lancashire, extending over an area of about 12 acres, and there are three reservoirs which provide fishing and sailing facilities. Grimsargh also has the benefit of Tun Brook Wood, which follows the line of the Tun Brook southwards to the River Ribble and is thought to be one of the largest areas of deciduous woodland in the country. The architectural heritage of the village is represented by St. Michael's Parish Church, which dates back to 1726, and by the Plough Inn, which used to be the main railway station building.

From Grimsargh the road continues north-eastwards up to **Longridge,** a much larger settlement of stone built terraces situated at the foot of Longridge Fell. Most of the houses here date from the Victorian period when Longridge was developing in importance as a cotton spinning town, although the terrace known as Club Row has a rather different story to tell. This particular row of cottages represents the cumulative efforts of a very early form of 'building society', in that it was constructed by 20 men who had banded themselves together as a club to build their own dwellings. Each man contributed a guinea every month, which was used to purchase materials towards the construction of a cottage which was to have both a 'necessary and a coal house'. The men acted as their own labour force, and when a house was completed a ballot was organised and the winner moved in. This process was repeated until all the original 20 were housed in the terrace, which then became known as Club Row.

Longridge has also been an important source of building stone for other places, as well as for its own houses, and alongside the road up to Jeffrey Hill there is evidence of the early quarries from which this stone was extracted. Several of the civic buildings in Preston were constructed using Longridge stone, as were Liverpool Docks when the port was expanding rapidly during the 19th century. The former Royal Sovereign Hotel on the roadside was once appropriately called 'The Quarryman's Arms', and as well as a date of 1808 the plaque above the doorway carries symbols which depict the tools of the quarryman's trade. From higher up the slopes of Longridge Fell there are some superb views northwards of the Loud valley and Chipping against a backcloth of the Bowland Fells, whilst to the south the land drops gently away down towards the River Ribble.

It is here, on the north bank of the Ribble, that the Roman settlement of **Ribchester** is to be found. Although some evidence of Bronze Age occupation has been unearthed it was in AD 79 that a permanent fort was first

*The White Bull, Ribchester*

established in this location by the Roman governor Gnaeus Julius Agricola, who probably chose the spot because it was at the junction of the important roads between Manchester and Carlisle and between York and the west coast. Whilst comparatively little of the fort's defensive wall still remains, several of the internal buildings have been excavated (including two granaries and parts of the headquarters building) and this has yielded some interesting coins, pottery, masonry, sculptures and inscriptions.

Once the Romans had left Ribchester it seems to have declined quite considerably, and by 1540 Leland was noting that 'Ribchester is now a very poor thing; it hath been an ancient town'. In contrast to Roman times Ribchester was no longer on an important highway and it had no regular market or market-place, and even the three fairs which were held annually did not provide any great wealth or prosperity. As late as the second half of the 18th century Ribchester was a small place of no more than a few hundred inhabitants, but during the latter part of the same century Ribchester began to grow into something like its present form with many new cottages being built to accommodate the growing number of handloom weavers in the village.

*The former Quarryman's Arms, Longridge*

Flax had formed the basis of local handloom weaving during the 17th century, but by the 18th century this had been largely replaced by cotton.

Many of the stone cottages built to provide living and working accommodation for these weavers still survive today, and good examples can be seen on Church Street opposite the very attractive White Bull public house. A common feature of these cottages is the wide windows of the 'loomshops', which were generally situated on the ground floor because of the need to have damp conditions in order to stop the yarn drying out too quickly. From about 1780 to 1830 handloom weaving and certain related trades such as bobbin turning were a major source of employment in Ribchester, but by the middle of the 19th century economic decline again set in because of the advent of efficient power looms — even in 1844 it was being noted that the village 'has every appearance of poverty, and offers a painful contrast with the historical recollections it awakens'.

Since that time Ribchester has recovered to become an attractive and thriving place full of character, particularly notable for its appealing vernacular architecture from the late 18th and early 19th centuries. It also has an interesting old parish church which dates from the 13th century, although there was almost certainly a pre-Norman place of worship on the site. Later additions to the Early English nave and chancel include the 14th century North Chapel as well as the tower dating from the 15th century. Inside the church can be found a very early font, above which is a gallery or 'singing pew' built in 1736 to accommodate musicians for the services, while at the other end of the nave is a fine 17th century pulpit.

If the Norman origins of St. Wilfrid's Parish Church are in some doubt, there seems no

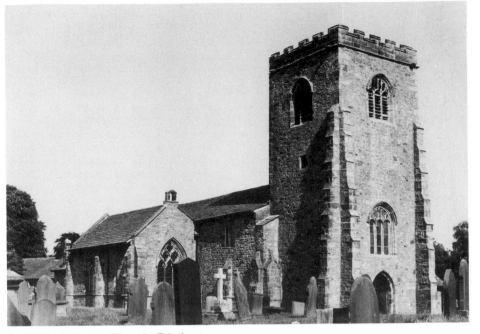

*St. Wilfrid's Parish Church, Ribchester*

dubiety at all that a church of this period was built at Stydd about half a mile to the north east of Ribchester alongside the old Roman road. This pretty little building, dedicated to St. Saviour, probably started life as a hospice for the religious order of Knights Templars or Hospitallers, although associated buildings such as the refectory and dormitory have since entirely disappeared. The earliest part of the building is the north wall, its semi-circular arches and zigzag ornamentation indicating that a church stood here during the first half of the 12th century, while the south wall contains an original Norman window as well as the 13th century doorway. In the west wall can still be seen the doorway which probably led from the Prior's lodging to a west gallery, while inside the church there is a 15th century font and a 17th century pulpit. It appears that the manor of Stydd was acquired by a preceptory of the Knights Hospitallers in about 1265 from a more ancient hospital, although there had been an organised community here for at least 50 years before this.

Just down the lane from Stydd chapel are the Shireburn Almshouses, a delightful building dating from 1728 and erected to accommodate five Roman Catholic widows or spinsters. These almshouses were endowed by John Shireburn of Stonyhurst in 1726, together with the provision of coals and a small allowance, and are still in the ownership of the nearby Catholic church. The attractive front features an arcade of rustic Tuscan columns with a gallery reached by an open staircase, whilst in the garden is an old well.

Between Ribchester and Hurst Green the area is rich with historic houses, one of the

most interesting being Dutton Hall on Gallows Lane just over a mile to the north east of Ribchester. This impressive house was built in about 1670 by the Towneley family, who held the manor of Dutton, and its principal features include the two cross-wings together with numerous mullioned windows and a balustraded balcony over the central bay. Nearly two miles to the north of Dutton Hall is Huntingdon Hall, which has stood on the present site since 1619 and again displays a lovely frontage of mullioned windows. The hall and lands in this part of Dutton are named after Robert of Huntingdon who came from the Abbey of Selby in 1277.

Then less than a mile from Hurst Green itself is Bailey Hall, surrounded by its own moat and probably one of the most intriguing houses in the area. The present Hall dates from the 16th century and probably occupies the site of the original mansion of the Clitherow family, which is thought to have been built in the 1300s. To the north of the Hall are the remains of the Chapel of St. John the Baptist, a small chapel which was founded in about 1330 by Robert de Clitherow but which gradually fell into ruin during the course of the 16th century. Parts of this building appear to have been incorporated within the principal front of Stonyhurst College.

**Hurst Green** is a very pretty village which encapsulates the best features of the Ribble Valley's picturesque settlements — some simple stone cottages, a couple of friendly pubs, a tiny village green upon which the rest of the village focuses its attention and panoramic views out across the neighbouring fields. Hurst Green also has a very distinctive building which immediately captures the

*Norman doorway, Stydd Chapel*

*Trough of Bowland*

*Waddington Village near Clitheroe*

*Shireburn Almshouses, Hurst Green*

visitor's interest, in the form of the Shireburn Almshouses (not to be confused with the similarly named almshouses near Ribchester). Unlike the rather unassuming terraced cottages just across the road, the Almshouses proudly boasts something of a cultured appearance by virtue of its central courtyard bounded by a stone balustrade with turned balusters. This intriguing building dates from 1706, when Sir Nicolas Shireburn had it sited at the east end of Longridge Fell to provide housing for poor people from the villages of Aighton, Bailey, Chaigley, Dutton, Ribchester, Wiswell and Mitton. At that time the Almshouses consisted of ten rooms and a chapel, but in 1946 the building was dismantled and re-built as workers' cottages close to the gates of Stonyhurst College.

Whilst the Shireburn Almshouses in Hurst Green may be something of an architectural oddity, **Stonyhurst College** nearby is nothing less than an architectural masterpiece and surely the most impressive house in the Ribble Valley. For nearly 200 years the building has been used as a world famous Roman Catholic school, although it was first of all the residence of the lords of the manor Hugh Shireburn began work on the present building in about 1523, with substantial additions being made by Sir Richard Shireburn who erected the gatehouse in 1592. Later extensions and alterations were made by future generations of the Shireburn family, but following neglect and a change of ownership in the 18th century the house was offered to the Jesuits of Liege by Thomas Weld in 1794. The Jesuits themselves introduced other buildings to the site, with the very substantial Church of St. Peter being built in 1835 in response to the Act of Catholic Emancipation in 1829. This was built as a

replica of King's College in Cambridge, and it houses one of the best Victorian organs in the country.

As well as being a remarkable piece of architecture enjoying a marvellous landscaped setting Stonyhurst College also contains many priceless treasures, including a 7th century copy of St. John's Gospel and a cope of Henry II which was later used by Henry VIII at the Field of the Cloth of Gold. The College is also noted for the contribution made by many of its former pupils, with one of the most famous being Sir Arthur Conan Doyle, the creator of Sherlock Holmes, who based the setting for his story 'The Hound of the Baskervilles' upon Stonyhurst.

To the east of Stonyhurst the River Hodder winds its tranquil way through woods and fields, and at a point just above its confluence with the Ribble is spanned by an ancient packhorse bridge. Here again we see the work of Richard Shireburn, who erected the bridge in 1562 at a cost of £70. Local tradition suggests that Cromwell and his army crossed over this bridge when staying at Stonyhurst in 1648, but it is more likely that he forded the Hodder at a point close to where it joins up with the River Ribble at Winckley. A footpath along the west bank of the Hodder connects this historic and picturesque structure, known as the Lower Hodder Bridge, with a rather more modern crossing of the river further upstream known as Higher Hodder Bridge. The stretch of river in between these two points is a delight for naturalists since dippers, grey wagtails and kingfishers are all to be seen here, whilst the shady woods lining the river are interspersed with all types of wild flowers.

From Higher Hodder Bridge at the foot of Longridge Fell it is a short distance to **Bashall Town,** once a sizeable settlement but now just a tiny hamlet. The dwellings that used to be here were clustered around Bashall Hall, a Tudor house which was the home of the Talbot family. At that time the

*Stonyhurst College*

conflict caused by the Wars of the Roses was a very real threat in places such as this where Lancashire and Yorkshire were uncomfortably close to one another, and the Talbot family would have maintained their own small army. Evidence for this is still to be seen in the form of the retainers' dwelling at the rear of the Hall, a barn-like building which is an example of a 15th century barracks. From the Hall a footpath follows a mediaeval route leading northwards to Bashall Eaves, passing over a single span packhorse bridge known as Saddle Bridge.

Both this mediaeval route and the more modern country road close by lead towards **Browsholme Hall,** the home of the Parker family since the 14th century. The Parkers' long history in the area goes back to the time when they were the traditional bowbearers, or legal administrators, of the Forest of Bowland. The present Browsholme Hall is a substantial house which reflects the importance of the family in the area, having been built in 1507

*The Lower Hodder Bridge*

*Browsholme Hall*

but then refaced in attractive red sandstone in 1604. Among the items of interest here are some pieces of stained glass which were rescued from Whalley Abbey upon its dissolution in 1537 as well as a gauge which was used to measure dogs — in the Forest of Bowland it was illegal for most people to keep a dog large enough to hunt deer, so those which could not pass through the gauge were deemed too large and either had to be killed or have their legs mutilated so that they could not pursue the deer.

From Browsholme Hall the road heads back towards Longridge again before turning to the north in order to bring us into the village of **Chipping,** lying between Parlick Pike and Longridge Fell. This delightfully tight-knit village of old stone cottages has two main streets, both of which are watched over by the parish church of St. Bartholomew standing in an elevated position close to the point at which they join. It appears that a church has occupied this spot from at least 1041, although a place of worship may have been established here as early as the 6th century. The earliest parts of the present building date from about the middle of the 13th century, although since then the church has been frequently altered and restored so that it now presents a fascinating array of architectural styles and periods. The tower is probably the least changed part of St. Bartholomew's, having been erected in the middle of the 15th century, while inside the church is a font dating from 1520 and a peal of bells cast in 1793. Outside in the churchyard can be found a sundial mounted on some stone steps with the date of 1708, whereas in the church porch one can see the initials of John Parkinson (a member of one of the area's most important families) together with the date of his death, 1771.

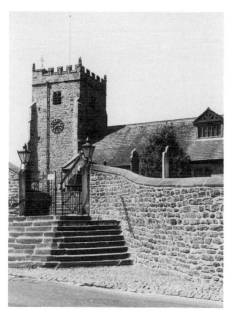

*Chipping Parish Church*

St. Bartholomew's was particularly important in the locality because it was a place of worship for the Shireburn family, who lived at Stonyhurst during the 16th and 17th centuries. One of the projects which the Shireburns undertook was to create the 'Wolfhouse Quire' within the church as a Shireburn chantry, and it was in this special section of St. Bartholomew's that members of the family prayed and were buried. Unfortunately such chantries had too many Roman Catholic overtones for Puritan tastes, and they were frequently removed in later 'restorations'; this proved to be the fate of the Wolfhouse Quire, which had taken its name from the family home at nearby Wolfen Hall.

With the parish church behind one can look down the narrow and rather appropriately named Windy Street, along the rows of terraced cottages which are hemmed in behind narrow cobbled pavements and courtyards. The most interesting building here is a 17th century school which was established under the will of John Brabin, a local dyer and cloth merchant who gained his wealth from the 'putting out' system of manufacture (in which he gave out weft and yarn to the local handloom weavers and received in return the woven cloth which he then dyed). Brabin's will also provided money for the uniforms of 16 pupils, shelter for the local poor through the building of almshouses and funds for three boys to be apprenticed to a trade annually. On the front porch of the school is the date 1684 and the inscription 'Doce Disce Vel Discede', which has been translated as 'Teach, learn, or cut your stick', i.e. 'if you don't want to be educated do not enter!'

John Brabin's house stands on Talbot Street, the other main street in the village, and bears the date of 1668 as well as the inscription 'Let him that loveth God love his brother also' - a motto which he seems to have put into practice. Elsewhere on Talbot Street there are more attractive 17th century cottages, many with datestones above their doorways, together with the local post office and a craft shop as well as two public houses (the Talbot Hotel and the Tillotsons Arms). A third public house, the 18th century Sun Inn, stands at the junction of Talbot Street and Windy Street just across from the parish church, and so it seems very unlikely that any visitor could fail to have his thirst quenched in this particular village!

Chipping's history goes right back to the Bronze Age, evidence of which was found in the form of a burial mound to the north of the church uncovered in about 1770. By Roman times the village had already begun to acquire its status as a market-centre, and the cultivation of wheat in the newly cleared Vale of the Loud brought about significant prosperity for the area. As well as the trade in wheat other major commodities such as

*Front porch on Chipping's original school*

horses, salt and lime were also being exchanged. The modern name of Chipping is in fact derived from the Old English word 'Chepyn' meaning 'market-place', which was probably situated at the base of the present church steps. Over time the name has gone through various changes, from 'Chipinden' in the Domesday Book to 'Chepin', 'Chipin', 'Chipindale', 'Chepyn', 'Chypne' and 'Chypindale' before the final form of 'Chipping' became widely used in the 17th century.

Most of the village's earliest inhabitants would have been involved in making a living from small-scale farming together with quarrying and forestry as well as peat cutting. By the 17th century the handloom weaving of textiles was providing additional employment, although most of the people living in Chipping were still engaged in working the land. By the latter half of the 18th century, however, the picture began to change quite dramatically with the coming of the Industrial Revolution, and places such as Chipping took on a new attraction by virtue of their abundant supplies of fast running water and the continually damp climate. The tributary of the River Loud running through Chipping was of particular interest to early investors in the textile industry, and along its length at least eight sites were developed not only for cotton spinning but also for trades such as spindle making, chair making, corn milling, brass founding and nail making.

The main result of all this activity was a considerable increase in Chipping's working population, but by the middle of the 19th century the village was in decline as trade

*One of Chipping's intimate streets*

began to be concentrated in the larger towns. Comparatively little evidence of this early industrial growth still remains in Chipping apart from Kirk Mill, which was used firstly as a cotton mill but was then taken over by John Berry in the 1890s for his chair making business. As the 19th century drew to a close the Berry chair making family emerged as the

central and most successful one in the village, from a group of five or so, and the business has continued to flourish right up to the present day. Now the firm of H.J. Berry and Sons produces around three thousand items of furniture every week, and its premises are one of Chipping's best known features.

From the outskirts of the village a narrow country lane heads back towards the Hodder valley, passing Leagram Hall with its majestic rolling parkland. Leagram probably began life as a mediaeval deer park but by the 19th century it was proving to be a valuable haven for wildlife, as is evident from the observations of owner and naturalist John Weld. From Leagram the road skirts the edge of the fells and joins the Hodder Valley at Burholme Bridge. The place name 'Burholme' may be from the pre-Conquest period and probably means 'the manor above the river'. Just to the north of the bridge is Burholme Farm, which in the 14th century was part of a small hamlet where what was known as the 'Woodmote Court' was originally held prior to being moved to Whitewell in about 1400. There was probably also a small chapel here.

**Whitewell** itself lies just less than a mile to the south of Burholme Bridge and consists

essentially of an inn and a small church. The inn was originally a manor house built by Walter Urswyck, 'Keeper of the Royal Forest of Bolland', at about the end of the 14th century, and some of its earliest walls still remain. This manor house was the Swainmote Court House, and the Swainmote and Woodmote Courts would have met here. It was also the place where the forest tenants would have come to give account to the Master Forester and his Keepers, while the present forecourt was once the old market-place for the district. The church of St. Michael next to 'The Inn at Whitewell' originally began life in about 1400 as a chapel of ease, in which a corpse from a distant place could be deposited for the night on its way for burial in a properly consecrated church, although it was substantially rebuilt in the early 19th century. Inside the church is to be seen a Jacobean pulpit and a Flemish tapestry.

The section of the Hodder Valley northwards up to Dunsop Bridge and Newton is often described as 'Little Switzerland', and so it comes as no great surprise to discover that the scenery in this part of the county is absolutely exquisite. The area was first mentioned as early as AD 934 when King Athelstan granted lands to the west of the rivers Dunsop and Hodder to Wulfstan, Archbishop of York, but **Dunsop Bridge** appears to have developed largely through the patronage of the Towneley family of Burnley who at one time owned nearby Thorneyholme Hall. Just outside the village is the Roman Catholic chapel of St. Hubert, dating from 1864 and in which there are not only numerous memorials to the Towneley family but also to Kettledrum, one of their horses which won the Derby in 1861 — it appears that the Dunsop area generally was important in the breeding of horses during the 19th century,

*The Inn at Whitewell*

*St. Hubert's R.C. Chapel, Dunsop Bridge*

and there are still many old stables remaining here. Outside in the grounds of St. Hubert's stands a large white angel, a memorial to Richard Henry Towneley.

From Dunsop Bridge the road leads westwards towards the Trough of Bowland, that magnificent route over the fells which is perhaps more reminiscent of Scotland than England, while in the opposite direction the road follows the River Hodder upstream to the very pretty village of **Newton.** Mentioned in the Domesday Book under the name 'Neutone', this village has a number of fine 17th century houses as well as a late Georgian public house known as the Parkers Arms. Newton was quite an important centre for the Quaker movement, and just on the edge of the village can be seen a Friends' Meeting House with the date of 1767 (although the Quakers had first established themselves here in 1670). In 1768 John Brabin left 20 guineas to endow a school for the education of 'all people called Quakers and six of the children of the poor not being Quakers', and the Old School House still stands on the main street. Nearby is the United Reformed Church, successor to a house known in 1691 as a 'meeting place for Protestant dissenters'.

*Some of Newton's pretty cottages*

*Newton Hall, Newton*

Situated two miles to the north east of Newton is the village of **Slaidburn,** which with its mellowed stone cottages and cobbled pavements is one of the prettiest places in the Forest of Bowland. The focal point of the village is the 'Hark to Bounty' public house, a 13th century building with a name which recalls the days when deer hunting took place in these parts. Until 1861 the 'Hark to Bounty' was known as the Dog Inn, but tradition has it that on one particular day the Master of the Hunt, the Reverend Henry Wigglesworth, was taking refreshment at the inn and he heard his favourite hound outside eager to continue the chase. His exclamation 'Just hark to Bounty' seems to have taken the fancy of the landlord and the name has stuck since that time.

As well as being an interesting old hostelry in its own right the Hark to Bounty Inn also contains an old court room with its original furnishings of oak benches, a dock and a

witness box. From about 1250 the Chief Court of Bowland, or the Halmote, was held here after Slaidburn had been chosen by the de Lacy family as head of the manor in preference to Grindleton.

The earliest references to St. Andrew's parish church in Slaidburn also go back to the 13th century, when it is recorded that Hugh de la

Val granted to the monks of Kirkby Priory some interest in the 'Church at Slaydeburn', although parts of the present structure may be even older than this on a site which was probably occupied by an earlier building. The substantial tower may well have given the villagers protection during the Scots' raids of 1322, shortly after Bruce's victory at Bannockburn, while the buttresses providing

*Along Slaidburn's main street*

extra support to the tower itself date from the 15th century. Inside the church can be seen a font dating from the early 13th century together with its Elizabethan font cover, a fine Jacobean rood screen and a three-decker pulpit introduced during the Georgian period, while in the churchyard is a 14th century stone cross shaft together with a sundial upon a stone base which might well be part of the old market cross.

Another important building within the village is the old Grammar School, which dates from 15 May, 1717 when it was endowed by a local farmer. There is also a youth hostel in Slaidburn, providing 'education' of a different type and accommodated within what was originally the Black Bull pub. Next door to the Youth Hostel is the local Post Office, with the Village Stores just across the road and the village War Memorial just round the corner, all of which go towards making this one of the best village scenes in Lancashire. Humble stone cottages line both sides of the narrow street as it makes its way down towards a lovely bridge over the River Hodder, and here there is yet another cluster of cottages which look out beyond the river towards open countryside.

*The village war memorial, Slaidburn*

To the north of Slaidburn is the very impressive Hammerton Hall, a symmetrical Elizabethan mansion with mullioned windows and a stone spiral staircase, while further north still is Stocks Reservoir. Beneath this large man-made lake is a 'village' of some 20 houses, a shop, post office and pub which were all submerged when the reservoir was created in 1925. With human occupation now very much reduced the 344 acres of water are a magnet for winter flocks of Canada geese, tufted duck, mallard, teal and wigeon, while birds of prey in the area include the sparrowhawk, kestrel, tawny and long-eared owl, the osprey, goshawk and hen harrier. In addition the reservoir adjoins the 4000 acre coniferous plantation of Gisburn Forest, which provides a habitat for woodcocks, ravens, redstarts and barn owls, while on the moorland above the trees can be seen short-eared owls and both black and red grouse as well as skylarks, meadow pipits and wheatears.

The tranquil villages of the Hodder valley are separated from those on the northern bank of the River Ribble by the lonely moors and fells in between, but the two scenic routes connecting them offer some unrivalled panoramas of the beautiful countryside in this part of Lancashire. The road from Slaidburn to Grindleton takes a slightly easier route around the side of Harrop Fell before dropping down towards the Ribble, after passing the tiny hamlet of **Harrop Fold** on its way there. This historic settlement lies within a secluded valley at the foot of the fells and is approached by one of the few remaining gated roads in the area. The name 'Harrop' means 'valley of hares', and during the Middle Ages it was one of the four wards of the Royal Forest of Bowland, these being Sclatbournewarde (Slaidburn), Baxsholfward (Bashall), Chepynwarde (Chipping) and Harropwarde (Harrop). Each of these wards was divided into 'vaccaries' or large cattle farms, with one of these being Harrop itself. Many of the farmsteads in the area date from the early 17th century, including Harrop Hall and Harrop Fold Farm, the latter being an original Lancashire 'longhouse'.

**Grindleton** is something of a linear village, with rows of cottages and houses rubbing shoulders together along both sides of the main street. It seems that the name 'Grindleton' was bestowed upon the district by Saxon invaders, who found this to be a place where the ancient Britons were continuing their sun or devil worship. In later times the village grew in importance as a textile centre, first through the introduction of handlooms in most of the cottages here and then through the construction of two cotton-mills. The neighbouring village of **West Bradford** also had its own cotton-mill, and no doubt both places benefited greatly from the swift flowing streams which came down from the fells before passing through the villages on the way to the River Ribble.

A mile down the valley from West Bradford is the very picturesque village of **Waddington,** which like its easterly neighbour enjoys the delights of a babbling brook running right through the centre. On either side of the brook are the beautiful Coronation Gardens, laid out to celebrate the coronation of Queen Elizabeth II, while overlooking this idyllic scene is the parish church of St. Helen. The tower was built at the start of the 16th century from stone quarried on nearby Waddington Fell, while the remainder of the church is largely the result of restoration and rebuilding work undertaken at the beginning of the 20th century. Inside the church is a mediaeval font, a mediaeval glass panel containing a picture of a 16th century figure (possibly that of Sir Richard Tempest, who was responsible for the rebuilding of the church in 1501), and some 17th century pews in the Browsholme Chapel. The Parkers of Browsholme have been connected with

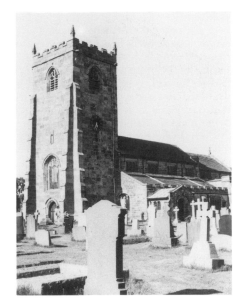

*St. Helen's Church, Waddington*

Waddington from as early as the 13th century, with the first family burial in the vault beneath the chapel taking place in 1500. Outside in the churchyard is the shaft of an old sundial, dated 1686, which stands upon a millstone.

Beyond the stream from the parish church is Waddington Old Hall, a mediaeval building which dates back to before 1464 when Henry VI took refuge there prior to being captured by the Yorkists as he fled across the river. The original walls and windows can still be seen in the Great Hall, a magnificent room panelled in oak and furnished with a beautiful oak dining table and carved chairs. As well as a 'secret staircase' leading to the large room above the Great Hall there is also the Monk's Room in the oldest part of the building, which probably dates back to the 11th century. It seems that this room may have been used by monks travelling between the two abbeys of Sawley and Whalley, although another story tells of the Black Monk of Abingdon who stayed there and betrayed Henry VI to the Talbots of Bashall Hall.

Another of Waddington's important buildings is Waddington Hospital, a group of alms-houses situated near to the start of the road over to West Bradford. These almshouses were first built in the early 18th century by Robert Parker to provide homes for ten widows of men from Waddington and the surrounding parishes in days when there was no welfare state. In addition to the ten cottages there was also a chapel where morning and evening prayers were conducted every day. By 1889 the number of cottages had risen to 26, but by that time too they had fallen into a very poor condition and it was decided to completely rebuild them. This was done, and the 'Hospital' now comprises 29 cottages for widows and spinsters as well as a house for the matron

*Entrance to Waddington Hospital*

*The Coronation Gardens, Waddington*

together with a chapel and offices, all built around the three sides of a quadrangle which encompasses a large open garden. Across the road from the Hospital is the Reader's House, which was built in 1876 as the residence of the Reader who was appointed by the Hospital's Board of Trustees to read the services in the Almshouses Chapel.

Waddington village has three public houses — the Buck, the Higher Buck and the Sun Inn — and it is interesting to note that the first of these, an 18th century building situated at the rear of the church, was sold in 1820 to the trustees of Waddington Hospital. The Higher Buck is at the head of The Square in the centre of the village, and at one time was called 'The Buck in the Vine' to distinguish it from the other Buck Inn; it also dates from the 18th century and originally included stabling facilities within a barn attached to the inn.

Running close to the Higher Buck is Waddington Brook, a stream which at one time was dammed to provide power for a corn mill and a cotton mill. Like many other villages in the district such water power provided the opportunity for several mills to be established here during the Industrial Revolution, and there was also a chair and bobbin mill located further downstream on a site close to the Sun Inn. Then just under a mile upstream can be seen the ruins of the old Feasor Spinning and Weaving Mill, a very substantial mill which was powered by a water-wheel fed from two water storage dams which can still be discerned amidst the undergrowth. Unfortunately a fire destroyed most of the mill in about 1860 and it was never rebuilt.

Waddington is also a place in which a large number of occupations connected with farming were carried out, and within the village can still be seen the old tannery, smithy and wheelwright's shop as well as the site of a former tileyard which produced land drainage tiles for agricultural use until the 1950s. The people of Waddington have a great deal to be proud of here, not only in terms of the village's long history but also in respect of its beautiful and well-groomed appearance. No doubt it is the latter which has given it the unusual distinction of winning the Best Kept Village competition within two different counties — in 1966 it was voted the best kept village in Yorkshire, while in 1975, and on several occasions since, it won the award for the best kept village in Lancashire!

From Waddington the road leads south-eastwards to the River Ribble and then on into Clitheroe, passing **Waddow Hall** en route. This impressive house was built in Tudor times as a dower house for the Tempest family, but later became their main residence in the area. The Tudor house was extended during the Jacobean period, but many of the original oak beamed rooms can still be seen. Waddow Hall is now a Commonwealth Training Centre for the Girl Guide Association.

*The Buck Inn, Waddington*

*Clitheroe Castle*

Crossing over the Ribble at Brungerley Bridge the road brings us straight into **Clitheroe,** an ancient market town which is dominated by the Castle at one end and the parish church at the other. The Castle occupies a strategic position on the top of a prominent limestone outcrop, from which one can enjoy some superb views of the Ribble Valley, and although the parish church is not as high as the Castle it commands an equally fine site. Between these two points the town developed as an important market and administrative centre from the very earliest days, although most of the current buildings here date from the 18th and 19th centuries. Later development spread into the surrounding countryside, but the main stretch between Castle Street and Church Street is still very much the focus point of Clitheroe.

All that remains of Clitheroe Castle today is its keep, one of the smallest Norman keeps in the country and amongst the earliest stone buildings in Lancashire. The much larger castle which existed here at one time was begun by Roger of Poitou, the first Lord of the Honour of Clitheroe, soon after the Norman Conquest. In addition to the keep there was a gatehouse, a chapel and a hall with a kitchen and stables, all of which were enclosed by the castle walls. The keep itself was divided into three floors - the ground floor was used for the storage of food and arms, the next level provided living accommodation and the top floor served as the sleeping quarters.

Although designed with defence in mind Clitheroe Castle became more of an administrative base than a military one, and during its early life it was the headquarters of the steward of the absent Lord of the Honour. With its court it also developed as a seat of justice, while the chapel of St. Michael served as the parish church for all the forests and lands of the Honour of Clitheroe. Despite its fairly innocuous role it was seen as a possible threat to the Commonwealth after the Civil

War, so in 1649 both the gatehouse and the chapel were demolished, a large part of the castle wall destroyed and the keep itself breached.

From what remains of the castle wall there are unrivalled views of the town below and also the surrounding countryside, including Pendle Hill to the east. Close by the Castle is Castle House, built in the middle of the 18th century as a residence for the Steward of the Honour of Clitheroe, whilst just beneath is the peaceful seclusion of the Castle rose garden. An interesting feature here is a turret which came from the Palace of Westminster, removed when the stone work was being renovated. The garden itself was laid out to commemorate the coronation of King George VI in 1937.

*An unusual feature in the Castle rose garden*

From the castle gates Castle Street leads down towards the Market Place, passing the Swan and Royal Hotel on the way. This is an old coaching inn and staging post which provided stabling for 28 horses and was the headquarters of the Royal Mail. Across from the Swan is another old hostelry, the Starkie Arms, which was originally known as the Rose and Crown. The Market Place was the site of all the town's fairs and markets from the Norman Conquest until relatively recent times, and within living memory both horse

fairs and cattle markets were held here and in the adjoining streets. This was also the location of the market cross, the stocks and the pillory, while both national and royal proclamations have traditionally been made from beneath the library clock.

On the edge of the Market Place is the former Town Hall, a building which dates from 1820 and which records that Clitheroe became a borough as early as 1147. This building replaced the earlier Moot Hall, and the sculptured heraldry on its front elevation includes the arms of the former Borough of Clitheroe as well as those of locally important families. Adjoining the Town Hall is the Public Library, which was financed by the Andrew Carnegie Trust.

From here Church Street climbs up to the parish church of St. Mary Magdalene, passing some attractive Georgian houses with their imposing doorways en route. A church is known to have existed on this site since 1122, with the probability that there was a place of worship here well before that date, and whilst the present building was erected only in 1828 it incorporates the earlier mediaeval tower and east window. Like the Town Hall the church was designed by Rickman, with the spire being added in 1846. Interesting features within the church include the recumbent figures of Sir Thomas Radclyffe (who died in 1441) and his wife Katherine Booth, as well as a brass memorial to Rev. Dr. Webster who wrote a celebrated book about witchcraft in 1677.

From the churchyard there are excellent views to the west of Longridge Fell, Beacon Fell and Parlick Pike, while at the bottom of the churchyard steps is a high wall built of the local limestone upon which the economy of Clitheroe has been largely based over the centuries. This limestone was burnt to

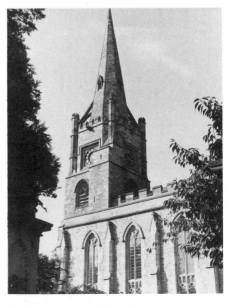

*Clitheroe Parish Church*

produce lime, and at the height of the trade as a thousand loads a day were sent out of Clitheroe by packhorse. Not far from the parish church, close to the junction of Church Brow and Waddington Road, is an attractive Georgian house known as The Alleys which occupies the site of an earlier moated manor house. Sir Thomas Radclyffe lived here, as did the celebrated 17th century botanist and herbalist Thomas Hesketh.

St. Mary's Well is situated along Well Terrace and is one of three similar wells which were the chief sources of water for the townspeople until the 1850s. Another well, known as the Heild Well, is to be found on Wellgate which runs off York Street near to the Market Place. Close by is Well Fold, an early industrial complex which embraced a foundry, a timber yard and a calico printing works and which became a haven for numerous artisans and craftsmen. The town's Grammar School occupies a site close to St. Mary's Well, although when it was founded in 1554 by a charter of Queen Mary and King Philip it was located within the churchyard and the vicar was often also the headmaster. The current building dates from 1914, replacing an older building which was erected on this site in 1829.

At its lower end Wellgate joins up with Lowergate and Duck Street, the latter so called because the ducking-stool for scolds and gossips was positioned nearby. Along Lowergate can be seen numerous old buildings constructed of local limestone as well as the brick built Employment Exchange, at one time the town's Court House, together with the 18th century Stanley House, one of the few large houses in the centre of Clitheroe. Directing us back up towards the Market Place from here is King Lane, this thoroughfare being named after Captain James King who was educated at the town's Grammar School before going on to become Captain Cook's navigator.

The limestone upon which much of Clitheroe is built has also been the foundation for its economic development, with one of the most important sources being Salthill Quarry to the north east of the town centre. The quarrying of limestone for walling stone and for lime was being carried out at Salthill at least as early as the middle of the 17th century, but its greatest exploitation took place in the 19th and early 20th centuries when the expansion of industry, better communications and improved methods of agriculture led to increasing demands for this raw material. The extraction process commenced with the use of explosives to loosen large pieces of rock from the quarry face, each piece weighing up to as much as 1,000 tons. These in turn had to be broken up by blasting, or by mechanical means if they were small enough. The limestone was then shovelled into small railway wagons which were pulled by horse,

*Looking along Castle Street in Clitheroe*

petrol-driven engine or 'endless chain' to the lime kilns or the crushing plant. By mixing the limestone with coal or coke and heating it up in the lime kilns 'cob-lime' was produced which farmers scattered on their fields, while plasterers and builders added water to it to make 'putty lime'. By the 20th century a considerable amount of crushed limestone was being mixed with tar to make tarmacadam for road surfacing.

As might be expected in a place which has enjoyed a long civic history, Clitheroe has some very interesting customs. One of these is 'Mayor Making', the annual meeting of the Town Council which usually takes place on the first Tuesday in May. A week or two before the Mayor Making ceremony itself the Council holds a closed meeting to elect the Mayor and consider the agenda for Mayor Making; this meeting is called the Cockle and Mussel Feast, at which cockles and mussels are traditionally eaten after having been brought through the Trough of Bowland especially for the occasion. On the day of Mayor Making the Mayor, Councillors, Town Clerk, Chaplain, Town Sergeant and Haberdiers meet at either the Swan and Royal or the Starkie Arms and then process to the Town Hall.

The first item on the agenda of the Annual Meeting is the election of the Mayor, followed by the election of the Deputy Mayor. Immediately after the election the Mayoral Party leave the Council Chamber and re-robe in the Mayor's Parlour. The Mayoral Party then returns to the Council Chamber and the new Mayor reads and signs the Declaration of Acceptance of Office, returns thanks for his election and then intimates his intention of attending Divine Service the following

Sunday. Traditionally for the new Mayor there is a Mayor's Dinner on the evening of Mayor Making, at which a specially prepared punch is used for the toast of "Prosperation to the Corporation". Mayor's Sunday takes place on the Sunday after Mayor Making, and on this occasion the Mayoral Party robe at the Mayor's Parlour before being led by a band to the parish church in the company of the councillors and ladies and gentlemen of the town.

On the south side of Clitheroe is the peaceful village of **Pendleton,** a small community of stone built cottages and working farms which has successfully retained its traditional charm. One of Pendleton's most endearing features is the bubbling brook which passes right through the centre of the village, crossed now and then by narrow stone bridges and providing a haven for groups of friendly ducks. This brook flows down from Pendleton Moor close to the Nick of Pendle, and like the rest of the village has probably changed little over the centuries as this was not a place which attracted any water powered industry. The existence of Pendleton was recorded in the Domesday Book under the name 'Peniltune', when it was part of the vast parish of Whalley covering over 1000 square miles, although the discovery of a burial urn in the village has indicated that there may well have been a Bronze Age settlement here as far back as 1600 BC.

As part of the parish of Whalley the villagers in Pendleton would have had to travel nearly three miles down the valley for their spiritual needs to be met, but they would also have been familiar with the sight of monks passing through the top end of the village en route between the abbeys at Whalley and Sawley.

At nearby Mearley Hall Farm are the remains of what was part of a building used by the monks from Sawley Abbey when grazing their sheep on Pendle. The people of Pendleton had to wait until 1847 before a church was built in the village itself, although some of them may have worshipped at the small nonconformist chapel which was built at Wymondhouses higher up on the slopes of Pendleton Moor. This largely resulted from the zeal and enthusiasm of a Puritan minister named Thomas Jollie, and it was really the beginning of the Congregational Church in this part of Lancashire.

Pendleton Village School was built in 1837, and this provided the first real opportunity to hold a Sunday service in the village instead of everyone having to go to Whalley or Clitheroe to attend public worship. By 1847, however, the village had its own chapel due to the generosity of Miss Jane Aspinall from nearby Standen Hall, although it was only in 1873 that Pendleton achieved independence as a separate parish. Then in 1893 the south aisle was added to house the organ, followed in 1906 by the introduction of a carved screen behind the altar as a memorial to the church's founder. Within the church the most interesting features are the windows, with the east window in particular having some fine stone tracery which frames its richly coloured glass.

Completing the admirable village scene which Pendleton's inhabitants enjoy is the Post Office and a public house bearing the unusual name of 'The Swan with Two Necks'.

*Pendleton Village School*

This is presumably a corruption of the words 'two nicks', which refer back to the practise of 'nicking' the bills of swans during the ceremony of 'swan-upping' on the River Thames. In addition there is a row of rather attractive 17th century cottages known as Rock Terrace, together with four working dairy farms along the main street which enhance the very rural atmosphere of this unspoilt corner of Lancashire.

From Pendleton the A59 road bypasses Clitheroe on the east side and heads northwards to the village of **Chatburn,**

*Chatburn*

*Pendleton's main street*

*Picturesque Downham*

situated in a hollow just above the River Ribble. In stark contrast to other villages in the Ribble Valley Chatburn is very largely an industrial settlement which still has its own cotton mill in addition to limestone quarrying and the production of road surfacing materials. Even so it is the stately spire of the 19th century parish church which dominates the skyline from miles around, and probably the most significant thing to be extracted from the ground was a large quantity of Roman coins discovered here in the 18th century.

In just less than one mile to the east of Chatburn we come to **Downham,** which with its dancing brook and historic parish church lays claim to being one of the loveliest villages in Lancashire. The church enjoys a prominent position overlooking the rest of Downham, and although the oldest part of the present building is its 15th century tower there was certainly a church here in 1283 with the possibility of a place of worship on this site even before the Norman Conquest. Tradition has it that the tower houses three bells brought from Whalley Abbey, while the last abbot of Whalley Abbey presented the font to the church over 400 years ago.

Across from the church are the village stocks and the Assheton Arms, an inn which until relatively recently was known as the George and Dragon. Successive generations of the Assheton family have in fact lived at Downham Hall since 1558, and they have all contributed to the preservation of this gem of

the English landscape. From the church gates the main village street, lined on both sides with ancient stone cottages, heads down towards the beck which flows from the slopes of Pendle Hill. On a sunny day it seems a far cry from the stories of the witches who were said to gather at Pendle summit during wild and stormy nights, and who have been associated with this and many other villages in the area.

To the north east of Downham is the village of **Rimington** and its associated hamlets of Stopper Lane, Martin Top, Newby, Middop and Howgill. In amongst the scattered cottages of this predominantly rural community is one which was the home of Francis Duckworth, a famous composer of hymn tunes including one named 'Rimington' after the village in which he lived. Strangely enough Rimington lacks a church of its own, although there is an old non-conformist chapel at Martin Top. A number of important archaeological finds have been made in the area, while Stopper Lane is the site of a disused lead mine.

From Rimington several footpaths head westwards over Swanside and then down into **Sawley,** although motorists have to double back on themselves and find their way through Downham and Chatburn before following the line of the Ribble upstream once again. Sawley is mainly important because of its ruined abbey. Originally known as Salley

*Downham's main thoroughfare*

Abbey, this was a Cistercian establishment like that at Whalley and was founded in 1147 by the third Baron Percy. The first monks here came from Fountains Abbey, while one of the most notable occupants of a later period was Sir William de Rymington who became Chancellor of Oxford. Also well worth seeing here are the views of the village and the curving River Ribble from Sawley Brow, a high point to the east of the abbey.

Over the Ribble from Sawley village a country lane takes the traveller northwards to the very picturesque village of **Bolton-by-Bowland,** situated in the little valley through which Tosside Beck runs. As is the case with many of the villages in this part of Lancashire, Bolton-by-Bowland displays the traditional features of stone cottages, village green, market cross, public house and parish church, all bound together by a fair degree of local pride. Hemmed in by mature trees and well-kept farmland the village also enjoys a remarkable atmosphere of seclusion and tranquility. Although now only a comparatively small place Bolton-by-Bowland was an important centre for the administration of the surrounding district, receiving its market charter in the reign of Edward III during the 14th century

The village was mentioned in Domesday Book under the name 'Bodeton', although this was later changed to Bolton-juxta-Bowland, and even at such an early period there would probably have been a place of worship on the site of the present parish church. This is dedicated to St. Peter and St. Paul and dates largely from the 13th century, with a tower whose design is more reminiscent of parts of Somerset than of Lancashire. This is reputed to be because Henry VI spent some time in hiding at nearby Bolton Hall when the tower was being rebuilt in the 15th century, and he may well have influenced its final appearance.

*Bolton-by-Bowland Parish Church*

Inside the church is a font dating from 1500, around which are carved the arms of important local families, while near the chancel is the famous Pudsay tomb. This consists of slab of Craven limestone measuring three yards long by two yards wide, upon which is engraved the figure of Sir Ralph Pudsay (who lived at Bolton Hall) in full armour. On one side of the tomb are depicted two of his wives and on the other

side is a third, while beneath the parents are the figures of their children — all 25 of them! Some of the children are in military costume, some in ecclesiastical robes, while the ladies are dressed in the costume of the period.

One of Sir Ralph's descendants, William Pudsay, is said to have minted his own 'Pudsay shillings' in order to stave off bankruptcy, using silver from a mine near Rimington. His activities aroused the opposition of Queen Elizabeth I, who sent soldiers to arrest him. As he fled Pudsay and his horse are reputed to have leapt from Rainsber Scar over to the opposite side of the Ribble, and from there he made good his escape and eventual pardon. This tale is told to explain what has become known as 'Pudsay's Leap', to be found in the woods above the river and close to the spot which was occupied by Bolton Hall before it was demolished earlier this century.

Eastwards from Bolton-by-Bowland is **Gisburn,** another delightful village characterised by old stone cottages and cobbled pavements. The parish church is a particularly attractive feature of the village, set back from the busy main road and incorporating Norman windows and some early stained glass. Gisburn is mentioned in the Domesday Survey as part of the Percy fee, but in 1241 it was granted to the Abbot of Sawley. Following the dissolution of the abbey the manor was disposed of by the king, and in 1613 it passed into the hands of the Listers. From that time onwards Gisburn's development became interwoven with the fortunes of the Lister family, and in 1797

*The Parish Church in Gisburn*

Thomas Lister was created a peer of the realm under the title 'Baron Ribblesdale of Gisburne Park'. From the centre of Gisburn the A682 heads northwards to Paythorne and Paythorne Bridge, a place on the Ribble where on a day known as 'Salmon Sunday' salmon can be seen fighting their way up the river to get to the spawning grounds.

To the south east of Gisburn is **Barnoldswick,** a town which owes its growth mainly to the Industrial Revolution — although its earliest roots go back to Saxon times when Bernulf arrived and established his 'wick' or settlement here. In later centuries Cistercian monks also came to the area, moving on to the more famous foundation of Kirkstall Abbey in Leeds but perhaps leaving their influence in the form of the church of St. Mary-le-Gill. Enjoying a relatively quiet and remote setting a mile or so from the town centre this church is one of the oldest in the area and features a 13th century chancel, a nave and tower dating from the 16th century

*Stone cottages along Gisburn's main street*

and a three-decker pulpit from the 17th century.

After remaining very much a village for several hundred years Barnoldswick was suddenly transformed by the coming of the Leeds and Liverpool Canal in the late 18th century. This not only opened up communication between the Mersey and the Humber but also brought in the basic raw materials of coal and cotton which enabled a considerable number of textile mills to be established here. In addition the canal provided the necessary transport to move not only finished textile goods out of Barnoldswick but also the local gritstone which was being quarried here at the same time. From a figure of 1,401 in 1801 the town's population grew to over 7,000 by 1901, helped largely by the coming of the railway and the expansion of the cotton industry. Textile recessions obviously hit the town hard, but it recovered somewhat with the arrival of Rolls-Royce just after the war. By virtue of its location away from main roads Barnoldswick is largely free of through traffic and is nicely compact, with the countryside little more than ten minutes away by foot in any direction.

On the east side of Barnoldswick close to the county boundary is **Earby,** a slightly smaller settlement but one which also developed as an important textile town during the latter part of the 19th century. Like its neighbour it is completely surrounded by open countryside, and from nearby vantage points there are open views of the Pennines and the Yorkshire Dales. One of Earby's features of interest is a mining museum housed within what was originally the old grammar school. Lead mining here and in the Yorkshire Dales was at

*St. Mary-le-Gill Church, Barnoldswick*

one time a considerable industry, supporting many isolated communities, and the museum's collection of equipment and relics gives a good idea of what life must have been like for those who found their livelihood in this industry.

From Earby the main A56 passes southwards through the pleasant village of Kelbrook before arriving at **Foulridge,** which at one time was on the county boundary until this was moved a few miles eastwards. Traditionally a farming area Foulridge also developed an early woollen textile industry, and many of the more substantial older stone houses were built with the proceeds from the wool trade. One of the most significant and enduring changes in Foulridge was the coming of the Leeds and Liverpool Canal together with its two feeder reservoirs. Foulridge Lower Reservoir (also known as Lake Burwain) was constructed on the south side of the village in 1793, whilst the famous Foulridge Mile Tunnel which connected the Lancashire and Yorkshire sections of the canal was completed in 1796. Then in 1815 Foulridge Wharf and Warehouse were built, in the same year that the Leeds and Liverpool Canal was opened along its entirety of 127 miles. This brought a considerable amount of traffic and prosperity into the area, and it became a common sight to see boats unloading their cargoes of raw cotton at the wharf.

In its day the Foulridge Mile Tunnel was quite a monument to early civil engineering, but as there was no towpath the boats had to be 'legged' through — a method which involved men lying on their backs and pushing with their legs against the tunnel walls. From 1880 until 1937 a steam tug was provided to make movement through the tunnel substantially easier, followed by the introduction of tunnel keepers and then traffic lights operating on a time switch. It is interesting to note that in 1912 a cow fell into the canal at the Barrowford end of the tunnel and swam to the Foulridge end, whereupon the exhausted beast was revived with alcohol — a photograph of the swimmer in the tap room of the nearby Hole in the Wall pub records the incident!

At the centre of the village is Town Gate, with its picturesque village green hemmed in by attractive stone cottages. This initially took the form of a thriving community of handloom

*The Old Grammar School, Earby*

*Town Gate, Foulridge*

weavers living in the cottages overlooking the green, together with beerhouses and blacksmiths catering for the bargees and their towhorses. Across Skipton New Road from Towngate is Stoneygate, from the top of which can be seen the 17th century building known as Ball House as well as Cragg Nook (dating from about 1740) and Foulridge Hall Farm.

Foulridge Hall was the traditional home of the lord of the manor of Foulridge, and an interesting boundary wall with three stone spheres on top of it still remains from that period. During the 17th and 18th centuries the area around Stoneygate was a place in which hat making developed as a cottage industry, as did handloom weaving and spinning. It appears that rabbit fur and wool were the principal ingredients used in the making of hats, whilst animal bones were boiled down to produce the necessary adhesive. Nearby stands Scroggin Hall, believed to be the oldest building in Foulridge, whilst opposite it is the former village primary school built in 1852-53 as a National School.

On the south side of the village is Breeze House (reputed to have been built in 1619), together with the New Inn which is included in the book 'The Haunted Inns of England'. The Hare and Hounds Inn is situated at the junction of Skipton New Road with Skipton Old Road, an ancient hostelry which dates from at least 1824. Further south still is Foulridge Parish Church which was dedicated in 1905, whilst across the reservoir from here is Hobstones. This early 18th century farmhouse has a history of hauntings, including the appearance of a maimed monk.

**Barrowford** is a small town to the south west of Foulridge, and for centuries it too was largely a farming settlement until the development of the textile industry. In the case of Barrowford this took the form of cottage homes and 'dandy shops', which were three

and four storey houses built especially for weaving and usually accommodating six or seven looms. When power looms were introduced most of the employers moved out to Nelson to be close to the canal and railway, so there was no large scale demolition to make way for the new mills and consequently the town has retained a great deal of its original charm. Amongst the fine old buildings to be discovered here are Bank Hall, built in 1696 to an Elizabethan style but featuring some Jacobean curved mullions on the second floor, the White Bear Inn nearby which dates from at least 1607 but is probably much older, and another 17th century house with gables known as Park Hill which is now the Pendle Heritage Centre. Other features at the Heritage Centre include Park Hill Barn

(now a farming museum for the Pendle area), an ancient cruck barn and an 18th century walled garden.

Just across the road from Park Hill is Barrowford Toll House, built in about 1805 to collect tolls from travellers on the Marsden to Gisburn and Long Preston turnpike road. Another interesting feature connected with travel through the area is the picturesque packhorse bridge over Pendle Water which dates from 1583, while at nearby Carr Hall is a famous avenue of lime trees planted in 1815 by Colonel Thomas Clayton. These are said to represent soldiers, with some trees standing out as officers, all in the actual formation of Colonel Clayton's regiment at Waterloo.

By following Pendle Water upstream from Barrowford the visitor quickly arrives at the village of **Roughlee** and the start of 'Lancashire witch country'. It was here, in the area around Pendle Hill, that two families in

*Barrowford Toll House*

*Park Hill, Barrowford*

particular were caught up in the accusations of involvement in witchcraft which were to lead to their deaths at Lancaster Castle on 20th August, 1612. The two families were essentially very poor vagrants who lived in squalid hovels such as disused barns and farm outbuildings, and they caused a great deal of superstition among local people as sheep were stolen and cattle slaughtered. One of the families was the Demdikes or Devices, who lived in an old barn called the Malkin Tower near Newchurch in Pendle and were headed by Old Demdike, the grandmother of the family, while the other family were the Chattoxes who lived further down the hill at Higham.

Things came to a head in March 1612 when Alison Device was accused of bewitching a pedlar from Halifax, an act which she confessed to when examined by magistrate Roger Nowell at nearby Read Hall. Nowell proceeded to round up first of all the Devices and then the Chattoxes as different members of the families gave incriminating evidence against one another, and by May all of them had been committed to Lancaster Gaol to await trial at the August Assize. Old Demdike died in Lancaster Castle before the trial could take place, but five other members of the two families were found guilty when tried and were condemned to death by hanging.

It was on the 20th of August that they were executed on Gallows Hill before a large crowd, together with Alice Nutter who had been drawn into the affair. Although she was a landowner rather than a vagrant like the others she was accused of assisting the Demdikes in one of their murders, and it may have been a conspiracy between the two families which played a large part in her conviction. Her husband was landlord to the Chattox family, hence the ill-feeling between them, but in the previous year to the trial it seems that she had been involved in a bitter legal dispute over estate boundaries with her neighbour Roger Nowell. He had lost the dispute at some financial loss and so perhaps saw the 1612 trial as a chance for revenge. Alice Nutter is Roughlee's main connection with the Pendle witches, in that Roughlee Old Hall was her home up to the time of the trial; the attractive stone built house with its mullioned windows is still to be seen in the village, hemmed in on two sides by modern residential development.

Despite the tales and legends of witches in the Pendle area it seems unlikely that witchcraft was really practised here. The stories which were circulated, and the two families and their neighbours who latched on to them, doubtless struck fear into the hearts of local people, but the 'witchcraft' may have been just a cover for petty crime. The Demdikes and Chattoxes were probably gangs of vagrants who contributed to each other's downfall by rash accusations about evil doings. Yet even if there was no talk about witches before these families came to prominence there was certainly plenty of talk for many years afterwards, because the Pendle Foresters had a real fear of witches and so they held on to their local charms until comparatively recently. The Pendle witches arrived on the scene at a time when great value was being placed upon farm stock by the up-and-coming yeoman farmers, and in a world which lacked veterinary science it was easy to blame witches or evil spirits for unaccountable 'bad luck'.

To the west of Roughlee is the attractive village of **Barley,** lying at the foot of Pendle Hill which is reached by a footpath leading directly from the main street. On Pendle Hill itself is a large pile of stones called 'The Beacon', which is essentially a Bronze Age burial mound used over the centuries as a warning-fire site. No doubt it alerted the local inhabitants of Scottish raiders entering the area and bent on plunder, but it was also used in 1887 for Queen Victoria's Jubilee

*On the fringes of Barley*

celebrations. On this occasion the fuel for the blaze was supplied by breweries in Burnley and Barrowford, their horses taking it to the bottom of the hill from where it was taken to the top by local farmers.

Farming has been the main livelihood of many families in this area for centuries, with the predominant activities being sheep- and cattle-rearing. By the early 18th century, however, the emphasis began to change, with a number of people becoming involved in the production of textiles through the introduction of attic handlooms as an extra source of income. Then by the 19th century two cotton mills were established in the village, one to the west of Barley Green with 200 looms and another known as Narrowgates Mill which has since been converted to residential use.

One of the current features of the area around Barley is the reservoirs which provide an opportunity for some enjoyable circular

*Roughlee Old Hall*

walks. These comprise the Upper and Lower Ogden Reservoirs and the Upper and Lower Black Moss Reservoirs, completed around the turn of the century to provide drinking water for the Nelson area. The work was undertaken by Irish navvies, who effectively doubled the population of the village overnight. Barley is an interesting and picturesque village in its own right, but it also fulfils an important function as a base from which to explore not only Pendle Hill but also much of the surrounding countryside.

Less than a mile to the south of Barley is the village of **Newchurch-in-Pendle,** a Pennine hill settlement which clings somewhat precariously to one side of the valley. Although there is just one main street along which the stone cottages jostle for space and a better view of the valley below, the village lies at the junction of four ancient trackways — one of these comes from the south in the direction of Burnley, the one from the west comes directly from Whalley Abbey, the one from the north from Barley and Twiston, while the last comes from Roughlee and Colne to the east. The name 'Newchurch-in-Pendle' actually originated in 1544 when John Bird, Bishop of Chester, consecrated a new church here within the larger area known as Goldshaw Booth, although it is thought that a chapel stood in the village from at least the 13th century onwards.

The first significant impact on the area was made by the Saxons, and the title 'Goldshaw Booth' is evidently derived from a Saxon lady Goldgeofu, whose bothy or booth (meaning a farm) gave the district its name. The terrace upon which the village sits, with a flat hilltop at the higher level, must have appeared a useful site for a defended farm, and the ridge above the village is still known as the Castle; a large square enclosure here was the place where animals were kept safe from man and beast. During the Middle Ages Goldshaw Booth was a cow and deer rearing centre as well as part of the royal hunting area of Pendle Forest, but by the time of Elizabeth I the area had become 'deforested' and the land mostly rented to or owned by small farmers.

After having survived the rigours of Scottish raiders rampaging through the area, as well as the conflicts of the English Civil War, Newchurch settled down to a period of prosperity in the 18th century when a boom in trade led to an increase in the number of handloom weavers. Most of the houses within the village seem to date from this period, and by 1826 a survey showed that Newchurch had 769 inhabitants within its boundaries with 387 handlooms. There was also an 18th century factory just below the village which carried out the washing and dyeing of wool for the local handloom industry.

The oldest and most interesting building in the village is St. Mary's Parish Church, originally erected in the 16th century to replace an earlier chapel of ease on the same site. The 16th century church was itself later replaced by the present building which dates from about 1740, although the earlier tower was retained; on the south side of this tower can still be seen the old priest's door, while on the western face is a piece of carving resembling a filled-in oval window which is said to represent the all-seeing 'Eye of God'. On the south west corner of the nave roof is a sundial dated 1718, while outside the south wall is a flat gravestone with the names of members of the Nutter family inscribed upon it; these were very probably relatives of Alice Nutter, the reported witch of Roughlee Old Hall. The village has been associated with witchcraft since the notorious trial of the Pendle witches in the 17th century, but it has also been the setting for numerous stories about ghostly apparitions and other shadowy traditions.

For the church, however, a continuing tradition of rather more substance has been that of 'rushbearing', which celebrates a simple ceremony of older times when church floors were strewn with reeds or straw in August as a prelude to the cold weather of winter. The reeds provided the benefit of not only keeping the draught from worshippers' feet but also of helping to stop the earth floor becoming a quagmire in wet conditions. In earlier days parishioners would carry the rushes to church in bundles, a procedure which later developed as a festival when the young men and women of the parish would decorate the church with garlands and flowers. Then by the 19th century rushes were traditionally placed into a rush cart and piled up to ten feet high in the shape of a bishop's hat before being paraded through the parish in procession. When the rushbearing ceremony was reinstated in Newchurch just prior to the First World War children taking part would carry not only garlands but also tiny pieces of doll's house furniture which they had made out of reeds and pins.

The road south from Newchurch-in-Pendle crosses the valley formed by Sabden Brook and then climbs up over a ridge of higher ground before descending sharply into **Fence** and **Wheatley Lane.** These two small villages comprise the larger area known as Old Laund Booth, with Fence taking its name from the enclosure within which stags were kept when hunting was abandoned in Pendle Forest. Both villages had farming as their main source of employment, but this was later supplemented by the spinning and weaving of cotton. Nonconformism appears to have been strong in this area, and Wheatley Lane was the chosen location for one of Lancashire's few Inghamite Churches, founded by followers of Benjamin Ingham.

The nearby village of **Higham** is remembered more for its pub than for any other place of worship, and 'The Four Alls' depicts a king ('I govern all'), a clergyman ('I pray for all'), a soldier ('I fight for all'), and a working man, reflecting somewhat ruefully 'I pay for all'! For centuries the Forest Halmote (the chief court of the area) was held in Higham Hall, whilst among the notable

*St. Mary's Parish Church, Newchurch-in-Pendle*

*Whalley Abbey Gatehouse*

*Hoghton Tower*

people associated with the village are Jonas Moore, the Surveyor-General of Ordnance and co-founder of the Greenwich Observatory, and Christopher Towneley, a Royalist and noted transcriber of many local deeds.

From Higham the A6068 road drops down into the valley of the River Calder and the small town of **Padiham.** Although it has a long history, being recorded as Padyngham in 1294 when it belonged to the de Lacy family, lords of the Honour of Clitheroe, it was not really until the 19th century that Padiham began to expand as a centre of the traditional Lancashire cotton industry. Many of the attractive terraced streets in the town date back to this period, when rows of workers' cottages were erected in conjunction with the numerous mills which were springing up at that time.

At the very heart of Padiham is the parish church, occupying the site of a mediaeval chantry which was rebuilt by the Abbot of Whalley in the early 16th century and then enlarged in 1706. The present church is built of stone in the Perpendicular style and dates from 1868, with a fine tower rising to 118 feet which can be seen from miles around. Interior features of interest include the 16th century font, sculptured with the symbols of the Passion and given to the earlier church by the last Abbot of Whalley, a well carved old chair in the sanctuary and a white marble memorial to Guy Le Gendre Starkie of Huntroyde.

The River Calder connects Padiham with its earlier 'spiritual' centre of Whalley, but lying between the two on the north side of the river are the pleasant villages of Read and Sabden. Like Padiham, **Read** has a history of early industrial development, although the hamlet of Old Read stands on a prehistoric track from Whalley through to Mereclough and Yorkshire. In the English Civil War a skirmish near Read Old Bridge in April 1643 resulted in the downfall of the Royalist cause in Lancashire. One of the most significant buildings in the area is Read Hall, at one time the home of the Nowell family — Roger Nowell was the local magistrate involved in the conviction of the Pendle witches, while Dean Nowell of St. Paul's Cathedral was another famous member of the same family. The village of **Sabden** lies within the same valley as Newchurch-in-Pendle, hemmed in by the well wooded slopes of Black Hill to the south and the more rugged slopes of Pendleton Moor to the north. From both of these ridges there are superb views of the surrounding countryside, while in between is some delightful farmland. The village itself consists of quaint rows of stone cottages, and is particularly famous for its historic associations with the industrial pioneer Richard Cobden.

About three miles to the west of Sabden lies the historic village of **Whalley,** famous for its ancient parish church and abbey. The present parish church of St. Mary's and All Saints dates from the early part of the 13th century, although it is certain that a church existed on this site in Saxon times and was known as 'The White Church under the Leigh'. Among the features of interest to be found here are the three Celtic crosses in the churchyard which date back to the 10th century, with local tradition suggesting that any person who can decipher the writing on the largest of these will learn the power of becoming invisible! Nearby is an 18th century sundial, while adjacent to the south porch are two stone coffins dating from the 13th century together with the base of a Roman pillar. A few yards away is the tomb of John Wigglesworth, whose inscription records that 'for more than fifty years the principal Innkeeper in this Town, withstanding the Temptations of that dangerous Calling, he maintained Good Order in his House, kept the Sabbath Day Holy, frequented the Public Worship with his Family, induced his guests to do the same'.

Inside the church the most interesting features are the choir stalls, which were originally carved for the abbey in about 1430 but then were moved to the church following the Dissolution. All of the 22 stalls have misericord seats which are richly carved on the underside — the third on the south side depicts a farrier trying to shoe a goose, while the twelfth on the north side shows a wife belabouring her husband with a frying pan! There are also some interesting pews for the benefit of the rest of the church congregation, including a portion of a mediaeval pew close

*One of Whalley's Celtic crosses*

to the lectern as well as the Starkie pew immediately in front of the pulpit and the Kage Pew at the head of the centre aisle. It appears that this large pew of cage-like construction was made for Roger Nowell when he was lord of the manor of Read, but the authorities refused to allow it to be placed in the church. After some 70 years it was eventually put in its present position, but then a quarrel arose between John Taylor of Moreton Hall and John Fort of Read as to who had the right to the pew. Despite a lawsuit costing thousands of pounds nothing was decided, so in 1830 the pew was divided with a wooden partition and each of the parties received one half.

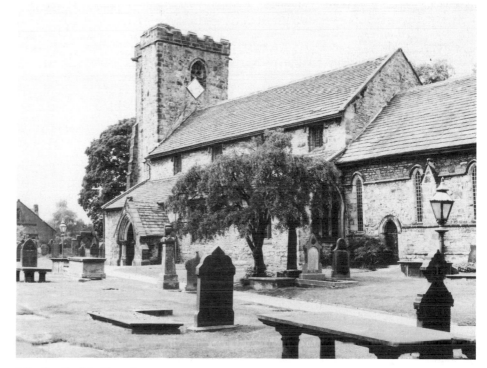

*Whalley Parish Church*

The chancel is dominated by its heraldic east window which bears the arms of 25 distinguished local families, while the chancel screen dates from the 15th century when it formed part of a one-time rood loft. The screen to the St. Mary's Chantry (now the Lady Chapel) is a fine example of 14th century craftsmanship, whilst that of the Mitton Chapel is only just a little older. This chapel was founded following the dissolution of a hermitage which stood midway between the church and the abbey, the hermitage having been used as the residence of a female recluse and her two maidservants. Unfortunately the time came when the incumbents in this hermitage were all 'found to be with child', and so it was decided to demolish the building and erect two chantry chapels in its place.

Other interesting features within the church include the 15th century font with its 17th century cover, the Churchwardens' pew dated 1690, the Vicar's pew dated around 1700, and the Constable's Pew dated 1714. The church chest dates from 1684 and has three locks according to the custom of the time, the incumbent and his wardens each holding a key in order to ensure that all three were present when the chest was opened. It is worth noting that one of the most complete set of registers in existence is also kept at the church, going back to 1538.

Not far away from the parish church is Whalley Abbey with its two imposing gateways, a Cistercian foundation which had its original roots in the small abbey which was established at Stanlawe in Cheshire in 1176. This was moved to Whalley in 1296 after the Rectory of Whalley was given to the monks in 1283 by Henry de Lacy. Despite some early troubles the Abbey flourished for two and a half centuries, exercising very considerable power and influence within the district. Together with the abbeys of Fountains, Furness and Kirkstall it dominated affairs in the north of England, and no doubt its great church built of local stone would have been an inspiring sight for pilgrims arriving here from both Lancashire and Yorkshire.

In 1536, Whalley Abbey and its last Abbot (John Paslew) were involved in the protest against the suppression of the smaller monasteries, known as the Pilgrimage of Grace. Abbot Paslew and some Whalley monks were eventually tried and executed for their part in this, and the Abbey was then seized by the king. It remained in the possession of the Crown until 1553 when it passed into the hands of the Assheton family, and during the course of the succeeding centuries it came into the ownership of various other local families until it eventually became the responsibility of the Diocese of Blackburn in 1926. Since that time it has

taken on a role as a conference centre and retreat for Church of England clergy, as well a being a place of historic interest for visitors.

It is well worthwhile taking time to discover the ruined Abbey and so learn something of the monastic life which would have been experienced here. The main feature of the site is the ruins of the great Conventual Church, which was more like a cathedral in size since it was 110 yards in length, 70 yards across and with a lantern tower rising 180 feet into the air. On either side of the chancel one can see the broad foundations of the columns which supported the roof, while to the west are the choir pits, one of the more unusual features of the Abbey. Over these elongated pits were placed oak boards to support the choir stalls above, with the aim being to give greater resonance to the voices of the choristers. These pits were situated in the nave of the church and not in the chancel as one might normally expect. The reason for this is that Whalley Abbey was built after the style of Westminster Abbey, which was restored for the coronation of Edward the Confessor. Edward had enemies at every hand and he determined that only those high dignitaries of the church required to perform the actual ceremony should stand behind him at his crowning; the choir was thus placed in the nave.

To the south of the church are the other ruined buildings of the Abbey — these include the lay brothers' house with its imprisonment cell, the monks' dormitory, the refectory, the lavatorium where the monks washed prior to taking their meals, the Chapter House where the major business of the Abbey was conducted, the reredorter or toilets (constructed so that any effluent would drop immediately into the mill race which flowed beneath), and the Abbot's Lodgings. The Abbot's kitchen was actually retained by the Assheton who first owned the Abbey, and over it he erected the long gallery of his manor house. The windows here are thus from the Tudor period and are different from those seen elsewhere in the ruins.

The Assheton family influence is also to be found in the imposing entrance to the Conference House, the portico and doorway being in a Dutch style as a tribute to the Royal family when the line of Orange ascended the English throne. For the lower orders there was a doorway 'below the stairs'. To the side of what is now the warden's entrance can be seen windows from three different periods - the pre-monastic windows of an earlier chapel, the Tudor windows of the Assheton occupation and the Victorian sashcord windows installed by Colonel Hargreaves. Then some distance away from the Abbey is the West Gate, astride what was originally the main road from Whalley to Ribchester and the first part of the Abbey buildings to be completed. This ancient gateway has unique

*Whalley Abbey Gatehouse*

*Cottages in The Square, Whalley*

features which are not found anywhere else in England, and above it was the chapel which the Cistercians used as a school until it ceased to function as such when the Dissolution came about. It was thus the forerunner of the local grammar school, which received its royal charter in 1547.

From the West Gate a road named The Sands takes us on to Church Lane and then into the centre of Whalley itself. Along The Sands is a row of late-Tudor houses known as Abbey Croft, built following the Dissolution as homes for employees of the Abbey estate of Sir Richard Assheton. More old cottages are to be found on Church Lane, which is probably the oldest street in the village. Of particular interest here are the three Tudor cottages known as Poole End whose rears now face The Square at the west end of Church Lane; originally the street continued past the front of these cottages and was the main road from Whalley to Ribchester. Poole House at the corner of The Square is said to have been the place where the monks of Whalley kept their fishing rods, while one of the main wells of the village lay beneath The Square and was the water supply for the adjacent premises right into the present century.

Church Lane joins up with the main street through Whalley at the point known as Town Gate, a place marked by four public houses. Three of these — the Whalley Arms, the Swan and the Dog Inn — each served a dual purpose in that each had its own farm attached until the later part of the 19th century. The fourth, the De Lacy Arms, was built in the 1860s on the site of the ancient

Manor house of Whalley. Several of the buildings around this part of the village still retain a number of metal rings and hinges attached to their walls, a reminder of the days when weekly sales of cattle and sheep were held in the streets — the rings were used to tether the cattle and horses while the hinges were used to secure the hurdles in which the sheep and smaller animals were penned. Opposite the De Lacy Arms are premises which were in use until the middle of the last century as the Rope Works, and the 150 yards of pavement stretching northwards from this point was the Rope Walk.

To the south of here King Street heads towards Whalley Bridge over the River Calder, passing some imposing Georgian houses on the way and what was probably the Abbey farm, as well as the old cottages which were originally homes for agricultural workers employed on the Abbey estates. There is also a Tudor farmstead bearing the name 'The Toby Jug' (its oak panelling reputedly taken from the Abbey following the destruction of its ancient buildings), as well as a row of small Victorian houses. In the opposite direction King Street leads us out to the old Grammar School, founded in 1547 but now used as an adult education centre; the school's cricket field was the venue for the first ever 'Roses' cricket match between Lancashire and Yorkshire. The building itself dates from 1725 and functioned as a school for day boys and boarders into the present century.

Before reaching the old Grammar School one can see The White House, which was at one time the dower house of the Fort family of Read Hall. The knocker on the door was

reputedly from 11 Downing Street, while recent alterations have revealed a deep well in the rear yard. The old Grammar School is situated close to the junction of King Street and Station Road, at a point known as Stocks Hill because it was here on a low eminence that the village stocks and pillory were located. Stocks Hill House nearby is said to have a well in the cellar which was used by the village doctors of former years for the preparation of their medicines. Down Station Road is a row of six almshouses set back on the north side, these having been built in 1837 with money provided by Adam Cottam, one of Whalley's greatest benefactors. Then at the end of Station Road is Whalley Viaduct, its long line of massive red brick arches acting as an unusual backcloth against which the rest of this historic township is set. The railway viaduct is the longest in Lancashire, a 19th century masterpiece completed in 1850 which carried the line to Whalley, Clitheroe, Hellifield and the north.

From this point the road carries on from the head of the viaduct and then underneath the Whalley Bypass to cross over the River Ribble at Mitton. The local guide book says that this area, comprising **Little Mitton** and **Great Mitton,** still has a breath of old England about it because of the way that it has remained unspoilt by modernity, and it would indeed be difficult to find a pleasanter spot. Situated above the river is the Church of All Hallows, built in the reign of Edward III and probably one of the most attractive features along the Ribble. As well as a low square tower the church also incorporates the Shireburn Chapel, standing on the site of the ancient chantry of St. Nicholas and founded by Hugh Shireburn in the 15th century. Sir Richard Shireburn built the present chapel, containing impressive monuments to the family which for generations were Lords of Stonyhurst.

Sir Richard died in 1594 and is described on his tomb as Master Forester of the Forest of Bowland, Steward of the Manor of Slaidburn, Lieutenant of the Isle of Man and Deputy Lieutenant of Lancashire. He also appears to have been a very diplomatic person in that he managed to find favour during his lifetime with four different monarchs who all held widely differing views, particularly about religion. Other interesting features of Mitton church include the roof and the great oak rafters which support it, together with the richly carved chancel screen dating from 1593 and the octagonal font which is very much older. There is also a 'leper's window', used by people in disgrace who were not allowed to hear the service from inside the church. Across from the church can be found Great Mitton Hall, a good example of a building of the Tudor or early Stuart period, while over the river is Little Mitton Hall, a substantial mansion in the early Tudor style.

Downstream from this point on the Ribble are numerous historic houses from the Tudor and Jacobean periods, one of the most impressive being Hacking Hall just to the north of Billington. This fine symmetrical Jacobean mansion stands at the confluence of the Calder and the Ribble and dates from 1607, having been built by Thomas Livesey and then re-built by Judge Walmesley of Dunkenhalgh. The great barn at Hacking Hall is an old tithe barn built by the monks from Whalley, its massive cruck frames giving it a church-like appearance.

Just three miles to the west of Billington is the small settlement of **Copster Green,** its main feature being the central common which was used to fatten local geese. During Victorian and Edwardian times this was also a popular place for people from the nearby towns to visit on a Sunday afternoon, and a number of the local inhabitants found employment in catering on such occasions. Others would walk to work to the cotton weaving mill at Langho, although for many years there was handloom weaving within the village itself and prior to that several small farms. The more important buildings here in Copster Green include Bolton Hall, a two storey farmhouse dating from 1665, and Lovely Hall situated on the south side of the village.

There has been a house on the site of Lovely Hall since 1246, when Robert de Boulton held lands in Salesbury, but the main building which can be seen today was completed in about 1530. The original layout of the house was the traditional 'H' plan of the times, but this was altered over the years with some major improvements taking place in the 18th

and 19th centuries. Many of the original roof timbers still remain, however, and there is also a considerable amount of wattle and daub incorporated within the roof structure. On the lawn in front of the house is an octagonal stone pillar with a sundial, the pillar bearing the date 1668.

Enjoying some superb views of the lower part of the Ribble Valley is the hilltop village of **Mellor,** situated just to the north of Blackburn on a high ridge overlooking the low-lying areas beneath it. This locality was of strategic importance to the Romans, who founded an encampment on Mellor Moor to act as a signalling station serving the more important settlement at Bremetennacum, now known as Ribchester. Quarrying and dairy farming developed as the main occupations in Mellor, although handloom weaving was also important during the latter part of the 18th century. A number of weavers' cottages can still be seen in the village, particularly those at Long Row which date from about 1800. St. Mary's Church is a notable feature of interest in Mellor, dating from 1829 and possessing a very fine peal of Guildford chimes. The internal woodwork is of English oak, while the very valuable chancel and organ screens are beautiful examples of the wood-carver's art. The stained glass windows on the south side of the church are 19th century Flemish work, with those on the north side being of modern English design.

At the foot of the hill on which Mellor stands is the small settlement of **Mellor Brook,** which during the last century had a bobbin mill and cotton-spinning mill as well as a local woodturning factory. Further north, however,

are the quiet agricultural parishes of **Osbaldeston** and **Balderstone,** consisting largely of scattered farms and secluded woods, the latter laid out on the fairly steep slopes leading down to the River Ribble. The meandering course of the river is particularly pronounced at this point, and Horseshoe Bend in Balderstone is a local beauty spot which is well worth seeing.

Watching over the Ribble's graceful curves here are some important historic houses, with Balderstone Hall and Osbaldeston Hall being especially notable, whilst a little higher up the wooded slopes above the river banks is the delightfully restored Oxendale Hall. The area is crossed by numerous footpaths which provide the visitor with tantalising glimpses of the river below, as it makes its way quietly but purposefully to the coast within the confines of its tree-lined valley. Another focal point in the area is the Parish Church of St. Leonard in Balderstone, which was built in 1852 on the site of a much earlier chapel of ease. Close by is the village school and Balderstone Grange, a substantial and attractive house which was built by the Archdeacon of Blackburn during the latter part of the 19th century.

One of the most important and impressive houses in this part of the Ribble Valley is **Samlesbury Hall,** dating originally from the second half of the 13th century when it was the home of the Deuyas family — after the manor which had been held initially by Gospatric de Samlesbury was split into two. In the 14th century the Hall passed to the Southworth family, who were very largely responsible for creating the historic house which we have today, but they were forced by poverty to sell out to the Bradyll family in

*Samlesbury Hall's elegant 'black and white' frontage*

94

*The rear elevation of Samlesbury Hall*

1679. Since 1679 there have only been a few years during which the Hall has had a resident owner, and by the beginning of the 19th century the fabric of the building was considerably decayed. Then in 1824 the new road which was built right up against one corner of the south range of the Hall brought increased traffic which led to the Hall's conversion into an inn, the Bradyll Arms.

For a time part of the Hall became a girls' boarding school, and then in the second half of the 19th century it was bought by Joseph Harrison who spent large sums of money on restoring the building. Before long, however, uncertainty again clouded the future of the Hall, and at the start of the present century it was even suggested that the whole building might be dismantled and sent to America. It was at this point that a campaign was mounted to save the property, a charitable trust being established to do this, and the money required was eventually raised so that the Hall could not only be bought but also restored and repaired. It has since become one of the most important tourist features of the Ribble Valley.

The oldest part of the present complex is the 15th century Great Hall, which probably replaced an earlier building on the same site. The rest of the Hall is very largely the work of Sir Thomas Southworth, who rebuilt the whole of the south wing and modified the Great Hall itself. When he died in 1546 the main parts of Samlesbury Hall which can be seen today were in existence, and it was he who introduced the first recorded use of brick for a manor house in Lancashire when the southern side of the south wing was faced in this material. At some point during the 16th century the west wall of the Great Hall was replaced in stone with a new fireplace and chimney, and it was probably at this time that the attractive bay window with its small room above was added. Other interesting features of the building include a window in the south wing, which is reputed to have come from Whalley Abbey, together with three splendid brick chimneys which are to be found on the same south-facing elevation.

The precise layout of the interior of Samlesbury Hall during the 16th century remains unknown, although it seems likely that the locations of the individual rooms today follow their original pattern. Whilst the Great Hall has been altered at both ends it has always been the single open room to be seen at present, and likewise the south range has

always consisted of two storeys except at its eastern end where the chapel extended up through both floors. This chapel was overlooked by a first floor gallery, perhaps used by the lord and his family while watching divine service, and was probably on the same site as an earlier one licenced by the authorities in 1420.

The Thomas Southworth who was responsible for much of the Samlesbury Hall to be seen today was buried at the unusually-named parish church of St. Leonard-the-Less, just two miles to the west. This ancient church dates from the late 12th century when Gospatric, lord of the Samlesbury manor, built a chapel of ease for the use of his dependants sometime between 1185 and 1190. For 300 years the chapel was served by Cistercian monks, who came firstly from Stanlawe near Chester and then from Whalley Abbey. By 1558, however, the building was in such a poor condition that urgent restoration work had to be carried out; this was followed by further major alterations in the 19th century, when the tower was added.

The features of particular interest within the church include a complete set of box pews (with the earliest dating from 1678), a 17th century communion rail, a fine pulpit which was originally constructed on three levels, a Sanctus bell over the south east door which dates from the 14th century and a very unusual chamfered oak draw-bar which still exists in the bar-hole behind the south west door. In the churchyard there is an old sundial near the south east door, while under a yew tree nearby lies a reputed witch. A beautifully engraved plough and scythe on the gravestone of William Lazonby to the north of the church still reminds people that Samlesbury was at one time the home of the champion ploughmaker of all England.

*St. Leonard-the-Less, Samlesbury*

The Samlesbury area in general has always been a rural one with the main employment being in agriculture, although by the middle of the 18th century a large number of people were engaged in the spinning and weaving of cotton. Most of these would have combined their textile work with other activities, particularly part-time employment on the land, as is borne out by the fact that many of the old farmhouses and cottages in the area were converted to this new use rather than having been specially built for the purpose. By the middle of the 19th century, however, more and more people were leaving the area to find work in the towns, and few new factories opened in Samlesbury itself to compensate for the decline of the old domestic handloom weaving industry. Two small textile mills were built, however, at Roach Bridge and Samlesbury Bottoms, but these did not employ a large number of people and they later changed from cotton spinning to papermaking. As the number of people living in Samlesbury gradually declined, a higher proportion of those who remained worked on the land, and by the end of the 19th century the local economy was again a predominantly rural one. The area is still very largely rural in character, despite the presence of a large new brewery and an aircraft works on the site of an aerodrome which was once intended to become an international airport!

Handloom weaving was also undertaken in the adjoining parish of **Hoghton,** to the south of Samlesbury, and whilst this area does not have a recognisable village centre it has numerous small hamlets where handloom weavers' cottages are still to be seen. The real focal point of Hoghton is **Hoghton Tower,** which dates from 1565

and is said to be the only true baronial residence in Lancashire. The de Hoghton family have owned land in this area since the time of William the Conqueror, and they trace their descent back to Walter, one of William the Conqueror's companions, and to Lady Godiva of Coventry, wife of Leofric the Earl of Mercia. The family home was built very much in keeping with their importance in the realm, and it is a thoroughly impressive piece of architecture which occupies a strategic position on top of a tree-clad summit above the River Darwen.

Hoghton Tower has enjoyed close connections with royalty over its long existence, particularly with James I, and this is reflected in the names of a number of its sumptuous rooms. The Buckingham Room with its magnificent oak panelling, for example, is named after the Duke of Buckingham, King James' favourite courtier, who had accompanied the King on his visit to Hoghton Tower in August 1617. Leading off the King's Ante Chamber with its fine Jacobean panelling is a room called the King's Bedchamber where King James I slept, with more panelling and a raised dais for the King's chair of state.

Then down on the ground floor one can find the King's Hall, where King James gave audience to several distinguished visitors, together with the famous Banqueting Hall

*Hoghton Tower gatehouse and its dignified approach*

with its minstrels' gallery where James I knighted the 'Sir Loin of Beef' on 17th August, 1617. Here one can see a copy of the original menu of the meals served to the King and the numerous guests during the King's visit, as well as the Jacobean table at which the King sat and the oak Tudor table on which the famous 'Sir Loin' had been placed. There is also a clock by Daniel Delander of London

*Front entrance to Hoghton Tower*

*The Rose Gardens, Hoghton Tower*

which is wound once a year, together with paintings of the Houghton family. The Banqueting Hall is known too as the place where William Shakespeare performed with Thomas Hoghton's troupe of players during the 16th century. Overlooking the Banqueting Hall is the Ladies' Withdrawing Room where the ladies retired after dinner whilst their menfolk continued drinking; the window between the two rooms had shutters which could be closed when necessary. Other interesting rooms in the house include the Guinea Room, named after the golden guineas which were painted in each corner of the wainscot panels and also on the doors, and the Ballroom with its beautiful examples of 19th century woodwork by Gillow of Lancaster.

According to the Lancashire historian Dr. D.T. Whitaker, Hoghton Tower is 'in exact conformity to Andrew Borde's directions in 1542 for the construction of great houses', and the house as it now stands still gives an excellent idea of the structure which its founder Thomas Hoghton had in mind - a manor house with two courtyards, the buildings around the first housing the servants and the second consisting of the banqueting hall and residential quarters. As well as its architectural and historic excellence the building also enjoys some delightful views of the surrounding countryside, particularly from the Gatehouse on the west side where one's eye is drawn down the long drive to magnificent panoramas of Wales, the Lake District and the connecting coastline.

The parish of Hoghton also has quite a history of 'unlawful' Catholicism during the period of persecution in the 17th century, and in the settlement of Gregson Lane is Arrowsmith House where Edmund Arrowsmith said his last mass before being captured and later sentenced to death for being a priest and a Jesuit. The sideboard on which he said mass is now used as an altar at St. Joseph's Chapel, itself dating from well before the Catholic Emancipation Act of 1829 and so situated in a secluded spot. Nearby in the midst of attractive parkland is Brindle Lodge, a handsome building dating from the 1770s.

Our tour of the Ribble Valley finishes at **Walton-le-Dale** on the south side of Preston, back once more on the banks of one of Lancashire's loveliest rivers. Formerly spelt 'Waletune', meaning an enclosure near a stream or a river, the manor of Walton was a royal possession in Saxon times, and its strategic position as the lowest fording point on the river must have assured its relative importance. After the Norman Conquest the manor was handed over to the de Lacy family, the wealthiest in Lancashire, and in 1301 Walton-le-Dale was granted a weekly market, two annual fairs and free warren. Then during the reign of Elizabeth I the manor passed to the Hoghtons of Hoghton Tower.

The Ribble bridge between Walton-le-Dale and Preston assumed particular importance during the English Civil War of the 17th century, then it became a strategic point in the defence of Preston by the Royalists. The battle for Preston continued for three days until at last the Royalists could no longer hold the vital bridge and the Parliamentarian army routed them. This victory was the prelude to many more which heralded the final triumph of the Parliamentarian cause. The bridge was also the scene of another decisive encounter in 1715 when the Jacobites rose in armed revolt against George I of Hanover becoming king. The oldest part of the present Ribble Bridge dates from 1872, although early records show that there was a bridge here as far back as 1302.

As well as its interesting history Walton-le-Dale enjoys an attractive setting amidst woods and undulating countryside, with the area around the River Ribble being particularly pleasant and featuring a walk through to nearby Penwortham along the route of an old packhorse way. Sited on a prominent point above the Ribble is the local parish church, which dates back to 1190. The oldest parts of the present building, however, are the 16th century chancel and the buttressed and embattled tower, the latter housing a fine modern peal of eight bells. Within the church is an ancient font and some notable memorials to the de Hoghton family. Then not far away is the smaller settlement of Higher Walton, situated above Walton-le-Dale and enjoying some picturesque river scenery along the course of the Darwen.

*The village of Wycoller and its picturesque packhorse bridge*

# Chapter 5: THE EAST LANCASHIRE UPLANDS

The area which we have called the East Lancashire Uplands is one of great physical diversity — ranging from the bleak heights of its open moorland to the colourful gardens of its historic houses, from the terraced streets of its industrial towns to the stone cottages of its farming hamlets. As we shall see, it is also an area whose economic and social history has been inextricably bound up with the development of textiles in Lancashire. To begin with this was very much a domestic activity, with the first weavers often being farmers who supplemented their living by making and selling cloth. Although it was normally the male members of the family who did the weaving, the women and children were also involved in carding (cleaning and straightening the fibres) and spinning. The production of woollen cloth was thus largely a homespun affair which was replaced by the weaving and spinning of cotton on a much more substantial scale during the late 18th and 19th centuries. What began in a small way at home as an additional source of income very quickly burgeoned into a huge industry which was to change the face of the country, and the towns of East Lancashire are a continuing testimony to the wealth and prosperity which the growth of the textile trade brought with it.

The starting point for our journey of discovery through this unique and fascinating part of the county is **Blackburn,** just a few miles further upstream along the River Darwen from the point where we ended the previous chapter. A settlement seems to have existed here as early as the Roman period, at the place where the road northwards to Ribchester forded the Blakewater, and even by Norman times the village had become something of a focal point for the surrounding area; and for the next 800 years the district around it was given the name 'Blackburnshire'. For the most part St. Mary's Church remained the dominant influence over the course of the Middle Ages, during which time Blackburn was essentially a small market town noted chiefly for its cattle market and woollen weaving. Then in the 18th and 19th centuries the Industrial Revolution brought about a major transformation of the area, with cotton replacing wool as the main industry and factory settlements replacing the smaller colonies of handloom weavers. The increased prosperity led to a spate of new building on the outskirts of the town, and during the 1800s Blackburn's population grew from 10,000 to 100,000.

One of the symbols of the prosperity which Blackburn enjoyed during this period is its Town Hall, an imposing stone building on King William Street which bears more than a passing resemblance to the Old Mansion House in the City of London. The Town Hall was built in the early 1850s after Blackburn

*Blackburn's impressive Town Hall*

had been granted a royal charter recognising it as a borough in 1851. On the south side of the Town Hall is a statue of William Hornby, one of Blackburn's most prominent industrialists and the town's first mayor. It was he who played the major part in acquiring Blackburn's charter, and he also came to be a Member of Parliament for the town.

Across from the Town Hall is the Exchange, built in the 1860s as the town's main trading centre for cotton and another symbol of its industrial pride. To commemorate the laying of the foundation stone two oak trees were planted in Corporation Park, one named Albert and the other Alexandra after the Prince and Princess of Wales on whose wedding day this ceremony took place. To the

north of both the Exchange and the Town Hall is Richmond Terrace, with its fine row of early Victorian houses dating from 1838 which are now in use as offices. At the centre of the row, above a columned doorway, can be seen the coat of arms of the Fielden family, the 19th century lords of the manor who owned most of the land both in and around the town.

From here Richmond Terrace leads down to St. John's Church, a fine Georgian building with a tower and cupola which was founded in 1788. Above the cupola is a weathervane fashioned in the shape of a weaving shuttle, an appropriate indicator of the source of the town's wealth. The graveyard is the resting place for a number of Blackburn's prominent industrial figures, including Daniel Thwaites, the founder of one of the town's breweries. Brewing, like textiles, was an important local industry, as was paper making, and both these activities are still going on in the town.

The historic core of Blackburn is located on the southern side of the town centre, beyond the modern shopping precinct and close to the Cathedral at the junction of Church Street and Darwen Street. It was here that the mediaeval market cross was situated, in the area that would have acted as the town's traditional meeting point. As well as being the place where important public announcements were made and soldiers recruited, it was also the site for public whippings (held as recently as the 19th century). Close by stood the old parish church, a mediaeval building which occupied a site used for worship since well before the Norman period.

This church was demolished in 1818 and replaced by a new building just a short distance away; the 19th century building now forms part of the nave of the Cathedral and

*The Broad Walk, Blackburn*

*Blackburn Cathedral*

was designed by John Palmer, a pioneer of the Gothic Revival style of architecture. Then in 1926 a new diocese was carved out of the Diocese of Manchester, and the Bishop's throne (or 'cathedra') was placed in Blackburn Parish Church thus turning it into the new Cathedral. Steps were consequently taken to enlarge the building so that it could meet its new functions adequately, and Blackburn now has one of the country's most interesting modern cathedrals. As well as some great works of art there are fragments of a 16th century window, some good examples of 18th and 19th century Flemish glass and also the contemporary glass of the lantern and St. Martin's Chapel.

To the west of the Cathedral is King Street, now largely a commercial area but at one time the most affluent residential part of Blackburn. Laid out at the end of the 18th century it was originally called Sudell Street after the family of Henry Sudell, benefactor of St. John's Church, who used to occupy a large house near the top end of the street. Number 39 King Street was probably the grandest house here and at one time was the home of the Hornby family; the date of 1778 can be seen at the top of the rainwater spout. Other buildings in the street also display dated rainwater heads, while one carries an old fire insurance plaque.

Away from the town centre Blackburn has a number of other imposing residential areas, particularly around Corporation Park (in the north west part of the town) where there are some splendid Victorian houses. Here one can also find The Broad Walk, a delightful tree-lined avenue which offers an opportunity to view the colours of the changing seasons at close hand. A little above here is Revidge, giving some lovely views of the open countryside to the north of Blackburn, while nearby Billinge Hill provides the prospect of some superb views over Witton Park (the one-time home of the Fielden family) and Blackburn town centre itself.

On the north east side of Blackburn is **Rishton,** whose name is Saxon in origin and means 'the fortified village or dwelling place amid the rushes'. During early mediaeval times the village grew in importance and by the mid-13th century it had a fulling mill in operation as the first step in the development of a local 'textile industry'. By the 17th century Rishton was noted for its manufacture of linen cloths, and then in 1766 the village made history as being the first place to weave calico. During the late 18th and early 19th centuries the textile industry moved from the homes of the villagers into the new mills which were springing up in all parts of the district; new housing was built around these mills but also close to both the Leeds and Liverpool Canal and the railway lines. Another dominating influence in Rishton during recent centuries has been the Petre family of Dunkenhalgh Hall, who owned the manor of Rishton as part of a much more extensive estate embracing Clayton-le-Moors as well. Dunkenhalgh Hall, now a hotel, is Elizabethan in origin (with later Victorian additions) and is said to owe its name to a Scottish raider called Duncan who settled here at a very early period.

If Rishton made its name in the textile trade through the weaving of calico, then neighbouring **Great Harwood** rose to prominence through 'mercerisation'. This new way of processing cotton to give it a sheen was invented in 1850 by John Mercer, a self taught industrial chemist who became Great Harwood's most famous 'son'. Mercer's invention had a profound effect upon the development of the cotton industry, and in 1852 he was elected a Fellow of the Royal Society. The Mercer Memorial, a lovely free-standing clock tower in the Town Square at the centre of Great Harwood, was erected in 1903 to mark Mercer's significant contribution to the life of the town.

As with many other Lancashire towns, Great Harwood's entry into the manufacture of textiles began during the 16th and 17th centuries when the area was famous for its woollen cloth and many of its inhabitants were engaged in the trade either as clothiers or weavers. By the end of the 18th century the manufacture of woollen and fustian fabrics was overtaken by cotton handloom weaving, which itself started to decline with the introduction of the factory system during the first half of the 19th century. The first true cotton mill in the district was erected in 1844, leading to a period of intense building as weaving sheds and rows of new terraced houses were erected in Great Harwood.

*The Mercer Memorial, Great Harwood*

Further commercial activity took place as a result of the arrival of the railway in 1877, with a final period of development occurring during the first years of the 20th century when a number of extensive weaving sheds were erected by local industrialists and mill building enterprises. One of the principal fabrics manufactured in Great Harwood was a material called 'dhootie', a cloth exported in enormous quantities to India before the First World War. At the height of the textile industry there were 22 mills in the town, employing over 80% of Great Harwood's working population, but now only one mill remains. The major continuing memorial to the cotton industry here are the streets of terraced houses which were laid out to accommodate the rapidly expanding workforce, but unlike some of the other towns in East Lancashire Great Harwood's terraced dwellings were substantially built with a good deal of space around them so that they are now one of its more attractive features.

*The Gatehouse at Martholme, Great Harwood*

Although the textile industry has been the major reason for the growth of Great Harwood, its history goes back much further than that. During Norman times it is mentioned in records as the Manor of Harwode Magna, and in 1177 it was bequeathed to Richard de Fitton by Henry de Lacy. It eventually passed by marriage into the hands of two local families — the Heskeths of Martholme, who owned the Upper Town, and the Nowells of Read, who owned the Lower Town. Great Harwood remained in the hands of these two families for nearby five hundred years, ensuring that it continued very largely as a self-contained community under the control of the lords of the manor. Then by the early part of the 19th century both the Upper and Lower Towns were sold to the Lomax family, and the pace of change in Great Harwood quickened considerably with the rapid development of the textile industry.

*Martholme, Great Harwood*

The manor house of Martholme still exists in Great Harwood and is the oldest domestic building in the area. Replacing an older one on the same site it was built in 1577 by Sir Thomas Hesketh, who had previously erected a gatehouse here. This latter building is a two storey structure with a central archway, above which is a large stone panel displaying the armorial bearings of the Hesketh family. A second gateway was added by Robert Hesketh to further improve the entrance to the house, this consisting of a wide circular arch carrying a wall and stone finial above it. In the centre of the archway is a shield displaying three wheatsheaves with the initials and date RH 1607.

Great Harwood's other important historic building is the Parish Church of St. Bartholomew, which was very much the focus of the township's life during mediaeval times. Surrounded by lime and sycamore trees most of the present building dates from the early 16th century, although the rather squat stone tower belongs to the 15th century. The stone flagged floor of the low entrance porch leads up to an ancient oak door and a holy-water stoup, while on one of the south-facing windows of the nave can be seen the Hesketh family crest with the date 1521. The impressive Roman Catholic church of Our Lady and St. Hubert dates from 1859, when it was built largely through the generosity of the Lomax family who had become lords of the manor during the early part of the 19th century. At that time, before the full onslaught of the Industrial Revolution, Great Harwood was a pretty village of farms and cottages built alongside two meandering streams and was no doubt one of Lancashire's beauty spots; then the growth of textiles changed the face of the township, although there are still some delightful places to be found on its outskirts. In particular there are some lovely views on the north side of the town, looking out across wooded stream valleys to Whalley Nab further beyond.

To the south of Great Harwood is **Clayton-le-Moors,** another settlement which grew significantly with the development of the textile industry. Its origins go back much further, however, to the Norman period, when together with neighbouring Altham it formed part of the Honour of Clitheroe granted to Robert de Lacy, although the name 'Clayton' is derived from the Anglo-Saxon word 'cleig' referring to the heavy nature of the soil here. By the early 13th century the manor was divided into ancient and enclosed lands on the one hand with common or waste land on the other, with the major landowners being William de Altham and Henry de Clayton. Farming was

*Sparth Manor, Clayton-le-Moors*

obviously the main activity in the area for several centuries, although mining and quarrying were also well established.

Textiles then began to appear on the scene towards the end of the 18th century in the form of calico printing, with further growth taking place as a result of the construction of the Leeds and Liverpool Canal through the middle of Clayton-le-Moors. Improved communications attracted more cotton mills to the area, and by the middle of the 19th century the cotton industry was the main source of employment. Following the depression during the first half of the 20th century Clayton-le-Moors' textile industry went the same way as that of Great Harwood's, and now there are no cotton mills left in the town. One of the few remaining memorials to the 19th century prosperity of Clayton-le-Moors is its parish church, which features a wealth of carved marble and has one of the finest Victorian interiors in the area. Also within the parish is Sparth Manor, dating from 1556 and a fine example of Tudor architecture with its mullioned windows and two storied porch, as well as the Elizabethan mansion of Dunkenhalgh Hall referred to in the account of Rishton.

The Leeds and Liverpool Canal which proved so significant in the development of Clayton-le-Moors also had a major role to play in the growth of neighbouring **Church,** although the early history of this township was largely dictated by the lords of the manor at Dunkenhalgh Hall. There appears to have been a settlement at Church as long ago as 1200, and it is generally accepted that it got its name from the place of worship which had been built here as a subsidiary chapel to the ancient parish of Whalley. One of the earliest industries was calico printing, established by an uncle of the famous Sir Robert Peel, to be followed by cotton weaving during the early part of the 19th century. Among the older buildings in the town the Parish Church of St. James is of particular interest because of its 15th century tower and ancient stone font, while in the Memorial Park is the one-time home of Frederick Gatty, a French textile printer who helped to make Church famous for its printed calico goods.

It was calico printing which also paved the way for the growth of **Oswaldtwistle** just to the south of Church, although its name is thought to derive from the words 'Oswald-Twistla' — possibly meaning the boundary of the kingdom of Oswald, the 7th century Northumbrian king. Parts of the area date back to the Norman period, but it was really the textile trade which led to its development from a village to a town. It was here that James Hargreaves invented his famous 'Spinning Jenny' in 1764 while he lived at what is now Stanhill Post Office, although he was forced to leave the area because of the opposition of local hand spinners who feared that the invention would deprive them of their livelihood. At its heart Oswaldtwistle is full of stone built terraced houses dating from its period of Victorian growth and prosperity, while on the outskirts of the town is open countryside laced with ancient homesteads and hamlets. On the south side in particular is some beautiful walking country with the added bonus of superb views of the Ribble Valley and Pendle Hill.

Nearer at hand, however, is **Accrington,** a Victorian town 'par excellence' and very much a creation of the Industrial Revolution — even though the name 'Accrington' is of Saxon origin. In 1801 it was really no more than a growing village, with a population of 3,000, but by 1911 this village had grown into an important town with a population of 45,000. With the invention of textile machines in the latter part of the 18th century the factory system of production was made possible, and Accrington developed rapidly as a factory town.

As trade increased so better communications became necessary, and the old routes were replaced by new turnpike roads. These were later supplemented by the Leeds · and Liverpool Canal as well as by three railway lines to Manchester, Blackburn and Burnley. As with many other textile towns, the early pre-eminence of calico printing in Accrington was soon superseded by cotton manufacture, and in particular cotton weaving. By the middle of the 19th century Accrington also began to develop as a town producing textile machinery side by side with the making and finishing of cotton goods, and this continued until the economic depression of the 1930s.

In addition to a multiplicity of factories, mills and terraced houses the growth of Accrington during the Industrial Revolution brought with it some important civic buildings, as a result of

*The Market Hall in Accrington*

the patronage of the early manufacturers. In 1815, for example, Jonathan Peel financed the construction of Peel Street and Church Street as well as St. James' National School, while in 1821-22 Thomas Hargreaves founded Warner Street. Many of the industrialists were also ardent churchmen, and a large number of churches in the town were established through their generosity. In 1850 it was decided to erect a monument to the statesman Sir Robert Peel, whose family were the biggest landowners and employers in the district, and as a result what is now the Town Hall was built in 1858. This was followed by the Market Hall in 1868 and the Public Baths in 1879.

Close by is the Parish Church of St. James which dates back to 1763 but is the direct descendant of the original Akerington Chapel first recorded in 1546. To the south of the town centre is Christ Church, an early Victorian church surrounded by some interesting groups of 19th century houses, while further south still is Oak Hill Park,

*Accrington Town Hall*

another private benefaction to the town. Next to Oak Hill Park is Haworth Park and Art Gallery, bequeathed to the Corporation of Accrington in 1920. This substantial property was built in 1909 as the private residence of William and Anne Haworth, the children of Thomas Haworth who had founded the family fortune as a cotton magnate at the height of the Victorian age. William Haworth developed the family business but also took an active part in Accrington's affairs generally, and it was his will that the house and grounds should be given over to the town as a public art gallery, museum and park.

*Doorway, Accrington Town Hall*

*Doorway, Haworth Art Gallery*

The house itself is built in an imitation Tudor style which is manifested externally by tall chimneys and high gables, and internally by oak panelling and the fine main staircase. As well as displaying several collections of important Victorian watercolour paintings the Haworth Art Gallery is also the home of one of the world's finest collections of Tiffany 'Favrile' glass, the highly decorative and intricately styled glassware in the Art Nouveau style that was the rage of American high society at the turn of the century. The 130 or so pieces represent the biggest single collection in Europe and are displayed within their own room at the Gallery.

Just half a dozen miles to the north east of Accrington is **Burnley,** a town that boasts of the same array of attractions which makes this and the other East Lancashire towns such fascinating places to visit — superb historic houses, a well preserved industrial heritage and some delightful surrounding countryside. It is hardly surprising then that Burnley should lay claim to the title of 'Capital of the Pennines'. The town prides itself on the fact that within its boundaries, encompassing an area of 50 square miles, are some of the finest examples of the region's historical, industrial and cultural heritage; it is also an ideal base from which to explore the many other places of interest which lie immediately beyond it.

Burnley itself is situated at the confluence of the River Brun (from which it derives its name) and the River Calder, and the first settlement was probably established here around 800 AD in the area now occupied by St. Peter's Church. By the end of the 13th century Burnley had grown sufficiently to merit the granting of a market charter and the

right to hold an annual fair, and in addition a fulling mill for the finishing off of woollen cloth. The latter was really the start of what eventually became the town's textile industry, but the market was also important because of the gradual growth which it produced during the succeeding centuries.

As with Lancashire's other textile towns it was the Industrial Revolution which really brought about Burnley's growth in size and prosperity, and during the course of the 19th century it developed into the world's leading producer of cotton cloth with a population of almost 100,000. The first weaving factory had been built on the banks of the River Calder as early as 1736, but it was the construction of the Leeds and Liverpool Canal towards the end of the 18th century that effectively opened up the town as a major industrial centre. One of the best examples of this industrial heritage is the Weavers' Triangle, an area astride the Leeds and Liverpool Canal to the south of the town centre which today constitutes one of the best preserved Victorian landscapes in Britain. Here can be seen numerous weaving sheds, spinning mills, warehouses, iron foundries and workers' cottages, representing a good cross-section of the buildings in a typical 19th century mill town.

Also important is the Leeds and Liverpool Canal itself, especially the Burnley Embankment which carries the canal from north to south across the town centre - this was regarded as one of the 'seven wonders' of the British waterways system, by virtue of its length of three-quarters of a mile and the fact that it contains some 350,000 cubic yards of earth. There were several problems which had to be overcome in taking the canal

*The Leeds and Liverpool Canal in Burnley*

through the town, so it is not surprising that the Burnley section was one of the costliest and most difficult to construct. The Leeds and Liverpool Canal, which constitutes such an important feature in Lancashire's landscape generally, was originally part of a larger but unfulfilled scheme to link the ports of Liverpool and Hull, and even the shortened version took a total of 50 years to construct from the first survey in 1766 to its completion in 1816.

Another facet of Burnley's industrial heritage is Queen Street Mill at Harle Syke, to the north east of the town centre. This is Britain's last remaining steam powered weaving mill, restored to working order as an authentic example of a 19th century weaving shed built when the cotton industry was at its height. The aim of this project has been to preserve an important part of Lancashire's textile industry by re-establishing a traditional cotton manufacturing enterprise through the creation of new jobs, as well as the training of young people in traditional manufacturing processes.

Queen Street Mill was built by the Queen Street Manufacturing Company, established in 1894 as a co-operative with 4,000 shares of £5 each; most of these were purchased by local people, with the shareholders being entitled to operate a number of looms in the mill. Even up to its closure in 1982 the Queen Street Mill continued to be run along 'co-operative' lines, and many of the last workers at the mill were direct descendants of the original shareholders. At its peak there were over 1,000 looms operating here, generally

*Queen Street Mill, Harle Syke*

producing plain calico cloth as a base for printed cottons. One of the particularly impressive features of the mill is the 500 horsepower tandem compound steam engine which provides the power required to run the looms.

The civic pride which is such a feature of the Victorian era in many of Lancashire's towns is epitomised in Burnley by the Mechanics'

Institute, recently restored by the local authority as an Arts and Entertainment Centre. This splendid building, designed by James Greene and opened in 1855, is a local example of the much wider Mechanics' Institute movement which began and flourished in the industrial areas of Lancashire and West Yorkshire during the early 19th century - a movement that recognised the need for better standards of education and expertise among the rapidly expanding workforce which was having to come to terms with the new technology of the Industrial Revolution. In addition to improving the education of this workforce the Burnley Mechanics' Institute also acted as a social and cultural centre, and for a hundred years or so it played a major part in the educational, cultural and social life of Burnley. Built by public subscription it symbolised the positive side of the Victorian era and became a venue for many of the greatest speakers of the age.

Yet Burnley's heritage consists of much more than its industrial legacy — it also embraces two historic houses whose owners have made a significant contribution to both local and national life. The first of these houses is **Towneley Hall,** one of Burnley's finest buildings and the home of the Towneley family from the 14th century until 1902 when it was purchased by the Corporation for use as an art gallery and museum. During the Middle Ages the house was built around a central courtyard and incorporated a Great Hall, where many of the normal household activities took place, but in the 1720s this Great Hall was replaced by a massive entrance hall in the Baroque style. Further alterations were made by Charles Towneley,

*Burnley Mechanics' Institute*

*Towneley Hall*

the Connoisseur (1737-1805), who also improved the gardens as well as the surrounding estate.

The gardens, laid out and planted in the English landscape style to provide winding woodland walks and uninterrupted views of the countryside beyond, are still the basis of today's park, while the brew house and laundry have also survived from this period. The present-day appearance of the Hall is largely the work of Jeffry Wyatt, whose plans for Peregrine Towneley were aimed at remodelling the whole building to give it a Tudor appearance. However, he was largely confined to replacing the 18th century sash windows with regularly placed mullion windows and to adding battlements and turrets as well as a new porch.

Inside Towneley Hall are some splendid period rooms furnished in the appropriate style and sumptuously decorated. The entrance hall, for example, has some fine 18th century plasterwork undertaken by two itinerant stuccoists from the Italian-speaking part of Switzerland, as well as the Towneley arms over the doorway and a long 17th century oak table brought from nearby Barcroft Hall. Elsewhere on the ground floor is the kitchen, furnished as it would have appeared in the second half of the 19th century and featuring a roasting spit driven by hot air from the chimney, as well as the housekeeper's room and the servants' hall.

On the first floor can be found the Towneley Chapel, with its intricately carved 16th century Flemish oak altarpiece brought over from Antwerp by Charles Towneley; there is

also a 15th century font cover originally from Scarisbrick Hall as well as an oak chest of the same period which is said to have come from Manchester Cathedral. On the same floor is the Parlour, the Family Dining Room and the Towneley Room, the latter featuring a fireplace dated 1737 signifying when this part of the house was built. Above these rooms are the two art galleries, which contain a collection of over 250 watercolours by 18th and 19th century English artists. There are also four works by Turner, who was brought to Lancashire in 1799 by Charles Towneley to illustrate Whitaker's 'History of Whalley'.

Of the other items on display at Towneley Hall the most important are the Whalley Abbey vestments, said to have been brought here for safe-keeping by Sir John Towneley at the dissolution of the monasteries in the 16th century. They date from 1390-1420 and form the only surviving complete pre-Reformation set of English High Mass vestments apart from a 16th century set at St. John's College. The mediaeval embroidery which they epitomise has never been equalled, and as an art form it has been compared to the finest painting and architecture of that period. Known as Opus Anglicanum it was exported throughout Europe and was an expensive craft practised by the highest ranks of society and by men organised in workshops.

The second of Burnley's stately historic houses is **Gawthorpe Hall,** on the north west side of the town, a beautiful Jacobean mansion set within secluded wooded grounds and the home of the Shuttleworth family for 400 years. Built to a design by Robert Smythson between 1600 and 1605,

this important building still retains its original drawing room with the fine plaster ceiling, panelling and fireplace in an unaltered state. The remainder of the house is largely the work of Sir Charles Barry, architect of the Houses of Parliament, who remodelled Gawthorpe for the Shuttleworth family between 1850 and 1852. He heightened the tower, added an open work parapet, installed new pinnacles to accommodate extra chimney flues and also altered some of the windows. Inside he constructed a new staircase, altered the entrance lobby, added more fireplaces and generally modernised the whole property. He also prepared an ambitious layout for the surrounding gardens, although this was not implemented until the 1890s.

All this work had been undertaken on the instructions of Dr. James Kay, later Sir James Kay-Shuttleworth, who had come into possession of the estate through his marriage to the heiress Janet Shuttleworth. Visitors to the Hall during their time included the Bronte sisters, Mrs. Gaskell and Thomas Hughes, author of 'Tom Brown's Schooldays'. Sir James Kay-Shuttleworth devoted his life to philanthropic works, with one of his greatest efforts being his successful campaign for free education for all.

Gawthorpe Hall's important features include not only the drawing room and its original plaster ceiling but also the Great Hall with its minstrel gallery, some beautiful oak panelling and a fine collection of period furniture. Also on display is the internationally famous Rachel Kay-Shuttleworth collection of lace, embroidery and costumes. The nearby Coach House has been converted into a craft centre and National Trust shop, whilst next door is the Great Barn. Built between 1600 and 1610 and featuring some magnificent timber beams as well as a huge stone flagged

*Gawthorpe Hall*

*Gawthorpe Hall in all its glory*

roof, this is one of the finest structures of its kind in the north of England and has recently been restored for use as a multi-purpose Arts Centre.

Leaving Burnley and heading northwards we come to **Brierfield,** which up to the start of the 19th century was just a small hamlet in an area known as Little Marsden. Then coal was discovered in the vicinity and within a few years three pits had been established employing many people who came across from Yorkshire. The advent firstly of turnpike roads and then of the Leeds and Liverpool Canal gave a further boost to industry here, as goods could now be conveyed at very cheap rates. By 1833 the growing transport systems of the area, coupled with the humid and equable climatic conditions, proved decisive in the establishment of a handloom weaving business in Brierfield, which laid a foundation for the subsequent cotton industry. The new business prospered, and soon power looms replaced handlooms and steam replaced waterpower for driving the machinery. By the end of the 19th century the cotton industry

*The Great Barn at Gawthorpe*

had become the main source of employment in Brierfield and remained so for many years.

To the north of Brierfield is **Nelson,** a town which is also very largely a product of the 19th century textile industry. Although there had been some handloom weaving in this area of scattered farms and cottages during the 18th century, it was not until nearly 100 years later that its industrial growth really took hold - firstly with the opening of the Leeds and Liverpool Canal, which gave access to the docks at Liverpool for consignments of raw cotton, and then with the coming of the railway. The focal point for this emerging town was the Nelson Inn, a public house named after the famous admiral, and it was from this inn that Nelson took its name — although it was actually situated within the parishes of Great Marsden and Little Marsden.

Despite its industrial growth Nelson has never lost touch with the countryside, helped very largely by its location on one side of the valley of Pendle Water. Consequently there are open fields and splendid panoramas on both sides of the town — to the west the lovely

*The Lord Nelson, Nelson town centre*

countryside gives way to the foothills of Pendle Hill itself, and to the east is open country for 15 miles or so until the outskirts of Halifax are reached. In the midst of all this is Pendle Water flowing along the valley

bottom, as well as the Leeds and Liverpool Canal a little higher up on the side of the valley. No doubt all this easily accessible natural beauty has helped to preserve the traditional character of the area despite its rapid industrial expansion.

Neighbouring **Colne** has a similar story to Nelson's in terms of its growth during the Victorian period, but its history as a settlement in its own right stretches back much further. There is some suggestion that a Roman military station was established in this locality, although the earliest relic to be found here was a 7th century cross indicating that Christian missionaries must have arrived in the area at about that time. After the Norman Conquest the manor of Colne was granted to the de Lacy family, who were probably responsible for the building of the first recorded church here in 1122, and by the following century the first fulling mill had been established on Colne Water.

During the mediaeval period Colne developed as a market centre for the surrounding district and experienced considerable prosperity through the growth of its wool trade. This was initially in the hands of local farmers, whose wealth enabled them to build large houses in and around Colne, but by the 18th century their role was taken over by master weavers. These new 'entrepreneurs' hired workers and accommodated them in tall houses, where they lived under cramped conditions on the lower floors and worked at the looms on the top floors. Such living quarters generally went with the job, and failure to maintain work meant the loss of a home.

With the continued expansion of the local wool trade a new Cloth Hall was built in 1775 to enable the master weavers to display their goods to the Yorkshire merchants, although this building was demolished during the

*St. Bartholomew's Parish Church, Colne*

*The Old Grammar School, Colne*

middle of the 20th century. Then gradually the nature of Colne's industry changed as it was found that the climate of much of Lancashire was highly suitable for the spinning and weaving of cotton, and by 1824 there were only three wool manufacturers left in the town as opposed to 22 mills manufacturing cotton. These were mainly producing calico, although as technology improved so they were able to make finer textiles. The town's reliance upon one main industry brought disadvantages, however, and the 'Colne Strike' of 1861-62 (during which over 1,000 weavers were kept on strike pay for eleven months) set back the growth of the town by 25 years whilst at the same time accelerating the growth of its neighbours. Gradually higher standards of living did return, although Colne also suffered from the recession in the textile industry which hit the Lancashire cotton towns during the early part of the 20th century.

Most of Colne's more important buildings can be found on either side of the main road through the town, and a good place to start a brief journey of discovery is at St. Bartholomew's parish church on the section appropriately named Church Street. The interior of this church still retains some later Norman pillars supporting 13th century arches along the north side of the nave, although the largest part of St. Bartholomew's is of the Late Perpendicular period when it was enlarged and enriched by the generosity of prosperous local cloth merchants.

Features of interest inside the church include a font and richly carved screens from the 16th century, as well as three lozenge shaped hatchments in the nave and chancel bearing the heraldic devices of the great local families.

Over the south porch is a large sundial. The churchyard was the original location for a set of unique stocks mounted on wheels which are now housed in the local heritage centre; these stocks have three pairs of holes and are said to have been last used as late as June 1850. Close by is the former Church School, an old grammar school dating from 1812, as well as the subterranean 'charnel house' where the sexton deposited fragments of bones brought up when new graves were being dug.

A little further down on the same side, where Church Street joins up with Albert Road, is the Town Hall. This was built in 1894 to a neo-Gothic style. Close by are Stanley Villa and Bank House, good examples of the

*The Town Hall in Colne*

imposing homes of some of Colne's wealthier residents during its 19th century period of prosperity. By way of contrast one can see some of the early 'back to back' cottages, which would have been occupied by the poorer working-class people, just round the corner in Spring Lane. Passing the rather grandiose Edwardian building which was originally a four storey Co-operative department store we come to The Gables, which was built for Nicholas England in 1870 after his rise in fortune as a pioneer in cotton manufacturing in the town.

Nearby is The Rectory of St. Bartholomew's, dating from 1829, and then at the bottom of Albert Road is the Crown Hotel, occupying the site of an old coaching inn which was re-built in 1853 in conjunction with the coming of the railway. Returning up Albert Road and Church Street on the south side we come eventually to the King's Head, another public house which was also a coaching stop at the end of the 18th century. During the Colne Chartist riots of 1840 the local magistrates had to barricade themselves in here until they were rescued by troops from Burnley. Further along Church Street is the site of the old Cloth Hall, used originally for the sale of worsted goods and then later adopted for public meetings, while beyond here on Market Street are another two of Colne's historic public houses (the 'Hole i'th Wall' and the Red Lion). It was this locality, at the junction of Market Street and Windy Bank, which acted as the focal point for Colne's growth during the 17th and 18th centuries, in comparison to its 19th century growth which took place lower down along Albert Road.

Colne is the birthplace of two particularly noteworthy people. One of these was Sir

*The Wallace Hartley Memorial, Colne*

William Pickles Hartley, whose fruit preserving empire in Liverpool began from rather more humble origins in Colne when he persuaded his parents to introduce jam making to their small grocery shop. The other was Wallace Hartley, the gallant bandmaster who led his band in the piece 'Nearer, my God, to Thee' as the liner Titanic went down on her maiden voyage in 1912.

If places like Nelson and Colne saw their most dramatic growth during the course of the Industrial Revolution, it was often at the expense of previously well established villages like **Wycoller** just a few miles to the east. Wycoller is now the prettiest spot you could imagine and a delightful place to visit, but until it was made into a country park fairly recently it was very much a 'forgotten village', on the verge of being lost beneath the sands of time as the forces of nature took their toll. Wycoller has its origins in farming, and for centuries it was a typical agricultural manorial village. In the late 18th and early 19th centuries, however, the manufacture of woollens and worsteds developed so rapidly as to make this the predominant local industry, with most of the village's population of 350 being employed within Wycoller as handloom weavers.

Then almost as quickly Wycoller became a 'ghost village' as the development of the power loom and the factory system during the Industrial Revolution led to the relocation and expansion of the textile industry in other places; the resident handloom weavers could not compete with the new technology and they were forced to seek work in towns such as Nelson and Colne. Alongside this went the decline of Wycoller Hall at the centre of the village, which was abandoned in 1818 after the death of the last of the Cunliffe family; during the course of the following years the centuries-old house fell into a crumbling ruin as people robbed it of its historic stones. The end result of all this was that Wycoller became almost deserted, a tumbledown place with only a handful of inhabitants who tended to live in the poor farm cottages rather than in any of the houses which lined the main street.

Then in the 1970s the local authorities and other interested bodies stepped in to rescue the village from oblivion by designating it a

*The ruins of Wycoller Hall*

country park and Conservation Area. This set in motion the process whereby not only have the houses been restored for people to live in again, but the village in general has been revived and facilities made available for visitors to the area. These facilities include a new information centre within the former coach house of Wycoller Hall as well as a car park on the edge of the village. Wycoller Hall itself was beyond restoration, however, and it remains a romantic ruin — particularly as it is said to have been the model for Ferndean Manor in Charlotte Bronte's book 'Jane Eyre', and so continues as a place of literary pilgrimage for Bronte lovers from all over the world.

The Hall is still a striking feature of the village nevertheless, despite its ruined condition, and of particular interest is the huge open fireplace in the former dining room, with its stone settle extending completely around the back of the fire. It is said that the Cunliffes kept 'open house' during the twelve days of Christmas and that the children of the neighbourhood used this settle as a gathering place because of its cosy atmosphere. To the right of the fireplace is an unusual keyhole-shaped opening which has been variously described as a powder closet, a cavity for containing pots and pans, or the head of a well.

Another unusual feature of this delightful village is its bridges — in a distance of less than a mile there are seven crossings over the bubbling Wycoller Beck, most of them being of considerable antiquity. Upstream from the village is the 'clam bridge', a solid slab of gritstone which is the most primitive of Wycoller's crossings, while nearer to the Hall is a 'clapper bridge' which ranks as one of the most interesting early bridges in England. Originally constructed of two long blocks supported on a central pier, the bridge now appears as three slabs of gritstone resting on two supports since it was damaged by the fall of a heavy tree during the 19th century. The

*The 'clapper bridge' in Wycoller*

clapper bridge is also known as the Weavers' Bridge because of its use by generations of handloom weavers who lived in the village, and it was also referred to as the Druids' Bridge in times past because of the legend that it led to an amphitheatre where the Druids made their human sacrifices.

Close by is an old packhorse bridge, said to date from the 13th century — here the voussoirs, or arch-shaped stones, extend the complete width of the bridge and for a considerable time were the actual paving surface of this structure, having to withstand the constant traffic of men and packhorse trains. Further downstream are two more stone bridges, one of which is said to have been constructed from the arch of the cellars of Wycoller Hall. In addition to these fascinating bridges there are also several fords crossing the stream as well as the remains of stepping stones.

From Wycoller our journey around the outskirts of Colne, Nelson and Burnley takes us firstly to the close-knit community of **Trawden** before reaching more of East Lancashire's isolated uplands. The earliest settlers here appear to have been farmers who mined their own coal from opencast sites around the village, although cotton weaving quickly became the dominant activity in Trawden during the early part of the Industrial Revolution. Like many other places the contraction of the textile industry brought considerable problems to a community whose workforce had been brought up largely on the loom. Immediately to the north of Trawden is the picturesque hilltop settlement of **Winewall,** whose main claim to fame focuses upon the Inghamite church which was built here in 1752. Winewall was one of the few places in Lancashire to have a

church of this little-known denomination, and it was from here in the 19th century that some members set off across the Atlantic to found the only overseas Inghamite church at Brantford in Ontario.

Between Trawden and the village of Worsthorne, immediately to the east of Burnley, the moorland is frequently characterised by a series of mounds, gorges and piles of stone. These are properly known as 'limestone hushings' and are the remains of an opencast mining industry which was directed towards the production of lime during the 17th and 18th centuries. As the limestone was not readily available on the surface, artificial streams or 'hushings' were created along the hill slopes in order to wash out the limestone, a method which was used with similar effect by lead miners and gold prospectors. This method of extraction developed into quite a fine art, with goits (or channels) being dug and streams being diverted. Water was also collected in head ponds, with outlet goits being excavated to direct the water over the hill slopes and so wash away the soil. The stones which were brought down by these artificial streams were then sorted, with the limestone being carried to nearby kilns or delivered to local farmers and the waste discarded in the form of vast spreads or 'sheddings'.

To produce lime required that the limestone be 'burnt', and in this area such burning was carried out in 'country' kilns. Generally of a moderate size they were constructed in a simple fashion using readily available materials, and were usually built into the side or on the top of the sheddings of previous workings. The process began with the chamber of the kiln being filled with fuel and limestone, which would burn for about 60

hours. It was then emptied, re-charged and fired again. In larger kilns the fires were never drawn, and fresh limestone was added as the burnt limestone was removed. The limestone was thus converted into 'quicklime', which on contact with water became a very effective fertiliser for the acidic soils in this area. The lime was also used to produce building mortar. The organisers of the limestone hushing industry employed local farmers who used these traditional 'country' techniques, but on a commercial basis. In certain instances both burnt and unburnt limestone was delivered to local farmers from the limestone hushings as some farmers chose to burn the limestone themselves, and the remains of their kilns can sometimes be seen in the corners of fields.

It seems that the work in this local industry was essentially seasonal, with hushing taking place in the winter and limestone burning in the summer and autumn. However, with the construction of the Leeds and Liverpool Canal at the end of the 18th century limestone hushing was brought to a finish since the raw material could now be transported much more cheaply from Craven. The extraction of lime was also now able to be undertaken on a much bigger scale, and when the limestone arrived in Burnley it was burnt in large commercial kilns. The days of limestone hushing were thus soon over and quickly forgotten, but recent archaeological explorations have revealed the very considerable extent of this local industry and have provided the basis of an historic 'limestone hushings trail' on Worsthorne Moor.

The village of **Worsthorne** itself is a pretty little place with the local parish church as its focal point. It is also a place which has remained relatively unchanged over the years, despite its proximity to Burnley. Worsthorne's roots are in farming (and there are still working farms at the centre of the village), although this was later supplemented with some local coal mining as well as the traditional handloom weaving which took place in many of Lancashire's early communities. Before the Leeds and Liverpool Canal came into being the village also saw some packhorse traffic passing through here on the limestone trail between Skipton and Burnley.

As well as its close association with the land, Worsthorne has also enjoyed a long and beneficial association with the Thursby family; during the 19th century members of this family proved great benefactors not only in Burnley generally but also in Worsthorne in particular, and the parish church of St. John the Evangelist was constructed and endowed largely through their generous contributions. This church has the unusual distinction of having its own licensed bar in a community room within the tower, which has obviously

*A typical 'limestone hushings' area to the east of Burnley*

contributed to its role as the centre of the parish's social life.

A short distance across the fields to the south east of Worsthorne is the village of **Hurstwood,** one of the finest Elizabethan hamlets in the north of England. This delightful little architectural gem lies peacefully in the midst of a wooded hollow alongside the River Brun, exuding great charm and character. Included amongst its attractive old buildings are Hurstwood Hall, built in 1579 by Barnard Towneley, and Tattersall's House, another late 16th century building owned by the Tattersall family who went on to found the famous Tattersall's bloodstock auction firm at Newmarket. There is also the very pleasing gabled Elizabethan cottage known as 'Spenser's House', the home of the grandparents of the Elizabethan poet Edmund Spenser who lived here for two years after obtaining his degree at Cambridge in 1576. His poetic lament 'The Shepherd's Calendar' was inspired by his unrequited romance with a local girl.

The village of **Holme Chapel,** situated in the Cliviger Gorge just two miles to the south of Hurstwood, is the setting for another important historic house whose owners have played a major part in the development of the surrounding area. Land here in Cliviger was administered from Kirkstall Abbey in the 12th and 13th centuries, but eventually part of this became the estate of the Whitaker family from the 15th century onwards. Their first dwelling was a half-timbered affair, but by 1603 this had been re-built in stone and was the beginning of the substantial house now known as The Holme. An impressive feature of The Holme is its main staircase with a beautiful stained glass window which overlooks the half-landing; much of this glass is said to have been recovered from Whalley Abbey, although it also incorporates a panel bearing the Whitaker family crest.

*Spenser's House, Hurstwood*

Probably the most important member of the Whitaker family to have lived here was Dr. Thomas Dunham Whitaker, whose 'History of the Parish of Whalley' was a pioneering work. He commissioned Turner to provide the illustrations for this, and the famous painter was a frequent guest at The Holme. Dr. Whitaker was also involved in the excavations of the ruins of Whalley Abbey and Ribchester, but perhaps more important for Cliviger he did much to enhance the appearance of the surrounding valley. The woodland areas which now clothe the formerly bare and rocky gorge are the result of his efforts, and he is said to have been responsible for the planting of 422,000 trees. In addition he laid out miles of scenic walkways as well as several lakes.

It was also Dr. Whitaker who was responsible for the building in 1788 of St. John's Church in Holme Chapel, an interesting Baroque-style edifice featuring an octagonal cupola mounted on a small square tower. As well as containing the private chapel of the Whitaker family this church is famous as being the burial place of General Sir James Yorke Scarlett, who led the successful charge of the Heavy Brigade at Balaclava. This had taken place on the same day in October 1854 as the heroic, but futile, charge of the Light Brigade against the Russian guns in the 'valley of death'. Scarlett's force of less than 600 men managed to rout over 3,000 Russian cavalry on ground that favoured the enemy.

From this point in the village one can enjoy another of Holme Chapel's assets — its extensive views up and down the wooded Cliviger Gorge. Looking across the valley and beyond the River Calder one can see the impressive escarpment of Thieveley Scout, a series of craggy rocks rising high above the tree-clad slopes beneath. Thieveley escarpment was the scene of at least two attempts to mine lead here during the 17th and 18th centuries, but both efforts failed. Beyond Thieveley Scout is Thieveley Pike and Beacon Rock, the latter being part of the countrywide chain of beacons which were used for warning-fires during times of national peril or celebration. In more recent years the site was put to its traditional use when a beacon was lit here to celebrate Queen Elizabeth II's Silver Jubilee.

A brief descent southwards from the high point of Beacon Rock overlooking Cliviger Gorge brings us to the headwaters of the River Irwell and another of Lancashire's

*The Holme, Cliviger*

famous industrial valleys — the **Rossendale Valley.** During the second half of the 19th century the prosperity and wealth of this part of the county was such that Rossendale became known as the 'Golden Valley', and excursions were organised from Blackpool for holidaymakers to come and see the area. There was also quite a remarkable movement in the opposite direction in that a number of Rossendale's more important industrialists banded together to build the Fylde resort of St. Anne's-on-the-Sea, the intention being that they could eventually live there and commute back to their workplaces. With the industrial recessions of the 20th century, however, the prosperity of the Golden Valley inevitably faded, leaving behind it a considerable legacy of dereliction, but with the environmental improvements of recent years Rossendale has suddenly become Lancashire's 'Green Valley' offering tremendous opportunities for leisure and recreation whilst at the same time retaining its fascinating industrial heritage.

During the period after the Norman Conquest much of the Rossendale area was in the hands of the Crown as a royal hunting ground — hence the name 'Forest of Rossendale' — and apart from one small monastic community in the 13th century no real settlement took place here until the 1400s when the Crown began to lease off parts of the Forest. The final clearance of the Forest of Rossendale began in 1504, when land was leased at 4d per acre. As it became the custom for inhabitants to split the land between their sons the holdings themselves became smaller and less economic, with the result that people were forced to supplement their income through the spinning and weaving of wool. This developed on a small-scale initially and was entirely 'home based', but by the early part of the 18th century it was producing a considerable expansion of population in the area which in turn led to the construction of many new cottages and farmhouses.

During the course of the 18th century there were some important advances in textile technology which brought about the introduction of water-powered mills in Rossendale, helped by the fact that here there were numerous narrow tributary valleys with fast-flowing streams. It was at this time too that cotton began to be imported into the area to challenge wool's traditional dominance, with the damp climate proving decisive in Lancashire's attraction of this new fibre. The handloom weavers of Rossendale could not compete with the new power looms, and the majority were forced to seek work in the mills. By 1844 there were 80 cotton spinning and weaving mills in Rossendale with a further 10 calico printing and bleaching mills, and with the mills came rows of workers' houses which led to a line of continuous building development along most of the valleys.

In addition to textiles coalmining was also an important local industry, and by 1820 there were seven coalmines operating in the area. This led to a gradual change from water power to steam power in the textile industry, and the development of new and larger mills in the main valleys because of their better communications. Quarrying was another significant activity in 19th century Rossendale, with Haslingden flagstone being much in demand as a paving material. By the latter 1800s most of the larger quarries and many of the coalmines were connected to the main railway lines or the main roads by a series of tramways across the moors.

It was at about this time that the Rossendale footwear industry was developed, although its origins can be traced back to 1854 when Edward Rostron came over the Pennines from Yorkshire to establish the first felt works here — and so set in motion the process which was to result in Rossendale becoming one of the leading felt manufacturing areas in the country by the end of the century. Slippers were the first product of the footwear industry, and at its height around the turn of the century 3,000 people were employed in 13 factories. Slipper production then began to give way to boots and shoes, and although the industry has been hit by recessions and overseas competition at different times during the present century it has managed to survive rather better than some of Rossendale's other industries. From about 1920 onwards quarrying declined dramatically and many of the mineral tramways fell into disuse; the coalmining industry also suffered a decline, as did the textile industry which is now very small.

Textiles were certainly the lifeblood of **Bacup,** one of Rossendale's main towns, and it is still said to be the best remaining example of a small Lancashire cotton town even though many of the mills and terraced houses have now disappeared. At its heart is the town centre, which encompasses a number of interesting Victorian buildings including the one-time Market Hall, the Maden Baths and the Conservative Club. One can also discover some old sandstone setted roads, indicating how Bacup's highways appeared in the last century, as well as a number of traditionally styled Victorian shopfronts. Overlooking the compact town centre, from their elevated position on the slopes to the west, are several 19th century residences, built to provide appropriately comfortable accommodation for some of Bacup's wealthier residents of the time.

From Bacup the road heads firstly southwards and then westwards as it makes its way to Rawtenstall, through the steep-sided gorge containing the River Irwell. En route it passes the settlement of **Stacksteads,** a community of attractive old buildings dominated by the Victorian parish church as well as by some older industrial properties. Further along the road is **Waterfoot,** a village which developed rapidly after the opening of the railway and attained some importance during the Victorian period as a manufacturing centre. Probably its most important building is the fine shopping arcade built by Sir Henry Trickett at the junction of Bacup Road and Burnley Road East. Sir Henry, one of Rossendale's most important slipper manufacturers during the latter part of the 19th century and five times Mayor of Rawtenstall, had wanted Waterfoot to become the shopping centre for the Rossendale area. A memorial plaque to Sir Henry can be found beneath the arcade clock.

The village's Victorian heritage is particularly evident from the fine front elevation of the Royal Hotel, which dates from 1876, as well

*Bacup Town Centre*

as from the similarly dated Barclays Bank and the fine National Westminster Bank which was built at the turn of the century. The Railway Inn appeared during the middle of the 19th century following the opening of the railway here. Just across the main road and over the River Irwell is the Duke of Buccleugh Hotel, which stands on the site of Waterfoot's earliest mentioned buildings. The building opposite and those just to the east backing on to the river are amongst the oldest remaining in the village, while just beyond the former railway line are some one-time railway cottages.

To the north of Waterfoot is **Newchurch,** a village with some well preserved 17th century houses as well as good views of the valley below. In addition to possessing some fine old pubs, in the form of the 17th century Boar's Head and the Bluebell Inn, the parish church of St. Nicholas is also of interest; although the present structure was largely rebuilt in 1824 it is located on one of the oldest religious sites in Rossendale. Newchurch is an attractive residential area, and one which judging from its imposing Victorian villas was obviously a popular place to live for some of Rossendale's 19th century industrialists — 'Ashlands' enjoys a fine landscaped setting and was built in 1863 for Richard Ashworth, a local felt manufacturer and orchid grower, while 'Heightside' is a magnificent mansion previously owned by the Bolton family, owners of a coalmine in Burnley, who greatly extended and remodelled it in the late 1800s.

From Newchurch the road down into **Rawtenstall** follows the line of the Haslingden-Newchurch turnpike road built in 1795, bringing us out onto the northern side of the town centre. The earliest recorded reference to Rawtenstall was in connection with the Hundred of Blackburn in 1323, when it was mainly a district of cow pastures amidst the moorlands of the Forest of Rossendale. Eventually Rawtenstall developed into an important woollen centre, with the processes all being undertaken by hand workers using water power until steam power was introduced during the early 19th century. At about this time the cotton trade began to make its appearance here, and local industrialisation was further assisted by the construction of turnpike roads. These linked the Rossendale Valley with Manchester in the late 18th century so that stage coaches were able to provide a regular service between there and Rawtenstall. Then by 1846 the railway line from Rossendale through Bury to Manchester was completed and in use, and in the later part of the 19th century Rawtenstall also benefited from the introduction of felt manufacture at Waterfoot and the consequent development of the slipper and footwear industry.

Close to where the road from Newchurch enters Rawtenstall there are a number of old cottages still in existence which highlight its pre-industrial existence. Among these are Newhouses Cottages in Grange Avenue, which date from 1695. Inside one of the dwellings is a witch post, with a cross marked on the main upright by the hearth to ward off evil influences. Outside on one of the walls is the remains of a hook indicating that shutters were once hung here in the times before glass came into common use. Evidence of Rawtenstall's early textile trade is to be found in the form of the interesting three storey Weavers' Cottages in Fallbarn Fold to the south east of the town centre. This late 18th century building is one of Rossendale's finest surviving examples of a 'loomshop', a half-way house between the small handloom weaver's cottage and the mill. The top two storeys feature the characteristically long ranges of mullioned windows, which were needed to provide the maximum amount of light required for woollen weaving. With the introduction of weaving mills during the early part of the 19th century buildings such as this were no longer necessary. and by the 1860s the handloom weaving trade had largely died out.

Woolcombing was another important local trade, particularly during the first quarter of the 19th century, and its presence in Rawtenstall is remembered by the Bishop Blaize Hotel situated to the north of the town centre at the junction of St. Mary's Way and Haslingden Old Road. This building, with its attractive stone carving, takes its name from the patron saint of the woolcombers, who was a bishop in Asia Minor during the 4th century. The festival in honour of Bishop Blaize was traditionally celebrated with great pomp and ceremony in this area. Across St. Mary's Way from here is the Ram's Head Hotel, known locally as The Tup's Head and dating from the late 18th or early 19th century. Its fine clock displaying Roman numerals was made by J. Greaves of Rawtenstall, indicating that clock making was also once a local craft.

Looking westwards from here one can see the terraced streets of a typical 19th century north east Lancashire housing area, while to the south is Bank Street and the main commercial thoroughfare in Rawtenstall. Here too are numerous Victorian buildings which typify Rawtenstall's industrial prosperity — these include the Jubilee Buildings, a property erected in 1887 by the owners of the Ram's Head Hotel to commemorate Queen Victoria's Golden Jubilee, and the National Westminster Bank, one of the town's most ornate Victorian buildings and representative of the imposing quality of bank architecture generally. Not far away is the Midland Bank, smaller but no less solid and having a very attractive stone balustrade along the first floor as well as a fine door with a lovely arched window above it.

The southern end of Bank Street is terminated by St. Mary's Way, and across this dual carriageway is another group of

*Fallbarn Fold, Rawtenstall*

buildings which date largely from Rawtenstall's industrial heyday. Among them is what remains of Lower Mill, started in 1840 by the Whitehead brothers who were some of Rossendale's early manufacturing pioneers. These three brothers and their families were also strong pillars of local Victorian society and their impact on the district was considerable and long lasting. Beyond the mill is Holly Mount House which was built by the Whitehead brothers in 1835 for their own use, while somewhat closer to hand is the clock tower of Holly Mount School, the school being built by the Whiteheads in 1839 for the education of the children of their employees.

The Whitehead brothers also played an important role in Rawtenstall's religious affairs, and after having contributed to the cost of Longholme Chapel just off Bacup Road they were also significantly involved in the building of the United Methodist Free Church along Haslingden Road. David Whitehead laid the foundation stone for this particularly impressive place of worship in 1856, after having left the Longholme Wesleyan Church in 1849. It seems that the Whitehead brothers had become disenchanted with growing centralisation within the Wesleyan movement, although they may also have been afraid of losing their dominant position at Longholme.

Other public buildings in this part of the town include the library, paid for by Andrew Carnegie and built in 1907 to a design resulting from an architectural competition, as well as St. Mary's Parish Church. This building dates from 1836 and was largely the result of the cotton trade and the associated population boom, which led to the need for a new church nearer at hand than the existing parish churches in nearby settlements. The church was remodelled in the 1880s when the tower was transferred to the south west side. Yet as well as some inspiring public buildings this part of Rawtenstall also has an impressive backcloth of domestic architecture, with Schofield Road exhibiting some of the most spectacular terraces of 19th century houses built up a steep hillside in the whole of north east Lancashire.

To the west of Rawtenstall is the town of **Haslingden** — like its neighbour its own history is very largely rooted in the Industrial Revolution and it has some interesting 19th century terraced houses which cling to the hillsides, but it is the Parish Church overlooking the town from an elevated position on the northern side which remains its dominant feature. The present church of St. James is very largely a Georgian building, with a tower dating back to 1827, although it was certainly in being as early as 1284 and probably stands on a site used for worship back in Saxon times. Despite the interior of the church being almost completely

*Typical weavers' cottages in the Rossendale Valley*

refurbished in 1878 it still retains a mediaeval chest and an old seven-sided font. Outside the tower of St. James is the base of a double Saxon cross sometimes known as 'The Plaguestone', while in the churchyard are a number of gravestones with humorous inscriptions. Across Church Street from St. James is Fountain House, a fine example of an early merchant's dwelling with its stone flag roof, elaborate entrance and original wooden door. Until comparatively recently this building was linked to the mill behind it.

Looking down Church Street from St. James one can see the old Market Place and an interesting cluster of three storey buildings which portrays something of the town's traditional character. Several of these properties feature 'watershot walls', a local method of construction which ensured that the stones incorporated into the wall were set at an angle so that rainwater did not run down the individual blocks but was kept away from them. On the far side of the Market Place is 'The Lindens', an important 18th century merchant's house, while around the corner on Regent Street is the Regent Hotel, with its fine sash windows, together with the Public Hall. This latter building is dated 1868 and is noted for being the place where in 1907 Mrs. Pankhurst and her suffragettes successfully disrupted a speech made by Lewis Harcourt, MP for Rossendale and a Cabinet Minister of the time. Close to 'The Lindens' on the southern side of the Market Place are more properties dating from the Georgian era, although these were generally remodelled during Victorian times. The Thorn Hotel, for example, situated on Bury Road, was originally built by the Lonsdale family at the end of the 18th century but its present appearance reflects some late Victorian influences.

Taking us southwards from the Market Place

is Deardengate, along which is situated the public library which began life in 1860 as the Mechanics' Institute, a frequently encountered Victorian institution in many of Lancashire's industrial towns. Halfway along Deardengate is the junction with Blackburn Road and Manchester Road, acting as a second focal point in the town. Here one can see a couple of late Georgian buildings, the Black Bull Hotel and the Commercial Hotel, as well as the imposing single storey Midland Bank with a clock over its entrance. The Commercial Hotel also has a fine clock, cantilevered over Manchester Road, and it was from one of the hotel's upper windows that Mrs. Pankhurst addressed her supporters in 1907.

To the west of Deardengate is an area of older properties which date back to Haslingden's early textile years, and here are to be found some particularly good examples of Pennine loomshops. One of these is Coal Hey, three pairs of early 19th century back to back cottages which had a loomshop on the top floor. On the gable end is a blocked up 'takin' in door' and the outline of an outside staircase, which indicates how access would have been gained into the loomshop. Another former loomshop is to be seen in the upper floors of the three storey building next to Well House off Blackburn Road, premises which were originally owned by the prosperous Hargreaves family who also owned other woollen loomshops in the town. Running off Blackburn Road is Townsend Street, which features some of the last 'watershot' houses to be constructed in Haslingden; erected in 1842 these still retain their original stone flag roofs and stone gutters.

Although much of the 'old town' which existed around the parish church has disappeared through demolition, a good deal of the 1827 Manchester-Blackburn turnpike road has remained intact. As well as the properties already mentioned, a number of others were erected in the name of religion and politics — including the Methodist Church and the former Liberal Club. The Manchester Road Methodist Church was opened in 1857 and is a particularly fine building in a neo-Gothic style, made all the more noteworthy because of the adjoining manse and caretaker's house, both built in a similar style in 1873. These and other buildings around the Victorian focal point of the town centre give some idea of Haslingden's wealth and importance during its industrial growth in the 19th century.

More evidence of Lancashire's early textile industry can be found in the smaller township of **Helmshore** to the south and in the nearby Musbury Valley, which was the setting for a number of water powered mills. At the heart of the area is **Higher Mill,** which is well worth a visit since it and the adjoining cotton mill have been restored as the Museum of the Lancashire Textile Industry to explain in full the development of this very significant activity. Higher Mill dates from 1789 when it was built as one of the first fulling mills in the Rossendale area; prior to that time local weavers had to travel over to Rochdale to make use of the fulling mills there, and the moorland packhorse routes would have been busy with 'chapmen' delivering and collecting cloth. Fulling was the process whereby woven wool cloth was subjected to pressure, moisture and warmth in order to interlock the constituent fibres and so produce a shrunken matted surface. The heavy dense fabric which resulted from this was then suitable for use as blankets, overcoats and numerous other items. At Higher Mill one can still see the early water driven fulling stocks which compressed the fabric by means of wedge-shaped hammers, which also partially turned it to enable the fulling to take place throughout the cloth. A 30-yard piece of cloth could take a whole working day to full in these 'fulling stocks', which ran at about 39 beats per minute. Prior to the introduction of fulling stocks the cloth would have been wetted and trampled underfoot — which may not have been a particularly pleasant experience since stale urine was often used to break down the lanolin grease in the wool before effective fulling could take place!

By the middle of the 19th century rotary milling machines had been developed which did the same job as the fulling stocks but in much less time, with the fabric being rotated in the machines as pressure was applied by spring-loaded milling rollers. After the milling (or fulling) was completed, the cloth was then passed through a scouring machine to have soap and other agents washed out of it prior to being taken through a mangle to squeeze out excess water before the cloth was dried.

At this point the cloth was crumpled and so needed to be straightened and dried under tension; in the early days this was done in the open air on the hillside to the east of the mill, but later the process was carried out inside when steam heating was available. To facilitate this long 'tenter frames' were erected on the ground floor of the adjacent mill, and so arose the saying 'to be on tenterhooks'. Once dry the cloth was finished off by being passed through a 'teasle raising gig', which pulled up the surface fibres to form a soft raised pile. In certain cases it was necessary to bleach the creamy woollen cloth and this was carried out in the 'sulphur houses'; here the wet cloth was hung on glass hooks (to prevent staining) and pots of sulphur were burnt causing sulphur dioxide to react with the wet cloth and so produce a whitened fabric.

Next door to the Higher Mill fulling museum is a three storey cotton spinning mill which now houses the Museum of the Lancashire Textile Industry. This mill was originally constructed during the early part of the 19th century but then had to be substantially rebuilt in 1859-60 following a disastrous fire. Unlike the earlier water powered fulling mill adjacent to it this mill was built as a steam powered enterprise, and although the steam engine was removed in the first quarter of the present century the mill continued in operation until 1978.

The mill was run as a 'condenser cotton plant' and made use of waste cotton produced at various stages in the manufacturing process; soft waste occurred in the early stages of yarn production before any significant twist had been applied to the fibre, while hard waste consisted of waste yarn after spinning and reeling. From this cotton waste a soft full yarn

was produced which could be used as weft (the yarn carried by the shuttle) in weaving, and among the fabrics made from this yarn were sheeting, flannelettes, cheap towels and cleaning cloths. In addition to a full set of condenser cotton preparation and spinning machines the museum also has a major display gallery outlining the development of the textile industry in Lancashire. Ancillary industries such as the manufacture of shuttles and bobbins are also represented and on the first floor there is an internationally important collection of early textile machines.

The growth of the textile industry often led to the explosive development of certain communities at the expense of others which went into serious decline, and Helmshore has two such 'deserted valleys' on its doorstep. One of these is **Musbury Valley** immediately to the west, a beautiful and isolated area which displays the scattered ruins of early industrialisation. In the latter part of the 18th century and the early part of the 19th this valley had three mills, two of which were initially water powered and then steam powered, but by the end of the 1800s these had been ravaged by fire and were never rebuilt. All that is left now is the occasional mill lodge and some meagre ruins. Interestingly, Musbury had been the site of a hunting 'industry' several centuries earlier when a Royal Deer Park was created here. It was laid out in 1305 and stocked with deer by Henry de Lacy, who also preserved hawks in the area; enclosing the park was a four and a half mile ditch and fence, and parts of this boundary are still evident today.

To the north of Musbury Valley, beyond the former quarries sited on Musbury Heights, is **Grane Valley** — another largely deserted

*Higher Mill, Helmshore*

*The Grane Valley*

area which had a population of 1,300 prior to the construction of the three reservoirs now dominating the scene. Ogden Reservoir is the largest of the three, having been officially opened in 1912, and beneath its placid waters lie the sites of two mills and a hamlet. Close by is the original site of St. Stephen's Church built here in 1868, but by 1926 the area was largely depopulated and the church had to be moved stone by stone to its present site just over a mile further down the valley. Elsewhere in the valley are numerous ruined cottages and farmhouses, which had all been occupied up to the middle of the 19th century. It was then that Calf Hey Reservoir was built by the Bury and Radcliffe Waterworks Company, starting the process which led to the almost complete desertion of the valley by the early 1900s. A number of the ruins in the valley have since been excavated to reveal more of the extent and nature of the earlier communities here.

The Grane Valley is a fairly remote and barren area, and the farmers who lived here could not have survived without an additional income. Initially this was derived from the traditional handloom weaving or work in the local mills and quarries, but during the 19th century it was obtained from illicit whisky distilling — particularly in the remoter parts of the valley. The whisky was made in great secrecy in hidden chambers and passages which ran beneath the isolated farmhouses, with one specially built complex costing the government of the day the very considerable sum of £50,000 in lost revenue.

Illicit whisky stills were also common in **Pickup Bank,** a small village midway between the towns of Haslingden and Darwen, and it is said that there were more illicit stills per acre in Pickup Bank than anywhere else in Lancashire. It is also said that the usual way of hiding the liquor produced from these stills, when the Customs men were in the vicinity, was to put it in the beds of women who were in labour! As with many other places in Lancashire one of the earliest industries here was handloom weaving, and a number of cottages in Pickup Bank still feature the large windows which were necessary to give light to the upper floor rooms where the weaving was carried out.

No doubt much of the cloth which was produced here would have been taken to towns such as Preston and Lancaster along the 'donkey pads' which passed through the district, these being the tracks worn by the feet of travellers and their donkeys as they made their way from one town to another along the shortest route. These pads were also used by local men employed in the nearby coal pits, and by the 1840s there were probably about 50 small pits being worked in this area in addition to one or two larger mines. Stone quarrying was also an important local activity, and the small 19th century chapel at the top of Pickup Bank was built very largely through the efforts of the village quarry workers who were allowed to take home one piece of cut stone every day, cut in their own time. The local quarry owner of the day, who was also a lay preacher, had been generous enough to offer to build a chapel for the residents for the amount of money that was put into the offertory box that Sunday - but only 1/6d was forthcoming!

Midway between Pickup Bank and **Darwen** is the line of the important Roman road from Manchester to Ribchester, although the first settlements here were established largely during the Saxon period. During the 11th century, when the area was granted to the de Lacy family following the Norman Conquest, the name of the place was recorded as Darwynd, becoming known as Superiore Derwent by 1280 and then as Over Darwen within the parish of Blackburn by 1616. The earliest industries in this part of Lancashire were farming and quarrying, but by the beginning of the 18th century many of its inhabitants were occupied as 'coal-getters'. By this time the traditional textile trade was also developing in Darwen, with many people being involved in the spinning and weaving of woollen cloth in their own homes.

This local 'industry' passed through various phases of relative prosperity and depression as master weavers gained more and more control, but then during the latter half of the 18th century it was discovered that the climate here was extremely suitable for the spinning and making up of cotton. By the early part of the 19th century the Industrial Revolution had brought about the displacement of handlooms by power looms and the concentration of work in mills and factories rather than cottages and houses. All this led to the rapid growth of the town, assisted not only by the coming of the railway in 1848 but also by the development of a local wallpaper industry which has since played a major part in the economic well-being of Darwen. Other industries which have been significant in the town include the production of paints and plastics, the manufacture of salt-glazed drainage ware and rope making.

Yet it would be an injustice to describe Darwen largely in terms of its industrial growth, since it is surrounded by some delightful countryside offering excellent walks and far-reaching views. In addition there are three beautiful town parks on the outskirts of Darwen, all within one mile of the town centre on the lower slopes of Darwen Moor and linked to each other by attractive moorland tracks. The natural mixed woodlands of Sunnyhurst Wood were created in the 19th century to provide cover for game birds and hunting, and visitors can wander along its seven miles of footpaths as well as enjoy the peace and quiet of a one and a half mile circular trail through the woodland in Earnsdale Clough. Somewhat closer to the town centre is Bold Venture Park, developed within several former stone quarries and incorporating a number of wooded cloughs around a small lake. One of the park's most impressive features is a 60-foot high waterfall which cascades downwards with great force after heavy rain. Then on the southern edge of the town is Whitehall Park, noted for its fine floral displays and a Victorian drinking fountain.

Situated high above these three parks on the

west side of the town is Darwen Tower, some 85 feet tall and 1300 feet above sea level. From the top of this dramatic monument, in appearance resembling a gigantic space-rocket, one can see most of Lancashire as well as the Irish Sea, the Lakeland fells and the Yorkshire peaks. Officially, Darwen Tower was erected to commemorate Queen Victoria's Diamond Jubilee in 1897, although unofficially local people were also celebrating their previous year's victory in gaining the right to use the footpaths crossing the moor which for centuries had been the cherished domain of the lord of the manor's gamekeepers. Lancashire folk have been quick to take advantage of this splendid opportunity, and Darwen Tower now forms part of the 'Three Towers Walk' — a 35 mile round tour of the West Pennine Moors which also takes in Rivington Pike to the south west and the Peel Monument to the south east.

From Darwen the line of the old Roman road, now incorporated into a pleasant high-level moorland route, takes us down to the village of **Edgworth** and the start of what one might describe as Lancashire's 'Lakeland' — a whole series of valley reservoirs situated on the margins of the moors. These were constructed largely during the 19th century to supply drinking water to Lancashire's rapidly expanding textile towns, making the best use of the high rainfall, impermeable rock and numerous streams which qualify this area as an ideal water-gathering ground. Close to Edgworth are the Entwistle and Wayoh reservoirs, situated within the valley of Bradshaw Brook and a vital component in maintaining Bolton's textile growth during the 19th century.

Even prior to this the manor of Bradshaw had been important in the earlier history of the textile trade, when weaving was a cottage industry and manor houses with access to water had fulling mills to thicken and improve the woollen cloth. By the 17th century pure wool textiles were being superseded by a mix of wool and linen and then later the linen was replaced by cotton. Although fulling was no longer needed cleaning and bleaching were, and the supply of clean water from Bradshaw Brook was ideal for these processes. In the mid-18th century Bradshaw Bleachworks

had established itself, later extending into dyeing and cotton printing, and in 1831 Entwistle Reservoir was started by a consortium of bleachers from works in the valley further downstream who were concerned to ensure a steady flow of water in Bradshaw Brook.

By 1863 Bolton's existing supply reservoirs were not yielding enough water for the town, which had grown rapidly in population through the development of the textile industry, and so Entwistle Reservoir was compulsorily purchased by the Corporation. However, it was only when Wayoh Reservoir was completed in 1876 that water from Entwistle could be made available to the people of Bolton. With the opening of Jumbles Reservoir in 1971 further down Bradshaw Valley, taking on all the compensation water responsibilities for Bradshaw Brook, Wayoh Reservoir was able to provide still more water for Bolton, so that

now Wayoh and Entwistle reservoirs supply about 50% of the town's daily drinking water requirements.

Edgworth itself is very largely a 19th century mill village situated within the older parish of Turton. The original settlement consisted of farming hamlets or 'folds' close to the old Roman road, but then the village grew in size as bleachworks and cotton mills were attracted to the water power available in the valley of Bradshaw Brook, within the area known as Turton Bottoms. Here one can still see the ruins of a 19th century bleachworks together with its mill lodges on the higher ground above it, as well as some very attractive rows of terraced cottages built for workers in the three cotton mills which also existed in this valley. The ancient highway which runs through this picturesque little community pre-dates the turnpike road nearby and passes over what is thought to be a mediaeval footbridge on its way to Bury.

*A picturesque footbridge in Edgworth*

*Some of Edgworth's cottages*

*The main elevation of Turton Tower*

Nearby **Turton Tower** was the manor house presiding over affairs in Turton, Edgworth and nearby Chapeltown, although it also exerted its influence across a much wider area extending from Darwen to Bolton. That was how it used to be during mediaeval times, but nowadays it sits within eight acres of its own gardens and woodland and is a fascinating museum open to members of the public. The oldest portion of the present building is a 15th century stone pele tower, with the remaining part being a half-timbered farmhouse which dates from the late 16th century. Turton Tower is particularly associated with Humphrey Chetham, the treasurer of the Roundhead faction in Lancashire during the English Civil War, and because of this the dining room walls are hung with paintings of people from that period.

As well as having a collection of old weapons and suits of armour among its treasures the Tower has one of the oldest surviving libraries in Lancashire, given to the people of Turton by Humphrey Chetham in 1655. Among his numerous benefactions was the founding of Chetham's School in Manchester as well as the endowment of a village school in Chapeltown, and it is not inappropriate that the 18th century Chetham Arms in Chapeltown should also bear his name. The impressive collection of period furniture at Turton Tower includes a huge four-poster bed which is said to be only second in size to the Great Bed of Ware. This was probably brought here by the Kay family who lived at Turton from 1835, although it originally belonged to the Earls of Devon and could well date back to Elizabethan times.

Heading westwards from Turton Tower we come firstly to the bleachworks village of Belmont and another cluster of reservoirs on the lower slopes of Winter Hill, before passing over the moors and descending quickly into **Rivington.** This well known beauty spot comprises not only a chain of 19th century reservoirs but also the historic village of **Rivington** and the delightful terraced gardens of Lever Park. Five of the reservoirs in this area were built under the 'Rivington Pike Scheme' which was designed to provide water for Liverpool's growing population, and the first supplies were being delivered by 1857. The High Bullough Reservoir was then

*Turton Tower's half-timbered splendour*

added to the system, but with the demand from Liverpool increasing all the time two further reservoirs (Upper Roddlesworth and Yarrow) had to be constructed in 1860 and 1875.

Even with these extensions the Rivington system was still not able to meet the demands being placed upon it, so Liverpool Corporation Waterworks turned to Lake Vyrnwy in North Wales for much of its water. The eight reservoirs in the Rivington area now hold nearly 4,000 million gallons and supply about 11.5 million gallons of water a day to Liverpool and other places in south west Lancashire. In addition to public supplies the reservoirs provide 'top-up' or compensation water to several rivers, ensuring that the needs of local industry are also adequately met.

The construction of these reservoirs involved building embankments across narrow valleys to impound the water of their rivers and streams, and in the Rivington area all the embankments are made of earth with a puddled clay core. In addition they are lined on the reservoir side and pitched with stone to prevent water erosion. This work was carried out by gangs of 'navvies', who lived in abandoned buildings and makeshift camps of wooden huts and tents. In such conditions alcohol was often the only relief which the navvies and their womenfolk had, so illicit beer brewers and spirit distillers in the area enjoyed something of a 'boom' when the reservoirs were under construction. The hard and dangerous life which the navvies led during the construction of canals and railways

*Rivington Chapel*

as well as reservoirs often took its toll, and forty years was considered a good age to reach.

As well as the beauty of the reservoirs' rippling waters amidst their verdant vesture this area has a number of important historic buildings which not only delight the eye but also arouse one's sense of heritage. Several of these date

back to the Saxon period, although there is evidence to suggest that human settlement here started at least 8,000 years ago. The parish church in picturesque Rivington village is one of the buildings which is thought to have originated in Saxon times, although it was re-built in 1541 with further restoration being carried out over the next 200 years, while Rivington Chapel dates from 1703 and is one of the earliest nonconformist chapels in Lancashire.

To the south of the village are the well known Rivington barns, which are also thought to be Saxon in origin but whose present structure dates largely from the early 1700s with a number of later alterations. Great House Barn is just a short distance from the east 'shore' of Rivington Reservoir and acts as an Information Centre for visitors to the West Pennine Moors, while Rivington Hall Barn adjoins Rivington Hall itself some distance away and is now in use as a restaurant. Inside both barns the dominant features are the high cruck trusses which support the roof. Each cruck is essentially the two halves of a tree sawn down the middle, with the timbers and tie-beams joined together by wooden pegs. The cruck frames rest upon large stone bases, which not only provided a solid foundation on which the buildings could stand but also protected the timbers from damp ground and possible damage by animals. They also raised the height of the buildings, so enlarging their storage capacity. In keeping with their solid internal structure both barns have outer walls of stone and steeply pitched stone flag roofs.

*Rivington Hall*

The most significant alterations to these barns

*Great House Barn, Rivington*

Although Lord Leverhulme's 'Bungalow' residence has since been demolished the Terraced Gardens still remain as an attractive feature for visitors to explore. Overlooking the meadowland and tree-lined avenues of Lever Park below, the Gardens today consist of about 45 acres of woodland within which are to be found pathways, terraces, stepped walks, garden shelters, ornamental pools, miniature waterfalls, stone footbridges and ruined buildings. The most impressive building which still remains within the Rivington Terraced Gardens is the Pigeon Tower, built in 1910 to house ornamental pigeons and doves but also providing space for Lady Leverhulme's sewing room on the top floor. Another prominent landmark introduced by Lord Leverhulme is Rivington Castle, standing at the edge of Lower Rivington Reservoir; this was built between 1912 and 1930 as an added attraction in Lever Park and is a replica of the ruined Liverpool Castle at the time of its demolition.

High above Lever Park and the Terraced Gardens is a still more prominent landmark which pre-dates Lord Leverhulme's ambitious transformation of the area. This is the well known **Rivington Pike Tower,** a distinctive feature on the West Pennine Moors skyline which was built in 1733 to mark the boundary of the Rivington Manor Estate. Rivington Pike is the site of an ancient defence beacon dating back to the 12th century, and stone used to build the Tower was taken from the original beacon fire platform already on the site as well as from the bed of the nearby River Douglas. The Pike beacon was one of a chain of beacons lit on

were carried out by William Lever, later to become Lord Leverhulme, after he purchased the Manor of Rivington in 1900. It was he who reconstructed the buildings in keeping with their original cruck composition, using them to provide shelter and refreshments for visitors to the area as well as to host a range of social functions. Throughout the alterations which he undertook only oak timber was used, this being worked with hand tools and joined with wooden pegs in the traditional fashion. Along with the barns Lever also acquired Rivington Hall, the residence of the lord of the manor, on a site which is thought to have been occupied for about a thousand years. The Hall was originally a half-timbered structure in the form of a quadrangle approached by an open gateway, although most of the house was pulled down in 1774 and the Georgian west front then incorporated; the later south wing was added in the 19th century.

William Lever was the Bolton-born son of a prosperous local wholesale grocer, and from humble beginnings in his father's business he went on to develop the very wealthy Lever Brothers' 'empire' through the manufacture of soap. His purchase of the Rivington Estate provided the opportunity for him to indulge in his long-held passion for architecture and landscape design, not only for his own benefit but also for the benefit of the people of Bolton. One of his first priorities was to set aside an extensive area of the heather-clad slopes leading up to Rivington Pike for the construction of an imposing residence as well as for the creation of equally imposing landscaped grounds. These became known

as the **Terraced Gardens,** incorporating the Ravine with its waterfalls, rockpools and footbridges as well as the dramatic Japanese Garden with its tea houses, lanterns and ornamental lake. On what had once been an open windswept hillside a large new woodland grew up, encompassing both native and exotic trees as well as many thousands of shrubs.

*One of the footbridges in Rivington Terraced Gardens*

*The Pigeon Tower, Rivington Terraced Gardens*

the night of 19th July, 1588 to warn people that the Spanish Armada had entered the English Channel.

In more recent years an annual Pike Fair has been held here on Good Friday, as well as the Pike Race which started in 1892 when it was organised by the Lancashire and Yorkshire Railway Company as part of their sports day. The race started from the recreation ground of the Railway Mechanics' Institute in Horwich but followed no set course; many of the runners took short cuts through gardens while the leaders often removed planks over streams once they were safely across so that their opponents would have to make a detour or get their feet wet! The race is now held every Easter Saturday and attracts around 300 runners.

For those whose exercise ambitions extend only to walking rather than running there are numerous trails around most of the Rivington reservoirs. The Upper Rivington Trail, for example, is a two and a half mile circular walk starting at Rivington Village, whilst the Anglezarke Woodland Trail takes visitors through 100-year old woodlands on the edge of High Bullough and Anglezarke Reservoirs. Along its route can be seen the old stone quarries which were extensively worked between 1880 and 1920 when quarrying was an important local activity. Stone from these quarries was also used to line the embankments of the Rivington reservoirs, and the small community of navvies and quarrymen which flourished here had a shop, a smithy, stables and a pub called 'The Clog'. In addition to providing material for the construction of the nearby reservoirs these quarries provided stone for building, for paving flags, for road kerbs and for millstones; in fact many of the roads in Manchester and Salford are paved with stone from here

transported initially by horsedrawn cart to Adlington and then by train to its destination.

An even earlier activity carried out in this area was lead mining, and an archaeological trail relating to the history of lead mining on Anglezarke Moor starts from the north east corner of Yarrow Reservoir and follows the lower stretches of Limestone Brook. The earliest record of mining taking place in what is known as **Lead Mines Clough** dates back to 1692, although the most active period of production was towards the end of the 18th century when between 10 and 16 miners were employed and 73 tons of lead were produced in the two years 1788 and 1789. After falling into disuse attempts were made to work the mines in the 1830s but without success, and a century later they were filled in to provide work for unemployed people in Chorley. The only evidence that now remains of the lead mining industry is a rectangular 'slime pit', used by the miners for recovering fine particles of lead ore, and an 18th century waterwheel pit which held a wooden waterwheel used to pump water from the shafts.

The material brought up from these local lead mines was known as 'bouse', which was first sorted by hand to collect the larger pieces of lead ore. The remainder was then crushed to the size of peas using either flat-headed hammers known as 'buckers' or a roller crusher. To separate the lead ore from the other materials required the use of a 'buddle', a sloping surface or trough over which water was continously passed; as the crushed material was fed onto the top of the buddle the heavier lead ore settled out whilst lighter materials were washed away. This was not the end of the collection process, however, since the water used for washing the bouse still contained small particles of lead ore and so was channelled into a slime pit. Here the lead ore particles settled out near the top of the pit, which periodically would be allowed to dry out prior to extraction of the lead-rich silt. The ore which was collected then had to be smelted to obtain metallic lead; initially this may have been done in single open hearths on the hillsides around Lead Mines Clough, but during the later periods of working ore was generally sold to smelt mills elsewhere.

One other trail in the area of the Rivington reservoirs, this time with natural history very much in mind, is the Roddlesworth Nature Trail immediately to the south of Roddlesworth Upper Reservoir. This one mile circular route through the glades and woodlands of the Roddlesworth Valley also offers the opportunity for a detour along an old coach road leading to a unique wellhouse and the ruins of Hollinshead Hall, which was built in 1776. Water from the well was reputed to be able to cure eye complaints. The trail also passes a number of ruined farms which had to be abandoned because of the risk of pollution when Liverpool Corporation

bought the land for water catchment in 1848.

Our chosen western boundary for this part of the East Lancashire Uplands is the Leeds and Liverpool Canal, but between its waters and the waters of the Rivington reservoirs there is some beautiful countryside as well as a number of delightful villages. **Adlington** is the largest settlement in the area, and it was here that some of the first British muslins were woven in 1764; this revolutionised the fashions of the time since ladies could now have light and attractive gowns which could also be easily laundered. Trade and industry developed further with the construction of the Leeds and Liverpool Canal, and when it was discovered that the local springs were suitable for mixing dyes so the dyeing and block printing of cottons became an important industry in its own right. The textile industry as a whole continued to flourish throughout the 19th century, bringing with it Adlington's main period of growth, but the closure of cotton mills from the 1930s onwards heralded the decline of textiles. Now Adlington is probably better known for being the place where Leonard Fairclough founded his civil engineering business, which has since become internationally famous.

To the north of Adlington is **Heath Charnock,** lying at the foot of the Rivington and Anglezarke hills and having an eastern boundary which runs down the middle of the reservoirs by the same name. The most important building in this parish is Hall o'th Hill, dating from 1724 when it was built for the Asshawe family who were the major landowners in the district. It is now the clubhouse for Chorley Golf Club and enjoys superb views on all sides. Further north again and just a little above Anglezarke Reservoir is the small hamlet of **White Coppice,** a pretty cluster of stone cottages which probably has the most picturesque cricket ground in Lancashire, framed by the encircling hills. Perhaps somewhat surprisingly this used to be a cotton village, with an old water-powered mill which provided most of the local inhabitants with employment until it was demolished early in the 20th century. Prior to the construction of the mill many of the people here in White Coppice would doubtless have worked as handloom weavers.

Further northwards still is **Wheelton,** its steep streets climbing the slopes above the Leeds and Liverpool Canal, and then the parish of Withnell, which encompasses the villages of Brinscall, Withnell, Abbey Village and **Withnell Fold.** The last of these is particularly attractive, being hidden from the main Chorley to Blackburn road but situated alongside the Leeds and Liverpool Canal. The village of Withnell Fold developed very largely as a self-contained industrial community, with the rows of pretty terraced cottages being built by the Parker family to

*Gawthorpe Hall near Burnley*

*White Coppice near Rivington*

accommodate their workers at the nearby paper mill which they had established here in 1844. The mill-owning family also erected a small village school and a chapel, as well as a Reading Room which acted as the focal point for village recreation. The inhabitants of Withnell Fold were not so fortunate, however, when it came to the provision of a public house, since the Parkers were staunch adherents of the Methodist Church and teetotalism.

The mill which brought the village into being has since been demolished, but its towering chimney still remains as an important landmark as well as a continuing reminder of Withnell Fold's original raison d'etre. The placid canal is also a silent witness to busier times, when it was the main artery feeding the mill with the coal and raw materials necessary to produce high quality banknote paper for export. Now its main use is as a leisure waterway, although it also acts as a magnet for wildlife and occasionally herons as well as kingfishers can be seen along its length. The village as a whole lies within the valley of the River Lostock and is hemmed in by woodland and the open countryside beyond it, making it a haven for flora and fauna.

*The rural hamlet of White Coppice*

In many respects Withnell Fold is a microcosm of the East Lancashire Uplands as a whole — an established community which owes its origins largely to an earlier industrial era, but which has retained its underlying characteristics of beauty, individuality and settled charm.

*The mill village of Withnell Fold*

*Church Street, Croston*

# Chapter 6: THE WEST LANCASHIRE PLAIN

Our tour around the West Lancashire Plain begins and ends with the Leeds and Liverpool Canal, which passes through some remarkably diverse and varied scenery along the course of its route from the intimate foothills of the East Lancashire uplands to the rolling farmland on the edge of the Merseyside conurbation. The starting point for our journey is **Whittle-le-Woods,** a very pleasing settlement of stone built cottages about six miles to the south of Preston which developed rapidly with the advent of the canal. Interestingly enough, however, it was a southern branch of the Lancaster Canal which brought prosperity to Whittle-le-Woods rather than the Leeds and Liverpool Canal, to which a connection was made at a somewhat later date.

The intention behind the Lancaster Canal was to provide a quick and easy transport link from the Wigan coalfields to Preston and Lancaster, and the first section from Aspull to Adlington was later extended to reach Whittle-le-Woods in 1797 and then ultimately Walton Summit further northwards by 1809. The canal should then have gone through to Preston to meet up with the northern branch to Lancaster, but the prohibitive cost of crossing the River Ribble forced the engineers to resort to the construction of a tram road instead. It was at Walton Summit that goods had to be transferred from barge to tram for the second leg of their journey, and here eight sidings were introduced so that four or five barges could be unloaded at once.

The southern branch of the Lancaster Canal has now largely been filled in, but in Whittle-le-Woods one can still trace its original route through the two substantial tunnels which were cut through Whittle Hills. These tunnels initially formed one tunnel which was 300 yards in length and had its own towpath, with the work being carried out largely by hand over a nine year period. The Lancaster Canal was opened in 1803, and was linked to the Leeds and Liverpool Canal in 1816 at Johnson's Hillock just to the east of Whittle-le-Woods. Here again the lie of the land presented problems to the canal engineers, but they overcame these by the construction

*The Leeds and Liverpool Canal on the outskirts of Whittle-le-Woods*

of a flight of seven locks enabling barges to be raised 60 feet from the lower to the upper level. The locks, bridges and lock-keepers' houses at this point on the Leeds and Liverpool Canal form an attractive feature throughout the year and are an enduring testimony to the skills of John Rennie, the engineer responsible for their construction.

The arrival of the canal in Whittle-le-Woods not only offered the prospect of new industry in the area but also gave a boost to the fortunes of one which had been established for centuries before — the production of millstones from the Whittle Hill quarries. Even as early as 1530 the map-maker Leland had recorded of this area that he had seen 'on a hillside a great quarry out of which men dig very great and good millstones'. The transport

of such heavy items was a major problem in the days when only horse and cart were available, but with the coming of the canal a much wider market was opened up — millstones could now be taken along the Leeds and Liverpool Canal in wooden horsedrawn barges south to Wigan and Liverpool or northwards to Blackburn and Leeds, while some were also taken on the Lancaster Canal to Preston. Millstones extracted from Whittle Hill were sent to every part of the country, and there are accounts of some going as far as Germany, America and even China.

During the 1800s nearly every township in Lancashire had its own water powered corn mill, so the demand for millstones was quite high. The quality of a millstone was of vital

*Passing through a lock on the Leeds and Liverpool Canal*

125

importance to the miller, and the best English stone was considered to be Derbyshire Millstone Grit — although the stone quarried in Whittle-le-Woods was of a comparable quality. French Burr stone was imported and used to grind hard wheat, but local gritstone was cheaper, easier to dress and used to grind softer grains such as barley, oats and peas.

An English millstone was on average four feet in diameter with an 'eye' of 10 inches across, starting from a thickness of 16 inches and being used down to three inches. The stones were always operated in pairs, with the lower or 'bed-stone' remaining stationary and level; the upper stone or 'runner' could have a convex upper side to add to the stability of the stone as it turned at approximately 120 revolutions per minute. The stones never touched each other because of the risk of fire but were set slightly apart, with the adjoining surfaces of the stones being dressed in a pattern of grooves. The whole arrangement was enclosed in a wooden casing and the grain fed in through the central hole or 'eye', and as the upper stone revolved so the cutting edges of the grooves ground the cereal with a scissor-like action. It is likely that a millstone would receive its final pattern of grooves from an itinerant millstone dresser, after having been kept in store for a year upon arrival at the mill in order to allow it to dry out.

As well as developing a reputation for the quality of its stone the area also acquired a name for the quality of its water, particularly in the 19th century which saw the growth of the township known as **Whittle Springs** close to the point where the Lancaster Canal joined up with the Leeds and Liverpool Canal. When boring for coal in 1836 workmen hit a spring which gushed out at 50 gallons per minute, and by 1847 a hotel and spa had been built on the site. This consisted of a public house, an entrance lodge, a well-house, alkaline and chalybeate springs of water, a gentlemen's alkaline swimming baths measuring 81 feet by 19 feet, a bowling green, pleasure grounds, observatory, kitchen gardens, stables and coach house. This spa at the newly created Whittle Springs obviously proved a popular attraction to the Victorians, and in 1852 it was recorded that over 30,000 visitors came here.

To the north of both Whittle Springs and Whittle-le-Woods is **Brindle,** a peaceful little village at the heart of a largely agricultural area. Numerous country lanes and footpaths run through the area, with seemingly no particular destination in mind, while the fields are hemmed in by leafy copses and rambling stone walls. There are some particularly attractive views from the road between Brindle and Whittle-le-Woods, while in Brindle village itself the Parish Church of St. James is well worth seeing. Parts of this building date from the 15th century, although a stone coffin in the churchyard has been linked with one of the kings who fought at the Battle of Brunaberg. There is a tradition that this battle took place on the plains overlooked by Brindle, partly borne out by the fact that in 1840 a buried chest containing ten thousand silver coins was discovered at nearby Cuerdale Ford, the chest supposedly being left by the retreating army of Anulf after his defeat. The victor was Athelstan, grandson of Alfred the Great, who became the first monarch of England.

In more recent times Brindle became the scene of another 'invasion', but one which was remarkably better natured. This was Brindle Steeplechases, usually held in April on the undulating fields behind the parish church, and an account of the event in 1905 states that there was an attendance of nearly 20,000 people. 'The vicinity of the starting post presented a lively scene as the betting men plied their calling and the crowd in the intervals of the races devoted themselves to refreshment which was provided. The needs of the crowd were well catered for in this respect as the local publicans had marquees and stalls in the crowd where both solid and liquid refreshments were obtainable'.

Just over three miles to the west of Whittle-le-Woods is the small town of **Leyland,** a place which has become internationally famous through its association with the manufacture of both motor cars and lorries by one of Britain's best known companies. Leyland's origins go back much further, however, to about the 8th century, and the earliest documentary evidence records that the manor of 'Lailand' was a Crown possession in later Saxon times when it was owned by Edward the Confessor. The name 'Leyland' stems initially from Old English and means a place of fallow land, consistent with the plain on which the present-day town is situated. The manor was held by the Bussel family at the beginning of the 13th century and then eventually passed into the hands of the Faringtons, whose lordship of Leyland continued until comparatively recently. During this time they played an important part in Lancashire affairs, with the most famous member of the family being William Farington who was comptroller to the household of three successive Earls of Derby during the 16th century; he is also said to have been the person on whom Shakespeare modelled his character Malvolio.

The most interesting part of Leyland is the area around the village cross, now on the south side of the larger township but marking the original centre of the old village. The cross itself consists of an ancient stepped base and shaft with a more recent top portion, introduced because the cross had been broken during Puritan times. For many years there were two gas lamps attached to the top of the shaft, but in 1887 the cross was reinstated to mark the Diamond Jubilee of

*Leyland Cross*

Queen Victoria. In the same year an iron pump and drinking trough that stood next to the cross were replaced by the present fountain and drinking trough.

A little distance along Church Road from Leyland Cross is St. Andrew's Parish Church, said to have been first built here in 1050. The oldest parts of the present building are the tower and the chancel, which date from about 1220 and are largely unaltered except for some restoration work undertaken during the 15th century. Fragments of characteristic early Norman masonry which can be seen in the chancel walls are from the original church on this site. The chancel is divided from the nave by a carved screen, whilst the high pointed chancel arch is panelled around with 19th century fresco work. The chapel in the south east corner of the nave used to be the chantry of the important Farington (or Ffarington) family, and the Ffarington Chapel Door is particularly impressive. The churchyard is notable for the number of old gravestones preserved there, many of which still retain their incised inscriptions — the one for William Walker dates from 1588 and depicts a life-size figure cut into the stone slab, whilst that for Richard Sherdley has a date of 1687 and is unusual in that it has 14 lines of continuous capitals.

Further along Church Road is the Old Grammar School, a building which dates from the middle of the 17th century when it was founded as Leyland's first educational establishment. Living accommodation for the schoolmaster was added in 1799, but in 1874 the school was closed due to the deterioration of the building. By 1977, however, the building was restored and converted into a museum and exhibition centre to house a range of collections including the finds from early excavations of the Roman site at Walton-le-Dale as well as a number of Victorian costumes. The building itself is also something of a 'museum piece', displaying the original box-frame timber construction together with 'clam, staff and daub' partition walls and mullioned windows.

Close to the Old Grammar School is Leyland's oldest inn, the Eagle and Child, which dates back to the 16th century although the main body of the building is probably of 18th century construction. Part of the premises were reputedly used as Leyland's Court House, with the cellars acting as holding rooms for offenders. There are also said to be secret tunnels running from these cellars to Worden Park and the Old Priory in Moss Lane, used by supporters of Charles I when escaping from Cromwell's forces.

Retracing one's steps back down Church Road and past Leyland Cross brings us into Fox Lane, along which can be seen a variety of 'domestic' buildings. On the north side is a

*The Old Grammar School*

row of handloom weavers' cottages, built in or before 1802 and known originally as the 'Friendly Society Houses'. It was the introduction of weaving to Leyland which really signalled the onset of the Industrial Revolution here, since up to the end of the 18th century Leyland had been primarily an agricultural community with a reputation for being 'The Garden of Lancashire'. Further down Fox Lane are several groups of almshouses, most of which date from the 19th century, while across the road from them is Leyland Cricket Club which dates back to 1847. By the end of the 19th century so many Leyland players had joined the

county side that Leyland became known as 'The Nursery of Lancashire'. Local people have obviously prided themselves on their wider contribution!

Running southwards from Leyland Cross is Worden Lane, along which can be found a number of elegant and more substantial properties built during the 18th and 19th centuries. One of these is Leyland House, a Georgian town house of brick with stone facings and Doric columns which was built in 1770 by William Pollard of Lytham. In the early 19th century it was occupied by the Baldwin family, who gave nine vicars to St. Andrew's Church over the course of time.

The most substantial property reached from Worden Lane is Worden Hall itself, the historic home of the Farington family. This impressive building is delightfully situated within the extensive parkland which surrounds it, although most of the main house was demolished in the 1960s after a disastrous fire during the Second World War. The remaining part was restored by the local authority and renamed 'The Derby Wing' to commemorate the Faringtons' long-standing association with the Earls of Derby. Also restored since then have been the 19th century stable block and an adjoining barn, to provide accommodation for a craft centre and an arts complex. A parkland trail which has been established through the grounds of Worden Hall allows visitors to amble at their leisure through a Victorian maze, a more recently planted arboretum containing over 120 different kinds of trees and the formal sunken gardens with their central water fountain.

*Almshouses on Fox Lane in Leyland*

Although it was handloom weaving which

was largely responsible for beginning the transformation of Leyland from an agricultural to an industrial community, it was the manufacture of rubber goods, paint and, above all, motor vehicles and engineering which brought about its development as a sizeable town during the 20th century. How fitting it is, then, that Leyland should be the home of the British Commercial Vehicle Museum, the largest such museum in Europe and representative of the whole of the British industry. The museum is housed on the site of the former Leyland South Works on King Street, close to the centre of the town, where commercial vehicles were produced for many years during the early growth of the industry. There are over 40 beautifully restored vehicles and engines on display, with exhibits ranging from the horsedrawn era through steam wagons and early petrol engines right up to the present day, and many of the buses, trucks, vans and fire engines are on show in realistic settings. The museum also takes a look at how changes in road vehicles occurred to meet the vast growth in demand for the carriage of passengers, heavy goods and local deliveries, which could not be met by the less flexible canal and rail networks. To the south east of Leyland is the rather larger town of Chorley, with the parish of **Euxton** lying comfortably between them.

Euxton is a very pleasant mix of open farmland, stone cottages and more recent residential development, and as well as several important historic houses which speak of the early significance of this area there are numerous footpaths which enable visitors to enjoy Euxton's rural setting. One of the most impressive buildings in the district is **Astley Hall,** situated between Euxton and Chorley. As seen now this is essentially a three storey Jacobean house, having been remodelled during the second half of the 17th century when the whole of the principal front was pulled down and rebuilt on a more lavish and imposing scale in line with the style of the time. Prior to this the original house was a half-timbered dwelling of two storeys with stone flagged roofs, built around a central courtyard. In the Jacobean remodelling of the house many of the characteristic features of the original plan were lost, everything being subordinated to external effect, and walls of brick with stone dressings were introduced which were later coated with plaster.

Over the years Astley Hall has been the home of several important local families. The first of these was the Charnocks of Charnock Richard, who held the house as tenants of the Military Order of St. John of Jerusalem until it came into their possession subject to a small quit-rent during the 16th century. Tradition has it that Astley became the principal house of the Charnock family following a disastrous fire at Charnock Hall towards the end of the 1500s. Robert, the 'one-eyed Charnock' who fought in the Civil War, was the last of the male line and the house then passed by marriage to the Brooke family upon his death in 1653. It was at this point in time that the remarkable Great Hall was built and the mansion enriched with oak carvings, panel portraits and the superb plaster ceiling for which Astley Hall is noted.

When the male line of the Brooke family also failed the estate passed through marriage to the Parker family, and after the death of the second Thomas Townley Parker in 1906 it came into the ownership of Reginald Arthur Tatton. It was he who gave the Hall and surrounding parkland to Chorley Corporation in 1922, as a war memorial and museum for the benefit of local people. The local authority has since carried out numerous improvements to the building, including the conversion of two bedrooms to form an art gallery as well as the restoration of the courtyard to its original state and the uncovering of the half-timbered west front with its tall Elizabethan chimneys. Extensive restoration work has also been carried out on

*Astley Hall, Chorley*

the Flemish ceilings in the main hall and the drawing room.

One of the principal features of this important house is the Great Hall, which rises to the full height of two storeys and incorporates one of the two semi-octagonal bay windows to be seen on the front elevation. The ceiling in the Great Hall is divided into eight compartments which are handsomely decorated by wreaths and figures of plaster, leather and lead. The frieze below the ceiling is decorated in a similarly ornate fashion and over the fireplace are the heraldic arms of the Brooke and Charnock families. Around the walls of the room are a series of wood panel portraits about nine feet high which date from the early part of the 17th century, whilst included within the furniture of the Great Hall is the famous 'Sirloin' chair which is reputed to have been used by James I when he knighted the loin of beef at Hoghton Tower.

Leading directly out of the Great Hall is the Drawing Room, with a ceiling which surpasses even that of the Great Hall in its degree of ornamentation. According to one observer earlier this century, the Baroque oval plasterwork with its decoration of shells and infants is the best example of its kind in Britain, and it is said to be a relic of the French fashion which came in with the Restoration before the more 'chastened' style of Wren taught people to prefer simplicity to display. The Drawing Room has been furnished in an 18th century manner, and on the walls are tapestries depicting 'The Quest of the Golden Fleece'.

To the left of the Great Hall in the south west corner of the building is the Morning Room, which incorporates the second great bay window as well as further timber panelling. The ceiling is again an important part of the room, with the moulding in the bay displaying mythological birds and animals whilst that in the centre of the room features male and female figures. The remaining rooms on the ground floor include the Inlaid Room with its full-length portrait of Thomas Brooke when he was Sheriff of Cheshire, the Dining Room which forms part of the east wing of the house, and the kitchen with its great fireplace. At the centre of the Hall is a stone flagged inner courtyard complete with water pump, and on the west wall over the kitchen one can find the date of 1600 inscribed in the timber frame.

On the upper storey, over the Great Hall and the Drawing Room, is the Long Gallery which runs the full length of the house. The most important feature here is the Shovel-Board (or Shuffleboard) table, over 23-feet long and supported by ten pairs of legs with elaborately carved panels. The game of Shovel-Board was played by two players, each of them having four flat weights of metal which they aimed to propel from one end of the table to the other; points were awarded to the respective players if their weights came to rest within a certain designated area, with the maximum points being awarded for any weights which came to rest over the very edge of the table without falling off into the trough beneath. This was a particularly popular game during the Restoration period, and the table here in Astley Hall is probably the finest of its kind.

Other rooms on the upper floor include the Cromwell Room (where Oliver Cromwell is reputed to have stayed in August 1648); the Plaster Room, with its elaborately ornamented walls; and the Oak Room, a bedchamber above the Drawing Room which contains a bed reputed to be the finest specimen of its age to have escaped destruction. Mr. Ralph Edwards, writing in Country Life in 1922, continued his overwhelming praise of this bed by saying that it was "a specimen so magnificent that the town of Chorley, to which it has been made over, must become a place of pilgrimage for every lover of English oak".

Astley Hall is fittingly surrounded by the 105 acres of Astley Park, which was donated to the town in 1924. At the main gates is a Memorial Arch and Cenotaph, while within the park itself are numerous well-wooded walks and footbridges that criss-cross the River Chor. Adjacent to the Hall are bowling greens, tennis courts, a picnic area and an ornamental lake as well as a Georgian stable block which now serves as the tearooms.

The town of **Chorley** has traditionally served as a market centre for the surrounding districts, and despite many changes over the years it has still managed to retain its compact form and the atmosphere of a market town. The official records of Chorley having a

*A fountain in Astley Park*

market go back as far as 1498, and nowadays there are two markets held in the town on a weekly basis; one of these is the unique 'Flat Iron' market held on Tuesdays, the name being derived from the ancient practice of trading by laying out wares for sale on the ground, without stalls, when no doubt 'flat irons' were sold.

*The Parish Church of St. Laurence, Chorley*

The oldest building in the town is the parish church of St. Laurence, with its 14th century chancel and 15th century tower. Although there are some attractive Georgian buildings in Chorley, the 'Swann with Two Knecks' public house being a particularly good example, much of the town today has grown up as a result of the industrial growth which it has experienced during the course of the past 150 years. A number of textile mills in the area testify to the one-time importance of cotton spinning, although in places like Coppull just to the south of Chorley coal mining was a significant source of local employment. Yet despite its industrial background Chorley has always maintained close contact with its surrounding countryside, as can be seen at Duxbury Park on the south side of the town. As well as an 18 hole golf course there is also the 100 acre woodland park with its picnic areas, path system and scenic viewpoints looking out across the River Yarrow to the distant hills beyond. The park also contains an abundance of wildlife including red squirrels, foxes and herons.

Chorley's position at the foot of the Pennines means that it enjoys the best of both worlds in terms of surrounding scenery — to the east are the more rugged outlines of the Anglezarke and Rivington fells, whilst to the west are the more subdued panoramas of the West Lancashire coastal plain. The first villages reached on this west side of Chorley are **Eccleston** and **Heskin,** both ancient settlements with a real country atmosphere about them whose names originate from the British tribes which populated the area in pre-historic times. Farming provided the liveli-hood of the first settlers here, and records of a corn mill and a fulling mill in the area together with the building of substantial moated manor houses during the mediaeval period all confirm that agriculture was well developed by the Middle Ages.

Agriculture continued to be the mainstay of the local economy over the course of the following centuries, although handloom weaving led to the development of a textile industry in Eccleston during the early part of the 19th century. By 1861 300 people were employed at an integrated spinning and weaving factory, and growing prosperity in the village brought about the construction of a Methodist chapel in 1863 and the 'new' school in 1874. Coal mining was also an important source of employment during the 19th century, although there are records of 'cannel' coal being mined in the area as early as 1590. During the 20th century, however, textiles became the dominant activity, with farming remaining static and mining dying out, but by the early 1980s the textile industry was itself terminated with the onset of foreign competition and financial problems. Nowadays most people living in Eccleston and Heskin find their employment elsewhere, although farming continues to make an important contribution to the life of the area.

As is the case with many Lancashire villages, the parish church is a good place to start when

*The Old School, Eccleston*

looking for interesting old buildings in the area. St. Mary's Church in Eccleston stands in a picturesque spot on the south bank of the River Yarrow, a site which has been occupied by a place of worship since the very earliest times although the first recorded mention of a building here only appears in 1094. The nave, chancel and west tower date from the 14th century, with the south aisles being added in about 1500 and restoration work being undertaken in the early 18th century and then again in the 19th century. Around the inside walls of the church are stone monuments to some of the more prominent families within the district, including the Rigbys of Harrock Hall, the Kershaws of

Heskin Hall and the Dicconsons of Wrightington Hall.

The main road runs southwards from the parish church to the centre of Eccleston, where one can find some quaint cottages as well as the old village school and the former Eccleston Savings Bank, now converted to residential use. The Old School, built of stone and featuring pointed arch windows, was constructed in 1834 by public subscription, whilst the Eccleston Savings Bank was established in 1818 as one of the first of its kind. The founders of the Bank are said to have been the rector and curate of Eccleston.

Another important building, this time in Heskin, is Heskin New Hall — so called because of the Old Hall which stood to the north west of the village, although this was pulled down in the early 19th century. The New Hall dates from the 17th century and is constructed of handmade bricks; tradition has it that Oliver Cromwell lodged overnight here and that it is haunted by a ghost which appears as a lady in white. As well as a good number of interesting old buildings Eccleston and Heskin also have their fair share of interesting old families, particularly the long established Moon family who represented the largest family group in Eccleston. In addition to being wheelwrights in the village for several generations members of the family are noted for helping to establish the Mormon Church in Salt Lake City, Utah and for providing a headmaster of Leyland school in the 17th century. They were also responsible for building some of the earliest motor vehicles in the district.

In terms of distance the village of **Croston,** situated on the north bank of the River Yarrow, is little more than a hop, skip and a jump away from Eccleston — but in terms of time one can easily imagine being back in the 1700s, since Croston's cobbled Church Street

*St. Mary's Church, Eccleston*

is a particularly fine example of an 18th century Lancashire thoroughfare. At one end is the very pretty parish church of St. Michael and All Angels, a largely 16th century building laid out on a plan first established in the 15th century, while at the other end is a stone cross standing on an ancient base dating back to Saxon times. The present cross was erected here in fairly recent times as a replacement for the original one, which may have been damaged or destroyed during Cromwell's time. Just around the corner is an old packhorse bridge bearing the date of 1682, but actually built in 1671 at a cost of under £30, while on the other side of the church the delightful village scene is completed by the Old Rectory. This 17th century building was re-fronted soon after 1755, although the downpipes carry the date of 1722.

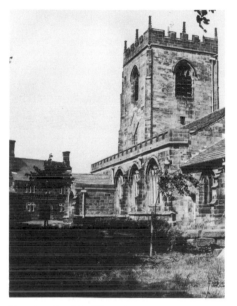

*Croston Parish Church*

The name 'Croston' probably stems from the 10th century and means 'village with a cross' — that is, a preaching cross, which in the absence of a church acted as a place of worship. Although the date of the first settlement here remains uncertain, it does seem likely that there has been a Christian community on the spot for well over a thousand years. No specific reference is made to the village in the Domesday Survey, although the mention of a priest suggests that there may have been a church either at Leyland or Croston. Certainly it is recorded that the church of Croston was among those granted to the Abbey of St. Martin of Sees in 1094 by Roger of Poitou, whilst the list of rectors is continuous from the end of the 13th century. There are also traces of the earlier mediaeval church within the structure of the present building.

As well as developing into an important ecclesiastical centre during the mediaeval period Croston also achieved some social

and economic importance, and in 1283 it was granted a charter for a weekly market on Wednesdays and a fair on the eve, day and morrow of St. Wilfrid. In addition there was a Michaelmas Wake and annual cattle fair, which survived into the present century. Several of the present street names in the village have also continued in existence from these very early times.

By the 18th century Croston was still very much what it always had been, a largely agricultural community of farmers and associated trades people. Yet the weaving of flax, obtained from Croston Moss, was also coming to be an increasingly significant occupation for a number of people — particularly poorly-paid farm labourers who were turning to handloom weaving in their cottages as a way of supplementing their income. A number of three storey flax weavers' cottages can still be seen along Drinkhouse Lane, while others from the 18th and 19th centuries are situated opposite the packhorse bridge in the centre of the village.

During the first half of the 19th century there was a growing number of handloom weavers working in Croston, most of whom were

concerned with weaving goods for the Manchester and Preston markets. By the middle of the century, however, the first cotton-mill appeared and the textile industry began in earnest, although Croston was later badly affected by the cotton famine; then by the end of the 1800s brick-making developed as an important local occupation. During this period Croston also benefited from the coming of the Liverpool to Preston line of the Lancashire and Yorkshire Railway, which provided new employment for local people and at the same time began to break down the inevitable insularity of this mossland village. The 19th century also saw a substantial increase in Croston's population, with many people being accommodated in the rows of Victorian terraced houses built during this period.

Improvements in transport in the present century have meant that Croston has effectively become a dormitory village, with many people travelling to work in Preston, Leyland, Chorley and Wigan — but thankfully it has still retained much of its charm and individuality. A major contribution to this has been the enduring patronage of both the church and the lords of the manor,

*One of Croston's Intimate corners*

helping to bind the village together and give it a quite unique sense of identity. The church has traditionally owned a substantial amount of land in the area, which it rented out to local farmers, but its dominating influence was particularly evident in the first part of the 19th century when Rev. Streynsham Master was rector for 66 years. Known as 'King Croston', he established a 'School of Industry' for the instruction of poor girls in Croston, took a leading part in the establishment of four almshouses built to celebrate the jubilee of George III and helped to found the Croston Savings Bank in 1818. His example was followed in the 20th century by Bishop Rawstorne, who was instrumental in the formation of a Croston and District Nursing Association to provide the area with the services of a qualified nurse and midwife maintained by public subscription.

The lordship of the manor was latterly in the hands of the de Trafford family, who resided at Croston Hall until the 1960s when the family line died out. The last of the de Traffords is said to have been a wonderful landlord who maintained his property without raising the rents. The Hall has since been demolished, although its Roman Catholic chapel (dating from 1857 and designed by Pugin) remains in use. Village life was also helped by the yearly celebrations held here — among them were Croston Wakes, held on the Monday nearest to Michaelmas (September 29th), and Coffee Day, which still draws people back to the village for family reunions each July. Community spirit has been further strengthened by having to deal with a common adversary — the floodwaters of the River Yarrow, which have caused considerable distress to the village over the centuries.

Just over a mile to the north of Croston is the village of **Bretherton,** which displays a completely different character to its southern neighbour — whereas Croston is a compact and tightly-knit village of cobbled streets and terraced houses which huddle together for shelter, Bretherton's cottages are spread out over a larger area with no immediately recognisable centre to act as a focal point. In this way the village reflects the great attachment to the land which those living here over the centuries have held.

The land has not always been particularly hospitable, however, and before the major drainage schemes of the late 18th and early 19th centuries much of the surrounding land was under water in the form of moss, marsh and swamp. The people of Bretherton generally had the area to themselves, since it was a low-lying region avoided by nearly everyone else. Even by the middle of the 19th century the introduction to the original minute book of Bretherton Congregational Church was recording that Bretherton 'is an

agricultural district, the land is low, and of medium quality, the principal produce being hay. The inhabitants are poor, and the majority depend upon the weaving of plain and coloured works in the handlooms for their subsistence'.

Things have changed dramatically since then of course, and there is now a prevailing air of prosperity — the land has been brought under control to yield its increase and the farmhouses and cottages are neat and tidy, with many local people finding work in the nearby towns. Yet the village remains happily off the beaten track, thankfully well away from the busy A59 road between Preston and Liverpool. Its continuing isolation well into the 20th century is demonstrated by the fact that a piped water supply only arrived in Bretherton just before the First World War, whilst main sewerage was only introduced as late as the 1960s.

Although the great charm of Bretherton is found primarily within the delightful cottages which line its roads, there are also several rather more substantial buildings which testify to the history of the area. One of these is Bank Hall, built by the Banastre family in 1608. The Banastre family had lived in Bretherton since the 13th century, but when the family line died out in 1690 the Hall passed into the hands of the Fleetwoods and then the Leghs of Lyme, after which it eventually came into the possession of the Lilfords. Bank Hall was extensively restored in the 19th century to a Tudor style, and it features some attractive curved gables as well as a clock tower with its original oak staircase. The 19th century also saw the Carriage Drive being laid out, a magnificent tree-lined road connecting the Hall with the village.

Another attractive and locally important building is Carr House, built in 1613 by Thomas and Andrew Stones for their brother

*The Old Windmill, Bretherton*

John. The front elevation of red brick is decorated by a diaper pattern of blue bricks and features a central porch which rises to the full height of the house. It was from the first floor room above the porch that Jeremiah Horrocks, a 17th century astronomer, observed the transit of Venus for the first time. Horrocks' observation led directly to Captain Cook's voyage to Tahiti in 1769 to observe the transit of Venus for himself, and from here Cook went on to his discovery of Australia and the exploration of New Zealand. As well as a massive oak beamed inglenook fireplace the house has an unusual 'cage newel' staircase, reputedly one of only two such staircases in England.

Carr House is situated some distance to the north west of Bretherton, but another 17th century building in the village itself is the Old School House. This was built in 1653 as

*Carr House, Bretherton*

Bretherton's Free Grammar School, with the cost being met by James Fletcher. On completion of the school a board of 14 trustees was selected, known as Feoffes, who drew up a constitution of 21 rules. One of these rules, understandably, was that 'no scholar shall wear or bring along with him to the school any club, cudgell or any other weapon such as sword, rapier or the like'. Another building of interest is Bretherton windmill, situated halfway between Carr House and Bank Hall and built in 1741 to replace a wooden peg mill. The mill was in full operation until 1904, but after that it became derelict and has since been converted into a luxury home. Nearly 100 years after the construction of the windmill Bretherton finally got its own parish church, being built of stone in an Early English style in 1840. Prior to this Bretherton had been included within the ancient parish of Croston, and for centuries the villagers had to travel over to the church of St. Michael and All Angels for worship. The Congregational Church was somewhat quicker off the mark, however, and an

Independent Congregational chapel was built here in 1819.

To the north of Bretherton is the village of **Much Hoole,** where Jeremiah Horrocks had been serving as a curate in the parish church at the time of his famous observation in November 1639. The church itself is a small red brick building dating from 1628, with a sundial on its tower bearing the inscription SINE SOLE SILEO - 'Without the Sun I am Silent'. Passing northwards through what is largely an agricultural area we come firstly to **Walmer Bridge,** which developed as a sizeable settlement through a cotton mill established here in the 19th century, and then to **Longton,** once described as 'one of the prettiest villages in Lancashire' and famous in its day for gooseberries. As well as the arable farming which has taken place here over the centuries, Longton has also seen the production of bricks, beer and baskets in the area.

It was probably the local brewing industry which gave rise to the large number of pubs to be found in the village, with The Black Bull attracting the attention of Sir John Betjeman because of its unusual first floor window. Despite this predilection for drink, however, there is also a Teetotallers' Walk which enables the abstainer to make a complete circuit of the village without seeing any licensed premises at all. As well as ensuring that the physical thirst of its inhabitants was met, Longton has also paid attention to their spiritual thirst — there are records of a place of worship here as early as 1153, and the continuing spiritual fervour is evident well into the 19th century when local women did penance in church wearing a white sheet and standing on a stool.

*The Black Bull, Longton*

Adjacent to Longton is **Hutton,** with its Grammar School dating back to the 16th century, and then further along the A59 as it makes its way towards Preston is **Howick Cross,** named after the old cross situated on the roadside. Archaeological evidence suggests that the area has a long history dating back at least to Roman times, although the name 'Howick' is Scandinavian in origin and means a landfall by a creek or inlet.

Next door to Howick Cross is **Penwortham,** which looks out over the River Ribble in the valley below and then across to the town of Preston just beyond it. A 19th century historian wrote that Penwortham 'probably possesses finer and more historic associations than any country place contiguous to Preston', and certainly its strategic advantages of high ground and a fording point over the river were recognised by the Romans. Under their rule Penwortham became an important centre, with the hill being fortified to guard the ford below, while during the Saxon period a castle was built here. Castle Hill was in fact the only hill listed in the Domesday Survey, demonstrating its significance in the eyes of the Normans as well as those who had been here before them.

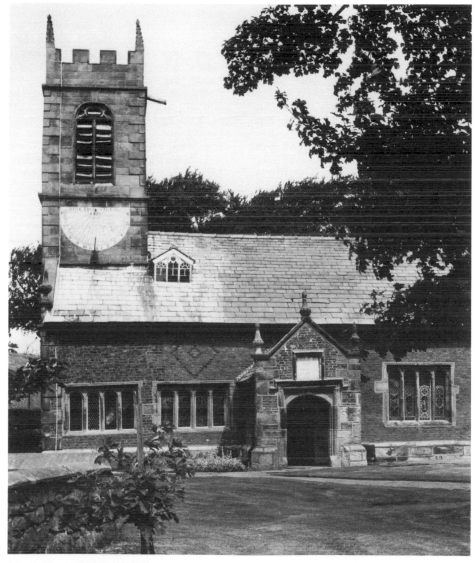

*Much Hoole Parish Church*

The area was also attractive in religious terms, and in 1075 Penwortham Priory was built here to take advantage of the crossing point of the river and the fact that the founding Abbot of Evesham could be given sixty salmon a year in part payment for the facilities which he provided. Castle Hill is now presided over by the local parish church, a largely 15th century building incorporating 19th century alterations, although there appears to have been a church on the site since AD 644.

Retracing our steps back along the A59 from this point high above the Ribble brings us eventually to one of the Ribble's tributaries, the River Douglas, and to the village of **Tarleton** situated along its west bank. Originally part of the parish of Croston, Tarleton had some ecclesiastical independence by virtue of the problem of crossing the Douglas and the Yarrow during times of flood, and in 1246 the 'island of Tharilton' was given to the monks of Thetford. Some time later it was transferred to the abbey at Cockersand near Lancaster. The village's early development came about through agriculture, focusing firstly on those fields above the river which were less likely to flood and then expanding through the increasing cultivation of the adjoining mossland.

Further significant growth then came about through Tarleton's entry into the seafaring world as the River Douglas was made navigable from the Ribble estuary to Wigan. An Act was passed in 1720 authorising the work to be carried out over the next eleven years, but the company responsible for the scheme collapsed at an early stage and the task was not resumed for 17 years; it was completed four years later enabling Tarleton-based vessels to make voyages to Dublin and the Lancashire ports with cargoes of hides, coal and limestone.

*The River Douglas at Tarleton*

Additional activity was generated when the Douglas Navigation was linked to the Leeds and Liverpool Canal, with Tarleton handling such a volume of traffic at the fortnightly spring tides that the scene was said to be "like a fleet of His Majesty's Ships" when they put to sea. There was enough maritime activity in the 'port' of Tarleton to support a village rope making business, in the form of a 400-yard long rope walk, and a 19th century census return included boat builders, sail makers and ship's carpenters in the list of occupations here. By the middle of the 19th century 300 vessels a year were sailing from Tarleton, although a severe decline set in shortly afterwards when dues were imposed and the customs officer withdrawn in 1859.

A resurgence of the Tarleton area came about in the last quarter of the 19th century with the arrival of the Southport to Preston railway, which provided much quicker access to the surrounding towns and their markets. Together with the introduction of piped water to the area this paved the way for the establishment of market gardening in Tarleton, with the first greenhouse being erected in 1894. Since that time market gardening has grown to become a major industry in the locality, with greenhouses becoming a permanent and widespread feature of the landscape.

Tarleton's first place of worship is mentioned in the records of Cockersand Abbey and appears to have been built in the 13th century under licence from the Pope. This chapel of ease was 'for the inhabitants of the said manor being far distant from the parish church at Croston and often prevented by the rising of the great waters and rivers from going there'. The chapel was pulled down at the time of the dissolution of the monasteries, but by 1719 money was made available for the erection of St. Mary's Church on the same site. This brick building can still be seen at the southern end of the village, adjacent to the A59, having remained largely unchanged over the years except for the addition of a stone turret, a cupola and a porch and vestry in 1824. By the end of the 19th century Tarleton's growth in population led to the building of the larger Holy Trinity Church on a more central site, designed to a 14th century style and praised for its 'seemliness and beauty'.

To the north of Tarleton are the villages of **Hesketh Bank** and **Becconsall,** which have grown up with a similar history of agriculture, maritime activity and market gardening. Both these villages have seen considerable changes in the surrounding landscape as reclamation of the Ribble marshes has progressed further and further northwards. The name 'Hesketh' is Danish in origin and means a landing place, whilst 'Becconsall' means Beacons Hill and stems from the artificial mound which was built to defend the fords across the river. The earliest

*St. Mary's Church, Tarleton*

reference to Hesketh Bank is in the 13th century, with most of the settlement's inhabitants being engaged in agriculture during the following five centuries. By the 18th century seafaring had developed as a significant activity, with larger sea-going vessels loading and unloading from barges at various points along the mouth of the Douglas and handling cargoes of coal, bricks and slates.

During the 19th century large parts of marshland were reclaimed from the sea through the efforts of itinerant Irish labourers, prior to which Hesketh Bank and Becconsall had been situated right on the Ribble estuary. This rather favourable location had led to the two villages becoming a popular spot for visitors, who came 'for bathing and marine recreation', and before the land was reclaimed and given over to agriculture the area also supported a lot of game and provided for coursing events. When eventually Blackpool and Southport offered more attractions than Hesketh Sands could offer the enclosure of the marshes and the arrival of the West Lancashire railway brought new prosperity to the area.

One of the prettiest spots in Hesketh Bank is at the end of Becconsall Lane, the site of some venerable farmhouses as well as the old parish church of Hesketh-with-Becconsall. The present brick building dates from 1765, although a church has existed on this site at least from the 16th century. Nowadays services are held here only occasionally, generally on Remembrance Day and on Old Church Sunday in July, since a more modern parish church was built alongside the main road in the village in 1926. Nevertheless it remains a place worthy of a visit since it has a quiet charm of its own and affords extensive views across Hesketh Sands to Lytham St. Annes and Blackpool.

The views from the churchyard certainly attracted the local historian A. Hewitson when writing in the latter part of the 19th century, and his description of the panorama is as enticing and accurate now as it was then: 'On the north-western side we noticed first the long level lands of Becconsall Marsh, reclaimed from the wash of many a tide, spread with young shooting corn and wheat, and rippling in the sunlight like a lake of emerald; beyond were long lines of creamy barren sandbanks; then the Ribble flowing down to the sea coolly and calmly; in the distance the Naze Point, Freckleton, Kirkham and the wide expanse of the Fylde; hills climbed up to the right; and still more to the right stood Preston — stately, cloudy, expansive; whilst to the south we had the winding defile of the Douglas and the fruitful fields of Tarleton'. Not far from the old church is a boatyard and marina, maintaining the area's important links with the sea. It was at this point on the Douglas that goods were brought by larger vessels before being loaded into barges for transport inland to Wigan.

Moving westwards round the West Lancashire coast from this point we come firstly to **Banks,** a village which grew substantially as nearby Southport developed during the 19th century. There had been a settlement of monks here during the 13th century, producing salt from sea water and then transporting it via the Ribble to Clitheroe, but up to the 1800s Banks was essentially an isolated hamlet of fishermen and farmers, some of whom were involved in handloom weaving. Cockles appear to have been a source of wealth for the village, although there was also mussel gathering, 'bobbing' for eels, and shrimping. During the early 19th century the mosses around Banks were recognised for their potential in growing vegetables, and Southport soon became an outlet for the produce of the village's market gardens. Lettuce, tomatoes and celery were all grown here, but the fertility of the soil hardly relieved the work required to sell the produce — to reach Preston market the growers had to leave at 10 o'clock in the evening in order to be there in time for the early morning opening!

From the 19th century Gothic-style parish church of St. Stephen's-in-the-Banks the road through the centre of the village takes us west again before joining up with the main road into Southport. Before arriving there the road passes close to **Churchtown,** a one-time shrimping port with some attractive thatched cottages which pre-date the rather more substantial gentlemen's residences to be found in Southport itself. In addition to St. Cuthbert's Church at the centre of the village there is the admirable Meols Hall with its fine range of stable buildings, as well as a couple of old pubs and the extensive Botanic Gardens.

*Picturesque Churchtown*

*Stately Meols Hall*

At one time Churchtown was probably a much larger settlement than the area of sand dunes and fishermen's cottages which eventually grew up into the major resort encompassing it in the present day, and **Southport** really owes its existence to the growing popularity of sea bathing along the Lancashire coast during the latter part of the 18th century. It was in 1792 that William Sutton of North Meols built the first lodging house for visitors to South Hawes, then an extensive area of sandhills, followed in 1798 by the South Port Hotel which gave the future town its name. These early developments took place at what is now the southern end of Lord Street, and Sutton was soon joined by others who saw an opportunity to cater for the growing number of visitors to this part of the coast.

Lord Street itself, Southport's most prestigious thoroughfare, began to emerge during the 1820s when the joint lords of the manor (the Bold-Houghton and Fleetwood-Hesketh families) laid out the spacious street on formal lines so as to ensure that the development was of a high-class nature. Planned residential development in Lord Street and other areas from the 1840s onwards ensured that the town grew as a seaside resort for the refined well-to-do sections of the community, and by the end of the 19th century Southport was well established in its role as a select residential town and high-class resort.

The wealth and opulence which must have been attracted to Southport during the Victorian and Edwardian eras is evident from the many fine buildings which grace both sides of Lord Street, particularly around London Square and the Town Hall. The Town Hall itself is especially impressive, designed by local architect Thomas Withnell in a Classical style and featuring a central portico above which is a balcony beneath a pediment displaying the figures of Justice, Mercy and Truth. Next door to the Town Hall, but separated by the Cambridge Arcade, are other attractive municipal buildings — the Southport Arts Centre, built of buff sandstone in 1872-74 and featuring a high clock tower, and the Atkinson Art Gallery, built again of buff sandstone in 1876-78.

In front of these buildings are the Municipal Gardens, which were originally privately owned but were taken over by the Improvement Commissioners in the 1860s for the purpose of creating a central boulevard. However, substantial progress was only made at the beginning of the 20th century when a plan for the Gardens was prepared by the landscape architect Thomas Mawson. A central feature of his design was a bandstand with cast-iron columns, balustrades and fountains, and although the

bandstand had to be dismantled in 1969 a new one has since been introduced on a site lower down Lord Street. Some of Mawson's classical stone balustrading from his original plan does still exist, however, around the edges of the Municipal Gardens.

Higher up Lord Street is London Square, at the centre of which is the town's War Memorial. This consists of a central obelisk sixty metres high flanked by two pavilions of Roman Doric colonnades. Southport was one of the first towns to embark upon a scheme for a memorial, with the £30,000 cost being met by public subscription after an appeal was launched in 1919. At the corner of London Square and London Street is a yellow sandstone building which now houses the National Westminster Bank, another fine example of Victorian Classical architecture, whilst next to it is a row of Victorian commercial buildings which includes Southport's main Post Office. Further along Lord Street on the same side, to the north east of the Town Hall, is a row of old Regency houses, with their long front gardens serving as a reminder of the reason for the generous width of this main thoroughfare. It appears

*Southport's Victorian elegance*

that the houses here had to be built well back from a chain of pools which used to flood in times of heavy rain, and an open ditch at the bottom of the gardens provided the means for

*Lord Street in Southport*

draining off the surplus water. It was in this way that the building line of Lord Street was established.

From this point one can look across the road to admire one of Southport's best known features — the cast-iron canopies which run the whole length of the west side of Lord Street. These canopies incorporate many different styles of ornamentation and decoration, and they are an important aspect of Southport's main shopping boulevard. Towards the top end of Lord Street on this west side is the Bold Hotel, one of the town's first substantial hotels but built in about 1830 at a time when Southport was little more than a village. Its excellent views of the surrounding coastline and countryside were a source of much admiration when it first appeared on the scene, as no doubt was its Classical style and portico supported by Doric columns. Passing beneath the canopies and over Nevill Street on the way back down Lord Street brings us to a series of richly decorated commercial buildings. Among the first of these are the Albany Buildings, built in 1884 and featuring Elizabethan-style half-timbered gables as well as some heavily carved Early English Gothic stone windows. Further along is the Midland Bank, built in 1889 in the Roman Corinthian style and incorporating an ornately carved facade which hides a splendid interior of only one storey. The polished granite columns support a triangular pediment, on top of which stands a crowned statue of Neptune. Adjacent to this building is a group of properties known as the Muslim Buildings, so named because their rounded and pointed 'horseshoe windows' give them a distinctly Oriental appearance, and then immediately after comes the ornate entrance to the Wayfarer's Arcade. Originally known as Leyland Arcade and opened in 1898, the Arcade's long narrow approach leads into a broad galleried area which is decorated with

*Lord Street's famous canopies*

moulded panels, friezes, ornate woodwork and stained glass windows and is covered over by a glass and iron arched roof.

A little further down Lord Street, but still on the same side, is another of Southport's stately banks — one built in 1920-24 of white Portland stone and reminiscent of a Grecian temple. The giant columns and huge bronze door help to portray the image of solidity and security which every bank is keen to communicate. The very diverse architectural tradition on display in Southport is underlined by a contrasting building still further along Lord Street, a four storey half-timbered property designed in a neo Tudor-Elizabethan style. Dating from the turn of the century it has an iron and glass canopy and incorporates some interesting boat-building features which can also been seen on other buildings in the same block.

Crossing over Lord Street at this point brings us to the Prince of Wales Hotel, one of Southport's most impressive late 19th century hotels. Dating from 1876-77 when it was built as part of a speculative boom in the development of the resort at that time, the hotel was named after Prince Edward following his visit to the town. Then across Portland Street and beyond more public gardens is Wellington Terrace, a row of Regency houses which date from 1816-1818 and include the oldest buildings on Lord Street. Not far from here, at the southern end of Lord Street, are two commemorative tablets marking the original site of Southport's first hotel, built by William Sutton who was 'commonly known as the Old Duke and the Founder of Southport'. Even he might have found it difficult to conceive how his initiative here was to set in motion the process by which a wilderness and sandhills was to be quickly turned into a highly fashionable and elegant resort.

It is interesting to note that as early as 1869 Green's Official Directory was recording of Southport that its 'delightful sea-girt position and the extreme salubrity of its climate have produced an almost unparalleled change in transforming it in a few years from a small and almost unknown village...into an extensive and prosperous town chiefly composed of villa residences of elegant structure, so that it has been styled with great appropriateness The Montpelier of the North'. Many of these elegant villas are still to be seen on the south side of the town centre, particularly in the Birkdale area, enjoying splendid isolation from one another in their delightfully leafy surroundings.

As well as developing into a high-class residential town with superb shopping facilities Southport continues to attract numerous visitors in its capacity as a major holiday resort. A very real and continuing link with the past is the Pier, which opened in

*One of Southport's early attractions*

August 1860 and at 1,211 yards long has remained the country's longest operational pleasure pier. The traditional donkey rides on the sands have also continued from Victorian times, but nowadays there are a host of other attractions — including the Pleasureland amusement park, the Steamport Transport Museum and the 86-acre Marine Lake. For those who prefer rather more peace and quiet Southport offers a wide range of parks and some magnificent floral displays — from the hanging baskets outside many of the Lord Street shops to the brilliance of formal layouts in Hesketh Park and along the Promenade. One of the most delightful features is the half-mile long herbaceous border along Rotten Row in Victoria Park, at its best during the month of August.

Further down the coast, through Birkdale and Ainsdale, is the town of **Formby.** This settlement is much smaller than Southport but has its origins much further back in time — back in the Viking era in fact. Norsemen appear to have been the first people to settle on this coast in any numbers, and the name Formby (originally spelt 'Fornebei') means either 'Forni's town', Forni being a well known Norse personal name, or 'the old town'. Forni could have been the leader of the expedition which took possession of this area, or alternatively there could have been a settlement of people here previously — hence the reference to 'the old town'. After the Norman Conquest there was a succession of landowners, although in the Domesday Book Formby is mentioned as being held under three manors. For a large part of the Middle Ages much of the land in this part of Lancashire was granted to various monastic foundations as a source of income, but at the Dissolution in 1536-39 the Formby and Blundell families eventually emerged as the owners of the manors of Formby, Ainsdale and Ravenmeols.

Formby Hall is situated to the north of Formby itself, a site which has probably been occupied

**St. Peter's Church, Formby**

since the 12th century. The present house was built for William Formby in 1523, although there have been several later additions. One of these was the introduction of battlements in the middle of the 18th century by John Formby, who had been impressed by the mediaeval-Gothic style of Horace Walpole's house at Strawberry Hill in London. John Formby is also said to have been responsible for the laying out of the grounds, plantation and lake.

The oldest church in Formby is St. Peter's, built in the Georgian style of architecture during the middle of the 18th century to replace an earlier chapel which was blown down during a storm in 1739. Some of the stones were rescued from the old site and used in the foundations of the new church, whilst the sundial was re-erected to stand near the porch. A bell dated 1661 was also retrieved and placed in the turret of St. Peter's. The new church was built some distance inland from the site of the old chapel, well away from the dangers of sand and sea, but by 1855 the site was again in use as the location for another church, this one being dedicated to St. Luke. Built at the time when plans were being made to turn Formby into a seaside resort like Southport, St. Luke's became rather appropriately known as 'The Little Church in the Sandhills' and was at first under the patronage of the Formby family. Many of the family graves are still there, some of them being buried under the sand, and there is a memorial stone referring to Richard Formby in the porch. Within the churchyard was an unusual stone about three-feet high bearing the carved symbol of a cross, standing on a pedestal of three steps and known locally as the 'Godstone'. Tradition suggests that at a funeral the coffin was carried around the stone three times before the burial itself took place.

For much of its history Formby was a straggling village made up of groups of thatched cottages which were occupied by families who had been here for generations and generations. Life began to change considerably with the coming of the railway, but even in the early 20th century Formby was still under a manorial system of

government which had altered little since the 17th and 18th centuries. The advent of the Liverpool to Southport railway, however, effectively brought in a new era, and a new Formby began to take shape as it became a desirable residential area for Liverpool businessmen. Up to this time Liverpool merchants had been forced to live close to their offices, but with the greater flexibility provided by railway transport they found that it was now both convenient and practical to live in the country. With the completion of the railway there were also proposals, launched by the newly formed Formby Land and Building Company, to establish Formby as a coastal resort in the same way that Southport had been developed. However, although a promenade and a number of boarding houses were constructed the scheme never really took off, and the company was wound up in 1902.

To the south of Formby is **Hightown,** built largely around the railway and close to what was the site of the Crosby lighthouse, whilst just over the main Southport to Liverpool road from here is the much smaller village of **Ince Blundell.** The name 'Ince' appears to come from the Celtic word 'Ynes' meaning an island within a watery meadow, and the area has obviously required a lot of drainage over the centuries before it could be brought into commercial use for agriculture. The addition of the family name of Blundell was added at a later date to distinguish it from a village of the same name near Wigan, although the Blundells appear to have held land here from at least the 12th century. Some time later the

Blundell family inter-married with the family of Weld, and in the 19th century Thomas Weld adopted the name of Weld-Blundell when the lord of Ince died unmarried.

The magnificent Ince Blundell Hall, now a convalescent home but for several centuries the residence of the Blundell family, dates from about 1777 when Henry Blundell decided to build a rather more stately house than the old Tudor hall which the family had occupied up to that time. The very first Hall on the site had been built during the later part of the 14th century. Attached to the New Hall is the Pantheon, a circular building constructed by Henry Blundell to house his magnificent collection of paintings and drawings, whilst on the other side of the Hall is the Garden Temple which accommodated his quite unique collection of marble statues gathered together from his travels on the Continent. All these splendid buildings are situated within a delightful environment of peaceful seclusion and wooded parkland.

Attached to the Hall is Ince Blundell's only place of worship, the Holy Family Church; originally a small chapel it was extended by Thomas Weld-Blundell in 1848 and given to the parish 100 years later. A custom which appears to be unique in this country is the annual candlelight service at the church, when people from the parish decorate the graves in the cemetery with candles and flowers prior to a procession and service there. This custom is traditionally found in Belgium but it was introduced to Ince Blundell at the start of the present century.

**The Pantheon, Ince Blundell Hall**

*Astley Hall near Chorley*

*Albert Dock, Liverpool*

The influence and patronage of the Blundell family is also evident within the village itself, with the village school being endowed by Charles Robert Blundell and built in 1843 on land given by Thomas Weld-Blundell. The local pub, the Weld Blundell Arms, also bears the family name.

Another Blundell family have been lords of the manor at nearby **Little Crosby** since the 13th century, although they are not related to the Weld-Blundells who lived at Ince Blundell Hall. The earliest mention of a Hall at Little Crosby is in 1275, although the present building dates from the start of the 17th century. To the north of this historic and dignified Hall are some early 17th century stables as well as the Great Barn, which may date from the 16th or even 15th century. This latter building is the oldest on the site and features some huge oak beams supporting the roof; it was also the place where the customary festivities of the township were being held well into the present century. Within the grounds of Crosby Hall, which are completely encircled by their own stone wall,

*Some of Little Crosby's old cottages*

stands the old village cross as well as a memorial chapel built on the site of the Halkirk Burial Ground where Roman Catholic recusants were buried in the 17th century.

The village of Little Crosby reflects the historic character of Crosby Hall and features some fine 17th century cottages together with an 18th century smithy and a 19th century church. There is also the centuries-old Well Cross, marking the site of the 'town well' and at one time situated on the village green. This well supplied water to the village until the 1870s, when the construction of a main sewer caused it to run dry. Much of what has gone on in Little Crosby has been the result of the patronage of the Blundell family, and this is particularly evident in the building of St. Mary's Church. This was largely the work of William Blundell in 1845-46, who not only built the church but also lowered the level of the surrounding roads in order to make the church look taller and more impressive.

His son Nicholas Blundell was responsible for some of the interior decorations as well as several of the church's sandstone features, and in the windows are to be seen the coats of arms of various members of the Blundell of Crosby family and the families into which they married. There are also memorials to members of the family on the nearby walls, whilst back in the village across the road from the Well Cross can be seen a memorial to Francis Nicholas Blundell in recognition of his devotion to the welfare of the people of Little Crosby. Due to the beneficent interest of the Blundell family over the centuries the village of Little Crosby has changed very little, and it is a delightful place which continues to bear a faithful testimony to generations and traditions which have long since disappeared.

**The Well Cross, Little Crosby**

From Little Crosby the narrow country lanes take us through the hamlets of Lunt and Sefton before bringing us into **Maghull,** which lies on both sides of the A59 road between Ormskirk and Liverpool. The first reference to Maghull is in the Domesday Book, where it is recorded under the name 'Magele'. In the ensuing years it developed as a township of enclosed fields, surrounded by substantial woods and mossland, with its own moated manor house. This has since been demolished, but an interesting survivor from the mediaeval period is the ancient chapel in the grounds of St. Andrew's Church. This is the oldest ecclesiastical building within what is now recognised as the Merseyside area, with its outstanding feature being the north window dating from the end of the 13th century. Also within the chapel is a fragment of ancient plaster on the east wall which displays some traces of a mediaeval wall painting. In 1650 the chapel of Maghull was made into a parish church because of the difficulty which the villagers were experiencing in getting to Sefton Church across the flood plain of the River Alt. During the course of the next 150 years Maghull developed into a prosperous rural parish, although most of the land remained in the hands of a few individuals.

Significant changes in the locality began to take place with the coming of the canal, which coincided with the re-building of the chapel in the 1770s. The canal provided transport for fertilisers, grain, manure, cotton and coal, and as a result farming production was boosted and a passenger service established to provide a smoother journey between Liverpool and Wigan. Maghull

*Chapel House Farm, Maghull*

already had facilities to cater for travellers along the main Liverpool road, but with the advent of the canal the number of inns and beerhouses rapidly increased.

Further development took place with the opening of the railway line from Liverpool to Preston in 1850, and the substantial Victorian houses along Brook Road were built to cater for the demand from richer Liverpool people who no longer wished to live in the crowded streets of the city. Almost 30 houses were built between 1850 and 1900 amid the hedged fields of Maghull, designed for wealthy clients. With the increase in population in the parish a new church had to be built, and in 1880 St. Andrew's was consecrated as a replacement for the old chapel nearby. Maghull continued to expand during the course of the 20th century, and by the late 1960s it was the largest civil parish in terms of population in the country.

One of the most attractive buildings in Maghull is Chapel House Farm with its stone flagged roof, mullioned windows and gabled dormers as well as a projecting porch with an upper room. This now forms part of the Maghull Homes for Epileptics, founded in 1888 as a pioneer colony for those suffering from epilepsy and the first such institution in Europe. The new Maghull Manor, built in 1780 close to the site of the original manor house, was also incorporated as part of the epileptic colony shortly after it was established here. Maghull is thus an interesting amalgam of new and old, a large residential area serving Liverpool which contains within it pockets of older buildings which give an insight into its long history.

As Maghull has grown in size it has effectively coalesced with the neighbouring village of **Lydiate** to the north, a pleasant settlement which borders the flat open farmland created on what were the West Lancashire mosses. The name Lydiate appears to come from the words 'Hlid-Geat' or 'Swing-Gate', suggesting an enclosure with a gate to stop cattle straying and thus indicating local animal husbandry in the area from very early days. Probably the

*Maghull Chapel*

most interesting building in Lydiate is the Scotch Piper Inn, a lovely cruck framed house with a thatched roof which has the reputation of being the oldest inn in Lancashire. Before the Highland descent in 1715 the Scotch Piper was called the Royal Oak, but it has also been named 'The Bag Pipes' and 'Old Lolly' at different times since then.

Another interesting reminder of earlier days is the ruin of St. Katharine's Chapel, a 15th century building erected by the Ireland family whose ancestral home was the nearby Lydiate Hall. When St. Katharine's Chapel became unsuitable for services Thomas Weld-Blundell built Our Lady's Church in the fields close by as a replacement for it; opened in 1854 the church contains four alabaster panels representing the martyrdom of St. Katharine, which originally came from the chapel.

Lying between Lydiate and Ormskirk is the parish of **Aughton,** comprising the original

*The Scotch Piper Inn, Lydiate*

village of Aughton itself together with later residential areas which grew up close to the railway stations at Town Green and Aughton Park. A wedge of open farmland separates the 'ancient and modern' parts of the parish, so much of Aughton remains as pleasant countryside with dairying, arable farming and market gardening important features of the area as a whole. The undulating nature of the countryside offers attractive views of both the Pennines to the east and the Lancashire coastline to the west.

The most important building in Aughton is St. Michael's Parish Church, which displays a slender 14th century spire rising from the octagonal upper storey of an otherwise square tower. The tower itself is unusual in that it sits between the nave and a side chapel on small Gothic arches. The main structure of the church dates from the 15th and 16th centuries, but there is also a doorway blocked by a massive old buttress which has been preserved from the original Norman church occupying this same site. Part of a Saxon cross is also preserved within the church, as is an old stone coffin beneath the tower and a font which has been in use for over 500 years. There are several 17th century memorial brasses on the walls, including a rhyming one which states that ancestors of the Mossock family have been buried here 'above 380 years', whilst in the churchyard is a sundial dating from 1756.

On the prominent ridge overlooking the rest of the parish is the second of Aughton's churches, Christ Church, which has an impressive nave roof as well as some fine sculptures and wood carving. There is also an excellent reredos which extends across the whole width of the east end of the chancel. It was probably from this elevated point in

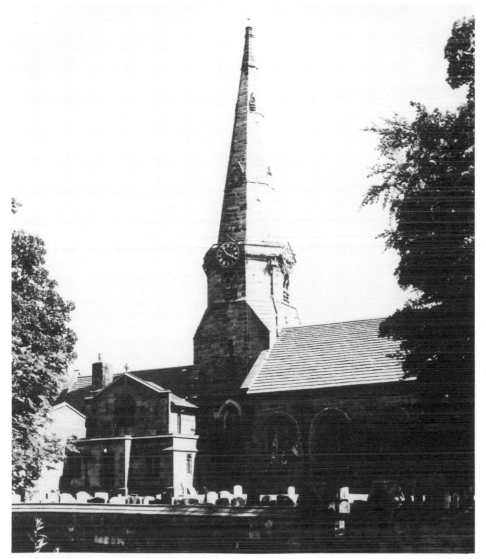

*St. Michael's Parish Church, Aughton*

*The Parish Church, Ormskirk*

Aughton that **Ormskirk** was bombarded during the course of the English Civil War in the 17th century, but happily the town survived this assault to become an important market centre at the heart of the West Lancashire plain.

Ormskirk's origins go back to Viking times, when according to one account a Viking leader called Orme landed on the coast in 840 AD and started a community here. The church which was built about that time, together with the small settlement around it, became known as 'Orme's Kirk' and has come down to us today as Ormskirk. In 1286 the town received its market charter from Edward I and was thus recognised as a borough, with the canons of Burscough Priory claiming the rights and tolls of a weekly market here. There was also an annual fair established at about the same time, although this has since ceased.

During the course of the next 300 years Ormskirk continued to develop in its role as a market town, and it was at this juncture that the Stanley family's long association with Ormskirk began. Largely by virtue of the Stanleys' association with the Royalist cause Ormskirk became the scene of considerable activity during the English Civil War, and the siege of Lathom House in 1644-45 was a major turning point in the course of the hostilities. When the fortified residence of the Stanley family was eventually taken the event was celebrated in London by a public thanksgiving, and orders were issued for the 'pride and glory of Lancashire' to be completely destroyed.

During the 18th century Ormskirk continued to grow in importance as a market town, with market clerks being appointed to check weights and measures. It was in this century that the Old Town Hall was built to hold meetings of the manorial and magistrates' courts, with the open ground floor space beneath being used as a butter and cheese market. Many inns were also built at about this time, to cater for the increased trade in the town as well as for the large number of stagecoach passengers on the well used routes through Ormskirk. In the latter part of the 18th century the town's prosperity was further stimulated by the partial drainage of Martin Mere, resulting in a considerable increase in rich agricultural land in the vicinity, and by the rapid growth of Liverpool's population which created a ready market for local farm produce. All these things contributed to a large amount of new development in the town, and even now Ormskirk has a very marked Georgian appearance and atmosphere about it.

Ormskirk was also affected by the Industrial Revolution, which brought cotton spinning and silk weaving to the town. Hat, glove and stocking making also took their place here alongside the more traditional activities of flour milling, brewing and coopering, tanning, clock making and cabinet making. Iron founding was also important from as early as 1796 and several cartage businesses evolved to serve the manufacturers, but because the Leeds and Liverpool Canal was routed some distance from the town Ormskirk was very largely denied any direct benefit from this new means of transport. This did not prove to be the case with the coming of the railway, however, and the Liverpool to Ormskirk section opened in 1849 to provide greatly improved travel for both freight and passengers. This also opened up the opportunity for people to work in Liverpool but live in Ormskirk, and the result was that many fine large houses were built in the locality during the Victorian period as residences for these early commuters.

By the early part of the 20th century, however, Ormskirk suffered a considerable decline due to competition from other manufacturing towns in Lancashire which were better suited for growth because of their role as ports or centres of working population. Ormskirk thus reverted to its more stable agricultural activities, with corn milling and brewing lasting rather longer than other industries because of their use of local products. Since then Ormskirk has become something of a dormitory town, experiencing a new period of growth as a pleasant residential area with good shopping facilities and the continuing advantages of a traditional market centre.

A good point from which to gain a full perspective of Ormskirk's character is the Clock Tower at the junction of Church Street, Burscough Street, Aughton Street and Moor Street, since this is the accepted centre of the town and the crossing of the main routes through it. The Clock Tower was erected by public subscription in 1876 on the spot which was originally occupied by the old market cross; this was the focal point of Ormskirk and the place where public announcements were made. Along Church Street can be found a number of old buildings which have important links with Ormskirk's past, including the Old Town Hall (which still bears the Stanley family crest of the 'Eagle and Child') as well as the unusually named Snig's Foot Hotel (a Victorian public house).

At the far end of Church Street is the parish church of Ormskirk, dedicated to St. Peter and St. Paul and without doubt Ormskirk's most important and visually impressive building. The first thing to be noticed about this church is that it possesses both a tower and a steeple, the latter having been built as the first of the two in the 15th century but appearing more modern because it has been re-built twice since that time. The massive battlemented tower immediately behind the spire was built in the 16th century with masonry from Burscough Priory, in order to accommodate the bells brought from the Priory after its dissolution by Henry VIII.

The oldest feature of the church is a stone carving on the outer face of the chancel's east wall, probably the work of a Saxon craftsman and indicating that a church has existed on this hill top site for more than a thousand years. Within the chancel itself one can find a later Norman window on one side together with an Early English arcade of two arches on the other. The east window of the chancel contains some of the finest stained glass in the north of England and was donated in commemoration of Nathaniel Heywood, a saintly vicar who was ejected from his office in 1662 for his refusal to conform to the restrictive terms of the Act of Uniformity. In the west part of the chancel is the Royal Chapel, one of the four remaining chapels or chantries in the church and featuring the Royal Arms at the apex of the first arch. It was here that Henry VII worshipped when he came to nearby Lathom House to visit his stepfather, the Earl of Derby, who had set the English crown upon his head after his victory at Bosworth Field.

Separated from the chancel by a 13th century arch is the Derby Chapel, now known as the Warriors Chapel. This is the burial vault of the Stanley family, who were the ancient rulers of the Isle of Man as well as being the Earls of Derby. It was the third Earl of Derby who built the chapel for his family, members of which had previously been buried at Burscough Priory. The four mutilated Stanley effigies on display here are of two men in armour and two women in period attire. The Scarisbrick Chapel is separated from the Derby Chapel by a hand-carved oak screen, and here can be found a life-size 15th century brass of a knight of the ancient Scarisbrick family. There is also a small brass nearby which states in a rhyming fashion that the ancestors of Henry Mosoke have been interred in this church for over 385 years. The fourth chapel is the Bickerstaffe Chapel situated in the north transept, with an interesting 15th century window near the pulpit.

The church's font is dated 1661 and was given by the Countess of Derby, who defended Lathom Hall against Cromwell's forces during the Civil War; it bears the Stanley insignia of the 'Eagle and Child' and has an hour glass fixed to the side of the bowl. Other interesting features within the church include a 17th century sundial just above the entry porch; a dog whipper's bench just inside the porch doors (fitted with a drawer for gloves, whips and tongs to separate and remove fighting dogs that had followed their owners into church); and a 17th century book rack which originally offered loaves of bread for the poor.

Looking northwards from the Clock Tower gives us a view along Burscough Street, another of Ormskirk's original thoroughfares and at one time part of the Liverpool to Preston turnpike road. Towards the far end of the street on the left hand side is the 'Buck i'th'Vine' public house, an old coaching inn with rounded stone quoins at its corners, whilst at the very end of Burscough Street on the same side is a fine Georgian town house. To the rear of these buildings is 29A Burscough Street or Swan House, probably the oldest building in Ormskirk after the church, while on the other side of the street several of the properties are timber-framed buildings with more modern facades. Derby Chambers, however, is a late Victorian building and is typically very elaborate.

To the south from the Clock Tower is Aughton Street, featuring some of the town's more recent architecture, while to the east is Moor Street leading down towards the Beaconsfield Monument and the town's bus station. From this point Railway Road takes us past some nicely restored terraced properties and up towards Derby Street, where a number of the town's public buildings are located and where some good examples of varied 19th century architecture can be seen. In the opposite direction from the Beaconsfield Monument, to the south, is Chapel Street with its humbler domestic architecture — on the right are some Georgian terraced cottages and on the left some later properties dating from the Victorian period. Further along on the right-hand side is a 14th century cruck framed cottage displaying a date stone which records the fact that the property was leased by William Arthur Grice in 1703, while further on again is a 17th century house associated with the Puritan upheavals of the 1660s.

The spire of Ormskirk parish church is one of a family of three such landmarks in this area — the others are St. Michael's in Aughton,

*Feature outside Ormskirk church*

which we have already noted, and St. Cuthbert's in **Halsall.** This lovely village lies within richly fertile farming land which has been won from the extensive Halsall Moss and is situated just over three miles to the north west of Ormskirk. Not far away from the village is the Leeds and Liverpool Canal, a very pleasant feature of this part of West Lancashire as it threads its way quietly through the flat countryside. St. Cuthbert's parish church is situated on the Southport to Aintree road at the heart of Halsall, and dating from the middle of the 13th century it is one of the oldest and most beautiful churches in the diocese of Liverpool. The spire itself is of particular interest, being added in the 15th century and rising from a tower whose upper stages are octagonal.

From St. Cuthbert's the main road through Halsall leads northwards for two miles before joining up with the Southport to Ormskirk road, at which point we encounter the village of **Scarisbrick,** pronounced 'Scazebrick' by locals and those who are in the know. This is the largest parish in Lancashire, with its 8,000 or so acres of rich agricultural land being intensively cultivated in the growing of vegetables such as carrots, Brussel sprouts, cabbage and early potatoes. Despite its size the population of the parish is comparatively small and is centred on a number of hamlets scattered throughout the characteristically flat landscape of this part of the West Lancashire Plain. Agriculture and allied activities still provide most of the employment for Scarisbrick's working population. The focal point of the area is Scarisbrick Hall, which has dominated the life of the inhabitants here for many centuries now. The name of the parish itself, and of the family which became so closely associated with it, first appears in the reign of Richard I when Simon de Grubhead of Lathom gave land here to his brother Gilbert de Scarisbrick, who had adopted the name of his property. So from the time that

*Scarisbrick Hall*

*St. Cuthbert's Parish Church, Halsall*

the first Hall was built in the reign of King Stephen right through into the 20th century the Scarisbrick family continued to exercise very considerable control over the district. The family's power and influence is particularly evident from the scale and grandeur of Scarisbrick Hall, said to be one of the finest examples of Gothic Revival architecture in England.

In the middle of the 19th century Charles Scarisbrick, reputed to be the wealthiest commoner in Lancashire, had set about remodelling the ancestral home with the help of the Victorian architect Augustus Welby Pugin. It was eventually finished in 1867 by his sister Anne, who had inherited the estate and enlisted the assistance of Pugin's son to design the one-hundred foot tower which is another of West Lancashire's distinctive landmarks. This slender clock tower and the turrets, gables and pinnacles of the two-hundred room mansion bear a striking resemblance to the Houses of Parliament in London, due apparently to the fact that Pugin senior worked with Sir Charles Barry on the buildings at Westminster. It was thus quite appropriate that the Prime Minister of the day, Mr. Gladstone, should be spectacularly entertained by Lady Anne at Scarisbrick Hall in December 1867 during his visit to Ormskirk and Southport. The last member of the family

to reside here was Sir Everard Scarisbrick who sold the Hall and its 450 acre estate in 1945 for use as an independent boarding school.

The north west part of the parish of Scarisbrick includes land which at one time lay beneath **Martin Mere,** in its day one of

*Some of Scarisbrick Hall's fascinating architectural detail*

*Scarisbrick Hall's imposing front entrance*

145

the biggest lakes in England with an area of 3,000 acres. This lake was known to the Romans, and during the Middle Ages the monks from nearby Burscough Priory fished here. The man responsible for the drainage and reclamation of this huge tract of land was Thomas Eccleston of Scarisbrick Hall, who brought in John Gilbert (the engineer involved with the Bridgewater Canal) to tackle the problem at the end of the 18th century. Eccleston's efforts to drain Martin Mere and reclaim the land for agriculture were successful enough to earn him the gold medal of the Society for the Encouragement of the Arts, Manufacture and Commerce, but even so part of the area reverted back to the wetland which for centuries had been the winter quarters for thousands of pinkfooted geese and other wildfowl.

It is not surprising then that this should become an important sanctuary for bird life, and in July 1972 the Wildfowl Trust acquired 363 acres of marshland here to create what has become an internationally known wildfowl centre. As well as the landscaped water gardens providing an ideal habitat for over 1600 resident swans, geese and ducks there is also a 300-acre wild refuge overlooked by hides which provide spectacular viewing of a wealth of other species of wildfowl. During the winter months there are thousands of pinkfooted geese arriving here from Iceland and Greenland together with large numbers of pintail, teal and snipe from Northern Europe. These are being joined by an ever growing number of swans, including whoopers from Iceland and Bewick's from Siberia. Often seen are oystercatchers, redshanks, common terns, herons, tufted ducks, gadwalls, shovelers and shelducks, whilst included amongst the birds breeding here are the black-tailed godwit, the little ringed plover and the ruff. A variety of birds of prey can also be seen here, including the short-eared owl, the hen harrier, the marsh marrier, the kestrel, the sparrowhawk and the merlin. Interestingly this is one place where the visitor is best advised to come in winter rather than summer, for it is then that the birds in the waterfowl gardens display their colourful courtship plumage as they prepare for the spring breeding season; it is also the time of year that the wild refuge attracts flocks of wintering ducks, geese and swans.

Less than three miles to the north east of here is the village of **Rufford,** the ancestral home of the Hesketh family who were also involved in reclaiming the mosslands on their estate. Their original home was Rufford Old Hall to the north of the village, now owned by the National Trust and featuring a remarkably well preserved Great Hall which is one of the finest examples of its kind. This half-timbered architectural gem was built by Sir Thomas Hesketh during the early part of the 15th century, its particularly important features

*Rufford Old Hall*

being the fine hammerbeam roof and its elaborate decoration.

The Great Hall was originally the central part of a house which had two wings — the west wing contained living accommodation for the lord and his family while the east wing incorporated the kitchen and domestic rooms. Of these two parts only the east wing remains, having been rebuilt in brick in a simple style in 1662. In the 1760s the family vacated the Old Hall and went to live in the newly constructed Rufford New Hall. By the 1820s, however, the Old Hall was re-occupied by Thomas Henry Hesketh; it was he who rebuilt part of the east wing adjacent to the Great Hall, in order to create a new dining room and anteroom as well as a first floor drawing room and a suite of smaller rooms served by a broad new staircase.

Inside the Great Hall is a unique 15th century moveable screen, seven feet wide and surmounted by three immense carved finials. The screen stands between two great octagonal spere-posts (gigantic oak trees of slightly differing girths) which support the roof. Also worth noting are the four hammerbeam roof timbers, decorated with carved angels holding shields and terminating in large bosses which display the arms of the Heskeths and related families from the 14th and 15th centuries. The wide stone fireplace here is believed to be a 16th century addition, superseding the original central hearth from which smoke would have risen through a louvre in the roof. The Great Hall also contains many examples of early furniture, including a collection of turned chairs as well as several 16th and 17th century cupboards.

More pieces of early furniture are to be found in the Dining Room, including a set of 18th century Chippendale-style dining chairs together with a bow-fronted mahogany sideboard and side-table. On the first floor is the 19th century Drawing Room, which makes use of what appear to be 16th century roof timbers rescued from the old west wing in 1662. The furniture in the centre of the room is predominantly from the 19th century, although around the walls are some 17th century chairs and cupboards. In addition to the oak furniture visitors to Rufford Old Hall can also view the collection of arms and armour drawn together by the Hesketh family, as well as a small museum of domestic life in Lancashire during the 18th and 19th centuries.

The concerns of the Hesketh family reached out into the village itself, and their patronage was of particular benefit to the local parish church. The present building dates from 1869, when it was erected in the Gothic Revival style and finished off with an attractive spire. Prior to that there had been an 18th century Georgian church on the same site, which itself replaced a 14th century chapel built by Sir William de Heskaith, grandson of the first Hesketh of Rufford. It was also Sir William who had obtained the Royal Charter for a weekly market in Rufford on Fridays, an annual fair on May 1st and a manorial court. Even now the annual Mediaeval Fair still takes place in Rufford on the first Monday in May.

**Burscough** and **Burscough Bridge** to the south of Rufford were originally small farming settlements which expanded rapidly with the coming firstly of the canal in the 18th

*Rufford Old Hall's half-timbered splendour*

**Top Locks, near Burscough Bridge**

century and then the railway in the 19th century. Prior to this time Burscough had attained some early significance through the Augustinian Priory which was founded here in the 12th century by Robert de Latham; subsequently it received such lavish extra endowments that it became one of the most important religious houses in Lancashire. At the Dissolution in 1536, however, the Priory was largely demolished, with much of the stone being taken to Ormskirk to build a bell tower from which to hang the Priory bells. Nowadays only a few crumbling ruins remain along Abbey Lane, adjacent to the main Liverpool to Preston railway line.

Early industries in the Burscough area were corn milling, basket weaving (using reeds obtained from Martin Mere) and cheese making, but the opening of the first section of the Leeds and Liverpool Canal from Liverpool to Newburgh in 1775 brought new employment opportunities and led to a dramatic growth in Burscough's population. Several mills were built in Burscough to handle the grain being brought direct from the docks at Liverpool, and the animal feed which was produced in these mills was then delivered to farms at all points along the canal. During the period when horse drawn boats were used considerable organisation went into the provision of stables and food for the horses, and Burscough canal yard was one place where feed for the horses, or 'provider', was prepared and distributed by means of a special 'provider boat' to different places on the canal. One of the most scenic spots in the Burscough area is the junction of the Leeds and Liverpool Canal with its Rufford Branch as the latter begins its journey north to Tarleton — the complex of canal cottages, locks, bridges and a canalside pub is really quite a delightful sight.

The Leeds and Liverpool Canal continues eastwards from here towards the picturesque villages of Newburgh and Parbold, but a brief detour to the south brings us to **Lathom Park** chapel and almshouses. This lovely group of historic buildings dates from the start of the 16th century, when they were established by Lord Stanley, the Earl of Derby, in grateful thanks for the benefits which were received by his family after the Battle of Bosworth. As well as endowing a chantry chapel the Earl of Derby also made provision for the maintenance of eight 'bedemen', who assisted the priest and were accommodated in what are now the almshouses. When the chapel was built it was also used for worship by the surrounding tenants, and the whole

**The chapel and almshouses at Lathom Park**

*Newburgh Post Office*

community was known as a hospice. During the early part of the 19th century much restoration work was undertaken in the chapel, including the renewal of the stained glass windows as well as the addition of a gallery and an unusual 'wagon' ceiling (copied from mediaeval churches in the west of England). The oldest features within the chapel are the chancel screen and the eagle lectern, both of which came from Burscough Priory after its dissolution by Henry VIII.

The village of **Newburgh** is probably one of the most attractive in West Lancashire, having everything you might wish to find in such a place — some lovely cottages and houses fronted by well tended gardens, an ancient Hall, an old post office, a traditional village green and a 17th century coaching inn which has been dispensing hospitality for the last 300 years or so. Neighbouring **Parbold** is an equally pretty village full of charming stone cottages and converted barns as well as some expensive houses on a grand scale, a number of which were built towards the end of the

19th century for wealthy Manchester cotton brokers. Some of the region's cotton merchants had their summer retreats here, and along Wood Lane one can still see the small cottages where their families spent what must have been rather blissful weekends, gazing out across the picturesque Douglas Valley from beneath shady verandahs. It is obviously a very desirable residential area, although it has also witnessed some limited industrial development in its time — there have been several boat building yards and a number of stone quarries. One of these quarries has since been used as the location for a select development of high-class houses, demonstrating the continuing desirability of this area as a place in which to live.

In terms of its history Parbold became part of the Barony of Manchester after the Norman Conquest and was held by a branch of the Lathom family of Lathom as early as the 13th century. The manor was later acquired by John Crisp in 1680, and it was his son who remodelled Parbold Hall in the Palladian style which we see today. For centuries Parbold was very largely a farming community, as is evident from the old stone windmill close to the canal at the centre of the village. This replaced a water powered corn mill which stood by the River Douglas, although it in turn was superseded in the middle of the 19th century by a larger mill originally worked by a steam engine. During the early part of the same century there were three collieries operating in Parbold, with the coal being shipped to Liverpool Gas Works from a canalside wharf.

Quarrying of the local gritstone has also been an important activity for several centuries

now, and during the last century in particular this stone was much in demand for the building of churches and other important public buildings. Parbold has two impressive churches of its own, a testimony to the wealth and standing of its residents during the Victorian period. Christ Church was built in 1875 to replace an earlier 15th century chapel, although several pieces of furniture were transferred from one to the other, while the impressive Roman Catholic Church of Our Lady and All Saints with its magnificent spire was built in 1884. Both buildings were very largely the gifts of wealthy local families.

An ideal spot from which to view the village as a whole is Parbold Hill to the east, a high point above the village which also offers some magnificent views of the surrounding countryside. On its summit stands a rough-hewn monument, known locally as 'Parbold Bottle' because of its shape, which was originally erected to commemorate the Reform Act of 1832. Another local landmark is Ashurst's Beacon just two miles to the south, re-erected in 1798 on Ashurst Hill by Lord Skelmersdale when a French invasion was regarded as imminent. The area surrounding the Beacon is included within a 300-acre country park, and from the summit 570 feet above sea level there are extensive views across the West Lancashire Plain.

*Ashurst's Beacon*

Immediately below is the parish of Dalton, still predominantly a rural area with a number of interesting old stone built farmhouses. The tiny village of **Dalton** was the site of the now-demolished Ashurst Hall, described in 1640 as 'a large castellated edifice', and although the Hall has disappeared its 17th century gatehouse and dovecote still remain. Another interesting old building which still survives is Priorswood Hall, a 16th or early 17th century house with well laid out gardens which may be the house mentioned in the Charter of Burscough Priory.

*Fairhurst Hall, Parbold*

The main local industry in this area has been flagstone mining, which took place largely from the 17th century to the late 19th century, and although there is nothing on the surface to hint at the existence of this industry the ground beneath is riddled with old mines which were once a hive of activity. These mines took the form of underground quarries and huge cavities, from which thousands of tons of roofing flags were extracted. Nowadays these mines are long forgotten, their entrances boarded up and their levels and cavities long since filled by rock falls.

Part of the parish of Dalton was included within the area designated by the Government in 1961 as the site for **Skelmersdale New Town.** The history of Skelmersdale goes back much further, however, to Roman times, when it was a resting place for soldiers marching from Wigan to the harbour at Crosby on the River Mersey. Skelmersdale was later mentioned in the Domesday Book as 'Schelmeresdele', a name which probably indicated Norse visitors to the area. The fact that the spelling of the name proved troublesome even for local inhabitants is reflected in the Up Holland parish church registers for the period 1600 to 1735, where Skelmersdale is spelt no fewer than 34 different ways!

By the early 19th century it appears that the inhabitants of Skelmersdale were mostly engaged in agriculture, but then came the discovery of coal and the birth of Skelmersdale as a sizeable township. From just a few hundred people in 1801 the population here grew to nearly 7,000 by the end of the 19th century, with a large contingent of Welshmen amongst the newcomers. Other industries also grew up in the area, brick and pottery being among the first followed by a cotton mill and straw rope making; the market hall became a boot and shoe factory and there was sand getting and washing for a glass and bottle works. This period of great prosperity came to an end in the 1920s with the decline of deep coal mining and the loss of many jobs, but Skelmersdale's fortunes revived with the advent of the New Town and the new employment opportunities which it brought. Instead of the unsightly colliery spoil heaps which once existed here the town has become a place of new residential estates interlaced by landscaped areas and parkland.

Immediately to the east of Skelmersdale is the historic settlement of **Up Holland,** which in the 16th and 17th centuries was an important market town encompassing blacksmiths, linen websters and shoemakers amongst its inhabitants as well as a butcher, carpenter, miller, spurrier and tanner. During the latter part of the 18th century Up Holland became notorious as a gathering ground for highwaymen, and the old 'Legs of Man' hotel in Church Street was said to have been the

*Up Holland Parish Church*

place where George Lyon conferred with David Bennett and William Houghton before taking part in the many robberies which they committed. George Lyon was the last of the highwaymen, and when he was executed at Lancaster Castle in 1815 was also one of the last to be hanged for stealing.

By the 19th century Up Holland had become the centre of the stone industry, with nail making and handloom weaving also being in full swing; in addition there were a number of collieries in the south and west of the district. Like Skelmersdale, however, Up Holland experienced a decline in its fortunes during the early part of the present century when the mining industry ground to a halt, although economic revival has since taken place with new employment opportunities arising from the newly erected factories in adjacent townships.

Up Holland still retains much of its traditional village character, exemplified by the narrow streets with their cobbled surfaces and steep gradients. School Lane, which was named after the grammar school founded here in 1658, is especially attractive with its very picturesque stone cottages and old Methodist Sunday School. Also along this street is Up Holland's 17th century courthouse, at one time the manorial court building of the Derby family but now a private residence. Around the corner is the 14th century parish church of St. Thomas the Martyr, together with the former Parsonage next door as well as Up Holland's oldest inn, the White Lion, just across the road. From here there are several paths and steps leading to the upper part of the village with its fine views out towards Orrell, Wigan and beyond, while a further climb up to the crossroads at Hall Green and then along Mill Lane offers extensive views towards Ashurst's Beacon on the one hand and the Pennines on the other.

From Up Holland narrow country lanes take us south-westwards across open farmland before bringing us into the village of **Rainford.** This settlement probably derives its name from the Rainford family who came across to this country from Denmark by way of France at the time of the Norman Conquest, yet despite its early beginnings Rainford was never composed of more than a scattering of dwellings until the 19th century. Throughout Rainford's early history the Lathams of Mossborough were the principal family of the township, and consequently the 14th century Mossborough Hall (at one time possessing its own moat) is the oldest building in the district. By the 18th century the Earl of Derby had bought Mossborough Hall and added it to his other Rainford estates.

Elsewhere in the parish are numerous other old farmhouses and cottages, many of which date from the 17th and 18th centuries; of particular interest is Dial House in Higher Lane, with an ancient sundial over the front door. The Parish Church of All Saints dates from 1878 and was built in a Gothic style to replace an earlier 16th century chapel of ease. Next door to the chapel was Rainford's first school, probably built as early as 1600, although it was later supplemented by a National School erected on land given by the Earl of Derby.

*Dial House, Rainford*

In terms of industry Rainford was one of the leading centres for the manufacture of clay tobacco pipes, and for more than 200 years this was the mainstay of the village economy. The early pipemakers appear to have been nonconformists, and it was perhaps because of the district's tolerance of their beliefs that they were first attracted to Rainford. Certainly the village does not appear to have offered any 'natural' advantages, since the local deposits of clay were unsuitable for making clay pipes and the necessary raw material had to be imported from Devon and Cornwall. By the early part of the 19th century there were more than 30 pipe shops and factories in Rainford, which then had a population of only 1,500. These workshops managed to produce an incredible annual profit to the village of £4,000. With the introduction of briar pipes in the 1850s the industry fell into decline, although it was only in 1956 that the last two clay pipe makers in Rainford retired. As late as the beginning of the 20th century the last remaining pipe shop employed 50 men who were turning out more than 15,000 pipes a day. The clay working traditions in the district were then carried on in the manufacture of earthenware drainpipes, although this too has since ceased. Apart from agriculture the other important local industry was coal mining, but this was brought to a halt through the coal strike of 1926.

Moving south-westwards again we come to **Kirkby,** another 'new town' development built around an older village centre. The name 'Kirkby' is Scandinavian in origin and is made up of 'Kirkja' ('church') and 'By' ('a fixed residence') — thus it literally means 'the abode of the church'. It appears that the Vikings or Norsemen who settled here also founded a church, the site of which can still be traced within the present churchyard. A new church was built on the same site soon after the Norman Conquest, although the current parish church of St. Chad dates only from the latter half of the 19th century. A feature of particular interest is the stone font, recognised as being one of the finest examples of Norman sculpture in the country. One of the figures carved on the outside of the font is thought to be St. Chad himself, who was made Bishop of Lichfield in 669 AD.

Our final port of call on the West Lancashire Plain is the village of **Melling,** situated between Kirkby and Maghull, bringing us back once again to the Leeds and Liverpool Canal. The name 'Melling' is derived from the Old English word 'Mellingas', which literally means 'the followers of Mealla', and it points to the settlement here in the 6th century of a small independent tribe which came across to England and reached Lancashire via the valleys of the Pennine rivers. The chosen spot for their permanent home was a peninsula of higher ground which has since become known as Melling Rock, above what was then the low-lying swamp of the coastal plain. This elevated place was also suitable as a burial ground, and it seems that from the very earliest days people were bringing their dead here. Even in 1319, when an enquiry was made as to whether the burial ground had ever been consecrated, it was discovered that burials had been taking place here from time immemorial.

At that point in history there was a chapel on the site which itself 'was from ancient times', dedicated to Holy Rood, and before that

*Melling Parish Church*

there is thought to have been a preaching cross even before the chapel was built. By the early part of the 19th century, however, the chapel had fallen into such disrepair that it was decided to build a new church to the north of the old site, although by 1872 the church itself needed restoration. Inside the church are some interesting memorials which were removed from the old chapel, while in the graveyard are some unusual gravestones. In 1908 Rev. Bulpit recorded that the most interesting one was 'one which I judge to be at least 700 years old. In relief upon it is a full-length floriated cross. Steps are represented at the base, so it is also called a Calvary Cross. There is no inscription, but under the left arm of the cross there is a shield which indicates the sex and rank of the one interred beneath it'.

Melling Church School also has a long history. The present building dates from 1844 when it was erected in a style very similar to the church, replacing an early 18th century school which was then used as a dwelling for the master and mistress. Another old building which has been very significant in village life here is the Melling tithe barn, built of local stone in about 1731. As its name suggests, its original purpose was to house the tithe which was due to the Rector of Halsall from the townships of Halsall, Downholland, Lydiate, Male and Melling. Originally there were two great doorways facing each other, which as well as enabling access into the barn also provided a through draught to assist in the winnowing of the grain when it was being threshed on the hard central floor. During the 19th century the tithe barn eventually became

used as a coach house when the nearby Vicarage was built, while in the present century it has been adopted as the Parish Room and Youth Club.

Lastly we come to the Leeds and Liverpool Canal, which cuts through the western side of the parish before heading towards Maghull. The canal was of principal benefit in serving the agricultural needs of the area, bringing coal and manure to Melling farmers, but it also fulfilled an important function in bringing raw material to the Midland Pottery here. With its three kilns, warehouses, sheds and six double cottages the pottery had been erected in 1877 as a relief works by a large Glasgow manufacturer, the object being to supply the increasing demand for pots which the rapid development of the jam trade had created in Lancashire. Hartley's jam works in Aintree was the principal customer for these jam pots. The large amount of clay required for this business was shipped from Devon to Liverpool and then conveyed to Melling along the Leeds and Liverpool Canal by the pottery's own barge. Towards the end of the 19th century it was recorded that nearly a quarter of a million articles had been turned out during a six week period. Sadly this came to an end in 1928 when a disastrous fire not only destroyed the pottery but also dispersed the community of skilled craftsmen which had grown up around it.

*Albert Dock, Liverpool*

# Chapter 7: LIVERPOOL AND ITS HINTERLAND

**Liverpool** is a city of unmatched architectural splendour, particularly from the 18th and 19th centuries. It is not surprising then that it has evoked the praise and adoration of many of its visitors, and even during the early 1700s Danial Defoe was drawing attention to its exceptional qualities:

> "Liverpool is one of the wonders of Britain, because of its prodigious Increase of Trade and Buildings, within the compass of a very few Years...There is no town in England, except London, that can equal Liverpool for the Fineness of the Streets, and the Beauty of the Buildings".
>
> (Tour through the Whole Island of Great Britain, 1724-27)

Liverpool's enduring attraction over the years has often centred upon its magnificent edifices, and in more recent times Sir John Betjeman was quick to nominate the City's Anglican Cathedral as one of the great buildings of the world. He was also happy to name St. George's Hall — 'surely the finest secular hall in England' — as one of the buildings for which he was willing to be burned at the stake in the cause of preservation!

Liverpool's growth as a great city is above all else intertwined with its development as a great port, and although it was not until the 18th century that it acquired national prominence, it was as early as the reign of King John that its future role was to be determined. It was he who saw in Liverpool a port which he could control and rely upon as a supply base for men and stores in his conquest of Ireland, and his Letters Patent of 1207 are commonly spoken of as Liverpool's original charter — its 'birth certificate'. Prior to this time it had been an area of no great significance, thought to be one of six outlying manors which belonged to West Derby and certainly subordinate to places like Speke, Kirkdale, Allerton and Childwall which were all mentioned in the Domesday Survey. It is interesting to see how the situation was to change over the course of the following centuries, a process which began with King John asking settlers to move to the 'town of Liverpool' in order to establish a royal borough there.

Despite its potential for trade the growth of Liverpool was fairly insignificant until the 17th century, with its historic core close to the Pool (a curving inlet of the Mersey) consisting of just seven streets — Castle Street, Dale Street, Chapel Street, Tithebarn Street, Water Street, High Street and Old Hall Street. Up to this time the population of the borough remained fairly static at around 500, with most of the inhabitants being engaged in fishing and agriculture; there were generally very few merchant ships entering or leaving the port, and any larger vessels which were seen here usually belonged to the King or his representative Lord Molyneux, the Constable of the Castle.

Liverpool's slow growth as a major trading centre, despite royal encouragement, seems to have been due to the fact that England's mediaeval trade was mainly with northern and western Europe, which obviously benefited ports on the eastern coast of the country. There was also the problem of Liverpool's considerable distance from both London and the profitable markets of south east England. By the latter part of the 17th century, however, things began to change and Liverpool saw the beginnings of its long period of commercial prosperity — doubtless helped by the fact that the Government began to use the port as a base for its attempted dominance of Ireland as well as by the threat to southern ports from the growth of French naval power.

Then in 1715 the first 'wet dock' in the country was built here, to accommodate not only the Navy's frigates but also to cater for the anticipated increase in commercial activity. This was not long in coming, and Liverpool soon began to benefit from trade with the newly-acquired British colonies, chief among them being the West Indies. Liverpool consequently became deeply involved with the slave trade, replacing Bristol as the chief port in this traffic by 1750, and other desirable overseas markets also began to open up as a result. All this was helped by the development of the port's hinterland, especially in coal mining and glass making, as well as by improvements to its communications network — including the development of various river navigational systems together with the opening up of roads and the growth of the canal system.

In addition Liverpool also benefited from a substantial growth in commercial and industrial expertise, and the release of land by some of the major families in the area not only led to developments in non-agricultural pursuits but also frequently provided assets for shipping and commercial enterprises. At the same time capital was attracted into Liverpool from other parts of the country, while local seamen and small traders played their part by building up flourishing businesses. One of the natural outcomes of this growth in trade was the development of the shipbuilding industry, and while there are records of 144 shipping and allied workers in Liverpool between 1700 and 1750 this had increased to 600 by the end of the century. Another measure of Liverpool's expansion during this period is the fact that the dock system was extended both northwards and southwards from the original walled town, with the town's population growing from 5,000 to 78,000 over the course of the 1700s.

In keeping with this growth in population the town itself expanded rapidly, with new streets

*Liverpool Town Hall*

*Bluecoat Chambers*

being laid out and a new Town Hall being built in 1754, although the present one dates from 1795 when the previous building on the site was destroyed by fire. The 18th century also saw a number of 'firsts' in Liverpool's history, including the publication of its first newspaper in 1712 as well as the compilation of its first street directory in 1766. This period witnessed the formation of the first Chamber of Commerce together with the creation of the first circulating library in the world and the building of the first Sailor's Hospital in the country.

Another pioneering venture was the Liverpool School for the Blind, founded in 1791 to help blind people lead a useful life. Alongside the town's burgeoning commerce went its blossoming culture, and towards the end of the 18th century a movement grew up which had a significant impact in promoting literature, art and social reform within Liverpool. One of its most influential adherents, William Roscoe, was largely responsible for the founding of the

Athenaeum Club and Library in 1797. It was thus not without good reason that one observer should write that Liverpool was 'now swelled into a vast emporium from an insignificant fishing town', while in 1791 Lord Erskine commented that it was 'fit to be a proud capital of any empire in the world'.

Yet there was much more to come, and the 19th century proved to be an even more remarkable period for growth and prosperity. Merchant shipping in particular grew rapidly, with the first ocean steamship route across the Atlantic being established from Liverpool. The port also saw the growth of large shipping lines, and by 1860 there were regular steam services to Rotterdam, Spain, Africa and the Americas, while clippers sailed to Australia and the East Indies. The owners of these shipping lines formed themselves into a particularly powerful lobby for the benefit of Liverpool and its trade, this being further helped by the establishment of the Mersey Docks and Harbour Board and the corn and cotton produce markets. The town itself

continued to expand rapidly, assisted by the advent of the railway system with the construction of the first passenger railway in the world between Liverpool and Manchester.

The outcome of all this was some quite remarkable statistics — by 1850 the town's trade was double that of London and more than half that of the whole nation; more foreign or overseas trade was carried out here than in any other city in the world; a greater tonnage of shipping was registered at Liverpool than at any other British port; and the property and income tax paid here was higher than in any other provincial city in the country. Liverpool also became the world market place for cotton and grain; it controlled the world's manufacture of sugar, soap, salt and oxygen; and its underwriting and insurance interests also dominated the world. With the health and welfare of its own citizens in mind, more parks were planned and landscaped in Liverpool than in any other provincial city in the world, before or since. It was hardly surprising that Thomas Erskine should describe Liverpool as 'that immense place which stands like another Venice upon the waters'.

Yet prosperity also brought pressures and problems, and Liverpool became a magnet for the poor of Europe. It also became the place to which over 300,000 Irish people were driven during the Irish potato famine of the 1840s, with the result that housing conditions here became deplorable. While the wealthy minority built their houses in spacious surroundings, workers' housing was cramped, cheap and utilitarian, with thousands of families being forced to occupy cellars which had perpetually wet floors. To meet these problems Liverpool appointed the country's first Medical Officer of Health in 1847 and through the building of Corporation flats and cottages became a pioneer in housing reform. New hospitals and developments in medical education made further contributions to the town's well-being, and the first children's hospital in the country was opened in Liverpool in 1851. To some degree the problems were further eased by the fact that many Irish people and other Europeans ejected from their own countries emigrated from here to the New World, although it took until the early part of the 20th century for Liverpool's worst social problems to be overcome for the benefit of those who stayed.

In terms of its culture Liverpool also saw some major new developments during the 19th century — in 1849 the Philharmonic Hall was opened, and in 1852 an Act was passed 'for establishing a Public Library, Museum and Art Gallery at Liverpool'. By 1880 this one-time fishing village had achieved the status of a city, with the title of Lord Mayor being conferred on its Chief Magistrate in 1893. The same year also saw the opening of Liverpool's Overhead Railway which ran the length of the City's dockland, stretching from Seaforth in the north to Dingle in the south. Less than ten years earlier the Mersey Railway linking Liverpool with the Wirral had been constructed, with electrification of the line coming in 1903. Despite the problems brought by industrialisation and urbanisation, the close of the 19th century saw Liverpool at the height of its prosperity, and as many foreign visitors found there was an awesome sense of civic grandeur here which was to be experienced in very few other places — '...no doubt can be entertained after a visit to this great City of the Mersey of the greatness of England, of its wealth and power...'

Yet it was in the 20th century that Liverpool saw the emergence of some of its more famous landmarks. In 1904 the foundation stone of the monumental Anglican Cathedral was laid by King Edward VII, although it was some 70 years later that the building was finally completed. Then in 1925 construction

of the first Mersey Tunnel began, being opened by King George V in 1934. A year earlier had seen the foundation stone of the Roman Catholic Metropolitan Cathedral being laid, in line with the Cathedral's original design, with consecration of a very different finished building taking place in 1967. This was followed by the opening of the second Mersey Tunnel in 1971, carried out by Queen Elizabeth II. In this way Liverpool continued its tradition of acting as host to royalty, a tradition which had begun during the 19th century when the hospitality of its mayors was said to be 'equal if not superior to the state dinners of the Governor-General of India'. Liverpool was so rich and so powerful that it conveyed the atmosphere of a national capital, and an American consul was moved to speak of it as 'the greatest commercial city in the world'.

The basis of Liverpool's commercial success was its shipping trade, which flourished within what eventually grew up to be a seven and a half mile stretch of docks and warehouses constructed on a quite remarkable scale. It is within the City's dockland that our tour of Liverpool must begin, for it is only here that Liverpool's roots are to be found and understood. Liverpool's emergence as a major port during the 18th century came about very largely through the slave trade between Africa and America, which not only made the city's merchants very wealthy

*Liverpool's shipping trade was the foundation for its commercial prosperity*

*Just some of Liverpool's characteristic dock warehouses*

indeed but also enabled them to control nearly half of the world's trade. By 1771 Liverpool had 105 slave ships, which carried more slaves that year than the total population of the City. By the 1790s Liverpool had a quarter of its ships carrying slaves, producing cargoes valued at over £2 million.

With the abolition of the slave trade in 1807 Liverpool was forced to look elsewhere for its trade, and it found an equally profitable substitute in the form of cotton brought from the American plantations. Other commodities such as sugar, timber and grain were also attractive, but it was cotton which largely ensured the continuing prosperity of Liverpool during the 19th century. The first import of cotton from the U.S.A. took place in 1793, but by the mid-1800s Liverpool had the largest cotton port in the country, feeding the Lancashire cotton industry which by that time had outstripped all its rivals. By 1911 over five million bales of cotton were coming into Liverpool every year, and the city was the greatest cotton market in the world. The result of all this was not only commercial prosperity but also technological advance — the Liverpool to Manchester railway was built very largely by those with business interests in cotton, as was the first trans-Atlantic cable laid in 1866.

The first dock to be constructed at Liverpool was started during the early part of the 18th

century and involved the conversion of the Pool into a 'wet dock' controlled by floodgates. This development in 1715 was to set the pattern for future docks all over the world, but by 1737 the 'Old Dock' was inadequate to handle the amount of shipping being received and so a new basin was created along with three graving docks. This basin was later reconstructed and named Canning Dock, while the dock just to the south (which was first introduced just a few years later in 1753) became known as Salthouse Dock. To the north an open harbour was developed into George's Dock, opened in 1771 to accommodate the new larger vessels, while to the south of Salthouse Dock two further docks were introduced (King's Dock and Queen's Dock) to cater for the increasing volume of shipping. By the end of the 18th century the docks and basins in Liverpool enclosed approximately 26 acres of water, at a spot where just a hundred years previously there had been only open riverside.

During the first two decades of the 19th century Prince's Dock was constructed just to the north of George's Dock, the first to be enclosed by walls and as such a model for the rest of the dock system. This was followed quickly by Union Dock, to the south of Queen's Dock, and its large outer basin, which together were to become known as Coburg Dock. Then in 1824 Jesse Hartley came onto the scene when he was appointed

engineer to the Dock Trustees, and it was he who brought the particularly distinctive architectural style and use of materials which is best portrayed by the restored Albert Dock and its warehouses. His contribution to the development of Liverpool's docks was enormous — between 1824 and his death in 1860 he not only constructed or altered every dock in the city but also added 140 acres of wet docks and some 10 miles of quay space, was consultant engineer to the Liverpool and Manchester Railway Company, and worked on both the high-level coal railway and on the Liverpool end of the Leeds and Liverpool Canal.

The first of Hartley's works were the Brunswick, Clarence, Victoria and Trafalgar Docks, but it was the Albert Dock which brought out the best in his considerable skills. Opened by the Prince Consort in 1845, the Albert Dock was unique in having a series of massive surrounding warehouses which were built immediately adjacent to the water's edge so that cargoes could be transferred directly into store from the ships' holds. The five storey warehouses, constructed of brick and cast-iron, present an impressive picture by virtue of their enormous scale and uncompromising simplicity, whilst at the same time providing some visually interesting spaces at ground floor level by way of the colonnades of cast-iron Doric columns which support the upper storeys. According to one commentator at the time, the warehouses 'cover a surface of 21,390 square yards and are wholly constructed of stone, brick, and iron, and perfectly fireproof, no timber whatsoever being used in them'. The massively-constructed quays built in granite are another characteristic feature of Hartley's approach, reaching a depth of 40 feet below the coping.

In more recent years the Albert Dock and its associated quayside warehouses have been comprehensively restored for shopping, commercial and cultural uses so that they now form one of Lancashire's foremost tourist attractions. Here too is housed not only the Merseyside Maritime Museum but also the Museum of Emigration (relating the history of the emigration of over 9,000,000 people from Europe via Liverpool to North America) and the Tate Gallery of the North, all accommodated within Britain's largest group of Grade I listed buildings.

The former Dock Traffic Office of the Albert Dock complex has also been restored for use by Granada TV as its main news gathering centre for the North West region. Built in the style of a Classical temple it is constructed largely of brick and iron and although very different architecturally from the warehouses nearby it is similar in its use of building materials. The main features of this impressive building are its central chimney stack and the Tuscan portico which has been created completely from iron. Along with the restoration of these important historic buildings a considerable amount of work has been carried out to improve the surrounding quayside areas, creating a heritage landscape

*The restored splendour of Liverpool's dockland*

which is unrivalled in Britain. A very important part of this is the enclosed dock at the centre of the development, its placid waters mirroring the huge warehouses around its sides and seemingly doubling their already substantial proportions.

Just one year after the completion of Albert Dock Hartley commenced work on the enlargement of Salthouse Dock and the construction of Wapping Dock to the east of King's Dock. Still more docks were built on the north side of the dock complex in 1848 and 1849, culminating with the opening of Canada Dock in 1859. This dock established a new massive scale of construction which was necessary because of the increasing size of shipping. By 1872 dock provision was again inadequate because of the growing demand and seven new docks were created in Bootle on the north side of Liverpool, together with another two new docks to the south. At the same time there was also a continuing increase in passenger traffic from Liverpool, and various landing stages and jetties were built to cater for this. By the end of the 19th century Liverpool's dockland frontage was completed when the Pier Head area was introduced, created through the draining and filling of George's Dock.

It is the impressive Edwardian buildings of Pier Head which perhaps represent better than any others the self-confidence felt during the height of Liverpool's success at the start of the 20th century. Three commercial buildings

*One example of Jesse Hartley's architectural style*

*The Mersey Docks & Harbour Board Building*

in particular convey the prestige and significance of Liverpool's business community at that time, creating part of what was to become the City's well known riverside skyline in a style which was imitative of some of the great North American cities with whom Liverpool was trading. The first to be built was the Offices of the Mersey Docks and Harbour Board, designed in the form of a 'Renaissance Palace' with cupolas at its corners and a large Classical 'church dome' in the centre. Inside was formed an octagonal hall reaching up to the dome, with arched galleries running round it at four levels.

Immediately to the north is the Cunard Offices, a well proportioned building with Greek Revival details, whilst next door to this is the world famous Royal Liver Building. Erected in 1908-10 this is a unique piece of architecture and one of the world's first multi-storey buildings to incorporate a reinforced concrete structure. Amongst its well-loved features are the mythical Liver Birds, perched on top of the domes above the building's twin clock towers. Over The Strand from the Royal Liver Building is the Tower Building, designed by the same architect two years earlier as one of the first steel-framed buildings in the country. It is so-named because it occupies the original site of the Tower of Liverpool, a fortified house which belonged to the Earls of Derby. This ultimately fell into disrepair towards the end of the 18th century and became a gaol for debtors and criminals.

Just to the north of the Tower Building is the Church of Our Lady and St. Nicholas, another of Liverpool's landmarks to be seen from the Mersey. In addition to being the parish church for the city it was also known as the Sailors' Church, since St. Nicholas is the patron saint of sailors. The oldest part of the present building is the tower, built by Thomas Harrison at the start of the 19th century and typifying the Gothic Revival style with its flying buttresses supporting an open lantern.

Tower Building stands at the lower end of Water Street, one of Liverpool's finest commercial thoroughfares and a suitable place from which to discover the city centre. Up to the early part of the 19th century this had been a high-class residential area for the city's merchants, but as they gradually moved out to take up rather more spacious accommodation it became a popular business location.

At the lower end of Water Street is Oriel Chambers, a building which was very much ahead of its time when it appeared in 1864. In those days the large proportion of glass in its external elevations was something of an affront to the commonly-held architectural tastes, and it was described rather unkindly as 'a great abortion' and 'an agglomeration of protruding glass bubbles'. In many respects it is one of the most important buildings of its date in Europe, being something of a forerunner of modern office buildings, and its elegant cast-iron window frames set within decorated stone surrounds have helped to earn it a Grade I listing.

Just across Water Street from Oriel Chambers is India Buildings, its neo-Classical style reflecting a North American influence. Built between 1924 and 1932 it is one of the largest office blocks in the city, having been designed in such a way that it could be converted into a warehouse if required. Another interesting feature of the building is the barrel-vaulted arcade running through the centre of the block and lined with small shop fronts. Then a little further up Water Street is the Barclays Bank Building, similarly completed in 1932 and likewise built on a grand scale. Here again the North American influence is evident, not only in its external style but also in its use of a steel-framed construction and the very advanced servicing design which incorporated completely ducted pipes and

*Part of Liverpool's famous Royal Liver Building*

wires as well as low-temperature ceiling heating.

At the top end of Water Street is Liverpool's prestigious Town Hall, the third to serve the City and another Grade I listed building. Originally built by John Wood of Bath in 1749-54 it had to be reconstructed by James Wyatt after it was badly damaged by fire in 1795. In addition to restoring the building he also added the impressive dome above it as well as the two storey Corinthian portico on its front elevation. Inside the Town Hall is one of the best suites of civic rooms in the country, featuring some excellent decorative work from the late Georgian period. It is interesting to note that the building has had to face a number of attempts to destroy it, including one when seamen protesting against a reduction in their wages attacked it with a cannon!

Just behind the Town Hall, on its north side, is the area known as Exchange Flags, created as an open-air exchange floor at the time that Liverpool's first Exchange Building was erected towards the end of the 18th century. At the centre of this open space is the Nelson Monument, erected in 1813 as Liverpool's first public sculpture and featuring four chained prisoners around a circular drum. This drum was designed as a ventilator shaft for the bonded warehouses beneath Exchange Flags, although these warehouses have since been converted into car parks.

To the north of Exchange Flags is Old Hall Street, which at one time led to the 13th century Old Hall but which is now marked by a good group of Victorian buildings. The finest of these is the Albany Building, constructed in 1856 and one of the best and earliest of the large Victorian office buildings in the city. At one time it was the meeting place for cotton brokers, prior to the Cotton Exchange being built next door to it. Among the interesting features of the Albany Building are the decorative elements incorporated within its Renaissance design, together with the spacious central courtyard crossed by two elegant cast-iron bridges.

The Cotton Exchange next to the Albany Building was also quite a remarkable piece of architectural extravagance, highlighting the importance and power of the cotton trade at its peak, but its impact was lost when the frontage was re-faced. Directly across Old Hall Street is City Buildings, another property which was remodelled but this time to rather better effect. Here the whole front of a mid-19th century sugar warehouse was given a cast-iron and glass 'skin' in 1906, sweeping around the corner in a manner which was soon to become popular in other major cities. Close to this building, completing a fascinating Victorian business complex, is Harley Chambers, a neo-Greek style office building dating from the 1860s and featuring

*Exchange Flags at the rear of the Town Hall*

Venetian windows and Ionic columns on its imposing facade.

Yet perhaps the best expression of Victorian business life in Liverpool is to be found in Castle Street, running southwards from the Town Hall at the junction of Water Street and Duke Street, for it is here that one can find a completely intact Victorian commercial street frontage. Castle Street is also important in that it was one of the seven original streets laid out at the beginning of the 13th century, leading down to the Castle before this was demolished in 1721 to make way for St. George's Church, in what was to eventually become Derby Square. This area then became Liverpool's market place and by the middle of the 18th century Castle Street was the most fashionable part of town, being filled with shops, but with the removal of the market elsewhere it developed into Liverpool's most important location for business and commerce. It was certainly not inaccurate then for Sir James Picton to comment that 'the history of Castle Street is the history of Liverpool', and to this day it remains the recognisable centre of the city.

A number of Castle Street's most visually interesting buildings are situated around the junction with Brunswick Street, perhaps none being more arresting than the Co-operative Bank with its contrasting bands of sandstone and granite together with some lively Victorian detail. It also features a corner turret mounted by an unusual green copper 'onion' dome, an element which is repeated in some measure on the building directly across from it at the corner of Brunswick Street and Castle Street. As with several other buildings in

Castle Street this one was designed in the Loire style, and as well as two turrets it features an elaborately decorated gable together with a balustraded balcony.

Across Castle Street from these two properties is the former Bank of England building (now the Trustee Savings Bank), built in 1845-48 by C.R. Cockerell, and its neighbour (occupied by the Furness Building Society) which enjoys the benefit of a portico of four giant Corinthian columns. Most of the other buildings in Castle Street have a similar sumptuousness of architectural style, reflecting the prosperity of Liverpool's commercial sector during the Victorian era. One last feature of interest before leaving

*The former Bank of England building*

Castle Street is the 'Sanctuary Stone' embedded in the road surface towards the top end of the street. This is the only surviving mark of the boundary of the old Liverpool Fair, held on two occasions every year, and it was in this area that debtors were able to walk free from arrest for ten days before and after each fair providing they were on lawful business.

At the top end of Castle Street close to the Town Hall is the start of Dale Street, another of Liverpool's important commercial streets and at one time the principal route into the town from Manchester and London. If Castle Street is lined with more than its fair share of important insurance buildings. Although the Liverpool, London and Globe Insurance Building next to the Town Hall is one of the earliest of these, having been built in 1855-57 to a design by C.R. Cockerell, probably the most impressive is the Royal Insurance Building at the corner of Dale Street and North John Street. Erected in 1897-1903 this is another of the city's giant early 20th century office blocks, a very impressive structure incorporating a steel frame hidden behind an exterior facing of granite and Portland stone. The building also features a sculptured frieze around three sides, depicting insurance in its various forms, as well as a striking campanile with cupola, dome and sundial which together make up another of Liverpool's well-known skyline features.

The building next door to this is known as The Temple, built in an Italianate style during the 1860s, while next door again is the Prudential Assurance Building which was designed by Alfred Waterhouse in a late Gothic style. Here one can see Waterhouse's typical use of brick and terracotta in producing what is a comparatively simple design, relying upon scale and rhythm rather than decoration for its effect. Further along Dale Street is the Municipal Annexe, built in 1883 as the exclusive Conservative Club in a French Renaissance style, while just over Sir Thomas Street is the large Municipal Buildings displaying a mixture of French and Italian Renaissance styles with French pavilion roofs, giant Corinthian columns and a range of 16 sculptured figures. The architect responsible for the Municipal Buildings also designed the City Magistrates Courts nearby, a mid-19th century building of ashlar stone with a central pediment and carriage entrance below.

From this point on Dale Street a detour down Crosshall Street brings us to the warehouse building known as the Midland Railway Goods Offices, situated between Victoria Street and Whitechapel. Built in the 1850s by the Midland Railway for the receipt and dispatch of its goods, this property features some massive loading doorways as well as an appealing concave elevation punctuated by windows set in giant round arches.

*Bluecoat Chambers, School Lane*

Before heading up towards the area around St. George's Hall, and more of Liverpool's superb civic buildings, a short diversion southwards via Church Street brings us to the Bluecoat Chambers. This delightful Grade I listed building and its cobbled courtyard dates from 1717, when it was built as a charity school in a 'Queen Anne' style. Constructed largely of brick with stone dressings around the doors and windows the Bluecoat Chambers has some lovely decorative features, particularly the cherubs on the keystones of all the windows as well as the Latin inscription below the pediment with its one-handed clock. The building is 'H' shaped in plan, with a centre link which originally contained the chapel and hall.

To the north of the Bluecoat Chambers is Church Street, originally laid out at the end of the 17th century and now one of the City's main shopping streets (as well as being the place where Frank Winfield Woolworth opened his first shop in Britain in 1909), while further north still is Williamson Square. During the 18th century this was a select residential area, but by the 19th century it had

*The Playhouse Theatre*

become more a place for public entertainment and in 1865 the Playhouse Theatre (then the Star Music Hall) was built here.

From Williamson Square Roe Street heads up towards the awe-inspiring St. George's Hall, a building in the Classical style whose design combines the massiveness of a Roman bath with the delicacy of a Greek temple. Praised as being one of the finest neo-Grecian buildings in the world, St. George's Hall was designed by the architect Harvey Lonsdale Elmes in response to the need for a new hall to accommodate a four-day musical festival held every three years in the City. There was also a requirement for new Assize Courts to be built in Liverpool, so the completed building provided a central Great Hall and a small eliptical Concert Hall (together with ancillary rooms) as well as two courtrooms. The Great Hall features red granite columns beneath an impressive tunnel vault, while the small Concert Hall has wood panelled walls, mirrors and chandeliers.

*In front of St. George's Hall*

Externally, the east front of the building facing onto Lime Street is especially dramatic, featuring 13 bays of giant Corinthian columns as well as a 200-foot long colonnade, while the south front is in the style of a Greek temple. On the east side of the building is St. George's Plateau with its unusual cast-iron dolphin lamp standards as well as monuments to Queen Victoria and Prince Albert, while on the west side is St. John's Gardens with a number of monuments commemorating the efforts of 19th century social reformers.

Beyond William Brown Street to the north of St. John's Gardens are a series of civic buildings in the Classical idiom which were constructed a little after St. George's Hall. At the centre of the group is the William Brown

*The Classical grandeur of St. George's Hall*

Library and Museum, opened in 1860 and featuring a portico of six Corinthian columns beneath a pediment modelled on that of the south side of St. George's Hall. This building was erected to house the 13th Earl of Derby's natural history collection which he bequeathed to the town in 1851.

On its west side is the Museum Extension and College of Technology, opened in 1902 and featuring a number of sculptures depicting the City's commerce, industry and education, while immediately adjoining it to the east is the Picton Reading Room and Hornby Library. Nicknamed 'Picton's Gasometer' because of its circular design, the Reading Room has a peripheral colonnade of Corinthian columns as well as a frieze and domed rotunda roof; it was also the first building in Liverpool to have electric lighting. At its rear is the Hornby Library, which features an Edwardian Imperial interior.

Next to the Picton Reading Room is the Walker Art Gallery, opened in 1877 and comprising a single storey Grecian stone facade with a portico of free-standing Corinthian columns, while next door again is the Sessions House dating from 1884. This is also a Classical style building incorporating a portico of four paired Corinthian columns above which is a pediment featuring the coat of arms of the Lancashire County Council. Within the building is a charming Italian Renaissance staircase hall with a series of small saucer domes.

Just across William Brown Street from the Walker Art Gallery is the Wellington Column, with its statue of the Duke of Wellington said to be cast in metal salvaged from guns captured at Waterloo. The fluted Doric column reaches to a height of 132 feet and is

an exact replica of the Melville monument in Edinburgh. From this point Lime Street runs southwards down towards the junction of Brownlow Hill and Mount Pleasant, passing the former North Western Hotel en route. This massive seven storey building designed by Alfred Waterhouse in the French Renaissance style was opened in 1871 as a 330-room hotel, offering an important facility for railway passengers arriving at Lime Street station. Behind the building are the Lime Street Station Sheds, one of which was the largest in the world when it was built in the 1860s.

Further along Lime Street are two more hotels, featuring the ornate decoration typical of Edwardian times. The first of these is the Crown Hotel, completed in 1905 and possessing one of the richest 'Art Nouveau' exteriors in Liverpool, while the second is 'The Vines' with its interior of mahogany, beaten copper and rich plaster. Then in Ranelagh Place at the bottom of Lime Street is the Adelphi Hotel, completed in 1912 with a cladding of white ashlar stone on a steel frame; the elegant interior features a wealth of marble panelling and plaster columns.

From Ranelagh Place, Mount Pleasant takes us eastwards up towards the Roman Catholic Cathedral and the University Precinct. Mount Pleasant itself began life during the latter half of the 18th century as an elegant residential district, and along its length there are still a number of attractive Georgian houses which remind us of its earlier history (although these are now largely in office or hotel use). At the top end of Mount Pleasant, where it again joins up with Brownlow Hill, is the University Students' Union building dating from the early part of the 20th century, while across the road from it is the Victoria Building designed by Alfred Waterhouse to house University College before it became the University of Liverpool. Waterhouse was also responsible for the Royal Infirmary close by, with its gabled dormers, turrets and round arches.

The Roman Catholic Metropolitan Cathedral of Christ the King is situated within this upper part of Mount Pleasant, a remarkable building of stained glass and concrete which was completed in 1967. The present structure is the work of Sir Frederick Gibberd, although

*The County Sessions House, just above St. George's Plateau*

it is interesting to note that it stands above the enormous crypt which was part of Sir Edwin Lutyens' proposed design in 1932. Lutyens' scheme would have given Liverpool a Roman Catholic Cathedral featuring a dome higher and larger than that of St. Peter's in Rome or St. Paul's in London.

Not far from the Cathedral, a short distance along Oxford Street, is Abercrombie Square which forms the focal point of the University Precinct. The Square was laid out during the early part of the 19th century, and it is enclosed on three sides by three storey Georgian terraces with continous cast-iron balconies at the first floor level. The architectural harmony of the Square is emphasised by the fact that each side was designed as a single composition based around a central stone Doric porch. The gardens at the centre, enclosed by iron railings, are rather reminiscent of residential squares in London.

Immediately to the south of the Roman Catholic Cathedral is Hope Street, which acts as a direct link to the city's well known Anglican Cathedral. Hope Street itself is lined with some impressive buildings from both the Georgian and Victorian periods, and its first noteworthy property is to be found at the junction with Oxford Street and Mount Pleasant. This is the Medical Institution, dating from 1836 and featuring a fine stone frontage with six large Ionic columns.

Further down Hope Street is a rather less 'restrained' building in terms of its architectural style — dating from the end of the 19th century the Philharmonic Hotel is another of Liverpool's fascinating 'Art Nouveau' creations featuring stepped gables, turrets and balconies. Inside one discovers a magnificent 'gin palace' interior together with some sumptuously tiled gents' toilets, much of the work having been carried out by artists and craftsmen from what was then the University's School of Architecture and Applied Art. Hope Street's educational links

*The Roman Catholic Metropolitan Cathedral*

are also evident further along at its junction with Mount Street, for here are to be found the former College of Art (dating from 1882) as well as the Liverpool Institute, which began life as the Mechanics' Institute back in 1835.

Both these buildings are constructed of ashlar sandstone, with the Liverpool Institute being fronted by an imposing portico of huge Ionic columns.

Across on the other side of Hope Street from this point is Blackburne Place, which was named after John Blackburne (Liverpool's mayor in 1788) who built a detached mansion here between 1785-90 in what was then open countryside. Part of his elegant Georgian house still survives, but perhaps of greater interest is the attractively restored Blackburne Terrace on the south side of the street — this row of three storey brick houses dating from 1826 is just one of a lovely profusion of similar terraces to be found in this part of the city. Blackburne Terrace is set back behind its own private driveway and landscaped gardens, with the four central dwellings having projecting Doric porches.

Returning to Hope Street takes us past another terrace of Georgian houses before bringing us to its junction with Upper Duke

*Abercrombie Square*

162

*The Anglican Cathedral*

storey houses over a basement. Other 'standard' features included iron balconies, iron railings, and Ionic columns framing panelled doors and rectangular fanlights.

One of the most impressive developments in the area during this period was Gambier Terrace on Hope Street, featuring two storey Ionic columns together with a ground floor arcade. The existing south wing was intended to form the centre section of a much longer terrace but building ceased during the slump of 1837 when the demand for large city houses declined due to the development of commuter homes in the suburbs, and as a result the design was never completed. Elsewhere in the district a number of previously unoccupied sites were developed for housing during the middle of the 19th century, introducing the 'innovative' bay window of the Victorian house but using similar materials to the surrounding Georgian properties so as to present a pleasing and unified appearance.

Immediately to the north west of the Anglican Cathedral is Rodney Street, which prior to the development of the Georgian terraces and squares to the east of Hope Street had grown up as one of Liverpool's newest and most popular residential areas during the later part of the 18th century. First proposed after Lord Rodney's naval victory in 1782 over the Comte de Grasse, Rodney Street developed rapidly as wealthy merchants began to vacate their houses lower down the town in Hanover Street and Duke Street.

Most of the splendid properties along Rodney Street are typically Georgian in their construction, being generally three stories high in red brick with two sash windows on the ground floor and three on the upper floors. They also usually have iron balconies to the first floor windows and ornamentation

*Part of Liverpool's Georgian heritage*

Street and Canning Street - and to our first full view of the Anglican Cathedral. This monumental piece of architecture in red sandstone, visible from many miles around, was first started in 1904 and only completed some 70 years later. Giles Gilbert Scott was the architect responsible for the Cathedral's ambitious but perhaps rather 'outdated' design in a somewhat simplified Gothic Revival style, and he succeeded in creating what must be one of the most awe-inspiring buildings in the world. Between Hope Street and the Anglican Cathedral is St. James' Cemetery, lying within a huge hollow which had originally been the quarry supplying stone for many of Liverpool's 18th century public buildings. The cemetery was created in 1825-29 by John Foster and it was soon to become the home of the Huskisson Memorial, a domed rotunda of Corinthian columns erected in honour of the Liberal politician and MP for Liverpool who had been killed at the opening ceremony of the Liverpool to Manchester railway in 1830.

As the Corporation Surveyor, John Foster (Senior) was responsible for the layout of many of the residential squares and terraces immediately to the east of the Cathedral, although his grid-iron street plan of 1800 really only became a reality as the Canning

Street and Falkner Square developments got off the ground sometime after 1835. In Falkner Square the central garden with its iron gate piers and railings was the first element of the scheme to be introduced by the Falkner family, who then followed it up with the terraces of houses around its four sides. Each side of the Square is symmetrical in design, with the terrace to the east incorporating some rather more formal elements such as a continuous iron balcony across the first floor and a central pediment. The relatively low two storey terraces on the other three sides, together with rows of plane trees along the pavements, all help to create the fairly informal atmosphere which prevails here, in what is one of Liverpool's traditional forms of residential development.

The long terrace of late Georgian houses on Canning Street are also typical of much of the new residential development which went on in this part of the city during the 1830s, with some slight variations in style indicating how a number of local builders were involved in erecting a few houses each to a standard design set by the Corporation Surveyor. The terraces in Canning Street are representative of much of the housing in this area in that they were built generally of brick (occasionally with stone facades) and incorporated large three concentrated around the doorway. Some, however, are rather more imposing in design, particularly 35 Rodney Street which has a five bay frontage as well as a pediment across its entire width. This is reputedly the first house to have been built here and was occupied by Pudsey Dawson (a Mayor of Liverpool) in 1799.

At the lower end of Rodney Street, close to its junction with Upper Duke Street just below the Anglican Cathedral, are several more Georgian terraces — one block on the east side, built as one architectural composition, features a five bay pediment and a continuous iron balcony, while on the opposite side is a smaller row of houses with some particularly fine doorways and delicate fanlights.

On Upper Duke Street itself is Mornington Terrace, an attractive row of five houses with its name picked out in gold leaf on the centre of the block. The work of the Corporation Surveyor is also evident in this locality, for it was John Foster (Senior) who designed St. Luke's Church in nearby Bold Place and his son John Foster (Junior) who built it between 1811-31. This is now a rather dramatic ruin after having been bombed during the Second World War, its decorated pinnacles and traceried windows remaining as good examples of the Perpendicular Gothic style of architecture.

From the foot of St. Luke's west tower one can look straight down Bold Street, back towards the commercial centre of Liverpool. Laid out in 1780 after having been a 'rope walk' used in connection with the making of ropes for sailing ships, Bold Street became a fashionable residential area attracting the city's merchants who generally had counting houses at the rear of their substantial dwellings. The area as a whole also became a focal point for gentlemen's clubs, newsrooms, libraries, concert halls and many other institutions, evidence of the wealth which was being generated in Liverpool as a result of the flourishing slave trade during the latter part of the 18th century.

Gradually Bold Street's original residential use gave way to shopping, and for over 150 years it was one of the most exclusive and fashionable shopping streets outside London, often being compared to Bond Street in the capital. At the bottom end of Bold Street is the Lyceum, designed by Thomas Harrison of Chester for use not only as a gentlemen's club but also to rehouse the Liverpool Library, Europe's first circulating library founded in 1757. One of the building's more unusual features was its weather vane, which controlled an indicator in the newsroom showing the direction of the wind for the benefit of the shipowners and captains using the club.

*One of Liverpool's restored Georgian terraces*

Built further up Bold Street on the same side was the former Palatine Club, constructed of Bath stone during the middle of the 19th century in the form of a Florentine palace on four storeys, while further along again on the opposite side is Marlborough House. This building replaced one of the first properties to be erected in Bold Street, a concert hall constructed in 1785 and capable of seating 1400 people. The present building no longer functions as a concert hall, but it still carries reliefs on its exterior elevations depicting musical instruments and musical scores. Running parallel with Bold Street, to the south west, is Seel Street; here one can find St. Peter's Roman Catholic church, dating from 1788 and the oldest in Liverpool, together with the Royal Institution at the junction with Colquitt Street. This was originally built as a private house for a

Liverpool banker in 1799, being later established as the Royal Institution for the cultivation of literature, science and the arts in 1817.

The final part of our journey through Liverpool's historic centre takes us onto Duke Street, which runs parallel to both Bold Street and Seel Street and acts as a direct link between the area around the Anglican Cathedral and that around the city's early docks. Duke Street was first laid out in 1725 in the form of a long avenue, and for a hundred years or so it was a fashionable residential area for many of the city's wealthiest merchants. A number of the families associated with Liverpool's development as one of the world's leading ports lived here, and along the street there are reminders of this period of prosperity.

Towards the top end of Duke Street are some Georgian terraced properties with stone dressings and decoration, while halfway along is 105 Duke Street which was opened in 1801 as the Union News Room on the day that England was united with Ireland. This building later became Liverpool's first public library and museum. Then right at the bottom end of Duke Street, close to the site of the Old Dock where Liverpool's development as a port first started, is an interesting group of Victorian commercial buildings in brick and stucco — an indication that Liverpool's considerable prosperity during the Georgian period was maintained and extended during Victorian times.

Liverpool is remarkable for its commerce and the quality of architecture which emanated from this, yet at the same time the city is perhaps better known to the world at large for its culture and the colourful characters who have conveyed this to us. Little needs to be said of The Beatles and those of their era, who brought about such a radical transformation in popular music, but then Liverpool has also produced far more than its share of internationally successful writers, comedians, playwrights and sportsmen.

Neither should we forget that local product which defies both imitation and export — the Liverpudlian accent, or 'Scouse' as it is known the world over. Perhaps this is a reflection of the rather mixed origins of Liverpool's population over the course of the centuries, and it is interesting to note that on various occasions Liverpool has been referred to as both the capital of Wales and the capital of Ireland! The influx of immigrants from both countries due to poverty and persecution has doubtless been a significant factor in not only extending the language but also enriching the culture.

Some minority groups have added to Liverpool life without being absorbed by its population — for many years Liverpool boasted the largest Chinese community in Europe, and prior to their arrival there was already a strong Jewish representation here. During the early years of this century their numbers were swelled by sizeable settlements of Jews from Germany, Poland and Russia, who eventually set up prosperous businesses in jewellery and tailoring. Even as early as 1775 John Wesley was speaking of Liverpool's great tolerance toward minority groups, and it is perhaps this characteristic handed down to today's generation which helps to make Liverpool such a welcoming place.

Liverpool is not only proud of its architecture and its people — it also boasts some of the finest parks and landscaped gardens in the country, many of which encircle the city centre within the boundary of the outer ring road. To the north east, for example, close to the districts of Anfield and Everton, is **Stanley Park** which was laid out in 1867-70. In addition to the lake crossed by a fine six-arched sandstone bridge the park features a glass conservatory (with Gothic decoration in cast-iron) as well as a small bandstand.

Further south is **Newsham Park,** another of the city's major parks laid out in the latter half of the 19th century to provide some recreational space for the new housing areas of the expanding city. As with a number of other parks in Liverpool, residential sites around the periphery of Newsham Park were leased by the Corporation to cover the cost of the park, and consequently a number of substantial semi-detached houses were built here during the 1870s and 1880s. Somewhat earlier than these is Newsham House, a large Georgian country house which became the Judge's Lodgings in 1864. On the other side of the park, beyond the ornamental lake, is Park Hospital; this was designed by Alfred Waterhouse and built in 1871-74 as the Royal Liverpool Seamen's Orphan Institution.

Further south again, this time in the Wavertree area immediately to the east of the city centre, the idea of housing integrated with open space led to the creation of a Garden Suburb here. The earliest origins of the **Wavertree Garden Suburb** can be traced back to the ideals of 19th century social reformers who first campaigned for lower housing densities in greener surroundings, although the suburb's development on the co-operative principle just prior to the First World War was very much part of a national movement to improve the living conditions of ordinary people.

The first step in the Suburb's development was the establishment of 'Liverpool Garden Suburb Tenants Limited' as a tenants' co-operative in 1909, followed by the construction of the first 100 houses by 1912. A further 260 houses were to come, all being planned at a density of twelve to the acre to allow adequate space for individual gardens. Open spaces and landscaping added further to the attractiveness of the development, and a wide range of community facilities was introduced for the benefit of residents. Wavertree's Garden Suburb was on a par with other similar schemes in Letchworth and Hampstead, and it attracted visitors from across the country who praised its layout, house designs and thriving community spirit.

**Wavertree Village** itself is obviously much older than the Garden Suburb named after it, but it was also a thriving settlement well before Liverpool came to prominence through the development of its port. In fact it remained an independent township until it was incorporated into the City in 1895, having grown considerably during the 19th century as a result of the influx of Liverpool merchants seeking to escape to a better environment. Looking westwards from the clock tower close to the centre of the village, a memorial to Sir James Picton dating from 1879, one can see a number of brick built Georgian houses along High Street as well as the Lamb Hotel, a late 18th century coaching inn with a Tuscan porch over the central entrance. Nearby is the former Wavertree Town Hall, dating from 1872 and featuring an imposing stone facade, while on the periphery of the village are some good examples of Victorian domestic architecture — in the form of both brick terraces and stuccoed villas.

To the east of Wavertree's clock tower, standing on what was the old village green, is another local landmark — the Old Lock-up, an octagonal-shaped stone building with a pointed roof which dates from 1796. Then leading south from the clock tower is Church Road, along which is situated the 18th century Church of Holy Trinity as well as the Liverpool Bluecoat School. This latter institution started life in 1717 as the Bluecoat Hospital on School Lane in Liverpool, but by the end of the 19th century the building had become too cramped and new premises were built here in Wavertree. The celebrated architectural historian Nikolaus Pevsner considered this building to be the most spectacular in Wavertree and one of the most outstanding half-dozen of its date in Lancashire.

**Sefton Park** to the south west of Wavertree covers an area of 233 acres and is the largest park in Liverpool. Named after the Earl of Sefton, from whom the land was originally purchased, the park was opened in 1872 as another fine example of the civic pride which prevailed in prosperous Liverpool at the time. The design and layout was by Andre and Hornblower, who also incorporated sites for a number of Victorian villas which not only helped to secure a financial return on the

*The Old Lock-up, Wavertree*

scheme but also provided a dignified setting to the park without being an intrusion into it. Some of these villas are of considerable architectural merit while others are of interest for their rather eccentric style, but all feature the solid craftsmanship which characterised the Victorian era. The most important building within Sefton Park is the Palm House, an octagonal-shaped three tier structure of glass and cast-iron which incorporates a central spiral staircase leading to an upper level catwalk. To the west of the Palm House is a chain of ornamental lakes, one of which surrounds the park's bandstand with its pagoda roof and domed lantern, while immediately to the south is a ravine landscape feature crossed by an impressive cast-iron bridge.

Nearby is the smaller **Princes Park,** laid out to a design by Sir Joseph Paxton and largely the result of an initiative by Richard Vaughan Yates (a prominent citizen of Liverpool) who in 1843 purchased an extensive area of land to the south of what was then the built-up area. This was Paxton's first independent commission, being quickly followed by one for Birkenhead Park, and the result was that his ideas such as ornamental lakes, artificially-mounded hills and curving paths to produce subtle views and vistas became the pattern for all future Victorian park design in Britain, Europe and America.

Here in Princes Park the 90 acres of greenery and water are fringed with residential development in the form of elegant brick and stucco terraces, individual houses in a Classical style and highly decorated Victorian villas. Probably the most attractive group of houses associated with the park is Windermere Terrace, a group of four dwellings of symmetrical design featuring a balustraded parapet and impressive front porches. Close by is Windermere House, a detached Victorian villa with a Classically-styled front porch incorporating four Ionic columns, and also Princes Park Mansions. At five storeys high this is the largest Victorian building in the area, and it has some

distinctive iron balconies as well as a central Doric entrance. The main entrance to the park is marked by some fine cast-iron ornamental gates designed by James Pennethorne (a pupil of James Nash) and by a red granite obelisk which stands as a memorial to Richard Vaughan Yates.

Running north-westwards from the main gates is Princes Avenue with its tree-lined central boulevard, an excellent example of 19th century urban design in Liverpool. The initial route was Princes Road, opened in 1846 as an important link between the city centre and the newly constructed Princes Park, but then additional land was subsequently acquired to widen the road to form the adjacent Avenue. By the 1890s this 'dual carriageway' had developed into a monumental approach on the Parisian scale to the rich southern suburbs of the city, with tramlines from the city centre terminating at Princes Park gates, and on both sides of Princes Avenue were built impressive terraces of stuccoed houses interspersed with some intricately detailed religious buildings.

Landscape design on the magnificent scale evident in Princes Park and Sefton Park did not end with the Victorians though — the more recent creation of the Festival Gardens in the area between Dingle and Otterspool alongside the River Mersey has demonstrated that the development of attractive open space is certainly not a lost art. What was formerly 125 acres of spoiled and derelict land was transformed into the luxuriantly planted site for Britain's first International Garden Festival, attracting over 16,000 visitors a day when it was opened in 1984 and setting the pattern for the development of other Garden Festivals in the rest of the country. Around the magnificent Festival Hall at the centre was laid out a vast array of theme gardens and natural habitats as well as numerous 'national' displays, such as the Chinese Garden with its temple and pagoda, all set against a backcloth

of expansive views across the River Mersey. Although part of the site has since been taken up by residential and commercial development most of the Festival Gardens remains open for the general public to enjoy on a year-round basis.

Part of this area along the Mersey was known as the 'cast-iron shore', possibly a reference to nearby **St. Michael's Hamlet** which has a distinctive tradition in the use of cast-iron for its architectural expression. It appears that one John Cragg, the proprietor of the Mersey Iron Foundry, settled here in the early 19th century and made considerable use of cast-iron for a variety of structural and decorative purposes in the group of five houses which he built. He was also responsible for the building of St. Michael's Church in 1814-15, a quite remarkable piece of architecture in that everything possible was made of iron — including the supporting columns and arches, the door and window surrounds, the window tracery and the parapets. As one might expect, even the churchyard is enclosed by iron railings. The architect involved in the work was Thomas Rickman, who had a very important influence on the great 19th century Gothic Revival.

The five houses built by Cragg shortly before the church also incorporate a significant amount of cast-iron in their design, particularly in the door frames and latticed windows as well as in the fireplaces, staircases and balustrading. A number of other houses in the locality which were built at the same time display a complementary architectural quality without making the same use of cast-iron, and the area as a whole enjoys a secluded atmosphere by virtue of the spacious gardens set amidst mature planting and leafy lanes.

**The Palm House, Sefton Park**

**St. Michael's Church, St. Michael's Hamlet**

To the east of St. Michael's Hamlet and across the green expanse of Sefton Park is **Mossley Hill,** probably Liverpool's most exclusive residential area during the 19th century. At that time the city's merchants and ship owners built for themselves large individual villas in extensive grounds, which had the advantage of fine views over the southern slopes of Mossley Hill down to the river. All this was made possible when the Aigburth Hall estates were broken up into smaller parcels by Thomas Tarleton at the end of the 18th century, with the intention of selling these off for the development of substantial mansions, this in turn being helped by the opening of a toll road in 1820 giving a direct approach to Liverpool.

With the coming of the railway in 1863 the area also became a magnet for wealthy professional and business people to live here, with the result that a number of new roads were laid out and lined by large houses (as opposed to substantial mansions, as had been the case earlier in the century). The next major phase of development took place in the 1930s, when a sudden surge in home ownership coincided with the sale of a considerable area of former farmland for building. The result was Mossley Hill's growth as a suburb of semi-detached houses, particularly on the lower slopes, but despite this it has continued to display its original exclusive character and has retained the sense of grandeur given by the detached mansions hidden in undisturbed privacy behind high sandstone walls.

One of Mossley Hill's most impressive buildings, situated close to its highest point, is Sudley Hall. Dating from 1830 this was the home of George Holt, a Liverpool shipowner, who lived here from 1883 until his death, during which time he gathered together a remarkable collection of paintings and sculptures. As the house was given to the City of Liverpool in 1944 this collection is now on display to the general public in what is the Sudley Museum and Art Gallery. Important features of the house itself include the iron Ionic verandah facing onto the garden, a conservatory with 'Chinese' glazing and the fine staircase with its tiered columns. Other impressive houses situated around the summit of Mossley Hill include St. Saviour's Convent, originally known as 'The Homestead' and built to an early Victorian Tudor style, as well as a mansion on Park Avenue designed by Alfred Waterhouse and now incorporated within Mossley Hill Hospital.

The focal point of the area as a whole is the Church of St. Matthew and St. James, sited on the very top of the hill and forming another of Liverpool's landmarks. Built in 1870-75 with money left by a local benefactor, the church is one of Paley and Austin's most impressive pieces of work and is very much in keeping with the opulent character of its surroundings. Cathedral-like in scale it is constructed of red sandstone in a Decorated Gothic style, its most prominent feature being the monumental crossing tower.

**Aigburth** is situated to the south of Mossley Hill just above the shoreline of the River Mersey, and the buildings here are rather more humble in appearance as befits their less elevated position. One particularly interesting building is Stanlawe Grange, said to be a late 13th century cruck framed building which belonged to Stanlawe Abbey, while nearby is the late Georgian church of St. Anne which is an interesting example of the Norman Revival style of architecture. Unlike the Church of St. Matthew and St. James perched on the hill above it, this particular church lacks any pretensions of grandeur, having a fairly small west tower together with some straightforward decorative touches.

As the main road here heads away from Liverpool towards Garston it passes **Grassendale Park** and **Cressington Park,** two residential areas laid out as a private speculative venture during the mid-19th century. The large Victorian villas which predominate in this locality are situated within well planted gardens which give it a spacious and mature character, and the tree-lined roads lead down to an elegant riverside promenade constructed and lined with sandstone plinth walls and cast-iron railings. Very few villas in the area are of the same design, the most attractive being the Classically-styled early Victorian houses in Grassendale Park with their cast-iron balconies, beautifully proportioned windows and doors, and stucco details.

Although the later Victorian and Edwardian properties do not exhibit the same unity of design, particularly in Cressington Park, the same noble character has been achieved through the adoption of similar restrictions on building lines and road treatment. It is interesting to note that the restrictive covenants relating to plot size, building lines and external materials which have safeguarded the distinctive appearance of this area are still administered by trustees for each park. It is also interesting to discover that the residents of these two private parks had their own railway station, the Cressington and Grassendale Station, built in the 1840s and a good example of early railway architecture. The elaborate details featured within the station complex include pierced bargeboards, half-hipped roofs and unusual eaves brackets.

Just two miles further up the River Mersey, beyond Garston and Liverpool Airport, is one of Liverpool's most important buildings — **Speke Hall,** an exceptionally fine and largely unchanged example of a Tudor manor house dating from the late 15th century. The house in its present form, a lovely half-timbered 'black and white' structure resting on a sandstone plinth around a central cobbled courtyard and sheltering beneath a sandstone slab roof, is predominantly the work of the Norris family who lived at Speke from the 14th to the 18th centuries.

Most of the work on the Hall was carried out

*An early Victorian house in Grassendale Park*

between the late 1400s and the late 1500s, rebuilding and enlarging a smaller existing timber-framed house on the same site. During this period the Norris family, important landowners in Lancashire and South Cheshire, were at the height of their wealth and influence, so it is not surprising to discover some elaborate and very rich decoration (consistent with the family's status) in both the Great Hall and the Great Parlour. In the 1730s, however, the house passed by marriage into the hands of the Beauclerk family, who held it until 1795 when the estate was sold to Richard Watt, a Liverpool merchant. Different members of the Watt family then owned Speke Hall up to 1942, when it was offered to the National Trust; since then the property has been leased to the local authority and opened up to the general public as a museum.

The four wings of Speke Hall look inwards to an attractively cobbled central courtyard dominated by two huge yew trees known locally as Adam and Eve, which are reputed to be older than any existing part of the Hall. It was across this courtyard that most visitors here would have passed before entering the

Great Hall by way of the Screens Passage. The Great Hall was erected sometime between 1490 and 1506, although most of its internal features seem to be of a rather later date. The fine oak panelling in this room includes the particularly impressive 'Great Wainscot' with its pilasters and carved heads in an early Flemish Renaissance style. Another notable feature is the fireplace with its unusually decorated chimney-breast — completed in plaster it consists of various motifs as well as a series of heads which are said to represent Sir William Norris and his family. The oak mantlebeam immediately below is carved with cable and vine decoration.

The size and grandeur of the Great Hall seems to have been for the benefit of visitors to Speke rather than for the benefit of its occupants, since it appears that the Norris family would have used this room only on relatively rare occasions. The Great Parlour next door, however, seems to have been one of the most important rooms in the house and was built during the early years of the 16th century as part of a wing to provide more spacious accommodation for family use. One

of the most interesting features of this room is the genealogical overmantle above the fireplace which dates from about 1560 and features the three generations of the Norris family who were mainly responsible for building the Hall. Another important feature of the Great Parlour is its early Jacobean ceiling, incorporating the stucco decoration which had become so popular during the Elizabethan period; each of its 15 square panels is covered by one of five designs — pomegranates, roses, lilies, grapes or hazelnuts.

The Great Parlour was kept mainly for entertaining and formal use rather than for the everyday needs of the family, which would probably have been met by the Little Parlour on the other side of the Great Hall. Now known as the Blue Drawing Room this has been restored to its appearance back in the 1850s, when it was fully redecorated and furnished with a suite made of tulipwood and rosewood. The use of William Morris 'Willow' pattern wallpaper in the room was a rather later improvement, dating back to about 1935, although this was recently replaced by wallpaper which is an exact copy of the

*Speke Hall*

*Speke Hall's impressive half-timbered frontage*

Although the tapestries in the appropriately-named Tapestry Room date from the 17th century, most of the furniture in the bedrooms at Speke Hall was introduced during a 19th century restoration of the building — many of the items are thus essentially Victorian but at the same time incorporate decorative motifs of the 16th and 17th centuries, particularly drawing on the style of the Flemish Renaissance. This part of the Hall also features several reminders of the time when Catholic priests took refuge here — in the Blue Bedroom is a spyhole giving a view of the main approach to the house, while in the Green and Tapestry Bedrooms there are hiding places in cavities next to the chimneys.

Evidence of the mediaeval moat which originally surrounded Speke Hall in its entirety is still to be found on two sides of the building, although what is left was drained by at least the mid-1800s. The earliest reference to the moat dates back to 1693 when it was stocked with carp and perch, but by 1781 it appears to have been present only on the eastern and north-eastern sides. From other records it also seems that there was a garden near the house from at least the Tudor period, with a gardener certainly being employed here in 1624, although the present basic layout of lawns, borders, paths and hedges was established when the whole garden area was redesigned between 1855 and 1865. There was also extensive planting of rhododendrons and azaleas at that time, and since then very few changes have been made to this pattern.

original having been printed from the original locks.

The ground floor rooms in the west wing are also furnished in a mid-Victorian style, having been restored during this period after they had fallen into disuse in the previous centuries. The east wing dates from the mid-16th century and forms the service quarters of Speke Hall, incorporating the kitchen and the servants' hall as well as a number of ancillary rooms such as the dairy and the butler's pantry. On the first floor of the north and west ranges of the building are the main family bedrooms with their accompanying dressing rooms — including the Blue Bedroom, the Green Bedroom and the Royal Bedroom. The last is so-called because of a tradition that Charles I slept here in 1630.

The district of **Allerton** lies just two miles to the north of Speke Hall, although the intrusive nature of Liverpool Airport and Ford's Halewood car plant between them makes this distance seem substantially greater. The most significant and impressive building in Allerton is Allerton Hall, a red sandstone mansion built largely during the 18th century but added to by William Roscoe (one of Liverpool's leading figures) in the first few years of the 1800s. Built to a Classical style in three storeys, the Hall features a central pediment with Roman columns above the main entrance, which is also marked by a large lion mask over the original panelled door; inside can be found some 18th century panelled rooms as well as some interesting plasterwork.

Not far away is Springwood House, another substantial mansion in a later Classical style which was completed by the shipowner Sir Thomas Brocklebank in 1839. Built of grey ashlar stone the important features of this building are its main facade, incorporating giant pilasters and sash windows, together with an inner staircase hall in the Regency manner with contemporary plasterwork and marble mantelpieces. Elsewhere in the Allerton area are several buildings which survive from a number of 19th century private

*The cobbled central courtyard at Speke Hall*

estates which dominated this part of Liverpool, reflecting the tremendous wealth held by the city's entrepreneurial merchants at the time. The fact that only the best architects available were called upon to design these buildings is further evidence of Allerton's general standing in Liverpool during that period.

The Cleveley estate to the west of Allerton Road was owned by Sir Joseph Leather, one of Liverpool's cotton merchants, and the buildings here were all the work of Sir George Gilbert Scott, better known perhaps for the buildings at St. Pancras Station in London. On the other side of Allerton Road is Allerton Priory, the estate laid out for the colliery owner J. Grant Morris in 1867-70, with Alfred Waterhouse being the architect responsible for the buildings here. Characteristic of Waterhouse's approach was the use of brick and stone in creating a distinctive Gothic style, an approach which features in many of his other buildings in both Liverpool and Manchester. Nearby is the Allerton Tower estate and a series of buildings designed by Harvey Lonsdale Elmes, the architect responsible for St. George's Hall in Liverpool. Another eminent architect who helped to shape the architectural character of Allerton was Thomas Harrison, who designed a mansion and gate lodge for Jacob Fletcher in 1815; these buildings now form part of Allerton Golf Club.

From Allerton an unusually pleasant dual carriageway takes us down into **Woolton Village,** a tight-knit community of terraced houses and early 19th century villas set in fine grounds. Most of the development which has taken place here dates from the Georgian and Victorian periods, and although there are variations in architectural style there is still considerable visual cohesion by virtue of the compact street pattern and the standard use of both local red sandstone and locally-made brick. Situated on the central reservation of the dual carriageway itself are two of the original gate lodges to Woolton Hall, one of the oldest buildings in the village and certainly one of its most impressive. Built of sandstone the house dates largely from 1704 when it was erected for Richard Molyneux, heir to Viscount Molyneux of Croxteth, although there is evidence that it also incorporates an earlier house on the same site.

Then in 1772 the Hall changed hands and Robert Adam was employed to remodel both the interior and the exterior; much of his work to the building can still be seen, particularly in the decorative ceilings and fireplace surrounds, although the huge 'porte cochere' on the front of the Hall is a later Victorian addition. Typical of Adam's work are the sculptured medallions on the front elevation, depicting classical scenes, and the ingeniously planned entrance hall with its cantilevered main staircase. Just a short

distance to the south of Woolton Hall is the pretty little enclave of Ashton Square, a terrace of prim stone cottages built during the latter part of the 18th century as accommodation for the Hall's estate workers. This terrace incorporates Gothic style arches over the windows and doors, and the fronts of the cottages are still edged by the original cobbled footpath.

The cul-de-sac along which Ashton Square is situated leads onto School Lane, named appropriately after the Old School further up the hill. This 17th century building constructed of large blocks of red sandstone is the oldest in Woolton and reputedly the oldest elementary school building in Lancashire, although the Gothic windows in the east and west gables suggest a somewhat earlier date than that of 1610 to be found on an inscription above what was the main doorway. In recent years the Old School has been converted into a unique single storey detached dwelling.

To the north of Woolton Hall from here is Woolton Stret, which leads into the centre of the village. Along the section of Woolton Street nearest to the Hall, and to the south of High Street, is an attractive terrace of early 19th century brick cottages as well as the old village cross with its unusual head stone. High Street itself is marked by several groups of Georgian terraced houses, many of which incorporate delightful door, porch and window details, while on the northern section of Woolton Street the Georgian character of the village is continued by a late 18th century group of farm buildings as well as by the early 19th century 'Coffee House' pub. Further along the street is a fascinating early lamp

*A Victorian lamp standard in Woolton*

standard dated 1873, which effectively marks the centre of the village, and then beyond that is the Elephant Hotel which dates from the early part of the 19th century.

To the north of this point Woolton Street gives way to Acrefield Road and another group of late Georgian houses, while across from the Elephant Hotel is Mason Street which leads up to Church Road. Here one can find not only more examples of attractive brick and stone terraces but also the rather grander edifice of St. Peter's Church, dating from 1886-87 and built of local red sandstone in the Victorian Gothic 'Perpendicular' style. Church Road is also the appropriate location of the 'Archbishop's House', an early 19th century Greek-style building of red sandstone which was once the residence of the Roman Catholic bishops of Liverpool.

The sandstone used in many of Woolton's buildings (and also in the construction of much of the Anglican Cathedral) was extracted from the quarry immediately to the west of Church Road, and the now cavernous

*Woolton Cross*

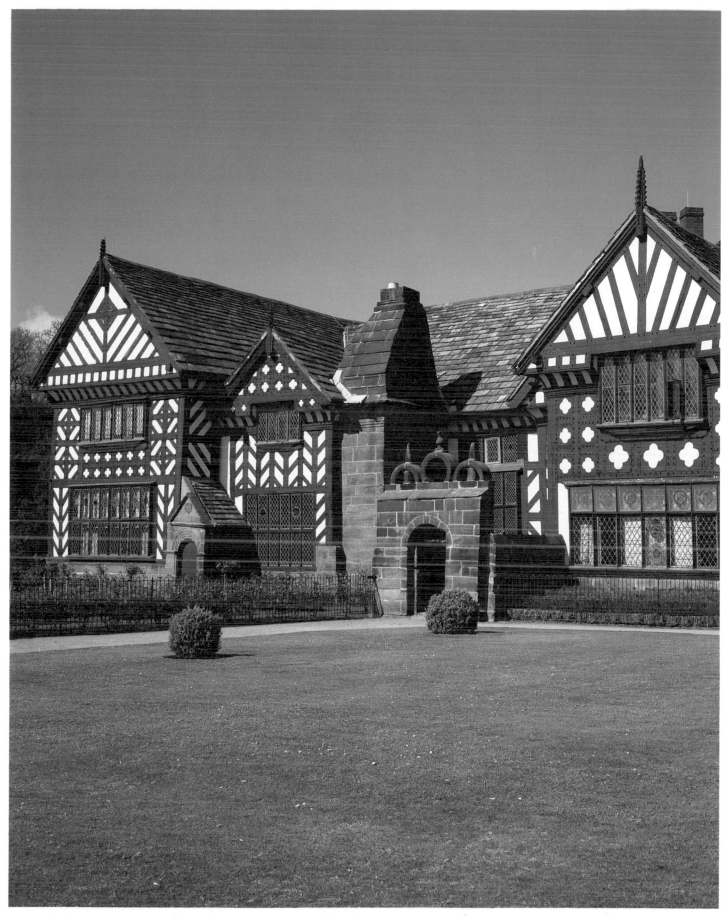

*Speke Hall near Liverpool*

*Croxteth Hall, West Derby*

depths of this quarry are traversed by what is effectively a high-level footpath situated rather precariously on top of a solid wall of sandstone dividing its two separate halves. The far end of this dramatic route brings us into Quarry Street, lined with smaller terraced cottages in brick and stone which were built for Woolton's working population. The nearby streets were also laid out during the 19th century to provide cheap housing for those employed in the quarries, the corn mill and other local industries; many of those engaged in these activities were attracted in from the surrounding rural areas, although there were also a good number of Irish immigrants who found their way here. At its southern end Quarry Street joins up with Allerton Road, which is lined with 19th century terraced houses as it makes its way down towards Woolton Street and the centre of the village.

*Gateacre's pretty Black Bull public house*

*Quarry Street, Woolton*

The village immediately to the north of Woolton is **Gateacre,** with Acrefield Road acting as a link between the two. At its lower southern end Acrefield Road is characterised by the early 19th century properties which seem to predominate in Woolton generally, but then further along the road are some fine Victorian villas in both the Classical and ornate styles. At its northern end Acrefield Road gives way to Rose Brow, along which is situated the red sandstone mansion with stone mullioned windows that is now a home for retired seafarers, while Gateacre Brow just below this point takes us down into Gateacre Village itself. The focal point of the village is the Green at the foot of Gateacre Brow, close to the crossroads which has been the traditional centre of this attractive settlement since the end of the 17th century when a cluster of cottages was established here. Over the course of the next 200 years or so Gateacre grew quite significantly, and at the centre of the village there is probably a wider range of buildings than is to be found in any comparable part of Liverpool.

The Green itself is marked by the Wilson Memorial Fountain, a small open-sided octagonal building of red sandstone with a pyramid roof, erected in 1883 in honour of the engineer who helped to bring Liverpool's water across from North Wales, this unusual structure features a French Renaissance frieze together with a large Gothic gargoyle and some other decorative touches. Also located on the Green is Gateacre's Jubilee Memorial, a red sandstone column supporting a bronze bust of Queen Victoria and introduced here in 1887, while nearby on the northern side of Gateacre Brow is a group of buildings which have been decorated in a mock half-timbered style. Chief among them is the Black Bull public house, pretty as a picture by virtue of its Victorian 'black and white' front, ornamental brick chimneys and cobbled forecourt.

On the opposite side of Gateacre Brow is a one-time brewery building, attractively finished with different coloured brickwork and decorative touches to its central ventilation tower, while a little further along the Brow are some traditional Georgian cottages built of brick in a somewhat simpler fashion to the old brewery. Next to these cottages the decorative Victorian approach to architecture reappears in the form of more mock half-timbering, this time above a ground floor built of local red sandstone set back beneath an 'oversailing' upper storey in the manner that was characteristic of Tudor buildings. This rather unusual property, designed by the architect of Liverpool's Liver Building, also features an octagonal corner turret beneath a bell-shaped roof as well as a plaster frieze of moulded panels depicting biblical scenes.

In marked contrast to this is the 18th century Unitarian Chapel standing in its own grounds on the adjoining plot, a much simpler building of red sandstone with tall arched windows and a small bell turret on top of the roof. This is one of Gateacre's oldest buildings, having been licensed as 'a meeting place for an Assembly of Protestants dissenting from the Church of England' on 14th October, 1700. The features inside the chapel's rather austere auditorium include an 18th century pulpit as well as some 18th century panelling.

Beyond the Green from here, on the east side of the village, is Belle Vale Road and a homely group of sandstone cottages set back behind long front gardens. These date from the first half of the 19th century and are characterised by nicely proportioned doors and windows.

*The Wilson Memorial Fountain, Gateacre*

*More of Gateacre's Tudor-style architecture*

Leading northwards from the centre of Gateacre is Grange Lane, the location of some of the village's oldest dwellings. York Cottages, for example, consist of two rows of small terraced artisan houses dating from the early 19th century which are set back behind Grange Lane, while further along are the rather older Paradise Cottages which are built of rough sandstone rather than the usual brick or ashlar. Next door to these are Soarer Cottages, built at the end of the 19th century in a Tudor Cottage style around an open courtyard and named after a Grand National winner. The architect was Richard Beckett, who was also responsible for the stable block on Grange Lane which was built in 1895 for Lord Wavertree's polo ponies; here again a Tudor style has been followed, with the building's brick base being topped by half-timbered upper walls. The final building of interest on Grange Lane is Grange Lodge, with its variety of architectural details from the 17th, 18th and 19th centuries; of particular importance is the panelled dining room from the Queen Anne period, similar in style to the early 18th century work at Woolton Hall and indicative of the involvement of an architect.

Grange Lane carries on north-westwards from Gateacre before arriving at the neighbouring village of **Childwall,** a settlement which dates from Norse times and whose name is derived from the Norse word 'Keldaville' meaning a spring or well in a field. Once part of a large parish stretching from Wavertree to Hale, and encompassing Gateacre to the south, Childwall still retains its village character — particularly around the Church of All Saints, which continues to be the focal point of the area. This is Liverpool's only remaining mediaeval church, dating from the 14th century, although sections have been rebuilt over the course of time. During

Further down Belle Vale Road is the Church of St. Stephen, completed in 1874 and constructed of red sandstone with a battlemented tower and octagonal spire, together with a group of cottages built of brick about the same time as the church and incorporating mock half-timbering on the gabled upper storeys.

Gateacre's predilection for Tudor-style decoration and architecture is also evident along Halewood Road, which runs southwards from the Green, particularly in the case of the Brown Cow public house which is a smaller version of the Black Bull. The two 19th century cottages which originally composed this pub now hide behind a late Victorian 'black and white' frontage and its gabled porch. Close by are some groups of early 19th century cottages built of brick and stone, while further along Halewood Road are a number of larger houses and detached villas.

*Childwall Abbey Hotel*

the early part of the 19th century, for example, the collapse of St. Nicholas' tower in Liverpool with the death of 21 people led some to think that Childwall's own tower might be unsafe, so it was demolished and rebuilt to the original design. Despite such events some elements of the church have remained unchanged, among them the windows in the north and south walls of the chancel which are reputed to be original 14th century work.

Another early place of worship, the chapel of St. Thomas the Martyr dating back to 1484, appears to have been incorporated into the Childwall Abbey Hotel situated just to the west of the church. Like many of the buildings in this part of Liverpool it is constructed of red sandstone, and made all the more noticeable because of its castellated parapet and the Gothic-style windows decorated by grotesque keystone sculptures.

In between the church and the hotel is the early 19th century Hearse House, similarly castellated and once the resting place for hearses as its name suggests, while to the east of the church is Elm House dating from the same period. Built of red sandstone like its neighbours it also shares similar architectural features, having some Gothic details as well as a battlemented parapet above the first floor windows. Had Childwall Hall not been demolished the composition of the village would have been well nigh perfect, but all that remains is Childwall Lodge some distance from the rest of the group. Yet here again a similar architectural style helps to pull all the buildings together, since the Lodge too shares the now expected Gothic details as well as a castellated parapet and lancet windows.

From Childwall one can follow Liverpool's Ring Road northwards to **West Derby,** one of the City's most attractive and historic settlements. Like Childwall, West Derby dates back to Norse times when its name meant 'the place of the deer, or wild beasts, in the west', and by the time of Edward the Confessor it was already established as a royal manor — probably incorporating a small castle or fortified hunting lodge since the forest here was greatly valued as a hunting ground. Mentioned in the Domesday survey of 1086 as the 'Derbei Hundret' it was given first place in the description of the land 'between the Ribble and the Mersey', and so well before Liverpool was ever heard of it had become well established as a centre of jurisdiction for an area stretching from the Ribble estuary south to Hale and inland nearly to Wigan.

West Derby is therefore a place with a long history, reflected in the interesting old buildings which are huddled together around the centre of the village. Although the 'Cross' or monument which acts as a focal point in West Derby only dates from the 1860s, when it was designed by Eden Nesfield, it marks the

*The Parish Church of St. Mary the Virgin, West Derby*

site of the altar of an ancient chapel which is known to have existed here as far back as 1360 (even though it probably existed some considerable time before that, and was doubtless contemporary with the castle). Rebuilt as a chapel of ease to Walton church in 1786, it was eventually demolished just before the completion of West Derby's own parish church in 1856.

Immediately to the south of the Village Cross is the Old Court House, a small red sandstone building which acts as an important reminder of West Derby's role as a centre of jurisdiction. Probably built during the latter part of the 16th century, the Old Court House was the place where 'copyholders' (tenants of the lord of the manor holding a copy of the Court Rolls showing their right to tenure) were called to pay their dues to the lord through his steward. Manorial courts such as this also dealt with disputes between tenants. Known formally as a 'Court Leet with view of Frankpledge and Court Baron', the manorial court is not only one of the oldest courts of justice still in existence in this country but also the oldest organ of local government. Presided over by

the lord of the manor it was in effect the village 'parliament', meeting to pass bye-laws, elect officials and arbitrate between disputing neighbours as well as to try petty criminal and civil cases. With the introduction of county courts the manorial court no longer has any practical value — yet despite this it has not ceased to exist but has simply passed into abeyance.

Close to the Old Court House is the Hare and Hounds pub, a stuccoed building with double gables and an attractive iron balcony, while just beyond are several early 19th century houses built of hand-made bricks underneath stone-flagged roofs. On the opposite side of the road from here is the Yeoman's House, a 17th century building constructed of red sandstone and featuring some attractive stone mullioned windows, while immediately adjacent to this are the village stocks which originally stood at the west end of the Old Court House — no doubt to ensure easier access in the dispensation of local justice! In 1800 the earlier wooden stocks were replaced by the present iron set, now standing within a small garden planted to commemorate the reign of Queen Victoria and the coronation of Edward VII. Apparently the most common offenders were drunkards who were punished by a fine of five shillings or else six hours in the stocks. The area now occupied by the stocks, together with part of the school playground behind them, originally formed the village pound or 'pinfold' — the enclosure where stray cattle, pigs and other animals were impounded until they were claimed by their respective owners. The fine for such 'misdemeanours' was a halfpenny per animal each night in the winter and a farthing in the summer.

In addition to the evidence of its early life as a manorial village, West Derby also has some significant Victorian buildings which demonstrate the continuing role played by the lord of the manor. The Parish Church of St. Mary the Virgin, for example, was built in the 1850s on land provided by the Earl of Sefton, who had the honour of laying its foundation stone. This imposing red sandstone building was designed by Sir George Gilbert Scott in the Decorated Gothic style which was so popular during the 19th century, although the original and more ambitious proposals had to be modified somewhat because of the considerable expense involved in providing secure foundations for the tower.

The tower itself incorporates three turrets of matching size together with a fourth larger one which accommodates the access staircase, while the interior of the body of the church features a magnificent west window as well as some fine woodwork and a unique display of heraldic shields representing the various dioceses within the Anglican Communion. On the outer wall of the south transept is a sundial dating from 1793 (removed from the south wall of the old chapel before this was demolished), a

*At the entrance to Croxteth Park*

*Victorian drinking fountain, West Derby*

forerunner of the rather more reliable timepiece in St. Mary's tower which was installed in 1888 and which has since become the most famous church clock in the area.

Close to the parish church is one of Croxteth Hall's entrance lodges, another fine Victorian building built in red sandstone to an imitation Tudor style and marked by the arms of the Earl of Sefton carved over the doorway. The features of particular interest here are the diamond-paned stone mullioned windows and the crouching beast on the rainwater head, as well as the gate piers on either side of the driveway which are topped by stone lions holding iron pennants. Immediately across from the lodge is a group of three red brick Victorian cottages, dating from 1861-70 and designed by Eden Nesfield, next to which is the West Derby Public House. This is a good example of a Victorian drinking establishment designed to fit into what was then the rural surroundings of West Derby, featuring a round arched doorway in stone with a traceried fanlight.

The Victorian theme around the centre of the village is continued by the West Derby Church of England Primary School, an unusual sandstone building dating from 1860 which is more reminiscent of a church than a school by virtue of its tower, spire and Decorated Gothic windows. The two adjacent houses also date from the same period and were built for the schoolmaster and schoolmistress. The last feature of

interest at the heart of West Derby is its Victorian drinking fountain, a typical piece of Victorian craftsmanship comprising a conical stone top surmounted by an ornamental street lamp. Erected here in 1894 as a gift to the village by teetotaller Richard R. Meade-King, it bears the confident slogan 'WATER IS BEST' and is significantly within spitting distance of West Derby's three pubs!

If the Victorian architecture at the centre of the village is comparatively restrained and 'humble' in appearance in order to blend with its homely forebears, the outskirts of West Derby provided an opportunity for a fuller expression of the style and grandeur of the Victorian era quite comparable to that which has been evident elsewhere in Liverpool. On Hayman's Green, for example, there are a number of substantial stuccoed Victorian villas standing in their own grounds which are characterised by rich ornamentation and balustrated stone balconies, while Broughton Hall on Yew Tree Lane is a High Victorian Gothic house dating from 1856. Built of rock-faced sandstone this property is elaborately decorated with castellated parapet eaves, flamboyant window tracery and tall chimneys with clustered octagonal stacks. Then attached to the south east corner of the house is an elaborate conservatory with a hipped roof and central lantern supported on iron columns, while internally the main rooms have carved timber wall panelling.

As well as being a noteworthy place in its own right, West Derby is also important because it provides a delightful setting for the entrance to **Croxteth Hall.** This palatial mansion is one of Liverpool's most beautiful buildings, part of a unique working country estate within the City's boundary which allows visitors to see for themselves how an Edwardian landed family would have lived. As well as admiring the Hall with its rooms sumptuously furnished in period fashion, visitors can enjoy a stroll through the walled garden, discover the Rare Breeds Centre in the original farm buildings close to the house, or amble at leisure through the 530 acres of surrounding parkland. This vast green expanse of fields and woodland, just five miles from the city centre, is particularly beautiful in May and June when the rhododendrons are in full bloom.

In terms of its history Croxteth was the home of the Molyneux family, the Earls of Sefton, whose coat of arms (the 'cross moline') and crest (a cap with peacock's feather) are displayed at various points throughout the estate. The family can be traced back to the Norman period, when they were granted land at nearby Sefton in about 1100, but during the course of succeeding generations they acquired land right across south west Lancashire. By the 15th century the Molyneux family had gained hereditary control over Liverpool Castle and over the Forest of West Derby, where the 'Park of

**_Croxteth Hall_**

'Crokstath' was situated, and by the end of the next century the first Croxteth Hall had been erected; part of this Elizabethan house is still to be seen at the rear of the present building.

Then by 1714 work on the construction of what is now known as the Queen Anne wing was completed, transforming the Hall into an imposing mansion and marking the final removal of the family seat from Sefton to Croxteth. This part of the Hall provides its most attractive facade, rising up from a wide terrace and embellished with decorative stonework incorporating the Molyneux family arms and symbolic trophies of battle over the entrance. Improvements to the Park were also made, including the laying out of drives and 'pleasure grounds'.

The Molyneux family experienced a significant rise in their fortunes when the 8th Viscount was created 1st Earl of Sefton in 1771, with the result that Croxteth Hall was further extended around 1800. This process of improvement and development continued throughout the 19th century, with the Earls of Sefton utilising their substantial income from agricultural rents to provide for themselves all the necessities of a well run self-contained country estate. As a result the home farm, stableyard, walled gardens, laundry, dairy and workshops were all built or enlarged during this period, with the rest of the Park being managed chiefly for field sports.

The Hall itself was enlarged substantially by the 4th Earl, who between 1874 and 1877 built nursery and gatehouse wings to enclose a central courtyard and extended the Queen Anne wing to provide a new porch and entrance hall at the west end as well as a large dining room and kitchens at the east end. Then the 6th Earl added the grand west front in 1902, producing what is now the Hall's main entrance in a style which echoes that of the Queen Anne wing.

During the 20th century the Earls of Sefton continued to be among the region's most influential people, holding important positions and becoming personal friends of the Royal Family, but with ill health and tragedy the line of inheritance narrowed and then was ultimately terminated with the death of the childless 7th Earl in 1972. It was the wish of the Earl's widow that the Croxteth Estate should pass into public ownership in the following year, and the Hall and its surounding Country Park are now open to visitors all year round as a place for leisure, education and environmental conservation.

Visitors to the Hall can learn something of the family's history and lifestyle in the ground floor display of Croxteth's heritage, while the adjacent courtyard features some of the carriages which would have been used for drives around the Park. Elsewhere on the ground floor are the domestic quarters of the Hall (including the kitchens, servants' hall, butchery and wine cellar), which reveal what the 'below stairs' life of a stately home was like. The focal point of the house is its grand staircase balcony, a splendid piece of interior design which forms a very marked contrast with the strictly functional service areas on the ground floor below. This balcony gives access to a number of rooms open to view in both the Queen Anne wing and the 1902 west front, including the original 18th century library and the card room. The latter still retains some of its original features, but following a disastrous fire in 1952 the library was stripped of its shelves and became a dining room. Also on display are the billiard and smoking rooms, together with their associated lavatories, a part of the house which was very much a male preserve during the 19th century.

From the grand staircase the main corridor leads to the private family rooms, beginning with Lady Sefton's sitting room or boudoir which connects with her dressing room and bedroom. This latter room is still furnished as it was in the Seftons' time, having the mahogany bed, massive wardrobe and matching furniture which was made for the 4th Earl in 1878. Then at the end of the wing is Lord Sefton's dressing room and bathroom, interconnected to form a small private suite. Like many large country houses of its period Croxteth Hall was the scene of lavish entertainment, being treated almost as a private hotel, and so there is quite a range of guest rooms in the house, situated above the principal rooms and also above the nursery.

During Victorian times the children of the family were generally kept away from those parts of the house given over to entertaining, a situation which especially prevailed for the servants who were required to move about unseen between their own rooms using a maze of back stairways. The Seftons were themselves seen at Croxteth for only part of the year, mainly when they wished to pursue their sporting interests, with the rest of the time being spent between their two other residences. One of these was in London, helping them to maintain their place in the social circles of their time, while the other was their 20,000-acre country estate at Abbeystead in the Trough of Bowland, famous for its grouse shooting and often visited by King George V.

An important feature of the Croxteth Estate, and one which quite naturally is closely associated with the house itself, is the two acre walled garden — not merely a kitchen garden but rather a showpiece which the Earl would delight to share with his frequent guests. The main function of the garden was to provide a continuous supply of fruit, vegetables, cut flowers and pot plants for the Hall, and to make this possible 25 gardeners were required for its upkeep. One of its advantages is that it enjoys its own unique climate, the high brick walls not only protecting crops and flowers from the wind but also radiating the warmth of the sun. These walls provided a very favourable environment for the training of young fruit trees, aided by the fact that a

system of flues within the brickwork itself distributed heat from specially-lit fires. With the development of greenhouses such 'heated walls' were superseded, although several chimneys can still be seen on one of the walls here. Bordering the main paths which divide the garden are some well established fruit trees, with a variety of crops planted between them as well as a pleasant area of formalised flower beds and borders at the southern end.

Like Croxteth's walled garden, the Home Farm was built to serve the needs of the Hall and the tenants of the estate, and for most of its history it was managed under the direct control of the Earl of Sefton through his agent and farm bailiff. Established in its present form in the mid-19th century it is very definitely a Victorian 'model farm', regarded then as having the best designed system of buildings available and providing accommodation for pigs, poultry, cattle and heavy horses as well as offering extensive overhead storage space for hay and grain. The wide variety of livestock and produce here was common to all farms in Victorian times, but the Home Farm in particular reflected the special interests of its owners and maintained pedigree herds of unusual cattle such as the Highland, the Dexter and the Redpoll. Despite the passing of the Seftons this tradition has been maintained at Croxteth and the Home Farm now plays an important role as an approved Rare Breeds Centre, enabling visitors to see some of the traditional breeds of the past at close range.

As well as the Hall itself and the Home Farm, Croxteth has a number of other interesting

buildings which emphasise how extensive an enterprise this country estate was. In addition to the entrance lodges there are cottages for gardeners and other estate workers together with loose boxes for racehorses, stud stables and kennels, with most of these buildings being constructed of reddish brick or sandstone and designed in the 'Old English' style favoured by the Earl's architects. Of particular interest is the 'model dairy', designed by Eden Nesfield in the 1860s and a typical example of the Victorian idea of quaint rural architecture; Nesfield was also responsible for the estate laundry, a building which was only partly modernised and which was in use for hand-washing up to the early 1970s.

Providing a fitting backcloth for the magnificent Hall and its associated estate buildings is the 530-acre expanse of Croxteth Country Park, which owes its rural character to the sporting interests of its former owners. The Park was managed with country pursuits such as riding and shooting very much in mind, and in addition to the pasture grazed by cattle from the Home Farm there were paddocks housing valuable racehorses as well as woodland planted with cover for pheasants and other game. Thanks to careful management over the years Croxteth now retains one of the most valuable areas of deciduous woodland for many miles around, which has contributed towards the creation of some splendid wildlife habitats. Then of course there are the gardens, lawns and shrubberies closer to the Hall itself, and here one can discover some fine specimen trees and ornamental ponds as well as the spectacular displays of azaleas and

*The West Front, Croxteth Hall*

*The Carriage Wash in Croxteth Stable yard*

rhododendrons during springtime.

One of the occasions when the Seftons would certainly be in residence at Croxteth, together with numerous guests, was the running of the Grand National steeplechase at **Aintree Racecourse,** situated just three miles to the north west of their mansion and the next port of call on our tour round the outskirts of Liverpool. The Molyneux family's connection with this great event goes back to the first running of the Grand National in 1839, although races had been held at Aintree over the previous decade on land which was leased from the Earl of Sefton. For the two years before that race meetings had been organised at Maghull by John Formby, a Liverpool landowner, but then an associate decided to organise his own races and so leased the land at Aintree and then staged the first Flat fixture on 7th July, 1829.

The history of racing in the Liverpool area actually goes back much further than this, to the middle of the 16th century in fact, when a chase over a four mile course at Crosby was held every Ascension Day for a prize of a silver bell worth about £6. Although there was a revival of the sport in the early 1700s racing was discontinued in the area in 1786 due to a lack of support, and there were no further meetings until 1827 when John Formby organised the first race at Maghull.

When the course at Aintree was first laid out it consisted of a stone wall, since replaced by the water jump, a stretch of ploughed land and two hurdles to be negotiated at the end of the four mile trip. Now the distance covered

is just a little more than 4½ miles, with a total of 30 fences being jumped over two full circuits of the course. The Grand National fences are regarded as the stiffest in the world, so it is not surprising that just three races are run over these huge obstacles and that it is only the National itself which extends to two complete laps. For a number of years Flat racing played an important part in Liverpool's racing calendar, but from the mid-1960s the number of races dwindled until the last one took place at the 1976 Grand National meeting. Now races over jumps are held at Aintree on just one occasion in the year, the three day Festival in the spring.

As well as having a hand in the development of Aintree Racecourse, the Earls of Sefton also figured in the growth of **Litherland** immediately to the west, for it was they who donated sites for both the Roman Catholic school and St. Philip's Parish Church. The latter building is in the Victorian Gothic style with a fine octagonal spire, having been consecrated in 1864. Although Litherland is mentioned in the Domesday Book, its name indicating that it was originally founded by the Norsemen who settled along the coast of Lancashire in the 10th century, the development of this area really dates from the construction of the Leeds and Liverpool Canal. Started in 1770 this provided cheap transport for local goods and brought the district into touch with the commercial life of Liverpool. The growth of Litherland was also encouraged by the construction here of the northern terminus of the former Liverpool overhead railway in 1893, as well as by the arrival of the Liverpool to Southport electric

railway in 1904, both of which made the town easily accessible and prompted the building of residential property.

To the south of Litherland is **Bootle,** which also benefited from the coming of the canal and railways but which ultimately became of much greater importance because of the line of docks established along its Mersey waterfront. Serving this dockland from the town's industrial hinterland was a vast complex of timber merchants, ship repair firms, warehouses and factories, particularly during the period when shipping and seaborne trade formed the entire life of the area, but in more recent years industrial diversification has ensured that Bootle's employment is no longer tied to shipping alone.

The name Bootle is derived from the Anglo-Saxon word 'botl' meaning a house or dwelling, dating back to about the 7th century when settlers were attracted here by the springs of drinking water and the plentiful supply of timber and soft building stone. Then at the start of the 10th century the Norsemen settled in this area and gave their names to nearby places such as Sefton, Litherland and Crosby. It was the good supply of pure soft water flowing from the Bootle springs which played an important role in the development of its earliest industries, among which were included tanning, paper making, bleaching, dyeing and cotton printing, and several attempts were made to supply water from these springs to Liverpool and its inhabitants.

By the beginning of the 19th century Bootle had also become a fashionable resort, and in 1801 it was recorded that '. . . the beach is covered with an immense number of people employing a number of caravans to conduct them into the water'. Consequently merchants and other professional people saw this quiet little village as an ideal spot in which to build their villas and mansions, although these were demolished later on in the 19th century when the docks were constructed. With the opening of the Canada Dock in 1859 Bootle began to expand rapidly, so that from a population of 6,414 in 1861 it grew to encompass 49,217 people just 30 years later.

Further expansion continued during the 20th century in step with the growth of the docks along Bootle's one and a half mile long waterfront, with the dock complex eventually incorporating the Gladstone docks, the Hornby dock, the Alexandra dock, the Langton docks and in more recent years the Seaforth container terminal. During the Second World War this dock system came in for particular attention from enemy bombers, as did the town in general. Of the 17,119 dwellings which then existed 2,043 were totally destroyed and a further 14,000 damaged. Large areas of Bootle have therefore had to be rebuilt since the war, creating a new heart for the town through its renewal and expansion.

To the north of Bootle along the coast is **Crosby,** a largely residential area which began to develop as Liverpool businessmen came to live here during the early part of the 19th century. The historic centre of this area is Great Crosby, originally part of the royal manor of West Derby and distinguished from what is now the much smaller village of Little Crosby. This latter manor was initially held by Richard Molyneux of Sefton up to 1362 when it came into the hands of John Blundell, and it has remained with the Blundell family ever since. The Blundells of Crosby are also lords of the manor of Great Crosby, having acquired it from the Molyneux family of Sefton in 1798.

It was at about this time that the land along the shore, known as Crosby Seabank, began to be developed as something of a resort, although limited settlement in the area had commenced nearly two centuries previously when Elizabeth I caused 200 acres of the common or marshlands to be enclosed and improved. Then at the time of the Battle of Waterloo in 1815 an hotel was built in this area, with the result that it was named the Waterloo Hotel (eventually becoming the Royal Hotel), acting as a focal point for what became a popular place for bathing served by a coach service from Liverpool. Then as development proceeded so the name 'Waterloo' came to be applied to all the southern part of Crosby, and to be inseparably linked to the elegant merchants' houses which were being built here.

The first of the late Regency and early Victorian properties to be erected in Waterloo were the six houses of Marine Terrace, begun in 1816 and originally called Waterloo Cottages; these were followed by those on Marine Crescent, built from 1825 onwards, then by Adelaide Terrace between 1831 and 1857 and finally by Beach Lawn between 1860 and 1878. The interesting features of these impressive terraces include their bay windows and the cast-iron or timber verandahs, which take full advantage of the wide views of the estuary and its shipping lanes. The terraces also have the benefit of public gardens running between them and the beach, helping to create a unique seaside environment.

Further north along the coast is the district of **Blundellsands,** dating largely from the latter part of the 19th century when Blundellsands Park was laid out as a high-class residential area by Nicholas Blundell of Crosby Hall. The estate was designed by Reade and Goodison of Liverpool, who based their layout on a central park of 20 acres surrounded by large plots accommodating substantial detached villas. The architects also made good use of the

seaboard location, retaining the original sandhills in certain parts and employing a curving avenue through the estate to emphasise the contrast between the leafy suburbs on one hand and the open coast on the other.

Most of the individual houses around Blundellsands Park are exceptionally fine examples of their period, with many of the late Victorian and Edwardian villas being built in a Gothic style but incorporating strong Romanesque and Italianate features — consistent with the influence which the Royal Palace at Sandringham was having on the popular taste of Victorian speculative building at the time. The layout of the estate around a 'key park' also reflects the influence of other developments, although in this case it was the much earlier work of Sir Joseph Paxton at Princes Park in Liverpool and Birkenhead Park on the Wirral. In addition to the 'pattern book' houses from the later Victorian period on the estate there are also some good examples of architect-designed houses from the early 20th century, including 'Redcot' on Warren Road in the 'Queen Anne' classic style and 'Littlecote' on The Serpentine in a style which illustrates the Voysey Tradition of English domestic architecture.

To the east of Crosby is the start of the M57 motorway, which can be followed south-eastwards past Kirkby and then down to Knowsley village, passing en route what was the site of Lord Sefton's tile and brick works close to the junction with the A506. The tiles and bricks for the whole of the Earl of Sefton's considerable estate would have been made at this works, which is located on Ingoe Lane in

*St. Nicholas' Fountain, Blundellsands Park*

Kirkby. **Knowsley Village,** however, has traditionally been the domain of the Earls of Derby since the 14th century when they established their home at Knowsley Hall, and many of the buildings here still reflect their patriarchal interest — particularly the

*Redcot, Blundellsands Park*

*The village green at Knowsley*

Almshouse, Parish Hospital and the Church of St. Mary.

Knowsley is one of the ancient manors of Lancashire mentioned in the Domesday Survey of 1086 (under the name 'Chenulveslei') and is situated in the last area of open countryside between Liverpool and St. Helens, its older village core of 18th century buildings huddled around an attractive green which is one of the best in Merseyside and a pleasant reminder of the area's rural past. Then in the Victorian period the Derby family extended Knowsley through the development of a 'model village' here based on the ideas of social reformers who rejected the misery of the new industrial cities in favour of a utopian vision of village life which looked back to a highly romanticised past. Landowners such as the Derbys were thus inspired to build well-planned communities for their workers, and at Knowsley the results are representative of those seen in similar developments elsewhere — typically spacious houses set in large gardens and designed to an ornate, picturesque style in marked contrast to the simpler cottages of the original village.

Knowsley consequently displays all the different elements which one might expect to see in an English village — church, vicarage, village hall, school, schoolhouse, several farmhouses with their associated buildings and a variety of cottages and houses in both brick and stone. There was even a village smithy sited on the village green, although only a monument now marks the spot where the anvil stood in the early 19th century, while on the northern outskirts of the village is located Dumbrees House, built in 1841 as a dower house for the widow of the Earl of Derby.

The home of the Earls of Derby since the 14th century has been **Knowsley Hall,** situated just a mile or so to the south of the village and set within delightful parkland which encompasses the well-known Knowsley Safari Park. Opened in 1971 the 360-acre Safari Park was a joint venture between the Earl of Derby and Mr. J. Chipperfield, allowing visitors free access to drive through the grounds in order to see the lions, giraffes, elephants and other animals which roam freely here. However, much of Knowsley Park still retains the character of the 18th century landscape which was created here by Capability Brown and which is one of the few remaining examples of his work in the north of England.

The Hall itself is one of the largest Georgian mansions in the country, featuring a range of architectural styles and incorporating parts dating back to the very earliest occupation by the Derby family in the 1300s; now the building is used largely by the Merseyside Police Force as its offices. During their time the Derbys have often played an important role in English history, supporting the kings and queens of their period and growing into the richest and most powerful family in Lancashire. In later times the family provided England with several government ministers, including a Prime Minister, and the 12th Earl attained particular fame for establishing important horse races such as 'The Oaks' and 'The Derby'.

During the 12th century Knowsley was owned by the Lathom family, but then in 1385 an heiress of the Lathoms married Sir John de Stanley and thus brought the property to the family which still holds it. Although Lathom House remained the chief seat of the family until the destruction of the building in the English Civil War, Knowsley was nevertheless regarded with some affection and was added to even in these early years. One of the first additions was the Royal Lodging, built for the first Earl of Derby's stepfather (Henry VII) and even now

**Knowsley Hall**

*Reflections of grandeur at Knowsley Hall*

incorporated into the southern side of the present forecourt. After the Civil War of the 17th century an initial attempt was made to rebuild Lathom House, but this was abandoned in favour of a general reconstruction of Knowsley, the work being carried out by the tenth Earl of Derby. His contribution was to remodel the picturesque huddle of buildings which then existed, of various dates and materials, and create a regular building of brick with stone dressing, quoins and balustrades and with tall sash windows. Even more ambitious alterations and additions were envisaged by the twelfth Earl, but the palatial plan produced by Robert Adam was eventually abandoned and replaced by rather more limited proposals carried out in a discreet Domesticated Gothic style by John Foster of Liverpool. During the Victorian period other alterations were made to the Hall, although a number of these were removed by the seventeenth Earl who set about to bring some visual order to what was then a vast architectural conglomeration. One of his improvements was to add a third storey to the main block, which harmonises with the earlier buildings and is surmounted by the family's 'eagle and child' crest in Portland

*Part of Knowsley Hall's south front*

stone. The eighteenth Earl continued this work, and as a result the house now appears very much as it was in the early 18th century.

From Knowsley Hall one of the estate roads leads directly southwards to **Huyton-with-Roby,** bringing us eventually to the original village core of Huyton which focuses on the parish church of St. Michael. **Huyton** appears to have Scandinavian or Saxon roots, and by 1086 the village was worthy of a mention in the Domesday Survey under the name 'Hitune'. Then by the 12th century at the latest the village was fortunate enough to have its own church, although the present structure built in red sandstone dates largely from 1663. Situated on a raised plateau and bounded by its own wooded grounds on one side and a small village green on the other, St. Michael's forms a particularly attractive feature within Huyton.

Enhancing this are the cottages facing onto the village green, which give it something of an 'estate village' atmosphere akin to that seen in Knowsley; this character is further emphasised by the Victorian mock-Tudor style cottages to be found nearby on Bluebell Lane. The village green is considerably older than the present buildings around it, and records indicate that both cock-fighting and bull-baiting took place here as did dancing around a maypole. Nowadays the main feature on the green is the village cross, a copy of an earlier one by Rickman and erected in 1897 to celebrate the Jubilee of Queen Victoria. Other buildings of particular interest around St. Michael's Church are its Georgian vicarage together with a number of Victorian houses and cottages.

As with many other villages on the outskirts

of Liverpool, Huyton developed rapidly as the coming of the railway line brought with it the opportunity for the city's merchants to live in rather more desirable settings well away from their places of work. One of the 'villa estates' built in Huyton during the Victorian period was situated very close to the railway station, characterised by large houses in an Italianate style set in their own extensive grounds. The exclusive nature of this estate is emphasised by its high boundary walls and an imposing stone arch at the entrance, while an air of gentility is created by the tree-lined serpentine road running through it. The most impressive buildings here include the stone-faced Huyton Hall, now the centre piece of Huyton College, and 'Greenhill', an Italianate villa in brick and stone. There are also a number of other large detached houses in their own landscaped grounds as well as a lodge in which the estate gardeners lived.

Not far away, on the other side of the railway line, is another Victorian villa estate which was developed some years after the opening of the railway as part of a grandiose scheme for a very large residential development to the east of Huyton, although this was the only part which was actually built. Here again the character of the area is typical of Victorian estates generally, with large houses set well back from the road behind mature gardens. The houses were built in a variety of styles typical of the period and include some good examples of the stucco, brick and cast-iron work which Victorian craftsmen were so adept at. The area also features two attractive neo-Gothic church buildings, including the Huyton United Reformed Church - built in 1890 on similar lines to Truro Cathedral, with red sandstone from Woolton Quarry, this is a prominent landmark in the district as well as

*Victorian cottages in Roby*

being an impressive piece of architecture in its own right.

Adjoining Huyton to the east is the village of **Roby,** which like its neighbour is characterised by an older mediaeval core extended by Victorian development which took place here immediately after the coming of the railway. Mentioned as 'Rabil' in the Domesday Survey of 1086, Roby is an ancient settlement which still possesses its original village cross — marking the site of the village stocks immediately next to it as well as the mediaeval market which was held in the vicinity. Facing the small village green on the north side of Roby Road is Toll Bar Cottage, which controlled the gate on the Huyton Loop of the Liverpool to Preston turnpike road of 1746, while a little further out from the centre of the village is Anderton Terrace, a good example of terraced housing from the period of the Industrial Revolution which still retains its original cobbled street to the front. The Victorian influence within the village is to be seen particularly along Station Road, which contains a group of elaborately decorated Victorian cottages as well as a number of Victorian houses built after the coming of the railway in the 1830s, although there are also two rather more substantial Victorian properties set within their own mature grounds on the opposite side of Roby Road.

To the north east of Huyton and Roby, on the other side of the M57 motorway, is **Prescot** — one of Lancashire's important but perhaps little-appreciated historic towns. It is certainly one of the oldest settlements in the Merseyside area, watched over by the parish church whose hill site and circular churchyard is indicative of Celtic origins. Interestingly, the name 'Prescot' signifies a priest's dwelling, and it is believed that an early Christian church was established here as long ago as the 7th century. Then by mediaeval times Prescot had developed into a thriving market town as well as the ecclesiastical centre of a huge parish covering much of south west Lancashire, extending across 58 square miles and embracing 15 separate townships. This made Prescot of sufficient 'national' importance to be included on the famous 14th century Bodleian map of Britain.

It was at about this time that the manor of Prescot became a royal possession through the family of John O'Gaunt, and in 1444 his grandson Henry VI bestowed it on 'my Royal College of Our Lady and St. Nicholas', which eventually became the now well-known King's College in Cambridge. This constituted the most valuable of all the College's endowments, and in return the townspeople of Prescot obtained many privileges which amounted almost to a state of self-government — including the right of their own courts leet to try all cases of debt and trespass, as well as exemption from jury service except within the manor and freedom from tolls in the Liverpool market. It is not surprising to learn, therefore, that the town adopted the King's College coat of arms as its own.

As well as being an important market town Prescot also developed as an early centre of the Industrial Revolution, particularly in connection with the watchmaking industry, although coal mining is recorded to have taken place here as early as the reign of Elizabeth I. At that time the 'copyhold' townspeople enjoyed what seems to have been a mineral right exercised nowhere else, in that they had the legal and financial freedom to mine coal deposits beneath any land of which they were the copyholders. Another early industry was the production of earthenware vessels, utilising the large clay deposits found in the vicinity and started in the latter part of the 16th century.

By the 18th century the craftsmen of Prescot had attained an international reputation for their precision work in the production of watch movements and files, and the town's rapid development was further helped by the fact that it had close links with Liverpool's expanding overseas trade and had become an important coaching centre on the Lancashire turnpike network. During the 19th century another thriving local industry here was the drawing of pinion wire, the process for which is claimed to have originated in Prescot. At the same time glass bottles were being made in the town and a mill was opened for the manufacture of cotton goods.

The historic importance of Prescot as a town lies in the fact that its mediaeval street pattern and plot layout has survived virtually intact, characterised by narrow streets and even narrower frontages to individual properties. Prescot is also important in that its topography is the best known of any similar mediaeval town in northern England, with Eccleston Street in particular conveying the atmosphere and character of a mediaeval thoroughfare. In addition the town still has the benefit of two surviving sections of its mediaeval wall. In the prosperous Georgian and early Victorian periods many of Prescot's older buildings were rebuilt within their original mediaeval plot layouts, and from this time there are still a number of fine Georgian properties remaining in the town — particularly in Vicarage Place, Derby Street and High Street. There are also a number of Georgian terraces in Prescot which have since been converted to shop use on the ground floor, some of which still retain watchmakers' galleries at the rear.

The most important building in Prescot is St. Mary's Church, a red sandstone building which dominates not only the town but also the surrounding countryside. Although there is evidence that a church occupied this site in Celtic times, the present structure dates mainly from 1610 and incorporates a 15th century vestry as well as an ancient base to the chancel. Externally the most dramatic features of this church are its tower and spire, added by Hawksmoor in 1729 to give it a classic 'Wren' appearance. Internally the church also possesses many beautiful elements, particularly the nave roof of 1610 — this is one of the finest Jacobean 'black and white' roofs in Lancashire and also one of the last examples of true Gothic ecclesiastical architecture in England before it was superseded by the Renaissance style.

*Prescot Museum of Clock and Watchmaking*

The oldest feature of St. Mary's is a sandstone font dating from Anglo-Saxon times, later superseded for church use by a marble font carved in 1755. It was in this font that John Philip Kemble, the famous 18th century actor, was baptised in 1757. Other notable features within the church include the alms box, choir stalls, wall panelling, misericords and altar rails of the chancel, all carved in black oak in the 17th century, as well as a finely carved chair (with a date of 1610) in the sanctuary. Let in to the chancel wall is a life-size effigy of John Ogle, buried here in 1612, whose family were hereditary stewards of the Prescot manor and who made a large contribution to the rebuilding of the church in 1610.

Another particularly important building in the town is the Prescot Museum of Clock and Watchmaking, housed within an attractive 18th century Georgian town house at the top end of Church Street close to St. Mary's. This museum provides the visitor with some fascinating insights into the development of the watch and clockmaking industry of Prescot, revealing the lives and working conditions of those employed in it. Clockmaking appears to have originated in the 14th and 15th centuries in conjunction with the blacksmith trade, and the earliest record in Prescot is of Richard Berry, a clockmaker, working here in Elizabethan times.

The skill of watchmaking, however, was introduced to Prescot in 1595 by Woolrich, a Huguenot refugee from France, and as there was a long tradition of metal working in Prescot the townspeople learned the new skill fairly easily. The successful development of

watchmaking in Prescot also seems to have been helped by the close ties which several local families had with the trade in London. It was not until the mid-1700s, however, that the industry became well established here, although by 1773 it was being noted that the district produced 'the best and almost all the watch movements used in England'.

The rapid development of the industry is especially evident from the writings of Dr. J. Aikin, who in 1795 described Prescot as 'the centre of the manufacture of watch tools and movements...All Europe is more or less supplied with the articles above mentioned in

this neighbourhood'. At that time there were 29 watch and clockmakers in Prescot, with eight toolmakers and one dealer, although since only the more prominent craftsmen would have been mentioned the true figure was probably much higher. By 1841 it was known that there were 252 watch and clockmakers of various types in Prescot, as well as 79 toolmakers, and these far exceeded the 63 people employed in coal mining, the 39 in the pottery industry and the 134 in the textile trade.

Throughout the late 18th and early 19th centuries clock and watchmaking in Prescot continued to grow in importance, with the work being done by hand in houses and small workshops. By the middle of the 19th century such workshops were attached to half the cottages and houses in the town, usually being two storeys high and about 20-30 feet long. The top floor of each workshop would generally be used for delicate watch work while the ground floor was used for heavier work such as casting and forging. Windows on two or three sides of the building ensured that the maximum light possible was available to the work benches fitted just below the window sills. As well as making some of the finest watches and watch movements in the world, Prescot was also famous for the manufacture of chronometers and marine navigational instruments — although this was a branch of the trade involving only the most skilled and able craftsmen.

However, success seems to have led to complacency, and instead of trying to improve methods Prescot watchmakers were content to carry on as before — with the result that the watchmaking trade remained at a pre-industrial craft stage. By the 1860s and the 1870s a noticeable stagnation and decline had set in, caused mainly by the industry's

*The former West End House in Prescot — now the Clock Face pub*

*Prescot's half-timbered heritage*

Watch Company in 1890 and called the 'Flat Iron House' because of its peculiar shape. This building is also notable because it was the site of the first Elizabethan theatre outside London, having been built by the 6th Earl of Derby who was a famous patron of drama.

From this point Eccleston Street heads westwards towards St. Mary's Parish Church, and along its length are a number of commercial premises which have retained their Georgian or Victorian character on the upper floors. Most of the buildings on this street have been built on the original mediaeval plots or 'burgages', helping to conserve the street's mediaeval atmosphere. The most important building here is number 30 (the Gas Board showrooms), which is the only half-timbered building in the town; one of its two gables is authentic and dates from 1614, while the other is a Victorian copy. Close by is the entrance to Stone Street, a narrow mediaeval cobbled passageway or 'ginnel' which is said to be the narrowest street in the country.

From the end of Eccleston Street one can pass round the north side of the Parish Church into Vicarage Place, an attractive Georgian street lined by trees and an informal arrangement of terraced houses. Marking the entrance to this street is the Deanes House Hotel, a partially rebuilt Georgian building in which the officers of the Leet Court met to have their annual dinner and in front of which are now located two cannon barrels reputedly from Lord Nelson's flagship 'Victory'. A new building on Vicarage Place bears the Prescot coat of arms, originally displayed on the Old Town Hall, while next door is a particularly fine example of an early Georgian house marked by brick lintels over the windows and attractive cast-iron railings and gateposts. Then at the end of the street is a Roman Catholic church, built of red sandstone in 1856 to a Gothic design by J.A. Hansom, the inventor of the hansom cab.

inability to adjust to the rapidly increasing demand for clocks and watches as well as by the devastating effects of competition from cheaper imported American and Swiss products. A last ditch attempt to save the industry from ruin was made with the formation of the Lancashire Watch Company along co-operative lines in 1888, but the venture failed and the company closed in 1910. So the curtain was drawn on the large-scale production of clocks and watches in the Prescot area, although trade continued in a small way until the 1960s.

Close to the Museum are several interesting buildings, including the Masonic Hall which is another fine example of a Georgian town house with its Doric porch and a traditional fanlight over the door. On the same side of the road is 2 Derby Street, believed to be a unique example of a purpose-built Georgian solicitor's office. This single-storey building also displays some typically Georgian features, being stuccoed with Doric pilasters and entablature. On the opposite side of Derby Street is the Sun Inn, designed to a Regency style and incorporating Corinthian columns on either side of the central doorway. Further down Derby Street, heading away from the town centre, is an interesting group of Victorian public buildings

(including a police station, courthouse, sergeant's house and the old Masonic Hall), while at the far end is a pleasant group of Georgian properties situated close to the junction with West Street. The main building in this attractive complex is the Clock Face pub, formerly known as West End House and built originally as a dower house for the widow of the Earl of Derby.

In the opposite direction, back towards the town centre, Derby Street leads on to High Street and to what was the town's Conservative Club. This imposing Georgian building has since been restored and converted to residential use, having originally been a substantial town house with servants' quarters attached. Further along High Street is the Hope and Anchor Hotel, an early 20th century building which displays some extravagant features — the front elevation is of particular interest, being surmounted by a Flemish gable supported by Doric pilasters and having Gothic tracery around the first floor windows.

Running southwards from High Street just beyond this point is Atherton Street, lined by Georgian terraced properties and former watchmaking factories, while a little further on is Chapel Street which joins up with Eccleston Street at its southern end. Located near to this junction is 72 Eccleston Street, a former watchmaking factory built by the Lancashire

*Vicarage Place, Prescot*

From here a winding mediaeval passageway known as 'The Wood', bounded by ancient high sandstone walls, makes its way around the southern side of the Vicarage grounds before arriving at the Market Place with its attractive Georgian buildings. Features of interest en route include an 18th century folly built to look like an Anglo-Saxon ruin and an ancient enclosure surrounded by sandstone walls which is the site of a holy well dating back to Celtic times. Then close to the Market Place is the Alphabet Stone, inscribed with letters of the alphabet and originally incorporated within the Old Town Hall which stood here prior to demolition in the 1960s.

From Prescot's Market Place, the venue for a weekly market first held in 1333 as well as the site of the town's market cross, stocks and whipping post, one can head north-eastwards out to **St. Helens,** a place which appears to have derived its name from the chapel of 'Sainct Elyn' which was then situated within the extensive ecclesiastical parish of Prescot. It appears that industry in this area goes back to at least Tudor times when the first coal pits were sunk at nearby Sutton Heath, laying the foundation for what was to become one of the largest production areas of the south west Lancashire coalfield. During the reign of Elizabeth I the district also became known for its ironstone quarries and the deposits of a particularly valuable type of fireclay. The extraction of coal here was further helped by technological advances in transport, particularly inland navigation — the opening of the Sankey Navigation from St. Helens to Warrington in 1762 gave the town the distinction of having the first artificial waterway in Britain, soon to be followed by the construction of the Bridgewater Canal in 1767.

If the extraction of coal was to pave the way for the town's early industrial growth, it was the manufacture of glass which was to continue this process and give St.Helens its worldwide reputation. It all seems to have begun when Jean de la Bruyere arrived here from France with some skilled craftsmen, and by 1773 the British Plate Glass Company had built a factory in Sutton which employed some 300 workers. Other glass works at Sutton and Eccleston were soon to follow, but it was the coming of the railway and the repeal of duties upon glass during the first part of the 19th century which really provided the opportunity for the industry to expand rapidly. At the same time a number of other industries also became successfully established in St. Helens, as a result of the trade expansion in both the home and overseas markets.

Consistent with the town's industrial growth during the Victorian era is the fact that most of its older public buildings date from this period, including the Town Hall which was completed in 1876. Even the parish church

*The Friends' Meeting House, St. Helens*

dedicated to St. Helen is not particularly old, having been built to a later Gothic style in 1916, although it occupies the site of the historic 'Chappell of Sainct Elyn' which was erected here during the 14th century. An ecclesiastical building of rather more interest is the Friends' Meeting House in Church Street, a charming little stone building with mullioned windows which features an old sundial above the doorway.

Returning to Prescot and its historic market place gives us the opportunity to travel southwards to the village of **Whiston.** This settlement has been in existence since at least the start of the 13th century, and whilst being eager to maintain its own identity it has often been closely associated with its larger neighbour immediately to the north. Although Whiston was largely independent in economic terms, with mining and watchmaking being the main sources of local employment, independence in religious terms was not so easily obtained — the parish church of St. Nicholas was only completed in 1868, prior to which people would have travelled to worship at Prescot or Huyton parish churches. Perhaps the most attractive feature of the village now is the extensive parkland which surrounds it, partly created through the reclamation of formerly derelict land and providing opportunities for both recreation and nature conservation.

Immediately to the east of Whiston is **Rainhill,** a very pleasant village full of red sandstone buildings and one of the 15 townships into which the parish of Prescot was divided during mediaeval times. The name 'Rainhill' is derived from the Old English personal name of Regna or Regan, and although the earliest known reference to the village is in 1190 it was really only in the 18th and 19th centuries that development occurred to any substantial degree. The cause behind this was essentially the improvement of communications — firstly through the turnpiking of the highway from Liverpool to

Warrington, facilitating the development of a coaching service, and then secondly through the coming of the railway which assisted the village's development as a residential area.

It was originally proposed that the railway should pass to the north of Knowsley and so be at least three miles from Rainhill, but vested interests prevented this from coming about and a new route was prepared which was given Royal Assent in May 1826. In Rainhill the main features resulting from this alteration were excavations through sandstone rock to make the Rainhill cutting and the erection of a 'skew' bridge to carry a road over the railway. Whilst the Sankey viaduct of nine arches was the railway's showpiece, the Rainhill 'skew' bridge was also important as one of the first examples of its kind.

Rainhill is also notable as the location for the famous Rainhill locomotive trials of 1829. At that point in time it had not been decided whether to operate the new railway by fixed engines or by the then unproved locomotive engines, and in order to settle the matter the railway company offered a prize of £500 for an improved locomotive which had to meet specified conditions. Competing engines were required to traverse the level portion of line from Rainhill Bridge towards Manchester and to cover a total distance of 70 miles (the distance from Liverpool to Manchester and back) by forty trips along the test length. Only George Stephenson's 'Rocket' successfully completed the trial and was thus declared the winner, establishing the steam locomotive as the only motive power on the railways for the rest of the century.

The railway doubtless had an influence on the establishment of an iron foundry in Rainhill, although like neighbouring Prescot to the north west the township was better known during the 18th and 19th centuries for its file cutters and watch toolmakers. Most of the file cutters were 'out-workers', obtaining their

*Sunnyside Farm, Cronton*

materials from larger organisations and working at home, a practice which continued throughout the 19th century and into the beginning of the 20th. The quarrying of red sandstone was also an important but somewhat earlier local craft, evident from its use in the construction of Rainhill's old walls and buildings. Yet for most of its life Rainhill remained a pleasant agricultural village, largely untouched by the worst excesses of the Industrial Revolution because of the lack of water power and the absence of coal workings.

Such an experience was certainly true of the picturesque village of **Cronton,** situated just two miles to the south of Rainhill but very definitely separated from it by the busy carriageways of the M62 motorway. First mentioned in the 11th century under the name 'Crohinton', Cronton is an ancient settlement possessing one of the last surviving groups of pre-18th century buildings in the Merseyside area. Situated at the centre of the village's historic core is Cronton Hall, an attractive building which displays the classic shape and proportions of a 'Queen Anne' house dating from the late 17th or early 18th centuries. Guarding the way to the front of the house are some fine wrought-iron gates mounted between stone piers, while to the rear is a group of interesting 18th and 19th century brick barns as well as a stone built coachhouse all arranged around a cobbled courtyard. Close by is Sunnyside Farmhouse, a rare local example of a cruck framed building clad in brick which dates from the early 17th century, while on the opposite side of the road from here are the Town End Cottages, formed from what was an early 18th century brick barn.

From this point Hall Lane continues up the hill to Rock Cottage, a 17th century

sandstone house with earlier mediaeval parts which used to be the 'Green Dragon' coaching inn. Standing nearby is the ancient Cronton Cross, which marked a resting place for coffin-bearers travelling from Prescot to Farnworth near Widnes, while at the junction of Hall Lane and Smithy Lane is Stone Cross Farmhouse. This sandstone house with its original stone barn dates largely from the 16th century, although it may also incorporate a much older dwelling.

Then at the western extremity of the village is Town End Farmhouse, another 16th century red sandstone building but with the extra interest of some half-timbered portions at its rear. Opposite the house is Town End Barn, built of brick and sandstone with parts which may be older than the house itself. A little distance from the historic centre of Cronton, alongside the main road from Warrington to Huyton, is the old village smithy — a place where cattle would be shod with horseshoes prior to being driven to market. Here too are the rather unusual village stocks, possessing five holes rather than the more normal two or four and one of only three such examples in the whole country.

In addition to the traditional occupation of farming, Cronton was also known for its cottage industry of watch part manufacture and watch tool making during the 18th and early 19th centuries — although this was generally carried out in conjunction with farming activities and as such was maintained at a limited level. The area was also the scene of some stone quarrying, particularly on nearby Pex Hill which had been used as the village's common pasture land since the 11th century. During the late 19th century Pex Hill was purchased by the Corporation of Widnes for use as a reservoir site, and since that time it has developed into a popular local beauty

spot — the sandstone outcrop on which it is formed supports the area's only true moorland, and the numerous footpaths through the heather and gorse provide splendid informal walks for the many visitors who find their way here.

Pex Hill is situated to the north east of Cronton, but on the opposite side of the village is flat open farmland traversed by narrow country lanes. These lead initially to the small settlement of **Tarbock,** one of the oldest in the Merseyside area and mentioned in the Domesday Survey of 1086. The eastern half of this settlement is known as Tarbock Green, consisting of several 18th and 19th century cottages and houses with well kept gardens which used to form part of Lord Sefton's estate, while the western part is known as Tarbock Village and is based around the Old Post Office. This property was re-built in 1884, as was the village smithy next to it which used to have a thatched roof.

This group of buildings at one time included the local school, while across Netherley Road from here is a house which was used as a brewery from the late 18th century up to the First World War. Nowadays liquid refreshment is dispensed, if not manufactured, at the nearby Brick Wall Inn which occupies the site of the village's original early 17th century hostelry. The village also retains its original manor house, in the form of Tarbock Hall Farmhouse on Ox Lane, while at the opposite end of the scale is Rose Cottage on Greenbridge Lane — an 18th century thatched cottage situated within an earlier moated site.

*The Parish Church, Halewood*

Just a couple of miles to the south west of Tarbock is **Halewood,** a much larger settlement on the outskirts of Liverpool which has grown substantially during the present century as one of the city's 'overspill' areas. Although Halewood is dominated by recent residential development as well as by the nearby Ford Motor Company complex it does still retain a sense of history around the parish church, characterised by some early Victorian red sandstone buildings within a pleasant setting of mature trees.

The Parish Church of St. Nicholas dates from 1838, although it was enlarged in 1847 and then further extended in 1882 by the addition of its tower. The surrounding group of buildings comprises the school and schoolhouse as well as the Rectory, being built to a consistent architectural style which is quite typical of the 1840s. Nearby is another group of buildings from the Victorian period close to the junction of Church Road and Hollies Road, made up of a white stuccoed villa together with a terrace of mock Tudor 'half-timbered' cottages and the Eagle and Child Inn. This inn was once thatched and originally contained a smithy and a room for cockfights.

Much of the land around here was in the ownership of the Earls of Derby, as is particularly evident from the development of some of the small farming hamlets to be found in this part of Merseyside. A good example is Hale Bank to the south east of Halewood, an interesting survival of a small rural settlement which has been subjected to comparatively little change over the years. Many of the cottages to be seen on both sides of Hale Bank Road date from the early 19th century when they were built for agricultural workers employed on the Derby estate, and like the older properties in Halewood they display a consistent architectural style typical of their period. Linner Farm is the most important building in the hamlet, a large stone property set in the midst of mature woodland and having the benefit of its own complete group of early 19th century farm buildings arranged round a cobbled courtyard and fenced in by stone slabs bolted together with iron braces. One of the buildings in this attractive farm complex was known as 'The Shant', offering shanty accommodation for Irish labourers during harvest times. Other estate buildings in this part of Hale Bank include Linner Farm Cottage, originally occupied by a groom, together with The Smithy House, Halsall's Cottages, Havelock Cottages, Laburnum Cottages and White Cottages. Here too can be found the Beehive Inn, dating from 1805 and originally comprising three separate dwellings.

At this point we have to cross what is now the current boundary with Cheshire to discover a number of places excluded from Lancashire as a result of the local government reorganisation which took effect n 1974, although all of them lie to the north of the River Mersey — the traditional dividing line between the two counties. One of these places is the village of **Hale,** a cosy little settlement situated between Speke and Widnes and surrounded by open fields which provide it with a measure of individuality as

*One of Hale's many thatched cottages*

well as some degree of protection against the urban sprawl.

Historically, Hale was a manor whose lord enjoyed various claims over the small agricultural community of serfs who worked his land and where ceremonies and traditions existed which were characteristic only of the village itself. One of these traditions, retained even up to the present day, is the election of a 'Lord Mayor' in a ceremony which appears to go back to at least 1320. Originally held by the oldest tenant farmer in the village, the office of Lord Mayor is now filled through the election of one of the 60 or so 'Freemen of Hale' — these 'Freemen' having been chosen originally by virtue of the service which they have rendered to the village and by the quality of their lives.

The most famous inhabitant of Hale, and certainly the one of greatest stature, was John Middleton (1578-1623), better known as the Childe of Hale and reputed to have grown to a height of 9 feet 3 inches before he was twenty! The whitewashed cottage where he lived still stands in the village, a neat dwelling hiding beneath a tidy thatched roof, while his

*The Manor House, Hale*

*The Town Hall in Warrington*

*Albert Square, Manchester*

grave can be seen in the churchyard just up the road, surrounded by iron railings and bearing an unusually laid out epitaph. Hale's thatched cottages are in fact quite a feature of the village, giving it a distinct and genuine 'olde worlde' charm which one might be surprised to find on the edge of the Liverpool conurbation. Many of these cottages date from the 17th century, although on the outskirts of Hale one can also find a very impressive group of thatched houses which were built during the early part of the 20th century. Set in spacious grounds amidst a mature landscape these properties represent a style and scale of domestic architecture which has long since disappeared, and they form a very picturesque entry into the village from the west.

Within Hale the most imposing property is The Manor House, a building with an attractive 'Queen Anne' frontage which started life as the parsonage to the nearby parish church but which eventually became the home of the local squirearchy. From here Church Road can be followed southwards down to Hale lighthouse, situated on a promontory overlooking the River Mersey. This perhaps unexpected structure was first erected in 1836 to help vessels negotiate their hazardous way around Hale Head, although the present building dates from 1906. With the reduction in shipping over the years the lighthouse became obsolete and was closed down in 1955, but it is still worth a visit for the excellent panoramic views of Helsby and Overton Hills in Cheshire which can be obtained from this point on the estuary.

Another unusual element of the Hale landscape is a 'duck decoy' on the Widnes side of the village, one of only a handful of such features which still remain in the whole country. This is a small wooded area encompassing a quiet pond at its centre which stands in lonely isolation on marshy land between the village and the Mersey, surrounded on all its five sides by a moat and reached only by a narrow swingbridge. The decoy had been in operation from as early as 1631 until comparatively recent times, with the ducks being lured from the pond along narrow channels into cages at the end where they were caught and killed. Happily, the area has since been taken over by local conservationists who have turned it into a wildlife sanctuary — a move which would doubtless have been appreciated by Sir John Betjeman, who described Hale village so aptly in the following way:

'The Manor House, the Green, the Church —
From Runcorn to West Kirby
You will not find howe'er you search
So sweet a rus in urbe'.

Following the Mersey upstream from Hale brings us shortly to **Widnes,** a town which

owes its growth to the development of the chemical industry here during the latter part of the 19th century. Prior to that time it was largely an area of tree-lined fields and small woods, with the main centres of population being located in the rural hamlets of Farnworth and Appleton further to the north. The name 'Widnes' is of Viking origin, taken from the Viking description of the distinct promontory jutting out into the River Mersey by the term 'Vide-ness' or 'Wide Nose'. Here the estuary is at its narrowest for several miles, offering a suitable location for a ferry service which operated from mediaeval times and which was immortalised by Stanley Holloway in his monologue "Tuppence Per Person Per Trip".

By the start of the 19th century Widnes had become a popular spot for visitors and pleasure-seekers, and when a railway link was provided in 1831 people were coming from as far away as Manchester in order to enjoy the fresh air and fine views. A local speciality was eel pie, available from the Boathouse Inn on the river side, and the waters of the Mersey were so clean at that time that shrimps and white salmon were also being carried up the estuary by the tides.

Things were soon to change, however, beginning in 1833 when the extension to the Sankey Brook Navigation was opened to link St. Helens with Widnes and so provide cheap transport for the export of coal south of the Mersey and the movement of salt from Cheshire to the St. Helens' glass industry. At the same time a dock was cut, thought to be the first railway dock in the world, which allowed the direct transhipment of cargo from the railway to river barges. Although Widnes lacked its own mineral resources it did have the very considerable benefit of a good

geographical position, being at the centre of a transportation triangle with rail, river and canal connections not only to the coalfields in the north but also to the salt fields of the south and the Port of Liverpool to the west. The result was that the area between the river and the canal, known as Spike Island because of the numerous lodging houses or 'spikes' which also grew up here, witnessed the beginning of the first large-scale production of chemicals in this country and the start of what was to become one of the world's major chemical centres.

The first development took place in 1847, when John Hutchinson from St. Helens opened his alkali works on the east side of the canal. He was followed three years later by William Gossage who set up an alkali works on the other bank of the canal and shortly afterwards started producing his 'World Famous Magical Soap' — a product which meant that for the first time soap was easily affordable by the nation's poor. Soon Hutchinson opened a further plant to the west of Gossage's, and other entrepreneurs in this new industry also began to establish themselves eastwards along the riverside. Among them were Ludwig Mond and John Brunner, whose joint business set up here in the 1860s was the embryo of the modern industrial giant I.C.I.

Despite the considerable activity taking place in Widnes during the latter part of the 19th century, the promontory which gave the town its name was kept free from industrial development and instead became established as a residential area hemmed in by chemical works. Known as West Bank it quickly became the most highly populated and densely developed part of the scattering of settlements which comprised the township of

*The West Bank area of Widnes and the Runcorn road bridge*

Widnes, and in this sense the area became the 'town centre' until at least the turn of the century.

Perhaps the most attractive part of West Bank is the promenade with its formal gardens running along the riverside, one of the few remaining Victorian riverside promenades in the country and now recently restored to form a section of the Mersey Way. From here one can walk through to Spike Island to see some of the restored features of the Widnes chemical industry or visit the museum which has recently been established in the Gossage Tower Building, originally built by John Hutchinson and later acquired by Gossages for use as an office and laboratory. This is now the permanent home of the Halton Chemical Industry Museum.

The West Bank area was also the location of the famous Transporter Bridge which was constructed at the start of the 20th century as the first vehicular crossing over the Mersey estuary. This bridge took the form of a 1,000-foot span supported by two pylons, along which a suspended car was hauled by electric motors. When the new service opened in 1905 West Bank quickly became an important traffic route and eventually developed into an area of regional significance, although all this came to an end in 1961 with the opening of the high-level Runcorn road bridge. Although the Transporter Bridge has since disappeared one can still see the loading pier, office and winding house.

The oldest building in the Widnes area generally is St. Luke's Parish Church at Farnworth, just a couple of miles to the north of the town centre. Founded in the year 1200 its most important historic features are the 13th century clerestory in the nave and the 14th century tower. It also has two chantry

*St. Luke's Parish Church, Farnworth*

chapels, one of which contains the notable Bold memorials. Among these are a splendid 17th century marble figure of Sir Richard Bold in Stuart armour carrying his sword, together with his lady beside him in period costume, as well as the painted effigy of a knight in armour which is believed to have been another member of the Bold family. Also of interest are the church records, dating from 1538 when it was first decreed that such records should be kept; only two other churches in Lancashire possess registers going back to that time.

To the east of Widnes is **Warrington,** a town which grew up initially because of the river crossing here — as early as the Stone Age the Mersey could be forded with some safety at this point, avoiding the high tides further downstream as well as the threat posed by the mosslands of Woolston, Rixton and Risley to the north. The river crossing was also attractive to the Romans, and by AD 100 a Romano-British settlement known as Veratinum had become established on the south bank of the Mersey at what is now Wilderspool. During the next three centuries this developed into an important industrial centre, manufacturing metal products as well as glass and pottery. By the 5th century this Roman settlement had been abandoned, to be followed some time later by a Saxon settlement established on the opposite bank of the Mersey near to the site of the present parish church and the river crossing. It seems likely that the first Christian church in Warrington, dedicated to St. Elfin, was founded during the later Saxon period.

With the coming of the Normans the overall control of the Warrington area was exercised by local barons, particularly the Boteler family who first lived in a wooden 'motte and bailey' castle built beside St. Elfin's Church to watch over the Saxon settlement and guard the ford. By the latter part of the 13th century the Botelers had moved to a new moated site at Bewsey, on the outskirts of the present town centre, and it was from here that they prompted the rebuilding of the old Saxon town by renting out burgage plots for development by local tradesmen and establishing the town's flourishing market which was recognised by royal charter in 1277. It was the flow of market-day traffic which brought about the building of the first bridge towards the end of the 13th century, this being replaced by a stone bridge erected by the Earl of Derby in 1495. By the early 16th century Warrington had become a sizeable town, with 'a better market than Manchester' according to Leland, and it was not surprising that it should be a strategic centre during the Civil War of the 1640s, the Earl of Derby using it as his Lancashire headquarters.

From the early 18th century the town further increased in size through the development of

local industries — including copper smelting and pin making as well as sail making and the weaving of linen cloth. Warrington also grew in importance as it found itself at the hub of the region's growing transport network, and by the end of the 1700s London-bound coaches were passing through the town nearly every day. Warrington was also quick to benefit from the development of water-based transport and by the 1760s it was assured of plentiful supplies of coal delivered from the St. Helens' coalfield by the Sankey Canal, whilst the Bridgewater Canal offered a reliable trade route with the rapidly expanding centres of Liverpool and Manchester. By the end of the 18th century Warrington had a broad industrial base of its own, encompassing trades such as brewing, wire drawing, sugar refining, iron founding, glass manufacture, file making and clockmaking as well as the weaving of fustian and other coarse cottons; it was also supplying at least half the British Navy's demand for sailcloth in a local industry which employed at least 300 weavers.

During the 19th century the increasing growth in Warrington's status was marked by plans for the renewal of the town centre as well as by the construction of several public buildings — after the town became a municipal corporation in 1847 a fine market hall was erected in Golden Square and in 1857 the library and museum were housed in purpose-built accommodation. At about the same time the Parish Church was renovated and a new spire added in keeping with the town's increasing stature in social and economic affairs. New residential areas were also developed in the outlying districts of Howley and Bewsey, as well as in the suburbs south of the river, and public parks were laid out in celebration of Queen Victoria's jubilees.

Warrington also continued its important connection with water transport through a link to the Manchester Ship Canal on the south side of the town, while its traditional role as a river crossing was further developed by the opening of the first section of the present Warrington Bridge in 1913. In more recent years Warrington's function as a 'crossover' town has been enhanced by the motorway network, while its physical development has been continued through the work of the Warrington and Runcorn Development Corporation. This organisation has not only created some splendid new residential and industrial areas on the edge of the town but has also provided several new recreational facilities in the form of district parks and the Risley Moss Nature Reserve.

The most important historic building in Warrington town centre is the Town Hall, a thoroughly impressive Georgian mansion designed by James Gibbs and built in 1750 for Thomas Patten. The Patten family were local merchants whose success in the copper

*The Town Hall, Warrington*

smelting industry here led to their rise as important landed gentry, and the house which they had built for themselves was appropriately surrounded by extensive landscaped gardens with nothing to obscure the views south to the River Mersey and the Cheshire countryside beyond. In many respects the Mersey had been the basis of their prosperity, in that an earlier Thomas Patten had realised the importance of the river in making Warrington a key distribution point for inland trade, and it was he who was responsible for making it navigable from Runcorn to Bank Quay so that copper could be brought to his smelting works there from Ireland, Cornwall and Anglesey.

The most impressive part of the Town Hall (originally known as Bank Hall) is its south facade, the centre of which features four Corinthian columns around the main entrance beneath a pediment which bears the arms of the Patten family. Leading up to the entrance is an open two-arm staircase with a fine wrought-iron balustrade, while on either side of the house itself are long detached service wings which originally functioned as the stables and coach houses and provided accommodation for the head servants. Inside the spacious entrance hall is a fine stone chimney-piece as well as a mosaic floor and various coats of arms, while elsewhere in the house one can discover two staircases of identical size which incorporate elegant wrought-iron handrails.

A unique feature of the Hall, and one indicative of the source of wealth of its original owners, is the fact that the whole house is built on a foundation made of moulded blocks of copper slag from the copper smelting works at Bank Quay. The window frames of the Hall are also unusual in that their delicacy is due to their being made from a combination of copper and iron, now painted in white. Setting off the front of the Town Hall is not only an attractive stretch of parkland but also some magnificent wrought-iron gates which are said to be among the finest in England. These were brought here from Ironbridge in Shropshire in 1893 by Mr. Frederick Monks, a director of the Monks Hall Foundry and a member of the town council at the time.

From the Town Hall Gates one can follow Sankey Street eastwards into the town centre, passing a number of impressive Georgian houses on the way. Just to the north is Palmyra Square, laid out as a high-class residential area in two stages during the latter part of the 19th century but subsequently taken over for office use as the pressures of commercial expansion reached into this part of the town. The eastern half of this attractive Victorian square dates from the mid-19th century and consists mainly of two storey terraced properties, while the western half was laid out in about 1890 and comprises three storey terraces as well as some larger individual buildings. One of these is the Parr Hall, home of the only remaining Cavaillé-Coll organ in its original condition. This organ heralded a new concept in console design which was widely adopted in France but not in this country, and as such the Parr Hall

*Palmyra Square in Warrington*

*The Town Hall Gates, Warrington*

organ is a national treasure comparable to a Reubens painting or a Stradivarius violin.

At the end of Sankey Street is Market Gate, which stood on a ridge of high ground overlooking the river and developed into the main crossroads of the town after the construction of the first bridge across the Mersey in the 13th century. The open area immediately to the north west of Market Gate was the location for the town's busy and prosperous market, and the elongated space which now exists here forms the centrepiece of Warrington's prestigious Golden Square Shopping Centre. The shape and proportion of the original space has been largely retained in the layout of the new development, although the market itself had to be relocated to a site on the east of Bridge Street to enable the comprehensive development of the Golden Square centre to proceed.

Dominating the Old Market Place is the Victorian cast-iron structure which was erected here in 1873, while on the site of an old meat market building is the Mad Hatter's Tea Party sculpture by Edwin Russell. Along the west side of the Market Place are replicas of buildings dating from the late 18th and early 19th centuries which occupied the site prior to redevelopment; chief among these are the Old Town Hall (now complemented by steps and an ornamental fountain) and the house originally occupied by William Beamont, the town's first mayor and a local historian. One building which was saved was the Barley Mow Inn, dating from 1561 and the oldest property in the town centre. Externally this building displays a half-

*The Mad Hatter's tea party, Golden Square*

*The Barley Mow Inn*

timbered front elevation featuring low wood-mullioned lattice windows and quatrefoil panelling of black wood filled with plaster,

while inside it has some good Jacobean panelling as well as a 17th century staircase.

To the north of the Golden Square shopping centre is Bewsey Street, developed mainly as a residential area between the late 18th and late 19th centuries, while to the east is Buttermarket Street which features several attractive Georgian buildings together with the Friends' Meeting House and the visually dominant tower of St. Mary's Church. Then to the south is Bridge Street, one of the best examples of a Victorian shopping street in this part of the country but which at the same time displays a variety of architectural styles from several different periods.

At the bottom of Bridge Street can be found the Old Academy, an attractive Georgian building now in office use which harks back to the time when Warrington played an important role in the nation's intellectual life. Soon after it was established here at Bridge Foot in 1757 the Academy was attracting scholars of a nationwide reputation, including Dr. Joseph Priestley (the discoverer of oxygen), John Reinhold Foster (who left the Academy to accompany Captain Cook on his second voyage around the world) and Gilbert Wakefield (a brilliant classical scholar). Many of the Academy's students distinguished themselves in the fields of education, philosophy and science, and eventually Warrington became known as 'The Athens of England' as more and more intellectuals were attracted here.

Two other buildings in Warrington are worthy of mention, although both are a little removed

*Part of Warrington's Georgian heritage*

from the town centre. The first of these is the Parish Church of St. Elphin, situated nearly a mile from the main shopping area but still dominating the town as a whole by virtue of its enormous spire. This is thought to be the fifth church on the site and the oldest dedication in Lancashire. Although originally founded by the Saxons the oldest part of the present building is the chancel which dates from 1754; the rest of the church has been rebuilt at various times since the middle of the 18th century. Inside there are a number of memorials to the Patten family, including a white marble effigy of John Wilson Patten (the Lord Winmarleigh of Bank Hall). There are also a number of very interesting buildings close to the Parish Church on both sides of Church Street, including a group of Tudor cottages where Oliver Cromwell is reputed to have stayed in 1648. The second building of special interest is Bewsey Old Hall, probably

the most romantic and historic house within the Warrington area generally. The first Hall to occupy this site was erected by the Boteler family in the middle of the 13th century, although the present building dates from about the year 1600. At that time the house consisted of two portions of similar design and connected by a hall and a porch, but all that remains now is effectively the southern wing with a much later porch.

Three miles due north of Warrington, just beyond the M62, is **Winwick.** This pleasant village on the edge of the town is notable principally for the 14th century Parish Church of St. Oswald, marked by a tall spire rising above its buttressed tower. It also enjoys a lofty nave with a richly panelled Tudor arch and a chancel dated 1847-48, although the clustered columns of the north arcade appear to be considerably earlier than the arches they

support. The west part of the south wall was rebuilt in 1530, with the Legh Chapel being somewhat older, while in the churchyard can be found part of a pre-Conquest Celtic cross as well as a 14th century font bowl.

Our final port of call before heading along the famous East Lancashire Road to Manchester is **Newton-le-Willows,** a small town with a long history. When the Domesday Survey was undertaken it was the centre of one of the county's 'hundreds', and fairly soon afterwards it became a barony. This barony was held successively by the Banastres, the Langtons and the Leghs, and it was the Langtons who were responsible for getting Newton recognised as a parliamentary borough in 1559.

For much of its early life Newton-le-Willows was a farming community, and to some degree this is still evident from the picturesque houses and cottages which line its wide main street. Then in 1830 the Liverpool to Manchester railway linked Newton with Lancashire's two biggest towns, and it expanded rapidly as Newton Junction grew into an important station. A wagon works associated with the railway acted as a further stimulus to growth, leading to the development of neighbouring Earlestown which was named after the railway pioneer Sir Hardman Earle. At the same time the Vulcan foundry for making locomotives was established just to the south of Newton-le-Willows, its rows of employees' cottages being constructed around a central green.

Newton-le-Willows' railway connections are epitomised by the gravestone of Peers Naylor, an engine driver who died in 1842. His memorial is to be found in St. Peter's Church, and along with a locomotive in relief it bears this fascinating poem:

> My engine now is cold and still,
> No water does my boiler fill,
> My coke affords its flame no more,
> My days of usefulness are o'er.
> My wheels deny their noted speed,
> No more my guiding hand they heed.
> My whistle, too, has lost its tone,
> Its shrill and thrilling sounds are gone.
> My valves are now thrown open wide,
> My flanges all refuse to glide.
> My clacks, also, though once so strong,
> Refuse to aid the busy throng.
> No more I feel each urging breath,
> My steam is now condensed in death.
> Life's railway's o'er, each station past,
> In death I'm stopped, and rest at last.
> Farewell, dear Friends, and cease to weep,
> In Christ I'm safe, in Him I sleep.

*The Clock Tower, Manchester Town Hall*

# Chapter 8: THE MANCHESTER METROPOLIS

One of the fascinating things about Lancashire as a whole is the wide spectrum of its character, ranging from classic industrial heritage on the one hand to beautiful unspoilt countryside on the other, and the fact that the county's industrial landscape is a fruit of its ample natural resources has ensured that such diversity has been marked by harmony rather than conflict. It is in the south east of the old administrative county, in what was to become very largely the new metropolitan county of Greater Manchester up to the mid-1980s, that much of Lancashire's industrial growth came to be concentrated within an epicentre of the Industrial Revolution. Few people will be surprised by the fact that this area has since developed into one of Western Europe's biggest single industrial conurbations, but eyebrows may be raised by the discovery that at least half of it has remained open countryside.

Old reputations die hard, however, and for some the very names of Manchester, Oldham, Rochdale, Bolton, Bury, Salford, Wigan and Ashton still evoke images of cloth caps, belching chimneys, cobbled streets and cotton mills. The persistence in some people's minds of the idea that Lowry landscapes are entirely typical of the Greater Manchester area is really quite remarkable, particularly as the reality is actually quite different — as we shall see! There is of course the long held misconception about Manchester's poor weather, dating back to the time when the historian Tacitus recorded for posterity that the soldiers of the Roman garrison in Manchester often complained about the incessant rain they faced there. The truth of the matter is that the Manchester conurbation has a lower average rainfall than many other places in Britain — with Bournemouth, Newquay, Douglas and Ilfracombe being among the more notable of these. Even some of the more desirable European holiday resorts have greater precipitation levels than Manchester, including Nice and Jersey as well as Pisa and St. Remo. So with one popular misconception dealt with let's press on and dispel a few more traditional myths!

At the heart of the area is **Manchester,** one of the first truly industrial cities in the world and a place where the 'Coronation Street' image has increasingly become outdated and irrelevant because of the transformation which has been taking place here in recent years. Manchester's history goes back to Roman times, when a military station and civil settlement were established on flat ground guarding natural routes to the north, south, east and west. It was at this point that the main Roman road from Chester to York crossed the important route northwards to Ribchester, the Lake District and Hadrian's Wall, so it is not surprising that the fort here became not only a significant base for controlling the

unruly Brigantes but also a major supply point for other stations on the associated network of Roman highways. In connection with this latter role the fort at Manchester supplied other forts with a variety of manufactured goods, and excavations of the adjoining civil settlement have revealed evidences of iron furnaces and other industrial activities.

With the withdrawal of the occupying Roman garrison at the end of the 4th century the area was overrun firstly by Anglian and later by Danish invaders, but by the 10th century it was brought under West Saxon rule; Manchester was then in the Hundred of Salford and a dependency of the capital manor of Salford. Further change took place under the Normans during the latter part of the 11th century, when William I granted the district between the Ribble and the Mersey to his vassal Count Roger of Poitou; he in turn passed on a large part of the Hundred of Salford (including the Manor of Manchester)

to Albert Grelley, whose family held the estate for 200 years or so. What became known as the Barony of Manchester was then governed from a manor house situated where Chetham's Hospital now stands, close to the Saxon church of St. Mary which had been built on or near the site of the present Cathedral.

In early mediaeval times the settlement at Manchester was a significant trading centre, its annual fair being confirmed by a royal grant in 1227. By the end of the same century it had also become a borough, whose burgesses were free from agricultural services to their lord and who held their houses (or burgages) by an annual rent of one shilling. At that point in time, too, Manchester was the centre of a large parish covering an area of 60 square miles, although proper administration of its ecclesiastical affairs was really only achieved when a college of priests was endowed at the end of the 14th century to

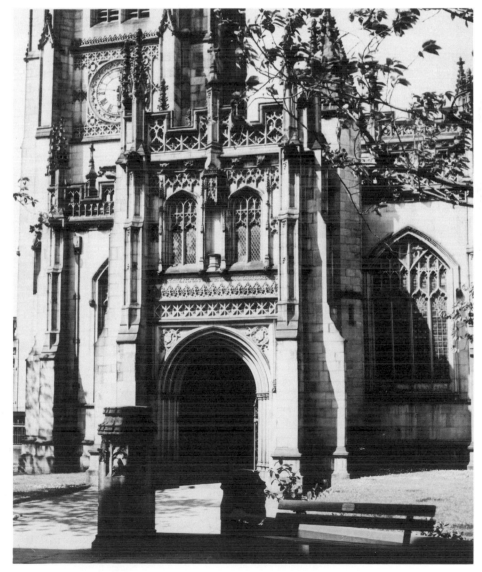

*Manchester Cathedral*

take charge of the church. This was closely followed by the reconstruction of the old building on a larger scale, with the erection of the present choir and aisles between 1422 and 1458; the addition of chapels on both sides during the late 15th and early 16th centuries further enlarged the church and provided the basis for its present spacious proportions. After a break caused by the Reformation the college continued in force up to 1847, when the Diocese of Manchester was created and the church became a cathedral.

By the middle of the 16th century Manchester had grown to such an extent that Leland described it as 'the fairest, best builded, quickest and most populous town of Lancastershire'. One of its earliest institutions was the free grammar school founded in 1515 and later to become the Manchester Grammar School, followed nearly one and a half centuries later by the founding of Chetham's Hospital and Library. Established by Humphrey Chetham in the building which had first been the manor house and then the College of Priests for the parish church, Chetham's Hospital initially provided accommodation for 40 poor boys who were 'the children of honest, industrious and painful parents'. At the same time a free library was provided out of an endowment of £1,000.

Just before Chetham's came into being Manchester had been the scene of some of the earliest bloodshed in the English Civil War when the town withstood a siege by Royalist forces under Lord Strange, later the seventh Earl of Derby. Following on from this the town was made the headquarters of the Parliamentary armies in the county and its garrison helped in the capture of other towns; by virtue of Manchester's part in the war it earned its first representative in Parliament.

By the latter part of the 17th century Manchester was already beginning to play a significant role in the textile trade of South Lancashire and North Cheshire, developing into the chief commercial centre as well as a place where many forms of manufacture and finishing took place. It was entirely appropriate, therefore, that it should be described as 'the very London of these parts, the liver that sends blood into all the countries thereabouts'. During the first half of the 18th century Manchester was famous 'for the Woollen, Linnen and Cotton Manufactories, whereby it is immensely enriched' and for 'its many noted buildings', and the result of this substantial growth in trade was the construction of navigable waterways to transport raw materials into the district and finished products out.

The opening of the Mersey and Irwell Navigation in 1736 was the first attempt to provide Manchester with a proper link to the

*Victoria Railway Station*

sea, followed by the eventual completion of the Bridgewater Canal through to Runcorn. By the start of the 19th century Manchester was linked to most of the surrounding towns by a network of canals ultimately giving access to Yorkshire and the Midlands. Road transport was also being improved at the same time, so that by 1804 it was observed that there were 27 different coaches running from Manchester, most of which operated on a daily basis. This considerable advance in communications was made possible by the turnpiking of the main roads out of the town.

With all these technological innovations it is not surprising that Manchester's commerce should go from strength to strength — the first Exchange was opened in 1729, the first bank in 1771 and a Commercial Society founded in 1794 which developed in the next century into the Manchester Chamber of Commerce. Neither is it surprising that Manchester's leading men were its linen drapers and merchants, who not only organised the putting out of linen yarn, cotton and wool to local workers but also provided the credit required to finance the trade as well as the warehouses to store its products. The growth in trade experienced by Manchester also provided considerable employment opportunities, with the result that the town's population increased from about 10,000 in 1717 to just over 70,000 in 1801.

Yet with growth came overcrowding and insanitary conditions, and so the Manchester Board of Health was established in 1796 as one of the earliest bodies to investigate health problems. The years just prior to this had seen

the formation of the Manchester Literary and Philosophical Society, an organisation which was to play an important part in developing the town's social consciousness as well as prompting technical advance. These two bodies not only helped to secure the first national census of population in 1801 but also laid a foundation for government action during the 19th century.

The 19th century furthermore saw the development of voluntary charitable institutions such as hospitals, dispensaries and homes for the destitute, as well as a rapid increase in the building of churches and chapels. Perhaps more significantly it was the period of Manchester's most rapid industrial and commercial growth, at a time when private enterprise found its greatest expression not only in the development of industry and commerce but also in the formation of societies devoted to cultural or social purposes. It is interesting to note that by 1841 there were 185 cotton mills in the Manchester parish alone, together with 28 silk mills and a number of other related establishments such as iron foundries, dye works and bleaching works.

An important factor in helping to maintain Manchester's position as the main centre in south east Lancashire's textile industry was the development of the railway network, and by 1846 there were seven railway lines directly serving the town. This followed on very appropriately from the opening of the world's first passenger station at Liverpool Road in 1830 (which has been recently restored and converted to form part of the

*The Royal Exchange*

Greater Manchester Museum of Science and Industry). As a consequence of its significant role in the growth of the railways Manchester became an important location for the production of steam engines, a skill which was to lead to the growth of the engineering industry in the town and which in turn eventually developed into the major industrial occupation of the area. The practical advances made in engineering here were also matched by some important scientific discoveries, such as those made by John Dalton (who formulated a sound chemical atomic theory for the first time) and J.P. Joule (who paved the way for the modern study of thermodynamics).

Complementing Manchester's industrial growth was its commercial expansion, reflected by the erection of increasingly splendid textile warehouses as well as by the prestigious facilities of the Royal Exchange, which in the latter part of the 19th century provided the largest room in the world devoted to commercial purposes. At the same time Manchester also offered the best banking facilities in the country outside London, with six private banks and five joint stock banks as well as what is now the oldest surviving provincial branch of the Bank of England. As one might expect Manchester additionally became a major insurance centre, playing a pioneering role in boiler and industrial insurance generally.

One of the greatest developments undertaken to assist the town's commercial growth was the construction of the Manchester Ship Canal, which was opened in 1894 despite considerable opposition from those with interests in the Port of Liverpool. This new communication line was an immediate success, reducing freight rates and encouraging the import of raw cotton and dairy produce as well as the raw materials for flour milling, food processing and engineering. It was also significant in that it enabled Manchester to rid itself of its dependence on the cotton trade and opened the way for the development of Trafford Park as a great industrial estate. At the opposite end of the commercial spectrum Manchester was an important centre in the development of the Co-operative movement, with the first small Co operative retail shop being started in Pump Street in 1858.

As was the case in Liverpool during the 19th century, a large part of this industrial and commercial 'progress' was achieved in the face of considerable poverty and squalor — much of which was the result of the factory system and the pressure of population, although some was due to unemployment, low wages and trade fluctuations. The social distress of this period made a considerable impression on Friedrich Engels, whose book 'The Condition of the Working Classes in England' was a formative influence in the development of revolutionary socialism. Yet changes were afoot, and it was in Manchester that the first two public parks paid for from the rates were created in 1846.

Manchester was also the venue for several important exhibitions which encouraged local art and history, with the Art Treasures Exhibition of 1857 proving to be the stimulus for the Halle concerts and Manchester's considerable reputation for music. In addition the 19th century saw a tremendous growth in the local press, led by the development of the Manchester Guardian in particular, and by the late 1800s the city had become an important news centre. Entertainment, too, was well represented by the dozen or so central and suburban theatres as well as by the three music halls, two large halls devoted to concerts, lectures and other entertainments, a circus, a Botanical Garden and the popular zoological garden known as Belle Vue which had been founded as early as 1836.

By the start of the 20th century most of Manchester's present physical fabric was already in place, dominated by the ornate warehouses, offices and public buildings of the prosperous Victorian era which are so characteristic of the city. Much of the current city centre street pattern was also in existence at this point in time, and the built-up area had been extended out as far as Blackley in the north and Didsbury in the south. The industrial and commercial development of Manchester continued during the early part of the 20th century, and although there was a major decline in the cotton industry this was made up for by the manufacture and use of man-made fibres. Manchester's engineering industry similarly saw further growth and diversification, with the city claiming an important spot in the history of the motor car — it was in a small workshop in Hulme that F.H. Royce built the motor vehicle which was to attract the attention of Charles Rolls and so lead to the famous partnership producing some of the world's finest cars. Since that time the engineering, chemical and electrical industries in Manchester have extended their activities into new areas such as guided missiles, computers and heavy electrical goods.

The best place to begin a closer examination of Manchester's architecture is Albert Square, right at the heart of the city, since this is a notable piece of Victorian townscape. The focal point is of course the Town Hall, designed by Alfred Waterhouse in the Gothic style which was very much in favour at the time. His scheme was chosen from among 136 entries submitted in an architectural competition, and although apparently not the most attractive his design was chosen on the strength of its practicality.

Built of brick with a facing of carboniferous sandstone the Town Hall occupies what is essentially a triangular site, at the centre of which is the Great Hall; this is lit by its surrounding courtyards, which also provide light for the main corridors and staircases arranged around them. The most impressive elevation is that facing onto Albert Square, dominated by a central clock tower rising to a height of 286 feet, although the other elevations have been treated with similar care

*Albert Square at the centre of Manchester*

Thomas Worthington was responsible too for the design of the Albert Memorial at the centre of Albert Square, the first such memorial in the country and just a little earlier than the rather more famous and elaborate structure in London by George Gilbert Scott. Worthington's design is in the form of a Gothic canopy ornamented by a rich display of carved heraldic panels and sculptures.

For a number of years the west side of Albert Square lay open to reveal the Roman Catholic church of St. Mary, known popularly as the 'Hidden Gem' and one of only two surviving city centre churches, but in more recent times this view has been closed off by two modern brick-clad office buildings. This has helped to enhance the sense of enclosure in Albert Square, which in turn has been further improved by work to extend the pedestrian zone in front of the Town Hall. The result has been a much larger open space attractively paved in stone and granite setts, providing a more dignified setting for Manchester's most prestigious building as well as a useful area for ceremonial and civic events.

*Central Reference Library and Town Hall Extension*

and inventiveness. One of the interesting aspects of the building is the way that a mediaeval story-telling approach was adopted to outline the city's history, and on display are numerous statues of the people associated with Manchester's past. The interior is also full of diverse architectural features, including the hammerbeam roof of the Great Hall as well as the cloister-like corridors and the three spiral staircases twisted around stone cylinders, which are in fact heated air flues.

By the time that the Town Hall was completed in 1877 the rest of Albert Square had also come into being, with the buildings along the south side in particular being attractively fashioned in a range of Gothic styles. On one corner, at the junction with Mount Street, is St. Andrew's Chambers, an impressive piece of architecture designed in 1874 by George Tunstall Redmayne (a pupil of Alfred Waterhouse), while on the corner with Southmill Street is the Memorial Hall, built in a Venetian Gothic style by Thomas Worthington to commemorate the 2,000 ministers who in 1662 seceded from the Church of England to form the Unitarian

Church. During its life this building accommodated not only the Manchester Unitarian Sunday School and Sir Charles Halle's choir but also numerous societies.

*St. Mary's Church — the 'Hidden Gem'*

Linking Albert Square with St. Peter's Square nearby is the Town Hall Extension and the Central Reference Library, two important components in an architectural grouping which is now one of the best pieces of town planning in Manchester but only a small fragment of the civic centre which was originally proposed to transform these two spaces. Both the Town Hall Extension and the Library were designed by Vincent Harris for an architectural competition in 1925, although the Library was only completed in 1934 and the Town Hall Extension some three years later. The latter building's simplicity of style and straightforward decoration makes it a very suitable link between the Town Hall's more elaborate Gothic architecture and the Library's uncomplicated Classical design, although its mullioned and transomed windows on the Mount Street side are somewhat reminiscent of an Elizabethan manor house.

St. Peter's Square itself is named after St.

*Elegant exterior of the Midland Hotel*

*The Portico Library*

At one time a canopied walkway connected the rear of the Midland Hotel with the former Central Station, now the G-MEX Exhibition Centre. Opened in 1880 as the last of the city's railway termini, Central Station featured an iron and glass arched train shed roof with a span of 210 feet, beneath which was a dramatic brick undercroft of intersecting tunnel vaults equipped with wooden platforms, lifts for goods trucks and railway turntables. Associated with the station were a series of warehouses, including the massive Great Northern Railway Company's goods station and warehouse complex dating from 1885.

Leading off St. Peter's Square to the west is Peter Street, marked principally by the old Theatre Royal and the Free Trade Hall. The Theatre Royal dates from 1845 and was Manchester's oldest and most famous theatre — until it became firstly a cinema and then a bingo hall — while the Free Trade Hall marks the city's part in the Anti-Corn Law League. The current building is the third 'Free Trade Hall' on the site, having been completed in 1856 to a Renaissance design which incorporates a feast of rich stone carving. The ground floor arcade incorporates shields of the Lancashire towns identified with the Anti-Corn Law Movement, while the pedimented windows of the floor above are framed by coupled Ionic columns; above these windows are a number of carved figures representing Free Trade, the Arts, Commerce, Manufacture and Agriculture, while higher still are some classical architectural details such as circular windows, a frieze of hanging garlands and a crowning balustrade. A plaque on the Free Trade Hall commemorates the fact that here on Peter's Field in 1819 was the scene of the infamous Peterloo Massacre,

Peter's Church, built in 1788-94 by James Wyatt but eventually demolished in 1907. In its place is the Cenotaph, designed by Sir Edwin Lutyens in a style similar to the one in Whitehall and erected here in 1924, while nearby is the imposing Midland Hotel, recently given a new lease of life after having been originally designed for the Midland Railway Company by its architect Charles Trubshaw and built between 1898 and 1903. In those heady days it boasted a Palm Court, Winter Gardens, a Concert Hall and Theatre, and French and Italian restaurants as well as 400 bedrooms — so not surprisingly it was described as being 'colossal in size, striking in magnificence, exceedingly pleasing in appearance, probably the most beautiful building in the whole of the city'.

when mounted troops brought death and injury to a crowd of demonstrators.

Heading from the north-eastern corner of St. Peter's Square is Mosley Street, known as 'the most elegant and retired street in the town' during the latter part of the 18th century. Surviving from that period is the Portico Library, a Classical building designd by Thomas Harrison and opened in 1806. This was the chief circulating library in Manchester until the Public Libraries Act of 1850, and initially there were 400 shareholders who paid an annual subscription of £2.10s for use of the ground floor newspaper reading room and the upstairs gallery with its books and periodicals. In more recent times the ground floor has been taken over for other purposes, although the library has continued to function from the first floor accommodation.

Another building which remains from Mosley Street's 'age of elegance' is the City Art Gallery, built for the Royal Institution of Manchester in 1825 for the purpose of 'futhering the interests of literature, science and the arts and the obtaining of a channel by which the works of meritorious artists might be brought before the public'. Designed by Sir Charles Barry (who later went on to design the Houses of Parliament), this building features an impressive portico at the centre of the bold symmetrical composition which marks the Mosley Street frontage, while inside the rooflit entrance hall remains comparatively unchanged with a staircase up to the gallery carried round on a Doric colonnade.

Next door to the Art Gallery, situated on Princess Street, is The Athenaeum, at one time a non-political club and cultural centre renowned for its literary gatherings but now an annexe to the City Art Gallery. Also designed by Sir Charles Barry, but this time in 1837, The Athenaeum has a special significance for Manchester's architecture in that it marked the introduction of the 'palazzo' style to the city, breaking the hold which the Greek Revival style had maintained on civic buildings up to that time.

From the south east corner of St. Peter's Square, Oxford Street gives us the chance to inspect some of Manchester's commercial

*Central Station — now the G-Mex Exhibition Centre*

*The tower of the Refuge Building . . .*

*. . . and its elaborately detailed entrance*

heritage as it leads down to the Refuge Assurance building and the dramatic warehouse architecture of Whitworth Street. On one side is the restored brick and terracotta facade of the Princes Buildings (dating from 1903), while on the other side of Oxford Street is the white Portland stone of St. James' Buildings, its tall and highly decorative frontage hiding a 1,000-room complex behind. Close by is the Palace Theatre, built in 1891 as the 'Palace of Varieties' in an Italianate style and becoming one of the city's 'respectable' music halls before being altered in 1913 and given its present tile exterior in 1956.

Then at the junction of Oxford Street and Whitworth Street is the former Refuge Assurance Building, its 220-foot high clocktower acting as one of Manchester's most familiar and best-loved landmarks. The original block on the street corner dates from 1891 and was designed by Alfred Waterhouse, while a second block further down Oxford Street was added in 1910 by his son Paul. In between these two blocks was introduced the clocktower, its base of grey granite constituting the main entrance to this thoroughly impressive office development. A third block along Whitworth Street was added in the 1930s, and is again a copy of Alfred Waterhouse's original design. Unlike many other large buildings from the turn of the century this particular one lacks the characteristic columns, pediments and rusticated masonry of that period; instead it displays a great deal of smaller detail which enhances the richness of the whole building and emphasises its overall scale.

The massive warehouses on Whitworth Street itself date largely from the Edwardian period, being built primarily in response to a boost in the city's flagging trade which was brought about by the opening of the

Manchester Ship Canal — so it is not inappropriate that Bridgewater House on the north side of the street should be named after the Duke of Bridgewater, who was responsible for initiating canal building in the North West during the 18th century. A little further east along Whitworth Street are two spectacular commercial buildings from the early part of the 20th century, India House and Lancaster House, linked together by a graceful gateway and representing the intoxicating prosperity which the city attained at the height of its development as an inland port.

Going eastwards again along Whitworth

*The main entrance to UMIST*

Street, en route for Piccadilly Station, we come firstly to the University of Manchester Institute of Science and Technology, originally built between 1895 and 1902 as 'the largest and best equipped Municipal School of Technology in the kingdom' although its roots were in the Mechanics Institute founded back in 1824. Just across from here and adjacent to the attractive Whitworth Street Gardens is another educational building dating from the same period, the old Central School which has since become a sixth form college. Of the two buildings the UMIST property is the more imposing, a formidable display of Renaissance inspiration with a particularly fine main entrance.

A short detour to the north takes us over the Rochdale Canal to the City Police Courts in Minshull Street, an attractive building dating from 1871 and designed in an Italian Gothic style by the Manchester architect Thomas Worthington. With its multifarious gables, towers and turrets this is a building which has plenty to say in architectural terms, amplified by the decorative carving on its exterior walls. Whitworth Street's final architectural statement is made by another civic building, this time the former Police and Fire Station situated at the junction with London Road. Built on a triangular site the three main elevations of this early 20th century property are constructed of brick and terracotta with a variety of decorative features, encompassing an open courtyard at the centre which acted as a focal point for the community living here. As well as providing accommodation for forty families the building also incorporated a bank, stables, fireman's library, gymnasium and

*The Police Courts on Minshull Street — by Thomas Worthington*

town into a great distribution and warehousing centre, a process which was continued and consolidated by the coming of the railways.

Despite the general demise of the canals which was brought about by the railways, some examples of traditional canal architecture still remain in the area — these include the humble offices of the Rochdale Canal Company on Dale Street as well as the stone-built Salt Warehouse nearby and a brick warehouse in Upper Stanley Street further along the Rochdale Canal. Salt Warehouse was built in 1817 with two wide-arched bays which allowed boats to be brought right inside the building for covered loading and unloading, while the Upper Stanley Street Warehouse dates from 1836 and features tiny round-headed windows.

The area between these old canal basins and the present Piccadilly Gardens forms one of Manchester's traditional warehouse districts, crammed with a mixture of 'severe' brick Victorian buildings as well as some rather more decorative properties from the Edwardian period exhibiting a range of architectural styles. Terracotta was particularly fashionable in Edwardian times because it was more resistant to industrial pollution than brick or stone and made possible the relatively cheap use of ornament on building facades. Many of the buildings in this area were extended backwards to fill the long, thin blocks of the grid-iron street pattern that had existed here previously, and Industry House is a particularly good example of this type of development. Dating from 1913 this building has an impressive terracotta facade as well as a long side elevation featuring a small stained glass window of a workman wearing a type of woollen vest which must once have been manufactured here. It is interesting to discover that the area as a whole is still concerned largely with the manufacture and distribution of textiles and knitwear.

children's playground, together with the other facilities required for everyday living here.

Originally known as London Road Station, the present Piccadilly Station on the east side of the city centre dates from 1842 when the first terminus was built here. At that time it was possible to reach London by rail in 9½ hours, compared to the fastest stagecoach journey of 24 hours. During the boom years of railway development there were no less than nine separate railway companies competing for access to the city centre, with the result that the heart of Manchester was encircled by a ring of stations, goods depots and arched viaducts. As the London Road station was station was extended and developed during the Victorian period so numerous warehouses and goods sheds grew up on the adjacent land, and one of the main survivors from this time is the brick-built London Warehouse on nearby Ducie Street. Dating

from 1867 this rather utilitarian piece of architecture incorporates cast-iron columns which are a feature of all the building's seven storeys, providing the support for its wrought-iron box girders and brick-arched floors.

Not far away from here are the Rochdale and Ashton Canals, both constructed during the great canal-building period of the late 18th century and acting as the main trade arteries between Lancashire and Yorkshire until the trans-Pennine railways were built in the 1840s. The canal basins in this part of the city centre are now largely filled in, but at the height of the canal era they were places of great activity and were at the hub of a system of canals which became vitally important in the development of the textile industry, linking the port of Liverpool with the cotton manufacturing towns of south east Lancashire. As a result Manchester was quickly transformed from a manufacturing

Like Albert Square, the area around Piccadilly Gardens is one of the focal points of the city centre, although its development over the years owes more to fortune than to formal planning. Up to the 18th century this part of Manchester was on the outskirts on the town centre, being characterised by large open pits from which clay was extracted for use in local house-building. Then in 1755 the land was given for the building of a new Infirmary here, with the result that the clay pits were linked together to form a single ornamental pond and were surrounded by walks and flowerbeds. By 1853 it was decided to fill the pond in and create a spacious Esplanade, thus establishing a suitable location for memorials to Peel, Wellington, James Watt and Queen Victoria.

During the course of the 19th century the area attracted numerous warehouses, shops, offices and hotels, but its appearance was then radically changed when the Infirmary was demolished in 1909 in favour of a new building on Oxford Road. The vacant site thus created remained vacant until the 1930s, when the present sunken gardens were laid out on the spot where the Infirmary's foundations had been. The warehouses which once stretched along the southern side of these gardens were then destroyed by fire in 1940, although it was only some 20 years later that the Piccadilly Plaza complex was built on this site in what was Manchester's first comprehensive redevelopment scheme. Interestingly this was only a small part of a much larger scheme proposed for the area down to Oxford Street, and which had it been built would have included several 50-60 storey skyscraper office blocks as well as an Arts and Educational Centre. Thankfully these proposals were never implemented, and Manchester's architecture has retained its rather more dignified and humane character.

On the north side of the gardens, along Piccadilly itself, are a number of substantial Victorian and Edwardian buildings which accommodate a range of commercial uses. For much of its existence Piccadilly was the location of Manchester's major hotels, and in recent years this tradition has been continued along Portland Street in particular through the Portland, Grand and Britannia hotels. The Portland Hotel occupies what was originally a group of three richly decorated Victorian warehouses, built in the 1850s and 1860s by the architect of the Free Trade Hall. At that time the traditional Manchester warehouse was being seen not only as a place for storage but also for display, and so buildings such as

*Piccadilly Gardens*

these were modelled rather grandly on the palaces of Renaissance merchant princes with the set purpose of impressing potential customers. Among the delightful features of the Portland Hotel are its carved window surrounds, the bold rustication of its stonework and its elaborate main doorway.

The Grand Hotel in Aytoun Street was a slightly later commercial 'palace', converted to hotel use in 1880, while the 'piece de resistance' is the Britannia Hotel a little further down on Portland Street, occupying what was one of Manchester's biggest and most spectacular warehouses. Portland Street as a whole was a particularly prime commercial area during Victorian times, and the centrepiece of its straight parade of impressive warehouses was the Cook and Watt's warehouse built in 1858; it is this building which now houses the Britannia Hotel. Although there was a substantial degree of harmony in the appearance of Portland Street's warehouse architecture by virtue of agreements about design and height, the individual buildings were distinct in their own right and even managed to incorporate a considerable diversity of architectural treatments within their respective structures — each floor of the Watt's warehouse, for example, is characterised by a different style, the building being finished off by four great roof pavilions with wheel windows.

Close by is Charlotte Street, the location of another of Manchester's warehouse concentrations and one in which the distinctive warehouse architecture has remained largely unaltered for over a hundred years. Most of the buildings here date from between 1855 and 1860, being characterised by some elaborate decoration and carved detail around the windows. As in other warehouse districts the architectural details and proportions were faithful to the Italian Renaissance style, producing a remarkable conformity over the length of the street, although the amount of ornamentation varied according to how much the individual client was prepared to pay. In general the principal office floor was

**Watt's warehouse — now the Britannia Hotel**

approached directly from the street by a flight of steps, with the floors above being used for storage and display while the half-basement was used for packing and delivery and the sub basement to accommodate the boilers, fuel store and steam engines required to power the building's hoists, cranes and pumps. The Italian Renaissance style is also evident in many of the imposing commercial blocks which line Princess Street, running off Portland Street further to the south, although there is evidence here of the growing strength of the Gothic Revival style which gained favour during the latter part of the 19th century.

Retracing our steps back up Portland Street to Piccadilly Gardens brings us face to face with a view of some of Manchester's major department stores over on the western side of Piccadilly. Lewis's success in the city during the latter part of the Victorian era appears to have been based upon the introduction of American-style advertising as well as the novel idea of free entry without the compulsion to buy anything. The store also learned the value of providing entertainment for its customers, and in the early days the sub-basement was filled with stereoscopic machines, distorting mirrors and penny in-the-slot Eddison phonographs; on one occasion it was even flooded with two feet of water to reproduce a Venice in miniature! With the addition of two major extensions in 1908 and 1929 Lewis's became the biggest store in the provinces, boasting of the first escalator and first cafeteria as well as a marble concert hall and a marble dance floor set on springs.

The building occupied by Debenham's across Market Street from Lewis's was built in 1932 as a textile warehouse for Rylands and Sons, only becoming a department store in the 1950s. Market Street itself is one of the city's main shopping routes and has been one of Manchester's principal thoroughfares since mediaeval days. By the 18th century it was built up with half-timbered cottages and a few more substantial brick houses, although it was only through a Parliamentary Bill of 1821 for the Improvement of Market Street that the width, gradient and direction of the street were given some consistency. In more recent times Market Street's character has again been transformed by the construction of the Arndale Centre and the completion of pedestrianisation.

From Market Street one can travel northwards along High Street and around the Arndale Centre before dropping down onto Shude Hill and Withy Grove, two more of Manchester's oldest streets. Shude Hill is a mixture of architectural styles from the last two centuries, while Withy Grove probably derives its name from the 'withies' or willows which were woven together as a supporting mesh for the clay filling used in timber-framed cottages.

*Victoria Station's imposing frontage*

At the bottom end of Withy Grove is the Corn Exchange, its long curving facade looking out across Corporation Street to the Arndale Centre beyond. The streets in this area were traditionally the focus of the grocery and provisions market, so it was not unusual for the first Corn Exchange to be built here in 1837. With Manchester's development as the centre of the North West's provision trade the Corn Exchange had to be considerably enlarged and improved over the years, and the current building was completed in 1904. As well as its appealing exterior the Corn Exchange also enjoys the benefit of a fine glass and steel roofed market hall where traders once set up their stalls, together with 519 offices.

*The Corn Exchange*

To the north of the Corn Exchange is Victoria Station, first erected in 1844 for the trans-Pennine Manchester and Leeds Railway but developing by the turn of the century into one of the largest stations in the country. One of its most distinctive features is the 160-yard Edwardian facade covering the full length of the station and incorporating an iron canopy which bears the names of the many resorts served by the Lancashire and Yorkshire Railway Company. Inside the station one can find an unusual map on white glazed bricks which shows the lines of the Lancashire and Yorkshire Railway, as well as a small cupola decorated with carved fruit located above the buffet.

A flight of steps opposite the front of Victoria Station leads down to a street called Walker's Croft, which follows the course of the covered-over River Irk and provides our first view of Chetham's Hospital. The name of this street is reminiscent of the days when cloth was laid out and bleached here after it had undergone 'fulling', a process for the cleansing and thickening of woollen cloth — in early times fulling was carried out by treading, and so those involved in this trade became known as 'walkers'.

Walker's Croft joins up with Victoria Street to the south west of the railway station, and from here one can gain access to two of Manchester's most important buildings — Chetham's Hospital and the Cathedral. The former consists of a group of long low buildings gathered around a central courtyard, having been built originally as the domestic quarters of the nearby Collegiate Church in the 15th century. By the time of the English Civil War the buildings were in a dilapidated state and were then bought by Humphrey Chetham, a wealthy textile merchant, just before his death in 1653. It was left up to his executors to open Chetham's Hospital as a school and make a collection of books as the basis of one of the first free public libraries to be established in the country. The library still exists today, although Chetham's is now in operation as a specialist music school.

The library was initially built up as a general scholarly library until the middle of the 19th century when it began to specialise in topography and history, firstly of Great Britain in general but more recently of the North West of England in particular, and the current stock now extends to about 70,000 volumes. The administration of the affairs of both the Library and the School is in the hands of twenty-four Feoffees, who are the successors of the twenty-four friends named by Chetham in his will. This historic complex has also been the traditional home of Manchester Grammar School, founded on the site in 1515 by Hugh Oldham, the Bishop of Exeter. Income for the school was provided from the revenues of three nearby mills which were purchased by Hugh Oldham for this specific purpose.

Like Chetham's the Cathedral is essentially a mediaeval establishment, and although most of the present building dates back only to Victorian times the reconstruction carried out then was very much in line with the style of the 15th century Gothic church which existed on the site up to the 1800s. In 1421 the lord of the manor had applied for a royal licence to found a college of clergy, offering his manor house as a convenient residence for the Warden, eight Fellows, four Clerks and six Choristers, and during the 15th century the

*Manchester Cathedral, above the River Irwell*

church was rebuilt on a scale which befitted its new collegiate status.

With a further improvement in status from a parish church to cathedral in 1847 rebuilding was again required, the Victorians not only enlarging and embellishing the structure but also replacing the seriously eroded red sandstone of the exterior with a more resistant stone from Derbyshire. In addition the tower was rebuilt to a slightly greater height in the 1860s, the north and south porches were added in the 1880s, and the ornate Victoria porch and vestries were added for Queen Victoria's Diamond Jubilee in 1895. Features of particular interest within the Cathedral include the Pulpitum or Choir Screen, a unique piece of mediaeval wood carving with three double doors, together with some fine carving on the choir stalls and misericord seats as well as the wall supports of the nave roof beams which take the form of angels holding 15th century musical instruments.

From the Cathedral one can head back in towards the centre of Manchester along Deansgate, an old street lying close to the line of the Roman road which made its way from the south via Chester to the fort at Castlefield and then continued in a northerly direction to Ribchester and Carlisle. With the development of a Saxon settlement at the confluence of the Irk and the Irwell, near to where the Cathedral now stands, Deansgate developed as an important thoroughfare linking two defensive sites and their

**The Old Wellington Inn**

associated centres of population, and after being built up firstly with half-timbered cottages it was then lined by rather more substantial brick houses and ultimately the shops and offices of the Victorian period.

Just off Deansgate at its northern end is St. Mary's Gate, which led up to the old market place with its mediaeval cross, pillory and stocks. These stood here until 1815, as did a number of mediaeval half-timbered buildings which existed in the area until 'redevelopment' took place with the creation of Victoria Street in 1837. In more recent years the area has been dramatically altered by the Market Place redevelopment scheme, which at least provided for the survival of the 16th century timber-framed Old Wellington Inn by elevating it some five feet on a reinforced concrete foundation to correspond with the level of the surrounding shopping complex.

The Market Place was the location for Manchester's first Exchange, built in 1729 to a Classical design and occupying the site where the Marks and Spencer store now stands. By 1809 a larger Exchange was built on the corner of what is now its present location, being extended in 1836 and 1845 to cope with the growing number of subscribers. By the 1870s the Exchange was being rebuilt

again, this time in a palatial Italianate style, but even this was not enough to cater for the increasing demand for accommodation and the building was further enlarged during the early part of the 20th century. Even by the end of the 1800s this important Manchester institution was becoming proudly known as the 'Royal' Exchange, and as well as providing office space for all the firms and organisations connected with the cotton trade it was the world's largest place of assembly for direct business transactions.

At its peak the Royal Exchange had a membership of 11,000 covering all parts of the textile industry, and on two days of every week many of these would be engaged in a frenzy of buying and selling from the floor of the Great Hall. In many respects the Royal Exchange typified Manchester's growth as a nationally important trade centre, and in the context of the cotton industry it was of international significance at a time when Manchester and cotton were synonymous. In the period between the First and Second World Wars, however, the cotton trade went into decline with the Royal Exchange surviving as just a memorial to former glories, although the Great Hall now accommodates the ultra-modern auditorium of the Exchange Theatre.

Following Exchange Street southwards from St. Mary's Gate brings us into St. Ann's Square, at one time a fashionable residential area but now the preserve of shops and offices. The focal point of the square is St. Ann's Church, built during the early part of the 18th century as Manchester's second church. This attractive Georgian building is the only survivor of twenty such churches which existed at one time in Manchester, and even St. Ann's was 'Victorianised' at the end of the 19th century as part of a restoration scheme which removed the old box pews, added new stained glass and refurbished the choir.

The construction of the church itself was quickly followed by the development of a residential square here, the square being lined by three-storey houses and planted with two rows of trees. These houses eventually became shops as the local residents moved further out to the Mosley Street area. A short detour down a narrow alleyway running from the west side of the Square brings us to Barton Arcade, a delightful structure of glass and cast-iron dating from 1871 which harks back to the time when buildings like Crystal Palace and the great railway train sheds were achieving particular popularity.

From the south side of St. Ann's Church one can follow the narrow St. Ann's Passage into the lower half of King Street, which like St. Ann's Square has remained a fashionable shopping area since the 19th century. Recently pedestrianised it is a very intimate thoroughfare with some splendid architectural details from both the Victorian and Edwardian periods, and in many respects it is one of the best streets in the city centre. Of a rather different character is the top half of King Street, very much the commercial heart of Manchester and lined by some quite remarkable individual buildings designed on an imposing and grand scale.

Along the northern side of the street, close to its junction with Cross Street, is Lloyds Bank occupying the site of Manchester's first town hall, while next door are the thoroughly modern buildings of the National Westminster Bank and Pall Mall Court. At the very top of King Street on the same side is the old Reform Club building, a good example of the Venetian Gothic style of architecture and richly decorated with polished granite shafts, sculpted capitals and carved panels. At the corners of the building's steeply pitched roof are delightful towers ornamented by gargoyles while below are the lavishly decorated rooms used by the former Manchester Club. The Club is no more.

On the opposite side of King Street from here is the Midland Bank, dating from 1929 and designed by Sir Edwin Lutyens, while a little further down is the monumental Ship Canal House, built in 1927 and faced with white

*St. Ann's Church*

Portland stone. An Act of Parliament had to be passed in order that regulations governing the height of facades in relation to street width could be set aside for the erection of this particular building, which is surmounted by a colonnade and statue of Neptune. Then on the same side towards Cross Street one can find the Trustee Savings Bank, a building which formerly housed a branch of the Bank of England. The architect here was Sir Charles Cockerell, who has endowed King Street with a building whose magnificent scale and character is out of all proportion to its size — although when work began in 1845 its Classical design was felt to be rather old fashioned.

From this point we can head back towards Deansgate via St. James' Square and John Dalton Street. St. James' Square is another interesting example of a formal Georgian residential area, laid out in about 1739 'for the residence of persons of a respectable situation in life', and although many of the properties were later demolished as the residents moved out to more favourable areas some of the houses still survive on the east side. One of the first buildings we come to after turning southwards onto Deansgate from John Dalton Street is the Rylands Library, a quite remarkable building of dark red sandstone which features a large traceried window and flanking towers on its front elevation.

Built by Enriqueta Augustina Rylands as a memorial to her husband, the philanthropic textile manufacturer John Rylands, the Library was designed along the lines of an Oxford college to house a collection of religious books and took nine years to complete after work began in 1890. From the vaulted entrance hall a staircase leads up to the first floor reading room, a long hall lit by stained glass windows at either end with galleries and study bays. This hall possesses one of the most beautiful interiors in the city, while the quality of the fittings here confirms that no expense was spared in the building's construction.

As we pass further southwards down Deansgate towards the Castlefield area one cannot help but be impressed by the range of architectural styles evident in the largely Victorian and Edwardian buildings which line both sides of the street — Elliott House at the corner of Jackson's Row displays Queen Anne features, while the Baroque 'grand manner' is evident in the design of Royal London House further along Deansgate. Yet at the same time there are also some remarkably bold departures from this general pattern, such as Sunlight House which towers over the smaller buildings in Deansgate from its position at the top end of Quay Street, reminiscent of American skyscraper blocks, this 1930s building was for a long time the tallest building in the city and the first to go higher than the Town Hall tower.

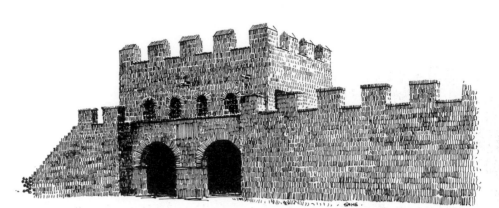

*The reconstructed Roman fort in Castlefield*

The Castlefield area to the west of Deansgate's southern extremity takes its name from the substantial remains of a Roman fort which still existed here during the 18th century, although by the end of the following century these remains had all but disappeared by virtue of the intrusions made by both the Rochdale and Bridgewater Canals and by several enormous railway viaducts. During Georgian times the 'Castle in-the-Field' enjoyed quiet isolation on the town's outskirts, but then the area became dominated by the architecture of the canal and railway eras which were so significant in Manchester's development.

In recent years part of the wall and North Gate of the extensive Roman fort which once stood here have been reconstructed, allowing visitors to gain an impression of Manchester's first settlement, while a short detour southwards from this point gives the opportunity to pass beneath the railway viaducts en route to discovering some of the glories of the canal age which are concentrated around the Castlefield Basin. This marks the junction of the Bridgewater Canal and the cross-city section of the Rochdale Canal, completed in 1805 to connect the former with the Dale Street Basin near Piccadilly. Construction of the Bridgewater Canal was begun in 1759 by Francis Egerton, the third Duke of Bridgewater, for the purpose of carrying coal from his mines at Worsley to the developing industrial town of Manchester, and this forerunner of all modern canals brought about the opening of the town's first wharf at Castlefield in 1765.

One of the surviving canalside warehouses still to be seen here is the Merchants' Warehouse, a brick and timber building dating from 1827 which is typical of the architecture of the period — of particular interest are the small semi-circular headed windows as well as the two shipping holes on the canal side of the warehouse. Just to the south of the canal is the Middle Warehouse, built around the same time as the Merchants' Warehouse, while beyond the railway viaducts to the west are the remains of the

canal arms which led to the now-demolished Staffordshire Warehouse as well as to the drainage weir known as the Giant's Basin. This latter feature was constructed by the canal engineer James Brindley to carry surplus water from the Bridgewater Canal to the River Medlock. In the opposite direction, along Castle Street, one can find not only the Castlefield Coal Wharf (opened in 1765) but also Gail House, a warehouse dating from the middle of the 19th century.

Although the passing of railway lines through this area contributed to the demise of its Roman remains, the railway architecture here makes some compensation for that by virtue of its use of Roman 'details' — Deansgate Station for example incorporates a mock portcullis and battlements, while the nearby railway bridges feature castellated brick and stone piers supporting cast-iron parapets with lancet arches. Cast-iron was also conspicuously used in the construction of the two massive railway viaducts which dissect the Castlefield area just to the north of the canal basin, these viaducts being built in 1877

*The Merchants' Warehouse, Castlefield*

*One of Castlefield's notable railway viaducts*

Storage accommodation for the freight brought into Liverpool Road Station was provided within a warehouse built just across the platform from the passenger facilities, this warehouse being similar in design to the Castlefield Canal Warehouses — constructed of brick and timber with an unusual curving frontage which follows the line of the railway track it incorporates openings on the railway side which allowed wagons to be brought inside for loading and unloading. By 1844 passenger traffic to this station was being diverted to the newly built Victoria Station with Liverpool Road Station developing as a focal point for goods traffic, and in order to cater for this the goods depot here was extended up towards Lower Byrom Street with the construction of the Goods Transfer Shed in 1860 and the Lower Byrom Street Warehouse in 1880. In the middle of this period the Grape Street Bonded Warehouse (now used by Granada TV) was also built on the northern side of the goods depot to provide further freight accommodation.

Following the closure of the goods depot in 1975 the complex was purchased by the Greater Manchester Council for restoration and conversion into the Greater Manchester Museum of Science and Industry, now the central feature of the Castlefield Urban Heritage Park which was established in 1982. Just across Lower Byrom Street from the Museum of Science and Industry is the Air and Space Museum, housed within a fine cast-iron and glass market hall which was built in 1876 for the Lower Campfield Market, while further along Liverpool Road near to its junction with Deansgate is the Upper Campfield Market erected just two years later. Next door to this on the corner of Deansgate and Liverpool Road is the Castlefield Visitors' Centre, occupying what was originally the former Free Library dating from 1882 and offering a comprehensive perspective on all

and 1898 to convey traffic to Central Station and the Great Northern Railway Company's goods warehouse respectively

A rather less dramatic piece of railway architecture, but no less important historically, is the Liverpool Road Passenger Station at the lower end of Liverpool Road. This was opened in 1830 as the original terminus of the Liverpool and Manchester Railway and the world's first passenger station, having been designed by George Stephenson and his son Robert to accommodate both freight and passenger traffic. Access to the station for passengers was by way of two entrances on Liverpool Road which led to the ground floor booking offices, with first and second class passengers being required to use different doorways. From the booking offices prospective passengers would then climb separate staircases to the waiting rooms and platform above. Next door to the station, at the very end of Liverpool Road, is an attractive brick-built house dating from the early part of the 19th century which was subsequently occupied by the Station Agent.

*Liverpool Road Station*

*Lower Campfield Market — now home to the Air and Space Museum*

*Ordsall Hall, Salford*

the varied facets of this quite remarkable piece of Manchester townscape.

The western boundary of the Castlefield area is marked by the River Irwell, which also forms the boundary between Salford and Manchester. In the minds of many people **Salford** in particular conjures up images of grime and depression, yet despite its reputation it holds numerous surprises for those who are prepared to take the time and trouble to look more closely. One such surprise is **Ordsall Hall,** situated just above the west bank of the Irwell and comprising a 15th century timber-framed wing richly decorated in Elizabethan times as well as a later brick-built wing dating from 1639. The Hall was originally constructed around a central quadrangle, but the other two wings have since disappeared. The site was also shared by extensive mediaeval farm buildings which once belonged to the Hall. The building which exists now has been carefully restored as a public museum, with one of its main features being the splendid Great Hall and 16th century spere truss.

Ordsall Hall was originally the home of the Radclyffe family, who featured prominently in Salford's history during the 16th and 17th centuries — in particular they made an appearance in the first armed clash of the English Civil War (the so-called Siege of Manchester) which took place on the only bridge spanning the Irwell. Salford's history

goes back much further than this, however, and it was a settlement of some importance in the ancient Kingdom of Northumbria as well as apparently being mentioned in the Anglo-Saxon Chronicle of AD 923. Salford also gave its name to the 'Hundred of Salford', an area stretching from the Mersey to Rossendale which was to constitute the south-eastern part of Lancashire when this came to be officially regarded as a separate county during the late 12th century. By 1228

Salford was given the right to hold a market and an annual fair, while in 1230 it was granted a charter designating it as a free borough. Early references show that the manor of Salford was one of the possessions of the Duchy of Lancaster, and since 1399 the lord of the manor has always been the king or queen of England.

Up to the end of the 18th century Salford was a small town of 7,000 people who found their

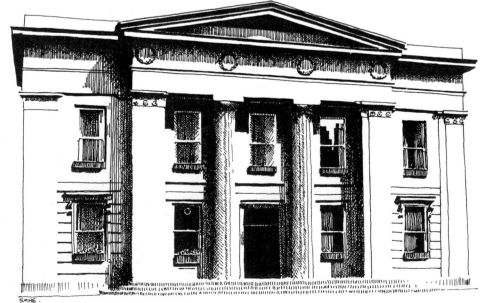

*The Old Town Hall, Salford*

206

*St. Philip's, Salford*

employment largely in silk weaving, dyeing, fulling and bleaching, but with the onset of the Industrial Revolution the character of the town was to change dramatically. By the end of the 19th century Salford's population had grown to 220,000 — an increase hardly exceeded anywhere else in the country — and it had developed into one of the greatest textile centres in the region with several enormous cotton mills. Brewing was also an important part of the local economy, which similarly benefited from the construction of Salford Docks at the end of the 1800s in conjunction with the opening of the Manchester Ship Canal in 1894. Such rapid growth was not without its attendant difficulties, however, and the vast areas of poor quality housing that were built during Victorian times brought with them overcrowding and great social problems.

One of the most interesting thoroughfares in Salford is Chapel Street, lined with several of the city's important civic buildings along its route westwards from the banks of the Irwell just across from Manchester Cathedral. Close to Victoria Bridge and the boundary between Manchester and Salford can be found the Church of Sacred Trinity, the oldest place of worship in Salford and the building which gave Chapel Street its name. Chapel Street also has some intrinsic interest of its own in that it is reputed to have been one of the first streets in the world to be lit by gas. Heading westwards along Chapel Street the next building of interest is the old Salford Town Hall dating from 1824, while close by is the Roman Catholic Cathedral of St. John built during the years 1844-48.

A little further along again is St. Philip's Church, erected to a Classical style in 1825, while adjacent to this is the Salford Royal Hospital which was established as the Salford and Pendleton Royal Dispensary in 1827. Chapel Street then gives way to The Crescent with its curving terrace of Georgian houses following a bend of the River Irwell just below, with The Crescent in turn leading to Peel Park and the University of Salford. Set in the midst of the University buildings is Salford's main museum and art gallery, its Italian Renaissance style retained from the 19th century mansion which first occupied this site. Within this museum can be found a complete reconstruction of a Victorian street as well as the largest collection in the country of paintings and drawings by Salford artist L.S. Lowry.

From Peel Park we head westwards again towards **Eccles,** passing en route Buile Hill Park with its Museum of Mining. Within a building designed by Sir Charles Barry in 1827 one can find simulated deep and drift coal mines as well as a display of mining history. At the Monks Hall Museum in Eccles one can also learn something of the area's industrial heritage through a display of machinery taken from James Nasmyth's Bridgewater Foundry, established alongside the canal at nearby Patricroft in 1836. Nasmyth was a Scottish engineer who became famous for his invention of the steam hammer. Monks Hall itself is a 16th century timber framed house hiding behind a mid-19th century mock Tudor frontage, while at the rear is a pleasant and secluded walled garden.

The oldest building in Eccles is St. Mary's Parish Church, parts of which date back to Norman times, although there was probably a place of worship here well before then because the name 'Eccles' is apparently derived from the Celtic word for 'church'. St. Mary's has played an important role not only in the history of Eccles itself but also in that of the surrounding townships which were originally included within the parish, and whose names are indicative of Saxon settlements.

Although Eccles remained largely free of industry up to the 18th century the area underwent a radical change in its character when the Bridgewater Canal was brought through the district in the 1760s. At first industrialisation took the form of silk spinning and weaving, but then as the suitability of Lancashire's climate for the making-up of cotton began to be appreciated so many of the mills in Eccles were attracted to this new commodity. Other industrial enterprises were also established here, including the production of a wide range of machine tools and locomotives as well as the development of England's first motor-driven fire engine. Yet it was canal engineering which gave the area its special place in the history books, particularly at Barton where in 1761 the engineer James Brindley constructed his famous aqueduct to carry the Bridgewater Canal over the River Irwell. This was matched by another remarkable feat of engineering more than one hundred and thirty years later — the completion of the Manchester Ship Canal, which not only gave Manchester direct access to the sea but also opened up the industrial and trade potential of all the towns along its 36 mile course.

Although the idea of a canal from the coast to Manchester had been raised as early as 1697 it was only in 1824 that serious consideration was given to the proposal, with the actual opening ceremony taking place on 1st January, 1894. The first steps towards the

*Monks Hall Museum, Eccles*

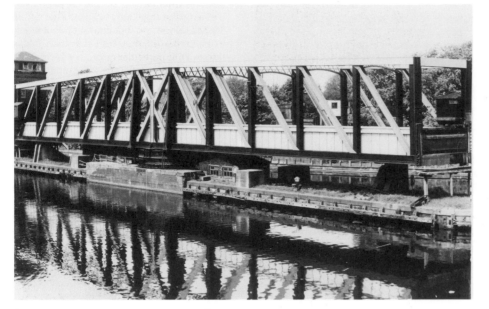

*The Bridgewater Canal aqueduct at Barton upon Irwell*

canal's construction were made by Daniel Adamson, who was successful in gaining Royal Assent for the project in 1885 despite two previous failures, although it was left up to Thomas Walker to initiate the first phases of actual work. Most of this was carried out by sixteen thousand 'navvies', who were employed to excavate the enormous ditch for just 4½d per hour.

Despite further difficulties the Manchester Ship Canal was eventually completed, with the opening ceremony being performed by Queen Victoria. By 1905 five million tons of traffic was passing through the port of Manchester annually, and in its peak year of 1958 this figure reached 18 million tons. Although this remarkable waterway has experienced a decline in recent years due to the contraction of its shipping traffic, a new era is being heralded for the Manchester Ship Canal through proposals for its use in leisure and recreation — particularly in conjunction with the revitalisation of its associated docklands.

As well as its canals Eccles has also been a significant place for the development of other forms of communication - the Liverpool to Manchester railway line was brought through here in 1830, despite some difficulties in crossing nearby Chat Moss, while Barton Aerodrome was the first municipal airport in the country.

The placid waters of the Manchester Ship Canal form Salford's southern extent, beyond which are Urmston and Stretford hemmed in on their southern extremities by the old county boundary of the River Mersey. **Urmston** probably originated as 'Ormestun', denoting the dwelling of Orme, the Orme in question being Orme Fitz-Seward whose land passed in the 13th century to Richard de

Trafford. Also incorporated within the district of Urmston are Flixton and Davyhulme, whose origins go back to at least the 12th century. Parish records suggest that before the opening of the Ship Canal in 1894 **Flixton** was still quite rural in character despite being part of the Hundred of Salford, and its enduring charm can even now be experienced within the beautiful gardens of Flixton House as well as in the vicinity of St. Michael's Parish Church.

*Doorway, St. Michael's Church in Flixton*

**Stretford** traces its historical roots back to even earlier times, its name being derived from the paved road ('streta') between Manchester and Chester which crossed the River Mersey at the 'ford' now marked by Crossford Bridge. A small settlement founded somewhat later on the north bank of the Mersey by the Saxons was appropriately called 'Streetford', and by the 14th century it

had grown in size through the development of the woollen trade here. A gradual growth in the area's prosperity was experienced during the course of the next four hundred years, after which Stretford enjoyed a rather more dramatic increase in its fortunes through its new connections with trade and communications.

The pace of development quickened firstly through the opening in 1761 of the Bridgewater Canal, which offered a convenient link from Worsley to Manchester via Stretford, while in 1772 an extension of this waterway through to Runcorn brought about a short, cheap route to Liverpool. Then in 1849 transport by rail was added to Stretford's increasing list of advantages by way of the opening of the Manchester, South Junction and Altrincham Railway, with 1894 seeing the completion of the Manchester Ship Canal to give Stretford a connection to the sea and thus make it accessible to ocean-going ships from all over the world.

One of the most significant developments in Stretford which followed on from the construction of the Ship Canal was the creation of Trafford Park Industrial Estate, an area of 2,000 acres which grew up as one of the most remarkable examples of industrial planning in the world. Prior to the coming of the Manchester Ship Canal Trafford Park had existed for several centuries as the rural estate surrounding the mansion of its owners the de Trafford family, but then in 1896 it was acquired by Trafford Park Estates Ltd. for the purpose of industrial development.

As well as enjoying a very favourable location at the centre of the most densely populated region in Britain, Trafford Park Estate had the benefit of unparalleled communications — in addition to having an extensive water frontage alongside the Ship Canal for ocean-going vessels it was also well served by main line railways and the Bridgewater Canal. There was too an excellent internal transport system, with the individual firms locating here being offered their own railway sidings, and every incoming company was guaranteed that its traffic could be hauled to and from the docks at the uniform rate of sixpence a ton regardless of the distance involved.

Trafford Park's early reputation was based upon engineering and manufacturing, but in more recent years it has developed as an important centre for storage, transportation and distribution — doubtless helped by easy access to the national motorway system. When it was first envisaged the Trafford Park Industrial Estate was a far-sighted and ambitious development, a unique concept which took advantage of the logic that building a complex of factories and workplaces on the very edge of an ocean-linked waterway would be of mutual benefit to both shipowners and manufacturers. The

*Longford Park gardens*

'gamble' paid off handsomely, and although the character of the estate has changed in recent years it is still a paramount industrial location in the country as a whole.

Of course not all Stretford's 'parks' are industrial ones, and the area has more than its fair share of ornamental pleasure-grounds. One of the best is Longford Park, encompassing eighty acres of parkland laid out around Longford Hall — originally the home of the Manchester textile manufacturer John Rylands. The lovely formal gardens around the house are a particular delight during the summer months, and each June they form a colourful backcloth for the famous Stretford Pageant. Then again the southern parts of Stretford are included within the Mersey Valley Park, a linear recreational facility which follows the course of the Mersey between Urmston and Stockport. In earlier days farmers flooded the meadows through sluices alongside the river to enrich their land, and in some parts these meadows still exist as nature areas supporting many kinds of birds and different forms of wildlife.

Immediately to the east of Stretford we come to some of Manchester's southern suburbs, many of which were developed as high-class residential areas during the Victorian era for the city's wealthy merchants — Whalley Range, Moss Side, Rusholme and Fallowfield all grew up during this period, offering a secluded haven well away from the grime and bustle of industrial Manchester. One of the most interesting areas is **Victoria Park** in **Rusholme,** which was laid out on formal lines during the early Victorian period to provide individual building plots on which substantial houses could be built for some of

Manchester's more 'well-to-do' people. The first stage was the formation of a company to purchase land in the Rusholme area, with the land then being sold off in blocks to shareholders and speculators who would erect houses in line with the agreed plan.

This plan was produced by the architect Richard Lane, whose layout centred on three crescents — Park Crescent, Hanover Crescent and a third crescent which was never actually built. Lane determined that the privacy of this select development would be upheld not only by laying out substantial gardens around each property but also

through the planting of numerous trees as well as by the erection of toll gates at points on the boundaries, so that outsiders would have to pay a charge if they wished to ride or drive through this particular neighbourhood. With an initial burst of enthusiasm the Park was 'opened' in 1837 after an Act of Parliament was passed giving the Victoria Park Company powers to lay out and embellish part of its property as an ornamental park with a wall as well as lay out streets, squares and crescents and erect private dwellinghouses.

However, as a result of the 1838-43 trade depression the Company ran into difficulties and failed in 1839, and it was only in 1845 that the relevant landowners decided that a Victoria Park Trust should be formed to carry through the original concept. With a new committee elected to manage the Park's affairs development proceeded as first planned, and magnificent houses were soon being built for Manchester's wealthy merchants. Victoria Park also became the preferred location for the city's artists and reformers, and as well as providing homes for people such as Ford Madox Brown, Charles Halle and Mrs. Pankhurst it attracted leading parliamentarians such as George Hadfield, Richard Cobden and Sir Henry Roscoe.

After the end of the First World War, however, the very select character of the Park was threatened by improvements in transport (allowing people to move further out of Manchester) and by the erection of terraces and semi-detached houses in the neighbourhood. The increase in traffic along Anson Road also brought about considerable public pressure for the removal of the tolls, and in 1938 the road was thrown open to all and sundry. The Trust then installed toll gates

*The old Toll Gates, Victoria Park*

on the side roads, but even this last-ditch effort at preserving the neighbourhood's tranquil seclusion came to nothing and the final toll gate was removed in 1954. Since that time the character of the area has changed quite significantly, with many of the larger houses being converted to institutions of one sort or another — schools, nursing homes and University halls of residence.

Although Rusholme's most extensive development took place during the Victorian period, its history goes back at least several centuries earlier. One of the oldest features of the area is what remains of the Nico Ditch, a defensive earthwork probably dating back to the 9th century which stretched from Ashton-under-Lyne to Chorlton. Tradition has it that this ditch was dug in one night (each man digging a length equivalent to his own height), indicating that the local population would receive very short notice of an attack by the marauding Danes. Similar defensive earthworks were constructed about this time to the east and south east of Manchester.

During the later mediaeval times settlement in the area was probably centred upon two substantial timber-framed houses, one known as Platt Hall and the other as Birch Hall. Occupation of the Platt Hall site dates back to the time of the Crusades, with the second timber-framed house here surviving until 1764 when it was replaced by the present substantial Georgian mansion. For the next century and a half the Estate was owned by the Worsleys and the Carrill-Worsleys, wealthy Manchester textile merchants, until the first few years of the 20th century when it was bought by the City Council for use as a public park. One of the ambitious improvements made at that time was the creation of a 6½ acre lake, and this together with the rest of Platt Fields Park was formally opened by the Lord Mayor in 1910. The red brick Hall is now an attractive museum displaying an interesting collection of English costumes. Although Birch Hall and its associated private chapel also had an important role to play in the area, the house was not so fortunate as Platt Hall and it was demolished in 1926 to make way for Manchester Grammar School.

As has been seen in the case of Victoria Park, it was the 19th century which brought about a change in Rusholme's character from a largely rural area to a residential suburb, and by the end of the century its development was practically complete. Such was the experience of **Fallowfield** too, which even up to the 1820s was described as being 'remote from town and sparsely populated'. All this began to change by the 1850s, however, as the industrial boom prompted Manchester's population to move out of the city centre to places like Fallowfield, assisted by the various improvements in transport. The large houses built along Wilmslow Road

and Wilbraham Road rivalled even the mansions of Victoria Park, and among the people attracted into Fallowfield was Alfred Waterhouse, later to become the architect of Manchester Town Hall. Perhaps the most impressive residence now remaining in Fallowfield is a delightful mansion known as 'The Firs', originally a farmhouse but then converted into its present form by Sir Joseph Whitworth. Standing in the midst of its own secluded and attractive grounds this eventually became the home of C.P. Scott, a famous Manchester Guardian editor, although since 1936 it has been the official residence of the University's vice-chancellor.

The road southwards from Fallowfield takes us through Withington and then on into **Didsbury,** first settled during Saxon times because of its defensive advantages and the fact that it was elevated above the impenetrable marshland alongside the river below. Further settlement was encouraged during the 13th century when the river was banked up to create a head of water for the local corn mills, providing an opportunity to create new valley farms on the drained pastures. At about the same time the church of St. James was built on a site to the south of the present 'village', again making good use of the solid higher ground just above the flood plain of the River Mersey. This church was the oldest ecclesiastical foundation in the parish of Manchester after the Collegiate Church, which eventually became the city's cathedral.

Up to the 18th century Didsbury remained very largely a farming community, but then the improvements in communications which were benefiting Manchester generally also began to make their presence felt here too. One of these improvements was the creation of a new through-road along the Wilmslow and Manchester Turnpike, providing a proper crossing over the Mersey at this point and opening up the opportunity for Manchester's rich merchants to build their large mansions in Didsbury. Initially many of these were

situated fairly close to the old village centre encompassing the church, pub and village green, but then in the middle of the 19th century new development began to take place further northwards, particularly in the Fielden Park area which became a residential suburb for the more well-to-do.

Gradually the village was moving away from the inns and church of 'old Didsbury' and establishing itself not only in Fielden Park but also around the hamlet of Barlow Moor, traditionally an area in which tradesmen employed on the local estates would live. This process was further encouraged by the coming of the railway through Didsbury in 1880, with Didsbury station being built close to Barlow Moor Road. The result was that most of the new development during later Victorian times was concentrated in the northern half of the village.

Westwards from Didsbury, on the opposite bank of the River Mersey, is the township of **Northenden** — which for most of its history was very firmly in the county of Cheshire until the City of Manchester began to look enviously at the surrounding area as a potential housing overspill site. The first attempts at annexing this northern part of Cheshire were made in 1926, although it was only after five years of acrimonious wrangling that the area was eventually incorporated into

*The Old Rectory, Didsbury*

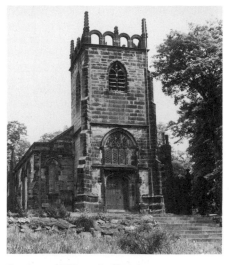

*St. James' Church, Didsbury*

*Fletcher Moss gardens, Didsbury*

*Wythenshawe Hall in its Tudor form*

*Wythenshawe Hall with Victorian additions*

*Baguley Hall*

Manchester in 1931. The eventual result of all this was the development of **Wythenshawe** as one of the world's first full-scale garden suburbs under the direction of Barry Parker, the foremost town planner of the period and a pupil of Ebenezer Howard, the 'father' of the Garden City Movement. The target in view was to provide housing for 100,000 people, and although there were problems due to the scale of such a development the wisdom of the garden city principles is now becoming apparent as Wythenshawe takes on an increasingly mature appearance.

Not all the buildings in the area are of such recent origin, however, and the visitor can also discover some fine historic houses — such as Baguley Hall, said to be the only existing example of Viking architecture in the world by virtue of its unusual roof trusses, and **Wythenshawe Hall,** an imposing mansion set in the midst of delightful parkland. This latter building was the home of the Tatton family for four centuries, but it was given to the City of Manchester in 1926 by Lord and Lady Simon of Wythenshawe who

had purchased it from R.H.G. Tatton, the last member of the family to own the house. Although the Hall dates back to the Tudor period much of its oak panelling and stained glass was introduced during the Victorian era, with the beautiful surrounding gardens being laid out in the 1850s.

Following the Mersey upstream takes us very close to the centre of Stockport before bringing us to **Denton** on the eastern outskirts of Manchester. Denton's particular claim to fame appears to have been the hatting industry, which was the main source of employment in this area for many years. The origins of hatting are related to the making of felt, which seems to have started here during the 16th century through local farmers seeking to supplement the living which they drew from the land. Initially the felt was sold to merchants in Stockport and Manchester, but then as the market for hats became established so local workshops were set up. By the beginning of the 18th century there was at least one concern in the area using outside labour, but by 1800 there were four sizeable hatting firms in the district increasing to twenty by 1825.

A vital factor in the development of the hatting trade was the improvement of communications brought about by the Industrial Revolution, and as communications improved so did production — by 1840 up to 2,000 dozen felt hats per week were being turned out in Denton and Haughton alone. Business was so good, and local labour so cheap, that several London firms were attracted northwards to the area. During the middle of the 19th century, however, a fairly significant decline in the hatting industry was experienced due to a change in fashion from felt hats to silk ones, and since the local hatting works employed women and girls as well as men so complete families became unemployed as a result of the depression. Fortunately Denton managed to weather the storm, and by the end of the 19th century new firms were being set up and the industry was achieving even greater

prosperity than before — although a more cautious approach became evident in the construction of the new factories, since these were so built as to be able to be converted into rows of terraced houses should troubled times emerge again.

Up to the middle of the 19th century most of the processes involved in hatting were carried out by hand. The first stage involved mixing the raw materials of wool and fur so as to form layers of even thickness, using a hatter's bow (a pole of ash with a catgut cord) which hung from the roof. As the bow was plucked so the fibres opened up and the material fell into even layers. This material was then pressed into batts to form conical shapes or 'hoods' about twice the size of the final product, these hoods being passed to the planking shop where large kettles containing water and sulphuric acid were heated over a fire.

Using a hatter's pin (a type of wooden rolling pin) the hoods were then gradually shrunk and thickened here before being shaped on a cylindrical wooden block. After drying and dyeing the hats were given their final shape by pulling and pressing on an appropriate wooden block, with separate blocks being used to shape the crown and brim of a hat. Then a precise curve was given to the brim using curler's parings formed of gauze bound with twine and covered with shellac. Then after checking their size with a hatter's rule the hats were lined and trimmed according to the

*The Moravian settlement, Fairfield*

*The Moravian church, Fairfield*

*The Moravian settlement, Fairfield —
cobbles and cottages*

fashion of the day; traditionally this was a woman's skill, often being done by women out-workers.

From Denton our route takes us northwards to Ashton-under-Lyne, passing through Audenshaw on the way there. At this point it is well worthwhile making a short detour to **Fairfield** in nearby Droylsden, where one can discover the intimate community created by Moravian refugees who settled here in 1783. After purchasing an estate of 54 acres the land was christened 'Fairfield', with the Moravians proceeding to erect a range of buildings to meet their particular needs; these included dwelling-houses for the married as well as a Sister's House for unmarried women and a Brethren's House for unmarried men. The Moravian settlement was also developed as a largely self-contained community with its own facilities, so in addition to the inn, bakery and dairy provision was made for a night watchman, an inspector of weights and measures, an overseer of roads and a doctor.

Over the years very little has changed in this delightful residential enclave, which proudly retains its neat Georgian houses on either side of the tree-lined cobbled streets. The Moravian church dating from 1785 is also well worth seeing, particularly for its fine cupola with a clock and weathervane. Just to the south of Fairfield Square is a later but equally fine residential estate of 39 houses built between 1914 and 1920 for the Fairfield Tenants' Association, a group of Moravians who wanted to live near the Fairfield settlement. Designed by the Manchester architects Edgar Wood and James Henry Sellars the detached, semi-detached and terraced houses vary in size but are all built of red brick in a neo-Georgian style with wide frontages and many changes in level. The delightfully spacious character of this unique estate is a reflection of its development during the heyday of the Garden City Movement.

Returning from this short detour to Fairfield we come to **Ashton-under-Lyne,** three miles to the north east, a town apparently founded by the Saxons. The name 'Ashton' signifies a place enclosed by ash trees, which were held in great reverence by the Saxons, while the appellation 'under-Lyne' may well have been added some time later to describe how the settlement was positioned below the earth ramparts, or 'lines', of the Roman road running through the area. An alternative view is that the 'lyne' refers either to the line of nearby hills or to the old boundary between Northumbria and Mercia.

During Norman times Roger Fitz-Orme de Assheton became the first lord of the manor of Ashton-under-Lyne, founding the House of Assheton which held the manor without break for several hundred years. Then in the reign of Henry VIII the manor passed into the hands of the Booths of Dunham Massey, who themselves held the manor until 1758 when it passed by marriage to the fourth Earl of Stamford. Although a charter had been granted in 1284 entitling Ashton to hold a market and two fairs it remained a village of only moderate size even up to the middle of the 18th century, when it comprised just four streets.

At that point in time the Industrial Revolution began to exert its influence here, with Ashton being recognised as a very suitable place for the manufacture of cotton cloth — it was situated in a rich coalfield, there was a plentiful water supply and the damp atmosphere was ideal for spinning and weaving. Consequently not only was there a very considerable increase in the number of cotton mills here, from nine in 1814 to thirty-three in 1839, but there was also a phenomenal growth in Ashton's population — between 1801 and 1851 the total number of inhabitants more than quadrupled. Most of this growth can be accounted for by the 'explosion' of the cotton industry, with workers flooding into the area not only from the more rural parts of north and west Lancashire but also from the surrounding counties and Ireland.

Such growth was not achieved without opposition, however, and the introduction of factory machinery to the textile trade was accompanied by violent social disturbances. Ashton in particular was affected by the 'plug riots' of the 1840s, these troubles being so named because one of the methods used to immobilise the machinery was the removal of plugs from mill boilers. These difficulties were gradually overcome, however, and by the start of the 20th century there were 35 mills in the town employing over 10,000 people. Yet despite the prosperity of those times the town suffered very badly during the depression of the inter-war years, and the cotton trade never recovered sufficiently to re-establish its once-supreme position in Ashton.

The physical character of the town owes much to the fifth Earl of Stamford, who in the later part of the 18th century laid out a new residential quarter to a grid-iron pattern at the west end of Ashton. Although a good deal of rebuilding has taken place since that time the original street layout is still discernible, and some of the street names are present-day reminders of the fifth Earl and his family. Later generations of the family left their mark on the town too, and in the second half of the 19th century the seventh Earl of Stamford made various gifts of land and money to Ashton. The Infirmary, the public baths and Stamford Park all resulted from his generosity, and during the cotton famine he also contributed £1,000 to the local relief fund.

In terms of individual buildings it appears that St. Michael's Parish Church is the most historic, with the Domesday Book recording that it was one of two churches which held land in Manchester (the other being St. Mary's Church, eventually to become the city's cathedral). Although Sir John de Assheton began a new church on the same site as the earlier one, in 1413, there has been so much alteration and repair since that time that none of the original structure remains. A major rebuilding at the end of the 18th century was followed by a disastrous fire which required the complete redecoration of the interior and the rebuilding of the south wall, while in the 1880s the tower was also rebuilt. The feature for which St. Michael's is particularly famous is its mediaeval stained glass, this being the best in Lancashire and comprising eighteen scenes from the life of St. Helen, four groups of figures representing members of the Assheton family and two English kings (presumed to be Edward the Confessor and Henry VI). These panels were inserted some time between 1498 and 1513, although some might have been painted as early as 1480.

Just to the north of the Parish Church is the site of the old market cross, which originally marked the centre of old Ashton at the junction of its four earliest streets. The local market was held here until 1762, eventually being replaced by the present market site near the Town Hall in 1830. The former market cross dating from 1793 was taken down in 1829 and now stands in Stamford Park. Just across from here are the Memorial Gardens, beyond which can be found Chapel Street and the location of Ashton's first Congregational Chapel opened in 1816. Associated with the chapel were the Albion Schools, opened in 1862 and achieving a national reputation by virtue of their impressive curriculum, excellent teaching standards and non-denominational admission requirements. Used as both a day school and Sunday School this educational establishment had at one time over 1,000 pupils.

Heading back into the town centre from here we come to Stamford Street, laid out as part of the westward expansion of Ashton from the 1790s onwards under the strict control of the Earl of Stamford. Stamford Street itself was begun in 1795 as part of a larger scheme of parallel streets following a grid-iron pattern, with the width of the streets varying according to their relative importance. At the western end of Stamford Street, close to the Parish Church, is a late Georgian house dating from about 1820 which is typical of the properties originally lining both sides of this important thoroughfare throughout its entirety. A little further along Stamford Street is Stamford Arcade, formerly known as Flag Alley because of the way in which it was paved with exceptionally large flagstones from the Saddleworth area. Some of the shops here date from the 1840s, and the alley continued across Stamford Street to give direct access to the Parish Church.

Further along again is Old Square, originally known as The Circus, with its three storey houses dating from the 1790s forming part of the Earl of Stamford's new development. The

*The Market Hall tower, Ashton-under-Lyne*

213

former Stamford Estate Office at the nearby junction of Church Street and Warrington Street is a fine Victorian house dating from about 1850, displaying the Stamford Arms over the doorway. Next to this building is the one-time Mechanics Institute, opened in 1862 and now in use as an Adult Education Centre. Across the road from here is the Stamford Street Methodist Chapel, built in 1832 to replace an earlier chapel dating from 1799, while on the north side of Stamford Street is one of the entry points to Market Avenue. This Victorian pedestrian development was created as a new thoroughfare by Joseph Fletcher in the 1850s. Passing through here and turning right into Old Street brings us finally to the former Booth's Cafe, the date of 1745 on a rainwater pipe bearing witness to the fact that this is one of the oldest buildings in the town.

In more recent times the Stamford Street which formed such an integral part of Ashton during the Georgian and Victorian periods has been extended eastwards beyond the Parish Church, and following it takes us out of Ashton and along the north bank of the River Tame just above Stalybridge town centre. At this point we are in what used to be the county of Cheshire up to 1974, but then heading due north we run into a considerably more confusing boundary situation when we enter **Mossley** — because this particular settlement was for part of its existence shared between the three counties of Lancashire, Cheshire and Yorkshire. In its very early days Mossley was included within the Manor of Ashton and had no separate existence of its own, but by 1864 a Local Government Act was passed which allowed Mossley to have a Local Board of Commissioners.

Despite many improvements Mossley's

*Hartshead Pike, Mossley*

unique geographical position at the junction of three counties gave rise to considerable administrative difficulties, and since no place with a population of less than 20,000 was allowed to have its own police force Mossley was looked after by three different police authorities. The confusion did not end with law and order, however, and in addition to being governed by three separate County authorities with three different County rates Mossley had the misfortune to have three Register Offices and three Members of Parliament. There were even three parish churches for the different parts of the town - St. George's (Lancashire), St. John the Baptist's (Yorkshire), and All Saints' (Cheshire).

As a result it was decided to petition Queen Victoria for Mossley's incorporation as a Borough, even though with only 13,000 inhabitants the town would probably be the smallest one in the country. Mossley's peculiar situation led to the petition being accepted and in 1885 the town was granted its Charter of Incorporation enabling it to become one of Lancashire's municipal boroughs. In more recent years, however, Mossley came back under the control of Ashton when it was included within the new metropolitan borough of Tameside in 1974 and so formally excluded from Lancashire.

Perhaps as a result of the vagaries of its administrative history Mossley has been keen to maintain its independence, partly helped by its isolated valley position over the hill from Ashton-under-Lyne. Its position has also provided it with some wonderful views of the surrounding hills, enhanced by tantalising and delightful perspectives of the stone built terraces which cling precariously to the steep sides of the Tame Valley. For much of its early history Mossley was a small farming settlement with many of its inhabitants engaged in woollen cloth manufacture, most of whom worked initially for the wealthier farmers who owned the looms. Then as new inventions in spinning and weaving were made during the course of the 18th century so the textile industry speeded up and the cloth merchants developed as a class on their own, building mills where the various processes involved in the manufacture of cloth could be carried out under one roof. These new inventions were introduced with cotton rather than wool in mind, but the long-established woollen trade continued to hold its own against the advance of its new competitor. Woollen manufacture in Mossley reached its highest point in 1830, by which time there were 20 woollen mills operating here, but with the invention of the power loom the manufacture of cotton made rapid strides and became the dominant industry by 1850.

The significance of the cotton industry in Mossley can perhaps be best gauged from the

experience of John Mayall, 'the Prince of Cotton Spinners', who started a business here which by 1876 possessed more mule spindles than any private firm of cotton spinners in the world. His brother George Mayall also had a significant influence on Mossley, for it was he who built 'Whitehall' in 1863 at a cost of £60,000. This imposing Italianate mansion situated on the wooded slopes above Mossley later became the Town Hall, and its pleasant grounds now constitute one of the area's public parks.

At an even higher level above Mossley is **Hartshead Pike,** an intriguing stone monument which watches over the surrounding countryside from its impressive vantage point 943 feet above sea level. The origins of the Pike are lost in the mists of time, although legend has it that King Canute (the Dane who ruled England between 1016 and 1033) halted his troops in the area and that a stone pillar was placed upon a neighbouring hill to commemorate the event. Another tradition suggests that the name 'hartshead' relates to the time when Prince Henry (later Henry II) was out hunting in the district and his companion slew a fierce werewolf, whose head was sent to grace the tower; after this had rotted another carved from stone in the likeness of a stag or hart was put in its place on top of the tower. The name 'Pike' is of Norse origin meaning 'a place of fires', so it is not surprising that the ground on which the monument stands is reputed to have been used as a beacon hill, probably acting as one of the chain of beacons used to herald the coming of the Spanish Armada.

*Colliers Arms, Mossley*

The first locally-recorded work to the Pike dates back to the rebuilding of 1751, when the monument was topped by a vane made in the form of a hart's head; there was also an inscription which read 'Look well at me before you go, And see you nothing at me throw', suggesting that vandalism was not unknown even in those days. Rebuilding was again necessary in 1863, with further restoration being required in 1928. By that time the Pike had become a popular local attraction, visitors being treated not only to refreshments but also having the opportunity to climb the stairs to the upper part of the structure. For present-day visitors refreshments are no longer available on Hartshead Pike itself, but nearby is a fascinating pub known as the Collier's Arms — one of the few drinking establishments remaining which also functions as a working farm, and which has somehow resisted pressures towards change and commercialism.

From Hartshead Pike and Mossley the River Tame can be followed northwards up into the foothills of the Pennines, venturing into the district of **Saddleworth** with its lovely villages crammed with picturesque stone cottages along the sides of the valley. Strictly speaking this area has always belonged to Yorkshire, or at least it did until the local government re-organisation of 1974 placed it very firmly in the hands of Oldham within the newly designated county of Greater Manchester. This was perhaps not the most popular of moves, but at least it gives us some excuse to visit these delightful valley settlements with their traditional wool weavers' cottages before heading into Oldham to discover more of Lancashire's own textile development.

The descent from Hartshead Pike takes us down firstly to **Brookbottom,** which prior to 1864 marked the boundary between Yorkshire and Lancashire — Mossley's rapid growth up to that point in time had made the establishment of unified local government essential, so the Mossley Local Board was formed and the county boundary moved so that the blossoming town lay entirely within Lancashire. From Brookbottom the main road can be followed northwards to the hamlet of **Quick,** which offers some particularly fine views not only of the Tame Valley but also of the Chew Valley which joins it just a little further to the east at Greenfield. Beyond Greenfield can be found Dovestone Reservoir, fed by Chew Brook and overlooked by the impressive Dovestone Rocks.

To the north of Quick is the small village of **Lydgate,** which despite its present size is said to have at one time supported seven public houses; now only the White Hart Inn survives, having been built in 1788 at the same time as the nearby St. Anne's Church. The simultaneous growth of both church and public house as the main centres of social activity appears to have been something of a local characteristic, taking place in many other settlements within the Saddleworth area. Here again there are some excellent views to be savoured, not only of the dramatic Pennine hills to the east but also of the great metropolitan conurbation sprawled out below in the opposite direction, beyond which can be picked out on one side the television masts of Winter Hill near Bolton and on the other the radio telescopes of Jodrell Bank in Cheshire.

Just to the north of Lydgate is the junction with the main route eastwards from Oldham,

*Higher Kinders, Saddleworth*

taking us into **Grasscroft.** This settlement started life as just a cluster of some of the earliest stone dwellings in Saddleworth, expanding considerably during the late 18th century when several mills were established alongside the local streams and also in the early 19th century when it became the junction of two turnpike roads. Then in Victorian times the area saw the construction of several large stone mansions, a number of which were associated with the Whitehead family (the main landowners in this district) as well as with other manufacturing or professional families. The main establishment owned by the Whiteheads was the Royal George Mill just to the south of Grasscroft, noted for the manufacture of felt and flags. The latter were often made for royal occasions, and the Whiteheads were presented with a carved Royal Coat of Arms which now hangs inside the nearby church (Christ Church) which they had built in the early 1850s. Here again there are good views eastwards of the Chew Valley, with the craggy Dovestone Rocks framed on one side by the Saddleworth War Memorial and on the other by Alphin Pike.

Across on the opposite side of the River Tame to Grasscroft is the settlement of **Greenfield,** an industrial village which only came into existence after 1850 as the cotton trade became established here. Prior to this the older houses and weavers' cottages tended to be situated on the hillside above the valley bottom, as were the ancient tracks and roads which only descended into the valleys when it was necessary to cross the streams below. One particularly interesting ancient route to the north of the village is Kinders Lane, which led up past Saddleworth Church and over Standedge to Huddersfield.

Close to the start of this old road is Higher Kinders, a fine example of a domestic weaving settlement which at one time provided accommodation for as many as seven families. Dating from the early part of the 17th century this fascinating little group of buildings displays numerous features characteristic of the domestic woollen industry, including the 'takin-in' steps which led up to the workroom extending the full length of the house as well as the long mullioned windows to provide maximum

*St. Chad's House, Uppermill*

light for those people working at the hand looms. There is also a small building nearby which functioned as a dyehouse, and here one can find the 'wuzzing holes' which were used in the drying of raw wool or weft - in removing excess water the wool was 'wuzzed' round in a basket slung from a pole, one end of which was inserted in the hole.

Upstream along the River Tame from Greenfield and in the valley bottom below Saddleworth Church is **Uppermill,** the largest single settlement in Saddleworth district and its administrative centre until the local government reorganisation of 1974. Uppermill has not always enjoyed pre-eminence in the area, however, and it was really only with the simultaneous creation of the turnpike road and the Huddersfield Canal along the valley floor that Uppermill began to rival Dobcross just to the north as Saddleworth's leading village. As was obviously the case with Greenfield most of the early settlement in Uppermill was on the hillsides, but from the late 18th century onwards woollen mills were being constructed in the small tributary valleys to the east of Uppermill as well as along the River Tame itself. Generally these early mills concentrated on woollen 'scribbling' or carding, with the other processes being carried on in hillside farms, although by the 19th century most of the finishing work had gravitated down to the valley mills with woollen spinning soon to follow.

During this later period Uppermill also saw a number of cotton mills established in the area, spreading across from nearby Lancashire. The site of one of these former cotton mills is now occupied by the car park to Uppermill Museum, with the museum itself accommodated within what was the mill's gassing room. Across the road is the

Alexandra Mill dating from the 1860s; this has traditionally been a woollen mill producing flannels in particular, a product for which the area has been famous even though shawl-making rivalled it during the late 19th century. This southern half of the village was largely owned by the Shaw family, who lived at St. Chad's close to what are now the village playing fields. This house occupies the site of a farm called Upper Mill, dating from the time when it and the corn mill were the only buildings in the valley bottom, although the farmhouse was rebuilt in 1798 as a Georgian house and then 'Victorianised' to a Gothic style in the 1840s. During the Victorian era St. Chad's was occupied by the prominent local architect George Shaw, who also took the opportunity to erect a small chapel alongside the house.

The northern half of the village belonged to the Buckley family during the first half of the 19th century, their residence being then known as the Manor House (after the manor of Saddleworth was disposed of in 1791 to numerous freeholders who designated themselves 'Lords of the Manor'); in more recent years, however, this property has become the Conservative Club. Uppermill's relative importance in the Saddleworth area is also evident from the fact that it has its own Civic Hall, erected in 1859 as the Mechanics' Institute which itself replaced an earlier Institute built in 1841.

Just about a mile to the east of Uppermill is Saddleworth Church, sitting prettily on the slopes of the valley above the rest of the village. The present church, dedicated to St. Chad, is a largely Victorian building, although there is evidence to suggest that as a place of worship this site dates back to at least the 12th century. It is hardly surprising, then, that the hamlet of Saddleworth Fold close by is probably one of the oldest settlement sites in the area. The word 'fold' essentially means a group of cottages, and these hillside hamlets grew up as descendants of the original landholders built cottages for themselves adjacent to the parental homestead, possibly as a result of the system of 'gravelkind' whereby land was divided between the male children.

On our way northwards to Dobcross from Uppermill we pass the Brownhill Visitor Centre, housed within a converted highways depot. High above the building is the viaduct carrying the main line of the former London and North Western Railway from Manchester to Huddersfield; completed in 1849 the line follows the course of the River Tame up to this point before heading on through the Diggle Valley. The growth of **Dobcross** as a

*Saddleworth Fold near Uppermill*

*The Square, Dobcross*

compact hillside village situated just to the north west of here dates largely from the construction of a new bridge over the River Tame in 1756, although the road through the village was not turnpiked until 1795. The erection of the bridge and the improvement of the road prompted the building of new houses, pubs and shops along Woods Lane from the latter part of the 18th century onwards, filling in some of the gaps between the earlier farmhouses and creating a more recognisable village settlement.

One of the oldest industrial sites in the vicinity is Walk Mill at the lower end of Woods Lane, the name being derived from the way that wool was 'walked' or trodden in the fulling process prior to the introduction of mechanical fulling stocks. Walk Mill was probably the earliest fulling mill in Saddleworth, having a considerable monopoly on the finishing of locally-made cloth — the size of the business here can be gauged from the fact that in 1792 there were 36,637 pieces of wool cloth produced in the Saddleworth district, each having a value of £7, and that a total of 1,480,000 lbs. of wool was used in their manufacture. Just up Woods Lane as it makes its way to the centre of Dobcross is Holy Trinity Church, the oldest church building still in use in Saddleworth. Built in 1787 in a simple 'preaching house' style, the cost of the building was met by local subscription — with the main donors being the merchants and tradesmen of this growing commercial district. Woods Lane continues on into the centre of Dobcross, bringing us to The Square with its shops, pub and one-time bank.

From The Square Platt Lane heads northwards along the contours of the Dobcross slopes before dropping down into

the village of **Delph,** stretched out along the banks of the River Tame. In many respects the development of Docross is paralleled by that of Delph, which was also largely a product of the Industrial Revolution and which only began to experience any significant growth during the early part of the 19th century. The name 'Delph' comes from the Old English word 'delf' meaning a quarry, and as such it is obviously related to the bakestone quarries which lay at the lower end of the Castleshaw valley just to the north of the village, although this does not adequately explain how the village grew up.

Perhaps the most important stimulus in Delph's expansion was the way in which most

of the land upon which the village was eventually built was sold off from the 1760s onwards, following on from the improvement of the old road crossing the river here and the consequent growth of road traffic. Although very much a creation of the Industrial Revolution Delph's expression of this radical development in the English economy is a thoroughly delightful one, reflecting the comparatively humane scale of the domestic woollen industry. Many of the village streets are lined with the characteristic three storey handloom weavers' cottages, often featuring a former 'takin-in' door on their top floors. This traditional means of access into the 'loom shop' or work room did away with the need to pass through the domestic quarters of the dwelling when raw material or woven cloth was being carried in or out.

In Delph, too, one can discover some interesting early mills, with Shore Mill along the riverside being a particularly good example. This three storey stone building has the mullioned windows characteristic of a weavers' dwelling but was in fact built as a water powered mill during the early 1780s; it is thus an 'embryo' factory whilst still retaining the vernacular style of architecture in its external appearance. Shore Mill's main function seems to have been the process of 'willeying', involving the carding of raw wool in order to prepare it for spinning.

Immediately to the north of Delph on the south-facing hill slopes is the hamlet of **Heights,** commanding good views of the surrounding countryside. A three storey house with its long lines of mullioned windows is evidence of the former domestic woollen industry which existed in these parts, while the nearby St. Thomas' Church together with the pub opposite are indicative

*Shore Mill, Delph*

of the larger population which once inhabited the area. To the east of here is the Castleshaw valley and the site of a Roman fort, situated along what was then the road between Manchester and York, while to the north is the small village of **Denshaw.** Like the other settlements of Saddleworth this village displays some interesting facets of the local woollen industry, from traditional weavers' cottages to early mills specialising in specific aspects of cloth manufacture.

The Denshaw area was part of the Friarmere division of Saddleworth, in which the land belonged to the Cistercian monks of Roche Abbey near Rotherham until the Dissolution, after which it eventually passed into the hands of the Gartside family who lived at the ancient settlement of Denshaw Fold. Descendants of the original Gartsides later built several of the farmsteads on the nearby hillsides, and the family continued to be important in the local economy well into the 19th century with Henry Gartside being rich enough to pay for the building of Denshaw Church in the 1860s.

If the Saddleworth district offers us some exceptionally fine insights into the development of the domestic woollen industry, then **Oldham** itself portrays the full glory of the Lancashire cotton trade. Above all else Oldham gives us a very good perspective of one of the county's best known features in terms of its physical and economic make-up — the cotton mill. During the latter half of the 19th century Oldham became the world's leading mill town, consuming more raw cotton and spinning more yarn than any other single centre of the cotton industry. Reinforcing its supremacy in cotton spinning was the fact that it also became the focal point for the manufacture of textile machinery, giving it a very considerable advantage over other cotton towns.

Even though Oldham played only a relatively minor role during the formative years of the Industrial Revolution it had certainly made up for this by the end of the 19th century, when it was finally being recognised as 'the heart of the cotton world'. This achievement was all the more remarkable considering its disadvantages as a hill town without either a river or any visible natural resources, being located a considerable distance from the raw cotton market in Liverpool and rather unfavourably positioned for connections to the canal and railway networks.

Yet Oldham did have some advantages in terms of its reserves of coal, a high level of humidity and its proximity to the two great factory regions of the West Riding and East Lancashire, as well as its closeness to the world's greatest yarn market at the Royal Exchange in Manchester. In addition it had the benefit of a local pattern of industrial organisation which facilitated the establishment and growth of new manufacturing businesses, enhanced by the availability of cheap land for the construction of mills. Oldham was also rather more successful in its response to crises within the cotton industry, meeting the challenge of the Cotton Famine better than any other manufacturing centre by becoming the most pro-Southern town in Lancashire and a strong supporter of the Confederacy because of its almost complete dependence upon the supply of American cotton.

Oldham also became the first Lancashire town to use Indian cotton in place of the American product, with the result that it not only survived the crisis but actively extended its productive capacity. The consequence of all this was that by 1866 Oldham had acquired more spindles than any other town in the world, surpassing both Manchester and Bolton in spindleage. Then over the next five years the number of spindles in Oldham was doubled to six million, giving the town the enviable reputation of having more spindles than any other country in the world with the exception of the United States of America — a position of supremacy which it held until 1937.

As the world market continued to expand so the number of cotton mills in Oldham increased, rising from 120 in 1866 to 320 by the end of the First World War. The result of all this was a quite remarkable impact upon the Oldham landscape, with the mills and their chimneys standing shoulder to shoulder against the horizon. One observer commented that the 'brick houses and shops go on forever, and at the back of them, blotting out all the rest of the world, rise great precipitous mills like frowning cliffs, at whose base are the small houses where the folks live like coneys at a mountain foot'.

Traditionally the Oldham mill was a five storey brick building with a warehouse and conditioning room in the cellar, together with an engine room which transmitted power to each floor by means of a rope race. In order to ensure that the structure was fireproof iron was used instead of wood for the main structural beams, with the invention of water sprinkler systems giving rise to the introduction of a water tower above the mill's external staircase. Hardwood flooring was another common feature, not only helping to maintain an even temperature but also permitting work in bare feet as well as making the recovery of waste cotton easier.

Externally the mills were made of brick rather than the more expensive stone, the bricks initially being made on site from the abundant local clay but then later supplied by specialist brick-makers. Approximately four million bricks were required for the construction of a relatively modern cotton mill, together with

*Oldham Parish Church*

*The Bridgewater Canal at Worsley*

*Barrow Bridge near Bolton*

*Foxdenton Hall, Chadderton*

two acres of glass and 2,200 tons of iron and steel. By the start of the 20th century mill architecture had become quite a refined art, paving the way for Oldham's massive 100,000-spindle mills to become Lancashire's dominant visual image.

Oldham had reached the peak of its importance in the world of cotton by 1890, by which time it was consuming one quarter of the imported raw material to this country. As well as becoming Liverpool's single largest customer it had also become the best example of a purely manufacturing town and the focus of the country's export industry. By the time of the First World War, however, overseas competition was beginning to curb the expansion of the British cotton industry, and in 1915 the Oldham Master Cotton Spinners' Association recorded the first decrease in spindles in the history of the Association since its foundation in 1866. After the War the slump within the cotton trade proved worse than expected, bringing in the long-term decline of the cotton industry. This seems to have resulted from the trade's traditional export markets equipping themselves with Lancashire-built machinery so as to capture their own home business. As the cotton industry in Oldham declined so its remarkable townscape was eroded, and between 1926 and 1976 180 of its 320 mills were demolished.

The success which Oldham enjoyed as a centre of the cotton industry also spread to a number of the outlying settlements, particularly the village of **Shaw** just to the north. With the benefit of advantages such as a good water supply, plentiful reserves of coal and a highly skilled labour force Shaw prospered as Oldham's entrepreneurs searched for cheaper and lower-lying land in their hunger to build more cotton mills. As a result it achieved a reputation as the 'richest little town in the country' and was home to some of the industry's most dynamic leaders. **Failsworth** to the south of Oldham also grew rapidly through the expansion of the

cotton trade, its first mill opening in 1834 and then being followed quickly by a succession of others. This was similarly the experience of Chadderton to the west of Oldham, where from the 1850s onwards cotton became of prime importance as the cotton mills and their associated engineering activities provided the

major source of employment. In 1844 there was just one cotton spinning mill and one flax mill here, but by 1914 there were over fifty cotton mills in the district.

The town of **Middleton** to the west of Chadderton also grew significantly as a result of the cotton industry, and by the middle of the 19th century it had been transformed from a small market town to a significant manufacturing centre with a population of about 8,500. The spinning, weaving, bleaching and printing of cotton were all carried out here, although in the earlier part of the 1800s silk weaving had been the dominant textile activity. Prior to this time Middleton was also well known for its clockmaking trade, and in the middle of the 18th century there were at least four well-qualified clockmakers working here out of a population of less than one hundred.

Middleton's history goes back much further than the textile or clockmaking trade, however, and although it is not mentioned in the Domesday Book its name suggests a Saxon origin. Despite the fact that the

*St. Leonard's Parish Church, Middleton*

Industrial Revolution brought about considerable changes in Middleton's townscape through the demolition of older timber-framed buildings and their replacement by new mills and shops, some of its earlier properties have survived to give us an insight into its original appearance. Among these are the Parish Church of St. Leonard, parts of which date back to the first half of the 12th century.

Prominently situated on a hill above the town centre St. Leonard's has connections with Cardinal Langley, a one-time Bishop of Durham and Lord Chancellor of England, who rebuilt the church in the early 15th century. It was rebuilt again in 1524 as a thank-offering for the victory at Flodden Field, and then in 1709 the peculiar wooden structure on top of the tower was added to the building. Other interesting features in the church include some rare monumental brasses of the Assheton family, one of the finest collections of brasses of any church in Lancashire, together with a stained glass window portraying Middleton archers at the Battle of Flodden Field and reputed to be the oldest war memorial in the country. Then there is the church clock, dating from 1807 and among the oldest in the Manchester area.

The Parish Church has also had important links with the local grammar school, which dates back to the 15th century when it was one of the very few such educational establishments in Lancashire as a whole. The school was later rebuilt in 1586 following an endowment from Brasennose College in Oxford, the new building being situated within a few hundred yards of the church and looked after by masters who were usually curates of St. Leonard's. Although the grammar school was built of local sandstone with millstone dressings, Middleton also has a small number of 'black and white' half-timbered buildings still surviving within the town — one of these is Ye Olde Boar's Head pub on Long Street, close to the Parish Church, whilst the other is Tonge Hall to the south east of the town centre.

Centuries ago Middleton may well have been part of the parish of **Prestwich** further to the west since the name 'Prestwich' is Saxon in origin and means a 'Priest's Retreat', suggesting that a church or monastery may have existed here even before the Norman Conquest. Certainly the parish presided over by St. Mary's Church was one of the most extensive in Lancashire during the 12th and 13th centuries, encompassing not only Prestwich but also Oldham, Hollinwood, Royton, Chadderton and Crompton as well as probably Bury, Radcliffe and Middleton. St. Mary's itself seems to date in its present form from about 1450, although a church had existed on the site long before that time. It was largely around the church that the settlement of Prestwich became established,

*Ye Olde Boar's Head, Middleton*

and although the present Church Inn dates back to the 18th century it was in the early part of the 17th century that the first hostelry was built here. Another cluster of cottages grew up in the area known as Great and Little Heaton, and during the early part of the 18th century Prestwich consisted primarily of these two centres together with a few outlying farms.

By the middle of the 18th century, however, Prestwich was beginning to change as farming gradually gave way to textiles as the most important occupation, with wool, fustian and silk becoming the main local products. Prestwich also increasingly became an attractive residential location for Manchester's wealthy merchants, and the large houses in the area are evidence of this trend which continued into the 19th century — by 1883 it was being noted that Prestwich 'contains a great number of genteel residences, principally occupied by Manchester merchants'. Local industry continued to expand and diversify, so much so that by the middle of the 1800s it included dyeing, bleaching and block-printing, together with broadloom weaving in many of

the individual cottages. All this was assisted and accompanied by the growth in communications, with Bury New Road being completed in 1826 and the Manchester to Radcliffe railway line being opened in 1879.

If Prestwich became the favoured location for Manchester's 'nouveau riche' merchant class during the first half of the 19th century, it was probably helped by the fact that it had already become home for one of the region's best-known aristocratic families. The Egerton family of Cheshire had acquired the Heaton settlements in the 17th century, and it was they who first started Heaton Hall in 1750. The present building dates largely from 1772, when James Wyatt carried out major additions and alterations for Sir Thomas Egerton to produce what is now acknowledged as one of the finest late 18th century houses in the North West. Designed in an impressive Classical style worthy of the Egertons' position in society the house also features some excellent plasterwork as well as a collection of 18th century furniture and paintings, and is set in the midst of extensive parkland which provides an appropriate backcloth for this architectural gem.

*Heaton Hall, Prestwich*

*The Bridgewater Canal and the Packet House, Worsley*

The name Egerton also figures significantly in the development of **Worsley** further to the west, a very attractive and popular residential area just beyond neighbouring Pendlebury and Swinton. The land here was held by the de Worsley family from just after the Norman Conquest until the latter part of the 14th century, when it eventually passed by marriage to a branch of the Egerton family. By the end of the 16th century ownership of the Worsley estate was in the hands of Thomas Egerton, who became a Chancellor of England, although it was his son John who became the Earl of Bridgewater, with a later earl being created the first Duke of Bridgewater in 1720. However, it was left up to Francis Egerton, the third Duke of Bridgewater, to make the biggest impact upon this inheritance through the construction of the Bridgewater Canal from Worsley to Manchester, an innovative project which ushered in the Canal Age.

Worsley Old Hall was the centre of the Duke's operations, although he had another Hall (known as The Brick Hall) built just to the south as his own residence. Following the Duke's death in 1803 the Worsley estate was administered by trustees before eventually passing to the Marquis of Stafford's second son Francis Leveson-Gower. In accordance with the third Duke's will Lord Francis took the name of Egerton, quickly making his own mark in the area through various philanthropic acts, and in 1846 he was made Earl of Ellesmere. The estate then continued in the ownership of the Earls of Ellesmere until 1923, when the land was sold to Bridgewater Estates Ltd.

The source of the third Duke of Bridgewater's wealth was the vast deposit of coal beneath his land in Worsley, and the Bridgewater Canal was constructed to enable him to exploit this resource. The value of his coal mines here was greatly reduced, however, by the high cost of transporting the coal and the fact that flooding became a significant problem as the shafts were dug deeper. By 1735 it had become necessary to start a sough or culvert to drain water from the Duke's mines to Worsley Brook near The Delph (originally the site of a stone quarry), and at the same time a canal was proposed as a cheap means of carrying the coal away from the workings. The result was a network of underground canals extending for 46 miles from two entrances at the foot of a steep rockface in The Delph.

With the problem of flooding dealt with the Duke then turned his attention to reducing the cost of transporting his coal, his solution being the construction of the Bridgewater Canal from his mines in Worsley to the industrial marketplace in Manchester. By 1765 this length was completed, reducing the cost of transporting coal by half. The obvious commercial success of the Bridgewater Canal inspired the construction of other canals throughout the country, facilitating the onset of the Industrial Revolution. Even before the stretch from Worsley to Manchester was completed the Duke of Bridgewater was preparing to build an extension from Stretford to the Mersey estuary at Runcorn, and by 1776 this too was open to traffic rivalling the Mersey and Irwell Navigation from Warrington to Manchester.

One of the interesting features of the canal is the way it was constructed on one level (at 82 feet above sea level) and totally free from locks except for where it descends to meet the Mersey at Runcorn. Another feature, and one which came to be regarded as one of the engineering wonders of the age, is the aqueduct at Barton near Eccles which conveyed the canal over the Irwell at a height of 38 feet above the river. This 'tour de force' of making water pass above water was a personal triumph for the Duke of Bridgewater's engineer, James Brindley, and one which particularly caught the public's imagination.

Looking at Worsley now one can hardly imagine that such a pretty place was once a busy industrial centre, full of workshops and warehouses which were stimulated by the construction of the canal and by the Duke of Bridgewater's various enterprises. Yet within Worsley's green and pleasant environment there are one or two tell-tale signs which point to its important industrial heritage — for example, the unusual rust-brown colour of the water in the canal is due to iron

*Worsley Old Hall*

compounds leached from the sandstone rock above the tunnels of the underground mines, while the attractive brick fountain on Worsley Green is actually converted from the base of a former chimney which bears an inscription in Latin verse commemorating the work of the third Duke. Then, too, there is the 18th century Packet House (with its 'black and white' frontage added in Victorian times) which stands imposingly at the head of the canal and from where passengers boarded barges heading into Manchester, while a little further along the canal are the dry docks built in the 18th century for the Duke of Bridgewater's own boats and still used for the repair of present-day barges.

If the third Duke of Bridgewater's contribution to Worsley was the canal and its associated activities, then his eventual successor Lord Francis Leveson-Gower (the first Earl of Ellesmere) was to make his mark through the erection of a number of impressive public buildings. The most important of these was St. Mark's Church, sited on the higher ground of Worsley Brow and completed in 1846. Its elevated position is enhanced by the building's tall spire, part and parcel of the imposing Gothic Revival style which was adopted by the architect Sir George Gilbert Scott. Externally the church is adorned by gargoyles and crockets, while internally it features pulpit and organ screens (decorated with 16th and 17th century panels from Flanders and France) as well as the Earl of Ellesmere's impressive tomb.

Close to the church is one of the entrances into the lovely Worsley woods, owned initially by the third Duke of Bridgewater but then later by the first Earl of Ellesmere who was the one responsible for the planting of trees here as well as the creation of a network of footpaths. The Earl of Ellesmere also constructed Old Warke Dam to produce a large artificial lake for fishing and boating, with the building known as 'The Aviary' being erected at the same time for use as a fishing and shooting lodge.

Although much of present-day Worsley reflects the contribution made by the Dukes of Bridgewater and their descendants there are nevertheless a number of buildings which pre-date their impact on the area. One of these is Worsley Old Hall, itself a former home of the Dukes of Bridgewater but dating from the Elizabethan period. At the south east corner one can still find a surviving fragment of the original timber-framed house, although most of the present Old Hall is the result of rebuilding work during the 19th century. Another notable building in the area is Wardley Hall, dating from the early part of the 16th century when it was a timber-framed house with an inner courtyard and a moat. Parts of this original building still remain in what is now the official residence of the Roman Catholic Bishop of Salford, together

with the brick north range and gatehouse of 1652.

Not content with connections from Worsley through to Manchester and the Mersey the Duke of Bridgewater's canal-building inspirations continued to preoccupy him during the latter part of the 18th century, with the result being an extension of the Bridgewater Canal westwards to Leigh. Originally there was only a short stretch feeding water to the Worsley-Manchester branch from Chat Moss, then a vast undrained peat bog, but by authority of an Act of Parliament of 1795 the canal was extended until in 1812 it was linked to a branch of the Leeds and Liverpool Canal at a point just to the south of Leigh. En route from Worsley to Leigh the canal passes **Tyldesley,** a settlement originating during Saxon times but which only rose to prominence during the period of the Industrial Revolution when coal mining and cotton spinning were the main activities here. Coal mining was also an important part of the local economy in the adjoining village of **Astley,** although many of the inhabitants were employed as fustian weavers.

**Leigh,** too, looks back to the Industrial Revolution as the time when its own development was considerably accelerated, although as early as the 15th century coal pits were being worked in the district with silk weaving being carried out as a local cottage industry during the reign of Elizabeth I. At the same time Leigh also became established as a thriving market town serving the surrounding farming community. However, construction of the canal towards the end of the 18th century was to prove significant in

Leigh's growth as an industrial centre, this new mode of transport providing improved access to new markets for locally mined coal as well as for the increasing products of the town's mills. This process of industrial expansion was further accelerated during the 19th century by the coming of the railways, with the country's first passenger line between Manchester and Liverpool being routed just to the south of the town.

One of the most attractive and enduring consequences of Leigh's industrial growth has been the creation of its distinctive and complex skyline, which now constitutes a prominent feature of the South Lancashire plain (particularly when seen from the East Lancashire Road). The most significant component in Leigh's skyline is the concentration of tall mill buildings with their ornate towers and chimneys, followed by the pit head gear and chimneys of local collieries as well as by numerous church towers. Among the latter is the tower belonging to the Parish Church of St. Mary the Virgin, a building which dates back to mediaeval times although its original foundation was probably much earlier.

Constructed of stone with an embattled clerestorey along its full length from east to west the church was completely rebuilt in 1873 except for its tower, which dates largely from the 15th century although it has since been refaced and strengthened. Features of interest inside the church include a finely carved Jacobean chair in the south chapel, an interesting brass in the north aisle marking the grave of Henry Travice (across which forty poor people would step every year on Maundy Thursday to qualify for his bequest),

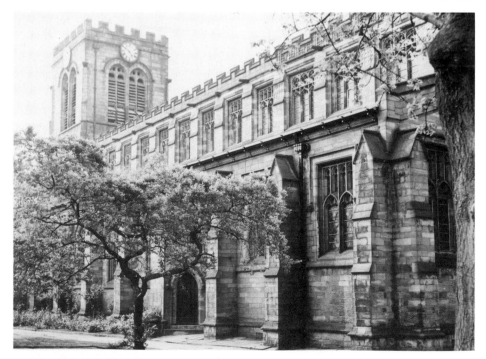

*St. Mary's Parish Church, Leigh*

and a richly carved oak reredos in the chancel.

It was in this parish church that the famous Richard Arkwright was married to Margaret Mullens in 1761, and it was his later inventions which led to a radical transformation of cotton spinning (paving the way for the development of the Lancashire cotton industry) and which drew upon some of the ideas being generated by people working here in Leigh. When Edward Baines wrote in 1825 that Leigh was 'entitled to rank high in the manufacturing annals of Lancashire. It was here that the era of improvements opened', he was probably referring to the fact that one of the first spinning jennies was made in the town in 1763, as was the first water-frame in 1767.

The canal which brought us to Leigh now takes us on to the town of **Wigan,** situated just a few miles to the north west. When Celia Fiennes visited Wigan at the end of the 17th century as part of her grand tour around England she described it as a 'pretty market town built of stone and brick', a description which is still remarkably appropriate even today despite the considerable industrial development which has taken place here during the course of the last two centuries. One of the reasons for this is that much of the town centre was rebuilt between 1865 and 1905, endowing Wigan with some impressive Victorian and Edwardian properties in distinctive red brick, stone and terracotta, while another is the fact that during the 1920s many buildings were re-fronted in an imitation 'black and white' Tudor style to re-create a market town atmosphere.

During the mediaeval period Wigan really was the market town which its present-day architecture still lays claim to, and at that time it served a considerable area of South Lancashire; it had also developed as one of the four most important boroughs in the county, ranking equal to Liverpool, Lancaster and Preston. By 1635, however, it had become the wealthiest of all four, paying Ship Money Tax of £50 compared with £25, £30 and £40 for the others. At that time these were the only towns in Lancashire able to send representatives to Parliament.

Wigan's earliest history, however, goes back to the Roman period when a fort known as Coccium was established here on the route of the Roman road from Chester to Lancaster. After the Romans had withdrawn the area was successively occupied by Celts, Anglo-Saxons and Norsemen before it eventually passed into Norman hands following the Norman Conquest. It was then part of the Hundred of Newton, with the rector of the parish church acting as lord of the manor under the lord of Newton.

As Wigan's trade and prosperity developed

*Wigan Parish Church and War Memorial*

during the early part of the mediaeval period so its importance began to be recognised on a wider level, and in 1246 it was made a Royal Borough by virtue of a charter granted by Henry III. This gave the burgesses or freemen of Wigan certain rights and privileges, such as the right to feed their pigs on the common land and exemption from market tolls as well as the right to form merchant guilds and to elect a common council of a mayor, aldermen, bailiffs and clerks. They were, however, still required to grind their corn at the rector's mills and bake their bread in his oven, although as the centuries passed so the burgesses became increasingly wealthy and gradually replaced the rector as the main source of power in the town. By the late 17th century most of the rector's manorial rights had already been taken over by the Corporation, although it was not until 1860 that this process was finally completed.

During the Middle Ages Wigan not only prospered as a market town but also developed as an early industrial centre, with brewing and tanning taking place here as well as the production of felt hats, linen and woollen textiles. Wigan's textile industry in particular became well-established over the course of the next few centuries, and by 1788

it was being stated that 'very considerable quantities of linens, checks, calicoes, fustians, etc.' were manufactured here, while in 1795 it was recorded that Wigan checks were 'in much estimation, nor have they lost their superiority over those of Manchester'. It is hardly surprising, then, that by the start of the 19th century Wigan had finally freed itself from the shackles of a feudal society dominated by the lord of the manor to become one of the more important manufacturing centres outside London.

As well as its textiles Wigan was also famous for its coal, with the earliest extractions being made in 1450. By the 17th century 'cannel' coal from the area was not only known throughout the country but also exported to America, and during this period there were at least twelve commercial collieries operating within five miles of Wigan. Then in 1771 Nathaniel Spencer wrote in his book 'The Complete English Traveller' that 'coals are in great plenty here...the coal dug up in the centre of the town is perhaps the best in the universe'. Spencer also noted that there were 'many forges for the making of iron', while an account of 1788 stated that 'the braziery, pewtery, brass foundry and iron forgery business find employment for great numbers'.

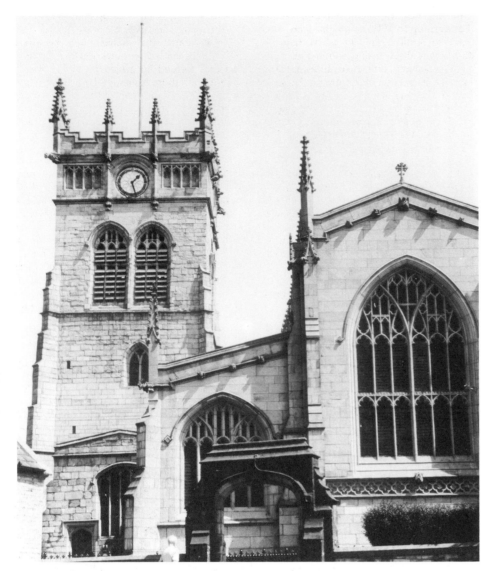

*The Parish Church of All Saints, Wigan*

people, while in 1863 there were 48 colliery companies in the Wigan area producing nearly four million tons of coal each year.

The manufacture of iron and steel was also significant in Wigan during the 19th century, with the first centre of iron smelting being at Haigh where furnaces using local ore operated from 1789 to 1815. Then in 1858 the Kirklees Hall Colliery Company opened an iron smelting works with the original intention of finding a profitable way to use the slack from its collieries; steel production began somewhat later in 1888. Between the First and Second World Wars, however, Wigan's traditional industries experienced a sharp decline, and although some of the larger textile conglomerates still maintain a strong presence in the area iron, steel and coal have virtually disappeared from the Wigan scene.

An appropriate place to begin a tour of inspection around Wigan town centre is at the Parish Church of All Saints, a building which dominates the town in both a physical and historical sense. First mentioned in 1199, All Saints is usually taken to be the Parish Church of Newton referred to in the Domesday Book, although the oldest part of the present building is the lower section of the tower which dates from the 13th century. The tower as a whole was remodelled in the 15th century and then heightened with pairs of windows and a pinnacled parapet in 1861, this latter work following on from the substantial rebuilding of the body of the church as a faithful copy of the 15th century Perpendicular Gothic church during the Victorian period. Architectural features typical of the Gothic style which are to be seen on the building include its shallow pointed arched windows divided by stone mullions, the upper level clerestory windows and carved gargoyles in the form of ghoulish heads or dragons. Features of particular interest inside the church include the timbers of the nave and aisle roofs (probably dating from the 15th century), the tiers of heavily carved stalls for the Mayor and Corporation, the effigies of Sir William and Lady Mabel de Bradshaigh in the south chapel, and the 13th century window and Roman altar which are built into the tower.

Immediately to the west of the Parish Church is Wigan's original Bluecoat School dating from 1773, a building which bears a cottage-like appearance by virtue of its stone-mullioned windows and dripstones over the window and door openings. Close by is an oasis of greenery known as Church Gardens, bounded on their northern side by the Magistrates Court and Crown Courts. These buildings were designed in an attractive 'Elizabethan' style during the latter part of the 19th century, and their chimney stacks, gables, stone finials and roof treatments combine to form one of the town's most

Bell founding and watchmaking were also important local industries during this period. Perhaps less well known is the fact that pottery flourished in Wigan during the 17th and 18th centuries, and that John Dwight (the founder of the English porcelain industry) lived in Wigan from 1662 to 1687. During this period he took out patents for a 'transparent porcellane and opacous redd and dark coloured porcellane', using local clays in his experiments. Another little-known fact is that Wigan was recognised as a medicinal spa town during the late 18th and early 19th centuries, until the springs of chalybeate waters became polluted by coal workings.

With such a solid foundation it was not surprising that Wigan's industry should go from strength to strength with the creation of the canal and railway networks from the latter half of the 18th century onwards. One of the first developments was the Leeds and Liverpool Canal, the section between Liverpool and Wigan being completed in

1777; then in the early part of the 19th century a connection was made to the Bridgewater Canal by a cut linking Wigan and Leigh. Railways, too, had a significant impact on the area, and Wigan was very much in the forefront of railway progress — with a large number of passenger lines as well as numerous mineral lines to individual collieries Wigan probably had one of the densest railway networks in the world.

The steam power which was behind the success of the railways also exerted a considerable effect on the nature and location of Wigan's industry, destroying the domestic textile industry and paving the way for the concentration of large mills in urban locations. The result of these changes in Wigan was the growth of its larger industries such as coal mining, cotton spinning and iron founding, together with a very considerable increase in its population from 11,000 in 1801 to almost 61,000 a century later. At the peak of the cotton industry there were 26 spinning and weaving mills in the town employing 11,000

*Wigan's Bluecoat School*

dramatic rooflines. On the opposite side of the church from here can be found an impressive War Memorial designed by Sir Giles Gilbert Scott in 1925, its intricate Gothic details harmonising nicely with similar decorative features on the church itself.

From this point a narrow alleyway takes us eastwards into the Market Place, which with the Parish Church constituted the core of the mediaeval town. The Market Place also formed the crossing point of Wigan's four main streets during this period — Wallgate, Standishgate, Millgate and Hallgate — all of which have continued into the present-day. During mediaeval times the Market Place was the focal point for the town's growth and prosperity, with markets being held here regularly from 1323 onwards. It was also the location of the market cross, the town stocks, a whipping post and the Moot Hall; this latter building dated from the 15th century and was the seat of local government as well as housing the borough treasury and various courts. During the latter part of the 19th century the Moot Hall itself was replaced by the Moot Hall Chambers, built to a French Renaissance style with oriel and Venetian windows. As well as being a traditional centre of commerce and administration the Market Place was also known for its public houses, and out of a total of 110 inns which were to be found in Wigan as a whole in 1869 ten were situated here.

Leading off the Market Place on its eastern side is a narrow alleyway known as The Wiend, a mediaeval thoroughfare which takes us past a row of 17th century cottages (now in use as shops) before bringing us to the thoroughly modern Wiend Centre. During the 19th century The Wiend gave access to Moore's Yard, a typical courtyard of the period crowded with back-to-back houses providing accommodation for 42 families as well as for a wide range of manufacturing trades. One of these trades was clog making, which so flourished in Wigan during the late 19th and early 20th centuries that by 1909 there were 63 cloggers recorded in the town.

Clogs were generally made with leather uppers and thick wooden soles of alder finished off with protective 'irons', a distinctive type of footwear which also resulted in a

distinctive pastime — clog fighting. It seems that even up to 1900 clog fights were often used to settle relatively trivial quarrels. Apparently those taking part in such fights were sometimes completely nude apart from their clogs, with women forming the larger part of their audience! The Wigan Master Cloggers Association met in a building on nearby Coopers Row, another narrow mediaeval street running off the Market Place and paved with setts.

At the northern end of the Market Place is the entrance to the elaborate Makinson Arcade, built in 1897 of brick and terracotta with French and English Renaissance features. These features are also to be seen on several of the buildings lining Standishgate further to the north, particularly the National Westminster Bank with its rich carvings in local sandstone. Another characteristic architectural treatment to be observed on numerous Standishgate properties are the

'black and white' Tudor style frontages displaying white plaster panels, gables with large boards and details such as carved brackets, leaded windows and overhanging jetties formed by projecting upper floors. Although these frontages date mainly from the 1920s they are somewhat reminiscent of mediaeval times when Standishgate was home to some of the town's wealthiest burgesses.

Millgate (running off the southern end of Standishgate) was also a popular residential street for Wigan's burgesses during the 17th and 18th centuries, and at its lower end is a fine Georgian town house with an elaborate door surround made up of a heavy triangular pediment supported by Ionic columns. Millgate's continuing importance during the Victorian period is evident from the former 'Raffles' establishment close to its junction with Standishgate — this building was known as the Ship Inn until quite recently and

*Makinson Arcade, Wigan Market Place*

features a fine Victorian interior with rich woodwork, ceiling panels and a tiled entrance. Ship Yard at the side harks back to the time when sea-going vessels from the Ribble Estuary could make their way up to Wigan along the River Douglas.

Over on the opposite side of the Market Place from this point is Hallgate, another of Wigan's main mediaeval streets and the one which provided a direct link from the Manor House and Rectory (known as Wigan Hall) to the Parish Church. The original Hall was probably moated and included a Moot Court and Gaol before the Moot Hall at the Market Place was built during the 15th century. For much of the town's early history the Rectors had considerable influence over Wigan's affairs in their role as lords of the manor, although this influence gradually waned as the burgesses and Corporation became increasingly powerful.

Wigan's other main mediaeval street was Wallgate, which can be followed southwards from the Market Place down to Wigan Pier Heritage Centre alongside the Leeds and Liverpool Canal. Running south-eastwards from the top end of Wallgate is Library Street, lined with a number of impressive civic buildings from the late Victorian and early Edwardian periods. Of particular interest is the Wigan Mining and Technical College at the lower end of Library Street, constructed of red brick and terracotta in a heavy Flemish Baroque style. This is certainly one of the town's most imposing civic buildings, marked by large gables and an impressive main entrance as well as by four massive cupolas over the 'lookout' turrets at roof level. Such architectural grandeur is really quite appropriate given that Wigan was one of the leading mining centres in the country, with over 1,000 coal shafts having been sunk within five miles of the town centre and over 750 million tons of coal extracted. Originating as the Wigan Mining and Mechanical School of 1857 this is the second oldest School of Mines in the country, although it is now being refurbished for use as Wigan's new Town Hall. Further down Library Street is the town's Central Library, designed in a Gothic style during the latter part of the 19th century by Alfred Waterhouse.

Running parallel to Library Street from a point further southwards along Wallgate is King Street, laid out in 1791 as Wigan's first planned civic thoroughfare and one which had developed as the town's major entertainment centre by the early part of the 20th century. Here were to be found not only the Palace, Theatre Royal and Hippodrome but also the Royal Court Theatre, the Court Ballroom, the Public Hall and the County Playhouse. Included among the variety of architectural styles to be seen along this street are the Italian Renaissance Palazzo designs of the Town Hall and Borough Courts as well as

the commercial Gothic style of the Victoria Buildings.

Wallgate itself also displays a similar range of architectural styles, from the Grand Manner or Edwardian Baroque of the Raven Hotel to the rather simpler Georgian architecture of the Bees Knees public house. The former is notable for its rounded pediment and sculptured tympanum, while the latter displays a characteristic arched doorway with Tuscan columns. The Italian Renaissance Palazzo style is also well represented on Wallgate, particularly by the town's Head Post Office (dating from 1884) and two nearby bank buildings. Wallgate's mediaeval origins are also not to be overlooked, and a narrow alleyway just across from the Head Post Office leads into the small enclosed space known as Rowbottom Square which is typically mediaeval in character.

Further down Wallgate are a number of significant buildings relating to the town's railway era, with the most prominent being Wallgate Station. The present building dates from 1896 — replacing an earlier one opened by the Lancashire and Yorkshire Railway Company in 1848 — and the main features of interest are its large cast-iron and glass canopy (providing shelter for horsedrawn carriages) together with some graceful arched openings and the use of red sandstone brought from Liverpool by rail. Close to Wallgate Station is the Victoria Hotel with its highly decorative frontage, whilst next door is Poole's Cafe bearing Wigan's best example of a Victorian shop front. Poole's Confectioners have been in business here for over a century, and their products may have contributed to the reputation which Wigan people have for

being 'pie-eaters'. Further along Wallgate again is the second of Wigan's railway stations, the more modern North Western Railway Station, but one which has its roots in the 1830s as being among the country's earliest railway establishments. Just across the road from here is Tower Buildings, designed in a Baroque style with an elaborate entrance canopy, while adjoining it is the Swan and Railway Hotel notable for its rounded oriel windows with 'Art Nouveau' terracotta details in the gables.

In many people's minds Wigan is remembered more for the music hall joke about its supposed Pier than for its history or architecture. Yet the funny thing is that Wigan Pier really does exist, having been recently restored as an important element of the Wigan Pier Heritage Centre which encompasses a fascinating group of canalside buildings situated at the lower end of Wallgate. The so-called 'Pier' was apparently a projecting landing stage alongside the canal, with a wagon 'tippler' which enabled coal to be transferred from colliery wagons into the waiting canal barges below.

As well as recent restoration work to the canal and towpaths one of the canalside buildings now houses an exhibition entitled 'The Way We Were', which captures in a thoroughly realistic fashion the atmosphere and life of Wigan in and around the year 1900. Here visitors are able to see just what it was like 'down the pit' at that time, to wander through the re-created tinsmith's shop and iron foundry, experience the life of the Pit Brow lasses and mill hands, sit in a restored Victorian pub and even attend a lesson in a reconstructed Victorian classroom. The other

*Wigan Pier and the Leeds-Liverpool Canal*

*Restored canalside warehouse at Wigan Pier*

*Haigh windmill*

restored warehouses on this fascinating site now provide accommodation for offices, a new pub and restaurant, a Tourist Board Information Centre, a souvenir shop and a study centre, while a few hundred yards away (and linked by a waterbus service operating on the canal) is Trencherfield Mill. This houses the world's largest working steam engine as well as a collection of historic textile machinery.

If Wigan's splendid industrial heritage is of no surprise, its remarkably fine landscape and range of natural habitats may well be. The ironic thing is that many of the area's outstanding ecological treasures are the indirect result of its earlier industrial development — ground subsidence from abandoned 19th and 20th century mineworkings has created extensive water areas and wetlands providing important habitats for resident and migrant birds, while rare plant species thrive on old pulverised fuel ash tips and the lime-rich slag heaps of abandoned iron and steel works. Among Wigan's three country parks is the Three Sisters Recreation Area at Ashton-in-Makerfield, created out of three giant colliery spoil heaps which reached a height of 50 metres; this now provides a location for karting and motorcycling as well as having links with the wildlife site of Wigan Flashes, where over 100 species of birds are recorded every year.

Another of the Borough's country parks is centred on Pennington Flash near Leigh, a large lake created by mining subsidence which is not only a major water sports facility but also a regionally-important bird watching centre. In winter especially hundreds of water species flock to the area, including herons and swans as well as grebes, Canada geese, shovelers and pochards. The third of Wigan's country parks is at Haigh just two miles to the north east of the town centre, where visitors can enjoy 250 acres of woods, gardens and rolling parkland linked together by nature trails and secluded walks. At the centre of this delightfully rural estate is Haigh Hall, an impressive stately house built of local stone between 1827 and 1840 for the Earls of Crawford. The air of tranquility which characterises this lovely country park is also a feature of Haigh village just to the east.

To the north of Haigh is the ridgetop settlement of **Blackrod** which enjoys some fine views of the surrounding countryside, particularly of the Rivington reservoirs further northwards from here. It was this elevated position which brought the area to the attention of the Romans, who probably built a fortification in this locality to guard the road between Manchester and Ribchester. Settlement continued even after the Romans left, although the earliest reference to a church dates back to 1338 when a small chantry was endowed here. The origins of the present parish church go back to the time of Elizabeth I, and although restoration and rebuilding work has been undertaken on

*Estate cottages, Haigh Hall*

*The Old Bell Tower, Arley Hall*

several occasions since then certain parts of the Elizabethan structure still remain, particularly at the base of the tower.

Another important building in the area is Arley Hall, a picturesque moated manor house situated on the site of an old abbey and now bounded by the Leeds and Liverpool Canal. According to local tradition there was an underground passage from Blackrod Church to the religious house which occupied the site, although from the time of the Reformation the building was used as a private residence with a new front being introduced in 1767. For much of its history Blackrod's main source of employment has been agriculture, its ridgetop location precluding any real response to the advent of the Industrial Revolution. However, coal was being extracted here as early as the 16th century, and by the end of the 19th century a significant proportion of the local workforce were employed as miners. Unfortunately the Depression put paid to this source of employment, and by 1938 the last mine had closed.

If Blackrod managed to remain somewhat aloof from the impact of industrialisation, the neighbouring township of **Horwich** was not so fortunate. The cause of this was the construction of the largest locomotive engineering works in the world, which took place here during the latter part of the 19th century. In the early 1800s Horwich was a stable community of 3,600 people employed mainly in weaving, bleaching and farming, but by 1909 the population had grown to 16,000 with the physical character of the town transformed by rows of terraced properties built to house those employed at the locomotive works. The Horwich workshops were built by the Lancashire and Yorkshire Railway Company in response to

the demand for more and better locomotives, and by the time the works were completed in 1888 they represented the height of Victorian engineering excellence.

The construction of a locomotive was carried out in several different stages, the first of which involved the preparation of iron and steel in the forge prior to the casting of the cylinders, wheels and boiler plates. The castings were then taken to the fitting shop to be trimmed and cleaned, after which they were transported to their various destinations — the boiler plates were riveted together to form boilers, while the wheels were taken to the wheel shop to be bored and turned on lathes prior to being put onto axles by hydraulic presses. The various components were then moved across to the erecting shop where boilers, wheels and cylinders were mounted onto the locomotive frame.

The final stage in the process was the painting of the locomotive, which took about three weeks. This involved firstly the removal of rust by scouring with sandstone and washing with turpentine, followed by the application of two coats of oil and white lead. After a coat of black stain to guide rubbing down to a smooth surface, an undercoat and second coat of black paint were applied followed by a third coat of paint and varnish mixture. The company's coat of arms was then affixed in the form of a transfer before three coats of varnish were given to the engine as the finishing touch. The whole locomotive building process generally took six weeks to complete, with the first locomotive from Horwich rolling off the production line in February 1889.

The construction of Europe's most modern railway engineering works was significant for Horwich not only because of the employment opportunities which the complex provided and the impact which it had on the local economy but also because of the social facilities which were associated with the works. One of the most important of these facilities was the Railway Mechanics Institute, which generated a completely new network of sports and social activities - as well as football and cricket teams a brass band was formed which went on to become 'Champions of Great Britain and the Colonies' by winning the Crystal Palace competition of 1922.

Horwich also benefited from the arrival of the works in other ways, too, and as well as the formation of the Horwich Fire Brigade, maintained at the Company's expense, the town also experienced an expansion of the local cotton industry as a result of the influx of labour encouraged by the Lancashire and Yorkshire Railway. One of the most successful mills stemming from this was the Victoria Mill built in 1904. Although the Engineering Works was eventually closed down in 1983

Victoria Mill has continued to produce cotton goods and is now one of the largest towel manufacturers in the United Kingdom.

From Horwich a road heading eastwards over some gentle moorland brings us to the outskirts of Bolton, passing on the way a one-time bleachworks at **Wallsuches.** The bleaching of locally-produced cloth was one of the earliest industries in this part of Lancashire, and the streams of soft water descending from the moorlands above Bolton gave the area a distinct advantage when large-scale bleaching became established in this country during the 18th century. In earlier times bleaching was very much a rural industry, with a bleacher or 'whitester' often being a farmer as well, and in the summer months it was a common sight to see the fields covered with cloth exposed for whitening by the 'crofting' or 'grassing' method.

Bolton's important role in this branch of the textile industry is confirmed by the fact that at least seven firms in the district on the Bleachers' Association list were founded before 1780, with some significant pioneering work being done by Thomas Ridgway who introduced chlorine bleaching and had a Watt steam engine installed at Wallsuches in 1798. The favourable physical advantages around the north-western and north-eastern outskirts of Bolton led to the development of a semi-circular line of bleaching and finishing works from Horwich to Little Lever, with this chain of works holding a position of importance within the industry well into the 20th century.

As well as being favourably situated for the production and finishing of woollen cloth Bolton also had the advantage of lying on the boundary of the linen producing country of West Lancashire, so that the spinning and weaving of flax as well as wool was able to be undertaken by the farmers who populated the Bolton countryside. However, it was the spinning and weaving of cotton which was to really bring about Bolton's development as an important textile centre, a process which began as early as the closing years of Elizabeth I's reign.

Cotton was initially used in the manufacture of fustians as warp to a linen weft, with the Bolton area soon becoming pre-eminent in this industry, although it was not for a hundred years or so that all-cotton fustians eventually replaced the cotton-linen material. As in the manufacture of woollen cloth the cotton industry was initially helped by natural advantages such as Bolton's humid atmosphere and the steady supply of soft water, but it was really the rapid growth of the port of Liverpool in the 18th century together with the growth of the West Indies as a cotton supplier which was to pave the way for Bolton's dramatic development as a centre of cotton manufacture.

Also important were the many technological advances in spinning and weaving which speeded up the process by which cotton was manufactured under the factory system rather than as a cottage industry, particularly Kay's 'flying shuttle' and Crompton's 'spinning mule'. The latter in particular provided an opportunity for faster and finer spinning, with the ready market for more delicate cotton goods encouraging many small works to spring up. By 1817 there were 20 cotton spinners in Bolton as well as 11 cotton spinners and manufacturers, 14 counterpane manufacturers and over 90 muslin manufacturers — indicating not only the development of fine cloth production but also the differentiation between factory spinning and manufacturing. By 1848 factory development had made even greater strides, with the sites of many of Bolton's greatest mills already being occupied, while in 1875 a concentration of mills in the north west of the town was developing by virtue of the cheaper land and lower rates here.

Throughout the 19th century as a whole technological improvements continued to be introduced in the mills, with the latter years of the century being marked by the invention of new finishing processes such as mercerisation and by the increasing use of ring spinning. Then in the early part of the 20th century there was a tendency towards a greater variety in yarn counts and less specialisation in the finest spinning, while the more economic use of cotton waste gave rise to condenser spinning. Like other towns in Lancashire, however, Bolton's cotton industry experienced a severe decline between the First and Second World Wars, and many of its mills have since been demolished or taken over by new uses.

*Workers' housing at Barrow Bridge*

One of the more impressive reminders of the better side of Bolton's industrial heritage is the village of **Barrow Bridge** on the north-western outskirts of the town, a model industrial settlement of the 19th century where the village's social, educational and economic life was completely integrated to form a close-knit community. The man behind this innovative approach was Robert Gardner, who in 1831 purchased what was then known as the Dean Mills Estate in preparation for establishing his model industrial settlement. In association with Thomas Bazley he proceeded to build two cotton spinning and doubling mills, each six storeys high with an engine house between

them and providing facilities which were then well in advance of those available in most other mills and factories. For instance, meals were taken in a separate room set aside for the purpose and workers had access to the daily newspapers; in addition hot water was in constant supply with hot baths and showers provided for all, while the factory ovens baked 150 loaves every day for the employees.

As well as a very desirable working environment Gardner and Bazley also provided their staff with accommodation close to their place of work, and whilst the model dwellings erected nearby were built as back-to-back houses with no back doors they were considered ideal dwellings and certainly far superior to the average workers' housing of the time. Each property had gas lighting as well as running water, while at the end of the terrace was a communal wash house in which individual mangles lined the walls. To cater for the community's educational needs Thomas Bazley opened the nearby Institute in 1846, offering tuition for 86 boys and 112 girls with all the necessary books and writing materials being provided by the mill owners. Other activities for the employees themselves were also organised at the Institute, including a library and a Reading Society as well as lectures on various topics.

A workers' co-operative shop was also established as an integral part of the community, being opened in 1835 by the mill workers with £200 borrowed capital. Although the prices were slightly higher than those in Bolton Market the workers took all the profits from the shop and by 1851 they had a balance of £1,500. One of the few things lacking in this largely self-contained community was a place of worship, for while

*Part of the Barrow Bridge 'model' industrial settlement*

Gardner and Bazley ran their village on Christian principles they were non-sectarian so no church or chapel was built here. They were also teetotal, so no public house was introduced either! The high standards attained in the community obviously made a significant impact upon its visitors, among whom were included Disraeli in 1840 — his novel 'Coningsby' includes an account of the village of Millbank, the last word in progress and thought to be partly based on Barrow Bridge.

In 1862 the estate was sold to William Callender, who not only continued the good work of Gardner and Bazley but even added further activities in the form of a Mutual Improvement Society and a night school for adults as well as enlarging the library and starting a Penny Bank. Problems unfortunately developed following the death of Callender and his brother, with the result that the mill was closed and then eventually demolished in 1913; the village too became deserted and the houses derelict. Articles about Barrow Bridge in the local press, however, brought the area to the public's attention, with the result that the cottages were restored to provide housing for local workers. The village itself also became something of a local beauty spot, with the shop selling Barrow Bridge rock and cane walking sticks as well as ice cream, sweets and fishing nets. Since that time during the early part of the 20th century Barrow Bridge has taken on a rather quieter residential character amidst its sylvan setting, the beautifully restored cottages and houses being very appropriately encompassed within a Conservation Area.

The Dean Brook running through Barrow Bridge village not only provided water for Robert Gardner's steam powered spinning mill but also supplied it for a bleaching enterprise owned by the Ainsworth family lower down the river. At that point in time the Ainsworths owned nearby **Smithills Hall,** a fine half-timbered building which is now one of the oldest manor houses in Lancashire. The earliest part of the building is the Great Hall and its screens passage, believed to date from about 1350 when a branch of the Radcliffe family acquired the property. Features of particular interest include the massive timbers with their characteristic Lancashire quatrefoil bracing as well as the 'speres' or projecting walls carrying the roof arch which mark off the passage from the Great Hall.

In the west wall one can still see the arched entrances into what was the kitchen, buttery and pantry, while at the opposite end is a door through to a chamber which acted as a bedroom for the lord and his family; above this is a solar or 'sun-room' where the ladies of the household retired during the day. During the 16th century the lower chamber probably became a dining room for the family while the upper one was a bedroom. Added on to the house here is a Tudor drawing room with early Renaissance linenfold panelling which is reputed to be the best of its period in Lancashire. The adjoining chapel of 1858 is a replacement for the one previously destroyed by fire, although it contains in its east window some 16th century heraldic glass preserved from the original building — among the designs included here are the arms of Thomas Cranmer when Archbishop of Canterbury (possibly the only contemporary record in colour) as well as the Royal Arms of the Tudors.

The courtyard format which probably characterised Smithills Hall when it was first built was continued during the late 16th century with the addition of a long west wing facing the chapel, together with the gabled wing projecting from it on the far side. The side of the wing facing the courtyard is of timber construction, while the western side is of stone like the gabled wing added afterwards. Further alterations to the house were made by the Ainsworths during the Victorian period, particularly in 1875 when the property was considerably enlarged in an imitation half-timbered style; the stables and coaching house were also built at the same time and in a similar architectural treatment.

Another notable timber-framed house which has featured prominently in Bolton's history is **Hall i'th'Wood,** situated a little further eastwards around the northern outskirts of the town. The impressive 'black and white' timber-framed wing of the present building probably dates from the Elizabethan period, although it may well incorporate an earlier timber-framed house built by Lawrence Brownlow, a Bolton clothier, when he established a fulling mill on the nearby Eagley Brook in 1483. By 1591 the Brownlows were extending their home with a rather more solid stone built wing, since by that time timber was scarce and the use of stone increasingly fashionable and prestigious. This new wing rather appropriately incorporates features which reflect the family's status at the time, particularly the spiked finials and the round-headed entrance arch of the porch. The house was later owned by the Norris family, with Alexander Norris being responsible for handling the confiscated estates of Royalist families in Lancashire after the Civil War; it was he who further extended the property in 1648 by the addition of a south west wing, and as a result Hall i'th'Wood displays a process of architectural development over a span of nearly two centuries.

Yet Hall i'th'Wood's significance to Bolton extends far beyond its architecture, for it was here that Samuel Crompton invented the spinning mule which was to later revolutionise the cotton industry. The Cromptons were farmers, spinning and weaving cloth when time allowed, and in 1758 Samuel Crompton came here with his widowed mother to take up the tenancy of the Hall after it had fallen vacant during the first half of the 18th century. It was in the attic of the house that Crompton experimented for several years in his attempt to produce a yarn which was both strong enough and fine enough to make muslin cloth, and the fruit of his endeavours was a machine which which helped to usher in the Industrial Revolution.

*Smithills Hall, Bolton*

230

composition, but Firwood Fold is the most famous and certainly in the best state of preservation. The original farmhouse in this delightful little group has since become two dwellings, while opposite is a 'Gothicized' house which was formerly the school but which was probably a barn in earlier times. On the edge of the small green (created when some obtrusive buildings were removed) is a small cottage with the remains of an external cruck in an end wall; this property may well be mediaeval in origin and is possibly the oldest house in Bolton. The whole scene is attractively finished off by some charming former stables with round windows, built by the owners of Firwood Hall to whom the fold belonged.

Like many other Lancashire towns **Bolton** owes its growth and prosperity to the Industrial Revolution, and its majestic Town Hall is a fitting symbol not only of the town's aspirations during this period but also of Victorian civic pride. Proposed in 1863 as a way of relieving unemployment during the

*Hall i'th Wood, Bolton*

However, the building's overwhelming importance to Bolton was only truly recognised at the end of the 19th century when as a crumbling farmhouse it was bought by William Lever (the first Lord Leverhulme) before being restored and presented to the Corporation for use as a museum.

If Hall i'th'Wood is important because it was home for Samuel Crompton when he devised the spinning mule, then **Firwood Fold** a little further eastwards is significant because this was his birthplace. A 'fold' was one of the earliest forms of settlement in the Bolton area, typically consisting of several cottages and outbuildings clustered round a farmhouse. Several still exist in the district, at least in name if not in their traditional

*Firwood Fold — Samuel Crompton's birthplace*

*The civic grandeur of Bolton Town Hall*

231

*The Town Hall Precinct, Bolton*

character is Preston's the Jewellers at the corner of Deansgate and Bank Street, which like a number of the properties on nearby Bradshawgate is built of terracotta. This material, easy to mould into intricate designs, was very popular in the early 1900s, when many of the local brickyards prospered. One of the more unusual features of Preston's building is the 'time ball' situated on top of the corner tower — at 9.00 a.m. every day the ball was raised to the top of its guide rods and at 10.00 a.m. exactly it dropped to the bottom of the rods on receiving a telegraph signal from Greenwich. As this 'time ball' could be seen from miles around local industrialists were able to set their clocks by it.

cotton famine caused by the American Civil War, the Town Hall was designed in a Classical style and opened in 1873 by the Prince and Princess of Wales. Above the imposing front portico is a pediment with sculptures representing Bolton's role in manufacture and commerce, while higher still is the lofty and elaborate clock tower which watches over the pedestrian precinct laid out below. This precinct in front of the Town Hall constitutes one of the finest formal open spaces in the country, providing a handsome and dignified setting not only for the Town Hall itself but also the Civic Centre behind it. The latter consists of a crescent-fronted municipal building in the Classical style on both sides of a central archway, begun in 1926 after slum demolition and completed in 1939.

At one point the site occupied by the Town Hall had formed part of Bolton's new Market Place, laid out in 1825 following congestion in the streets around the old market (held since 1251 at the crossing of Deansgate, Bradshawgate, Churchgate and Bank Street). Overlooking this new Market Place was a handsome Classical building designed by the notable Manchester architect Richard Lane, since retained as an important feature around the edge of the pedestrian precinct in front of the Town Hall. Known as the Old Reference Library and now occupied by a building society, this building was erected in 1824-25 by the Bolton Exchange Company for use as a newsroom and private library. Then in 1852 the upper rooms were let off to the Corporation for the purposes of establishing a public lending facility, and the following year saw the inauguration of Bolton Free Library.

Across the other side of the Town Hall Precinct is the Corliss Engine, part of the town's industrial heritage and now on display at the Oxford Street entrance to Victoria Square. Built in Bolton in 1866 and then in operation at a Yorkshire mill until 1969, the engine was brought here in 1973 when it was set in motion to declare the Precinct open. From the end of Oxford Street Deansgate heads eastwards towards the Market Cross situated in Churchgate, passing on the way a number of impressive bank properties built of stone during the latter part of the 19th century.

Equally impressive but of a rather different

The present Market Cross at the western end of Churchgate was erected in 1912 to replace an earlier one which had been removed in 1786. Here, too, stood the local pillory, providing a means of punishment for local criminals, while the rather more severe punishment meted out to the Earl of Derby on this same site in 1651 had been his death by execution. John Wesley also experienced the displeasure of the townspeople when he came to preach from this spot on 28th August 1748, finding 'many of them utterly wild'. One reason for this may have been the ready accessibility to alcohol, since Churchgate in particular seems to be lined by most of the town's oldest inns. A clever rhyme rather appropriately records the drinking establishments which were to be found on the south side of the road:

> 'The Cock in Churchgate never crowed,
> Angel and Trumpet never blowed,
> Legs of Man never strode,
> Man and Scythe never mowed'.

The last of these is in fact Bolton's earliest

*The Man and Scythe Inn, Churchgate*

hostelry, reputedly dating from 1251 — the same year in which the town received its charter granting the right to hold a weekly market and an annual fair. Just two years later Bolton received a seignorial charter establishing it as a free borough. Bolton market very soon became important in the clothing trade, and by the first half of the 17th century Blome was recording that the town was 'a place of great trade for fustians'. Then in 1662 Thomas Fuller confirmed Bolton's pre-eminence to fustian dealers when he wrote that the town was 'the staple place for this commodity, being brought thither from all parts of the County'.

Next door to the Man and Scythe is the Swan Hotel, a coaching inn dating from at least the 17th century as well as the meeting place for the half-yearly Court Leet during the 18th century. Then on the other side of Churchgate is the Boar's Head Inn, built in 1721 and quickly becoming Bolton's main drinking establishment. As well as being a posting house and a meeting place for the licensing sessions it also became a venue for a Book Club, where the literary-minded members of the town would meet together. This same side of Churchgate also gave access to a number of courts, yards and entries, although the only one still remaining is Gaskell Court approached down the passage by the side of the Bear's Paw public house. Cotton velvet is thought to have been produced for the first time in this locality in 1756, and the now demolished Velvet Walks is reputed to have had some connection with this early industry.

Churchgate's significance in the development of the textile industry is also remembered by a plaque on one of its buildings commemorating the fact that Richard Arkwright lived and worked here prior to moving to Nottingham where he invented his famous water-frame spinning machine. Bolton's rather more famous son, Samuel Crompton, is buried not far away in the churchyard of the parish church, his tomb bearing witness to his invention of the spinning machine called the 'mule'. The Parish Church itself is a comparatively modern building for this part of the town, being built between 1867-71 in a Victorian Gothic style produced by the architect E.G. Paley of Lancaster. As a parish church it is quite magnificent in scale with some rich mouldings and an excellent vaulted roof, reflecting the town's pride and confidence during the Victorian period.

The church which it replaced dated from the 15th century, and although this was completely demolished some monuments from the previous building were retained, including several mediaeval choir stalls and three misericords. There are also fragments of carvings from an earlier Norman church and a good collection of pre-Conquest carvings as

*Bolton Parish Church*

well as part of a 10th century 'Ring of Glory' cross and the most complete Anglian preaching cross in the area, possibly dating from the 7th or 8th century. All these relics underscore the importance which this church has held in Lancashire, particularly in mediaeval times when it was the centre of a large parish extending to about 30 square miles. Just behind the church itself is the Parish Hall, formerly the town's Grammar School — the present building dates from 1881-83 when it replaced an older school built during Cromwell's Protectorate, a building which in turn had replaced an earlier Tudor school situated close to where the front gates of the church now stand.

Having seen some of Bolton's mediaeval heritage the return journey to the Town Hall gives us the opportunity to discover more of the town's fine Georgian and Victorian architecture. Close to the parish church are Silverwell Street and Wood Street, both of which feature some elegant terraces of Georgian town houses. Wood Street in particular is notable for being the birthplace of William Lever, later Lord and then ultimately Viscount Leverhulme and one of Bolton's

greatest benefactors — he not only bought and restored Hall i'th'Wood for the benefit of the town but also gave Leverhulme Park and generously endowed Bolton School. Parallel

*Memorial to Samuel Crompton*

to Wood Street is Silverwell Street, which was the home of Sir John Scott (founder of the Provincial Insurance Company) and of Major John Pilkington, a cotton manufacturer and friend of Samuel Crompton.

Across Bradshawgate from the western end of Silverwell Street is Nelson Square, presided over by a statue of Samuel Crompton. Like many great men Crompton was not fully recognised during his lifetime, and his friend John Pilkington had sought to raise money from the rich beneficiaries of Crompton's invention to ease his impoverished state; even the monument to him only appeared in 1862, some thirty-five years after his death. At the top end of Nelson Square is the site of Bolton's first infirmary and dispensary, while Infirmary Street close by leads into Mawdsley Street and the County Court building. Opened in 1869 this displays an impressive Italian Renaissance style of architecture on the ground floor, with the keystones over the windows being decorated by flowers and leaves while those over the doors display a crown and the letters V.R. This building also occupies the site of an old theatre and concert hall in which Samuel Crompton played violin for a local orchestra. Mawdsley Street leads on to Exchange Street, which in turn brings us back into Victoria Square and the Town Hall Precinct, the grand focal point for the civic life of the town.

Beyond the town centre there are some important buildings to be discovered around Bolton's southern outskirts, beginning with St. Mary's Church at **Deane.** This is one of the town's few mediaeval monuments, being built during the 15th century by monks from Whalley Abbey. Despite some later changes

it is still a very good example of a North Country village church in the Perpendicular style, displaying the characteristic battlements and a pinnacled squat tower. When first built it was a chapel of ease for the northern part of the parish of Eccles, which included Farnworth as well as Halliwell and Horwich, but by 1536 it had become a parish church in its own right. In addition to its architectural significance the church has important connections with George Marsh, martyred in 1555 after a trial at Smithills Hall, and vicar John Tilsely, who was ejected from the parish three times during the English Civil War.

Further eastwards is to be found the district of **Farnworth,** which in Rock Hall boasts a fine example of a Georgian residence now in use as a visitors' centre for the Moses Gate Country Park and the Croal-Irwell valley recreation area. The mansion was built in the early 1800s by the Crompton family, with Thomas Bonsor Crompton inventing the continuous drying process which came to be so important in paper manufacture. Some of the lodges which supplied water to the mills here have recently been restored for informal recreation such as fishing and boating, while landscaping and tree planting have helped to transform what was once an eyesore into an important local beauty spot.

Just across the River Croal is **Little Lever,** one of the first places to be producing cloth woven entirely from cotton from the beginning of the 17th century onwards. By the end of the 18th century it had developed a reputation for the fine yarns being spun here, particularly in the factories grouped along the banks of the Croal, but it was also important for the mining of coal which was

assisted by the opening of the Bolton to Manchester Canal in 1791.

Little Lever lies close to the confluence of the Croal and the Irwell, and the latter can be followed eastwards upstream to **Radcliffe** just before it meets the River Roch at a point to the south of Bury. The name 'Radcliffe' probably dates back to Saxon times, perhaps taken from the natural feature of the red cliff or rock on the south east side of the River Irwell close to its confluence with the Roch, although the Romans had already passed through the area by virtue of the road which they constructed between Ribchester and Manchester. By Norman times the name 'de Rugemont' was being given to the village, and was also used as the surname of several members of the local manorial family.

It is from this latter period that the parish church in Radcliffe is thought to date, although there may well have been an earlier place of worship established here by the Saxons, and whilst we know for certain that the earliest part of the present building was erected in 1282 there is mention of Robert, the parson of Radcliffe, in a deed almost half a century before that time. The church still preserves a few Norman features, with the south transept dating from the 15th century and the tower being rebuilt in 1665, while inside one can find some ancient stained glass as well as a parish register dating from 1558 and a 17th century carved oak reading desk.

Whilst there is now little left of the manorial residence known as Radcliffe Tower it is thought that it was one of the most substantial in the country, comprising 'a hall and two towers of stone'; it is also reputed to have been the scene of 'The Lady Isabella's Tragedy', a gruesome mediaeval ballad which alleges that Lady Isabella had her stepdaughter killed and cooked in a pie!

The earliest steps in Radcliffe's industrial growth were taken by the Peel family, who were the first to establish a mill here, although they were quickly followed by the Bealeys and their bleaching business. During the course of the 19th century the textile industry continued to flourish by virtue of the town's proximity to Manchester and its own provision of coal and water, as well as because of the canal and railway. In the same period engineering also developed as an important trade, as did the paper manufacturing industry which has been established locally since the early 1700s.

The Roman road which passed through Radcliffe also appears to have passed through **Whitefield** immediately to the south east, as it made its way down towards Manchester. During the Norman period much of the area encompassing not only what is now Whitefield but also parts of Radcliffe and Heywood was conferred upon Leonard de

*St. Mary's Church, Deane*

*A lane in Holcombe near Bury*

*Hey House, Holcombe*

*All Saints Church, Stand near Whitefield*

some richly-coloured stained glass in the east window.

Three miles to the north of Stand and Whitefield is the town of **Bury,** which derives its name from the Saxon word 'byri' meaning a castle or fortified place. Such a structure may well have occupied the same site as that of a 14th century fortification which has been unearthed in the town. The existence of a settlement here during early Norman times is confirmed by the Domesday Book which records the presence of a church, with the manor being held initially by the lords of Tottington and then by the de Bury family before eventually passing to the Pilkingtons. In 1469 Thomas Pilkington was granted a licence by the king 'to build, make and construct walls and turrets of stone, lime and sand around and below his manor house...also to embattle, crenelate and machicolate those towers'. Recent excavations have shown that the outer walls which Pilkington built were nearly two feet thick, encompassing a quadrangle about 113 feet by 110 feet, while the inner walls were more than six feet thick.

By 1536, however, the castle was in ruins, with some of the stone probably being used for the re-construction of the nearby church. This rather sad state of affairs was noted by John Leland on his travels in 1540, when he wrote 'Byri on Irwel Water, IV or V miles from Manchester but a poore market. There is a ruine of a Castle by the paroche churche yn the towne. It belongged with the towne, sum time to the Pilkingtons, now to the Erles of Derby. Yerne (yarn) sum time made about it'. Things were not much better by the end of the 17th century, when it was recorded that there was 'great decay in the streets of Berry for want of pavements'.

With the onset of the 18th century, however, Bury began to experience steady commercial and residential growth, particularly in the area of the Market Place and along The Rock and Bolton Street, as a result of the development of the textile trades and the inventions associated with them. One such invention was the flying shuttle, produced in 1733 by John Kay of Bury, while another locally-devised innovation was the 'drop-box' made by his son Robert, although both these improvements had to wait until the local manufacturers transferred their interest from wool to cotton before they could be widely adopted. Helping to pave the way for Bury's transformation from a small market and woollen town of comparative insignificance to a considerable industrial centre was the Glebe Act of 1764, which permitted the Rector of Bury to lease his extensive church lands for housing and commercial development.

Of even greater significance to the town was the decision made by the prosperous Blackburn firm of Howarth, Peel and Yates in

Pilkington, who proceeded to create a 'park' bearing his name which remained in his family's ownership for 400 years. He chose the highest point in this park for his own residence, an area which came to be known as Stand from the very earliest times — this may have been because it was an appropriate spot on which to erect a special platform or 'stand' from which guests could observe the hunt as it took place in the surrounding area.

Despite the influence of the Pilkington family, later to be replaced by the Earls of Derby, Whitefield appears to have derived its own name from one of two sources — either from the practise of Flemish weavers spreading their fabrics in the fields to bleach in the sun's rays, or as a corruption of the word 'wheatfields' relating to the area's rich farmland. The tradition of weaving brought in by Flemish settlers at the end of the 15th century continued to develop over the course of the next few centuries, so that by the early 1800s Whitefield was a centre of handloom weaving with most families having a loom in their homes. There was also some cotton manufacture, but the heavy industrialisation which took place in other districts appears not to have occurred in Whitefield. Instead it developed more as an important residential area, benefiting not only from its proximity to Manchester but also the arrival of the Manchester to Bury railway line.

The most impressive building in the Whitefield area must surely be the Parish Church of All Saints at Stand, a splendid piece of architecture in the Gothic Revival style designed by Sir Charles Barry and erected in 1822-26. This is just one of many churches throughout the country built with money from the 'Waterloo fund' of one million pounds provided after Napoleon's defeat. All Saints is a tall building of grey ashlar, with a tower which appears much higher than even its 186 feet makes it because of its position on high ground; it is consequently an impressive landmark which can be seen from some considerable distance. Entering the church through high open arches at the base of the tower one can discover a galleried interior featuring tall clustered columns and a rib-vaulted ceiling. There is also a fine rood screen as well as

1773 to build their new works for the printing of calico at Bury Ground. After just a few years they had added to the printing works by putting up a factory in the heart of the old town, where the carding, stubbing and spinning of cotton was carried on, and by the early 1780s the Peels had six cotton mills in the area. Within a couple of decades the population of Bury had trebled, with wool giving way to cotton as the basis of the town's economic life. Assisting the increase of both trade and population was the coming of the Manchester, Bolton and Bury Canal in the 1790s, bringing with it an influx of coal and many kinds of heavy goods which helped to diversify the town's industrial base.

The result of all this in physical terms was a considerable extension of the town centre, with Silver Street and Manchester Road developing into one of the finest residential areas of central Bury. Silver Street in particular was the home of many of Bury's top people during the early Victorian period, and its name may even refer to the affluence of its residents; it also housed several private

*The Central Library and Art Gallery, Bury*

*Memorial to Sir Robert Peel, against the background of the Parish Church*

schools as well as a number of the more exclusive shops which served the 'carriage trade'. Bury's developing industries continued to produce the wealth which allowed the town to grow and prosper during the latter half of the 19th century, prompting the redevelopment of much of the town centre. As a result of this Market Street was created and the Derby Hall, Derby Hotel and Athenaeum built in a Greek Revival style; new buildings were also erected on the opposite side of Market Street in both Classical and Gothic styles to help enclose the Market Place.

After 1870 buildings such as the Derby Chambers, Barclays Bank, the Royal Hotel and the tall brick and stone offices at the Market Place end of Silver Street were introduced to the town centre, with Bury's Victorian reconstruction being completed by the building of the Arts and Craft Centre on Bond Street, the Textile Hall (originally used as the headquarters of the local textile unions) and the Central Library and Art Gallery. This latter building displays the best Victorian architecture in Bury, an impressive neo-Classical edifice decorated by columns, pinnacles, pediments and porticos as well as by a host of symbolic figures representing the arts, sciences and every branch of culture.

Another building of major importance to the town is of course the Parish Church of St. Mary the Virgin, situated just to the north of the Market Place. The present structure dates largely from 1876, when the church was rebuilt to a 'Geometric Decorated Gothic' design produced by the architect J.S. Crowther, although it also incorporated an earlier spire dating from 1844. Crowther's design made use of features from the

*Peel Tower, Holcombe Hill*

mediaeval abbey at Tintern as well as details from Westminster Abbey and other buildings, and his introduction of the French-looking apse is also characteristic of his work. The height and splendour of the chancel are similarly typical of his zeal for the Gothic Revival style, while the use of red brick walls and Minton tile floors was also unmistakably Victorian.

As might be expected the furnishings of the church are appropriately splendid, with no expense being spared — many of the fittings were designed by the architect, particularly the fine pulpit and much of the church woodwork, while the stained glass is all contemporary. Throughout the interior can be found scenes connected with St. Mary, the patron saint, as well as themes relating to soldiering since this is the church of the Lancashire Fusiliers. Outside the church in the graveyard can be seen headstones dating back to the 17th century, while of comparable interest are the carved stone heads above the windows. Although some of these are fanciful 'mediaeval' heads, many of them depict the actual people who helped to create this impressive building.

In the nearby Market Place is a statue of Sir Robert Peel, a one-time Prime Minister and Bury's most famous 'son'. It was his father who had helped to introduce the spinning, weaving, bleaching and printing of cotton to the Bury area at the end of the 18th century, and which heralded the town's industrial

prosperity, although Robert Peel the younger was to make his own particular contribution in the political sphere. He is particularly remembered for his work in creating the Metropolitan Police in 1829, as a consequence of which policemen came to be known as 'Bobbies', and also for the repeal of the Corn Laws in 1846. As a result he had become endeared to the working population, because these laws had kept the price of bread at an artificially high level.

Another memorial erected in memory of Sir Robert Peel is the **Peel Tower** standing on Holcombe Hill just above the village of Holcombe to the north of Bury. This 120-foot high structure was built of locally-quarried millstone grit in 1852, just two years after Peel's death, and paid for from money collected by public subscription. The Tower has recently been restored and now offers visitors the opportunity to climb its 148 steps for some magnificent views of the surrounding countryside — to the south and south west one can see beyond Manchester into the Peak District, Cheshire and North Wales, while to the west is Winter Hill with its television masts and then to the north Pendle Hill and the Rossendale Valley.

Our route northwards from Bury to the Peel Tower at Holcombe brings us firstly to **Tottington,** an area known during mediaeval times for its deer and wild boar. In the following centuries farming became established as the main activity here, although industry came to Tottington in a small way towards the end of the 18th century with the manufacture of cotton, bleaching and calico printing. One of the area's most unusual buildings is the old Dungeon in Turton Road, frequently in use after it was first opened in 1835 but now an architectural curiosity for passing sightseers.

Another architectural curiosity is the Garden Folly at Nabbs House in the neighbouring village of **Greenmount,** built during the middle of the 19th century by a rather eccentric gentleman named John Turner. His 'folly' consists of a castle-like summerhouse with battlemented walls, from which protrude numerous gargoyles said to represent the faces of Greenmount villagers to whom Turner had taken a particular dislike. The inside of the summerhouse was originally panelled with richly carved oak and was the place where Turner and his friends would retire for a drink and a smoke. He also devised some devious water spouts along the approach to his house, one being concealed in the cobbles at his front gate and another over the front door, with undesirable visitors being given an unexpected soaking. Linking Greenmount with Tottington is a pleasant linear footpath created from the former railway track which ran from Holcombe Brook; electrified in 1905 this is reputed to have been the first example of electrification in the country.

**Holcombe Brook** itself is a pleasant residential area which has grown up around the older settlement of Pot Green, which in turn grew out of agriculture and a small-scale domestic textile industry established here during the 17th and 18th centuries. With the gradual expansion of more centralised textile manufacture employment for local people came to be concentrated in two mills, both of which were powered by the brook which gives the settlement its name. These mills remain now only as ruins, with Pot Green consisting of modest stone built cottages and larger houses which illustrate the detail of building styles from the 17th century through to the 1890s.

From Pot Green Holcombe Old Road can be

*Part of Holcombe Village*

*Shoulder of Mutton public house, Holcombe Village*

followed northwards to **Holcombe Village,** a little-changed settlement which looks down onto Ramsbottom in the Irwell Valley below. The name 'Holcombe' is derived from the Saxon word 'Hol' and the Celtic word 'cwm', which taken together refer to the village's position in a semi-circular hollow on the hillside. The earliest recorded written reference to Holcombe dates back to 1220 when Roger de Montbegon gave 'my forest called Holcombe' to the Priory of Monk Bretton, although after the dissolution of the monasteries the area came under the control of the manor of Tottington.

For centuries the area around Holcombe was used for hunting by the lords of the manor, although at the same time the village itself also developed as a farming community based along the important packhorse and coaching route which ran northwards from Bury through to Haslingden and beyond. The greatest growth appears to have taken place during the 17th and 18th centuries when the income from farming would have been supplemented by handloom weaving, and most of the buildings in the village date from this period. Then during the 19th century new building began to be concentrated in the valley bottom, particularly through the emergence of Ramsbottom, with the result that Holcombe's own development virtually ceased. Consequently it is now an excellent example of a largely unchanged pre-industrial hillside village.

At the centre of the village is the Shoulder of Mutton public house, formerly known as 'Lower House' to distinguish it from Higher House, a little distance away, which itself was an inn at one time. The 'lower house' was built in 1751 and has changed little since then, its

frontage and side elevation constructed from finely-cut coursed stone in a traditional Georgian style. During the last century this building was known to have been a venue for cock-fighting, and is thought to have been the first in the area. Like its near neighbour, Higher House also dates from the 18th century although it displays a rather more vernacular style of architecture by virtue of its stone-flagged roof, mullioned windows and drip mouldings. The fact that these two buildings were the only inns in Ramsbottom prior to 1800 is an indication of the importance which Holcombe held at that time.

Not far away on the north east side of the village is Holcombe Parish Church, a visually

impressive landmark by virtue of its elevated site. A church has existed in the village since at least the 15th century, although the present building dates from 1853 when it was constructed of local stone in a Gothic style. Then on the opposite side of the village is Hey House, built by Roger Browne in 1616 and undoubtedly the finest historic building in the district. This is a typical 17th century 'grand' house built from coursed stone in the local vernacular style, with mullioned windows and a castellated parapet as well as shaped finials decorating the chimney stacks and main entrance porch. The interior features some equally ornate decoration, with a variety of carved woodwork said to be from Whalley Abbey together with some late 17th century carved fireplaces and some early painted windows. Close to Hey House is a footpath leading up the hillside to Peel Tower, the monument's precise position apparently being influenced by the Ramsbottom mill owner William Grant who determined that it should be in line with St. Andrew's Church tower when viewed from the doorstep of his own home!

The development of **Ramsbottom** from an insignificant hamlet into a sizeable town is also inextricably linked with the Grant family, who first arrived here in 1806 but were actually preceded by Peel and Yates who in 1783 built a mill alongside the Irwell to bleach and print woollen cloth. The Grants had made a name for themselves as merchants in Manchester, but when the opportunity came to buy Robert Peel's factory they leapt at the chance to extend the family fortunes. After some years establishing themselves in the business they built their own new works in 1822 — known as Square Mill because of its four great bays it was completely surrounded by water and required entry by means of a drawbridge. By 1825 it was being hailed as the foremost

*The Market Place, Ramsbottom*

'manufactory' of its kind, and people came from all over the country to see the bleaching and printing of cloth here.

The Grant family built several other factories in the Ramsbottom area during the first half of the 19th century, while the wealth created by this spread of industrial development also enabled them to contribute to some significant civic building work in the town — in addition to their factories they built roads, a library, a mechanics' institute, an orphanage and two churches. Between the 1820s and the 1860s they also constructed rows of terraced houses along Bridge Street and Bolton Street to accommodate the influx of mill workers, although many of these have since been converted to shops.

The stone buildings at the centre of Ramsbottom typify the local achitectural style to be found in this part of Lancashire — the Market Place, for example, contains a number of fine individual buildings such as the Civic Hall, the Grant Arms Hotel and the Methodist Church, while several of the other properties still retain many of their original features. The setting of these buildings in the Market Place is enhanced by the open sett-paved area and pleasant gardens fronting the Grant Arms Hotel and the Civic Hall, and whilst some changes have taken place many of the properties remain relatively unspoiled.

As well as bringing about the large-scale development of Ramsbottom the Grant brothers also had a hand in the rejuvenation of Nuttall village to the south of the town, which they purchased in 1812. At that time the mills were unused and many of the workers were unemployed, but following its purchase by the Grants the village prospered so that at its busiest there were some 100 houses here. Then in 1817 the Grant brothers built Nuttall Hall for themselves nearby and laid out 14 acres of gardens around it; although the Hall was demolished this century the gardens still remain in the form of Nuttall Park. The next major building project was the construction of St. Andrew's Church just over the other side of the Irwell from here,

*Brooksbottoms Mill in Summerseat*

formally opened in 1834 and paid for entirely by William Grant. One of the remarkable features of the church was that it was originally heated by hot air from Grant's Square Mill, drawn a quarter of a mile up the hillside by means of a brick tunnel which was high enough for a man to walk through.

In between the church and the site of Nuttall Hall is the old East Lancashire Railway line connecting Bury with Rawtenstall, recently restored as a tourist attraction and for everyday commercial use. Less than a mile to the south of Nuttall Park on the way back into Bury this line passes close to **Brooksbottoms Mill** in Summerseat, the most prominent feature in the valley bottom and saved from destruction by its conversion to luxury flats. The present structure dates from 1873 when it was built by Edward Hoyle

to replace an earlier mill, although the first mill on the site was erected here in about 1773 when Peel and Yates introduced centralised cotton cloth manufacturing to Summerseat. As the mill companies owned most of the land in the vicinity each phase of expansion and rebuilding brought with it the construction of workers' cottages nearby, and so consequently Brooksbottoms Mill (now known as 'The Spinnings') together with the adjacent groups of brick terraces and earlier cottages provides an excellent example of industrial river valley architecture from the 18th and 19th centuries.

From Summerseat the East Lancashire Railway heads southwards back into the centre of Bury, passing several sites of industrial interest before arriving at the terminus and Bury Transport Museum. This museum, headquarters of the East Lancashire Railway Preservation Society, has a splendid collection of both steam and diesel locomotives for use on the line, including the former Western main line diesels 'Western Prince' and 'Onslaught' as well as the former Southern Steam Pacific engine 'Taw Valley'.

Another similar example to Summerseat's industrial architecture, but this time in an upland location rather than a river valley, is to be found in **Mount Pleasant** just one mile due east of Brooksbottoms Mill. This settlement is an isolated and important example of a 'factory village', illustrating an important aspect of early industrial growth in the Upper Pennines area. In its original form the village consisted of a centrally-placed mill

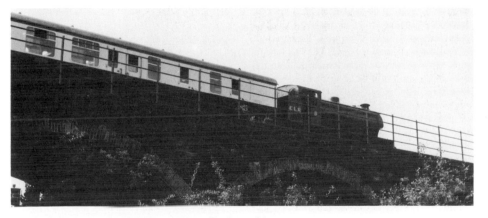

*Steam engine on the East Lancashire Railway Line*

with some outbuildings, a half-acre lodge surrounded by a stone wall and seven separate stone terraces which enclosed the mill on three sides. Although the mill and its outbuildings have been recently converted to residential use, this unusual industrial enclave still accurately portrays the development of a textile business over the course of the 19th century.

In 1819 John Hall bought part of an estate which had belonged to the late Captain Nangreaves, on land adjacent to Walmersley Old Road, transferring his business to the farm buildings on the site. At first the business acted as a collecting point for the cottage weaving industry, and weavers from Holcombe, Tottington, Affetside, Bradshaw, Harwood and Bolton would bring their cloth to Nangreaves before returning home with the warp and weft; at this point in time the business employed well over 1,000 weavers. Soon after arriving at Nangreaves John Hall began building a new mill incorporating weaving sheds, power looms and later a spinning shed. As the prosperity of the business increased so further additions were made to the mill building, with terraced cottages being erected to provide homes for the spinners and weavers. The last alterations to the mill were made in 1893 and the last workers' houses built in 1903. One of the interesting and enduring features of Mount Pleasant village is Walmersley Old Road alongside it, which is paved with stone setts for much of its length as it makes its way southwards into Baldingstone.

Just over the hill to the east of Mount Pleasant is the valley of the **Cheesden Brook,** at one time lined by water powered textile mills which paved the way for later industrial development in Heywood and Rochdale. During the 18th and 19th centuries the cotton and print mills which initially flourished here provided employment for several hundred people in what was then a hive of activity, but as the cotton industry became centralised in towns so the mills in this valley went into a sharp decline. All that is left now in this once-busy area are some romantic ruins suggestive of former industrial glories — half-hidden chimney stacks, placid mill ponds, ivy-clad walls and cobbled roads running through damp woodlands. Apart from these fascinating remains indicating man's previous activities in the valley the return back to nature is now virtually complete, and the Cheesden Brook has probably never been so quiet or peaceful since mediaeval times. A footpath through the valley provides walkers with a splendid opportunity to experience a sensuous seclusion in the present while at the same time learning something of Rochdale's industrial past.

As the Cheesden Brook makes it way downstream towards the River Roch it joins up with the Ashworth Valley, along which is

*Rochdale Town hall*

to be found a small group of buildings called Ashworth Fold and the 17th century Ashworth Hall, built on the site of an older house. Further northwards up the valley is the Egerton Arms public house, probably dating from the 15th century and at one time part of the original Ashworth Hall estate. The Egerton Arms is known locally as the Chapel House because of its close proximity to St. James' Chapel and the adjacent graveyard, and apparently at one time the landlord of the public house also acted as both sexton and gravedigger!

Following the Ashworth Valley southwards from here brings us quickly to the town of **Heywood,** on the other side of the River Roch, a place which perhaps more than most owes its existence to the cotton industry. It was originally part of the township of Heap in the parish of Bury, and up to the middle of the 18th century consisted of just a few scattered houses, but then in 1780 the textile firm of Peel and Yates established the first cotton spinning and weaving factory in the area. From these relatively humble beginnings Heywood grew rapidly, and by 1834 the town had developed so much industrially as to warrant the cutting of a canal to the nearest railhead at Castleton. Heywood's dependence on the cotton trade left it particularly vulnerable during the acute depression caused by the Cotton Famine of the 1860s, but by the end of the century the town was thriving again and when Yew Mill was built in 1891 it was reputed to be the world's largest spinning mill under one roof.

To the north Heywood is linked to open countryside by Queen's Park, which also features the unusually constructed Queen's Park Bridge providing a crossing over the River Roch — at a formal ceremony this concrete bridge was actually declared open as a 'bazaar' by the dignitary who forgot his lines on the day! From this point the River Roch can be followed upstream into the very heart of **Rochdale,** which like neighbouring Heywood grew rapidly during the 19th century as a result of the expansion of the cotton industry and whose splendid Gothic town hall is a fitting memorial to the wealth and confidence generated during that period.

Unlike Heywood, however, Rochdale has a significant history which goes back well before the Victorian era — a settlement existed here in the Saxon period, and then in the Domesday Survey the manor of Rochdale was recorded under the name 'Recedham' with an estimated population of 300 people. It later became one of the most extensive parishes in the Hundred of Salford, and in 1251 a weekly market was established here under a royal charter granted to Edmund de Lacy. This marked the start of Rochdale's development as an important commercial and industrial town, focusing initially upon the domestic manufacture of woollen cloth carried out in three storey weavers' cottages, many of which still exist in the town today, their upper floor workrooms easily identified by the continuous rows of mullioned windows.

Woollen textiles remained the principal local industry until the end of the 18th century, complementing Rochdale's role as a small market community, but then with the onset of the Industrial Revolution the installation of the

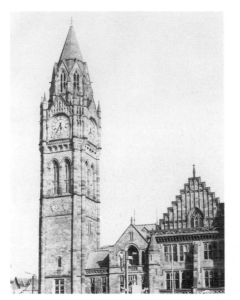

*The Clock Tower, Rochdale Town Hall*

new cotton spinning and weaving processes completely altered traditional patterns of work. Consequently the town experienced a major surge of growth as numerous cotton mills sprang up and rows of terraced houses were built close by as necessary accommodation for the employees. Other industries such as hat making, engineering and the manufacture of clocks and watches also developed alongside the spinning and weaving of cotton, but these were not sufficient to protect the town during times of recession in the textile trade, and it was during one such recession in 1844 that an attempt was made to establish co-operative trading. The result was the formation of the Rochdale Society of Equitable Pioneers, from which sprang the world-wide Co-operative Movement that even today largely adheres to the first Rochdale principles of trading.

If Rochdale people are justifiably proud of their history, they are equally proud of many of the town's buildings. The most impressive of these is undoubtedly the magnificent Town Hall, an outstanding product of Victorian ambition which was completed in 1871 at a cost of £155,000 (although the original estimate for the building was only £20,000!). Designed in the Gothic style so popular during the Victorian era the Town Hall is faced with local millstone grit and has a frontage of 264 feet along Rochdale's Esplanade, and whilst the present handsome clock tower is a replacement for the original one which was destroyed by fire in 1883 it is very much in keeping with the rest of the building.

The most important feature of the Town Hall's sumptuous interior is the Great Hall, reached by way of a fine Gothic Revival staircase and reminiscent of Westminster Hall by virtue of its mediaeval-style hammerbeam roof supported by angels. The stained glass

windows in the Great Hall are particularly impressive, providing a record of all the monarchs in England and said to be the finest modern examples of their kind in the country. The Mayor's Parlour also has some excellent stained glass, depicting each of the twelve months of the year, together with much of its original decoration, while in the Members' Lounge the walls display shields of all the town's mayors since 1856 (when Rochdale was granted its Charter of Incorporation as a Borough).

Immediately behind the Town Hall, situated high above the rest of the town centre on a wooded escarpment, is Rochdale Parish Church. Dedicated to St. Chad the present building largely reflects the renovation work carried out in the late 19th century, although it incorporates a restored 15th century font as well as some 13th century arches. Whilst St. Chad's is known to have existed in the 12th century it may well occupy the site of an early Saxon church, and indeed part of a Saxon wall still remains in the church grounds. Notable interior woodwork includes the handsome nave and chancel roofs, the beautifully carved 16th century screens and some pews carved by Tudor craftsmen who also made the communion table and parish chest. From the same period are some of the church brasses, depicting three knights in Tudor armour. Close to the church is the 18th century Vicarage, now in use as a museum, while another 'church connection' nearby is Broadfield Park. This was laid out as Rochdale's first public park on what was then church-owned land, and it now constitutes one link of a chain of parks and gardens around the heart of the town.

*Rochdale Pioneers Museum, Toad Lane*

Rochdale's other main historic building is the Rochdale Pioneers Museum on Toad Lane, at the opposite side of the town centre, and to reach it from the church we have to cross what is effectively the widest 'bridge' in the world — a covering over the River Roch which extends for a distance of 1,460 feet. This project was started in 1904 and completed in 1926, making possible the construction of Rochdale town centre as we see it today. The Toad Lane Museum is regarded as the home of the worldwide Co-operative Movement because it contains the original store opened by the famous Rochdale Equitable Pioneers Society on 21st December, 1844. Whilst this Society was not

*St. Chad's Parish Church, Rochdale*

the first Co-operative in Britain, nevertheless the Rochdale Principles of Co-operation which evolved from its decisions, methods and practices did provide the pattern for consumer co-operation not only in this country but also overseas. When the Pioneers first rented the ground floor of this building in Toad Lane they converted the front room into a store from which they sold a few basic commodities such as butter, sugar, flour, oatmeal and candles, and visitors can still see the original shop with its rudimentary furniture and scales. An upper room has been appropriately converted into an assembly room for meetings and small exhibitions, as the Pioneers originally used it for educational purposes themselves.

To the north of Rochdale is **Whitworth,** a pleasant township of stone built cottages stretching out along the main road which was to help put the district firmly on the map during the 18th century. In mediaeval times Whitworth was included within the parish of Rochdale as part of the Hundred of Salford, one of the eleven main divisions into which the County Palatine was divided in Norman times. Over the centuries the gradual destruction of the Forest of Rossendale in this part of Lancashire led to the extension of sheep farming here, and although small in area these farms led to the growth of weaving as Whitworth's first 'industry'.

Industrialisation, however, remained essentially a 'household' affair until an Act of Parliament in 1755 authorised the construction of a turnpike road through the valley. This ran from Manchester via Rochdale and Whitworth to Bacup, Burnley, Colne and Skipton, and it provided a ready means of transporting locally-manufactured goods to Manchester or Yorkshire. Impetus was thus given to local industry, with cotton gradually ousting wool in importance, and Whitworth slowly began to increase in size. Together with the spinning and weaving of cotton came the manufacture of textile machinery, while quarrying and coal mining also continued to make a contribution to the local economy. The stone from quarries on the moors above Whitworth has been used as the local building material for centuries, while at one time clay and shale were also excavated and used in the making of bricks. Whitworth stone is traditionally a hard, fine-grained sandstone with an exceptionally high crushing strength, so it is not surprising that stone from the local quarries should be used in the foundation for the Eiffel Tower.

Situated between Whitworth and Rochdale is **Healey Dell,** now a popular beauty spot but at one time an area which mimicked Whitworth's own industrial growth by virtue of the coal mines and cotton mills which were to be found on the wooded valley slopes here. As steam superseded water power so factory chimneys began to appear between the trees,

*Healey Dell near Whitworth*

but the chimneys have long since disappeared and the river once more flows through the Dell without any hint of industrial pollution. There are still, however, remains of old mills and weirs in the valley bottom which remind visitors of those days when cotton reigned supreme in the area. The dominant features now are two spectacular viaducts, one built in 1867 to carry the Rochdale-Bacup railway line and the other providing road access to nearby Broadley station.

Yet it is the natural features rather than the man-made ones which are of greatest importance in Healey Dell, not only the indigenous woodland of oak and birch which has established itself on the north-western side of the river but also the rather more varied plant life on the south-eastern slopes which has spread from the formal gardens of nearby Healey Hall. Then of course there is the wide range of animal life sheltering in the

natural habitats which now characterise the Dell. Even Homo Sapiens has found a place here, and a nature trail has been laid out through the area to help visitors enjoy its many distinctive facets.

Just over Brown Wardle Hill to the east of Whitworth lies Watergrove Reservoir, beneath which lies the ruins of Watergrove village, a once-thriving community. During the early part of this century over 200 people lived in the village, which then comprised 40 houses, two pubs, a chapel, a smithy and two mills, but in 1930 Rochdale Corporation chose Watergrove as a suitable site on which to build a large reservoir — so the villagers and many of the neighbouring hillside farmers had to go. Up to that point the village had sustained its existence by making use of the natural resources which surrounded it — coal was mined locally for heating and the generation of power, gritstone from nearby

*Terraced cottages in Wardle*

stood at the junction of two ancient highways — the road over Blackstone Edge and the packhorse route climbing out of the valley and then on to Todmorden — but the coming of the canal and railway changed all that, and by 1860 what had been a fairly remote Pennine clough used mainly by packhorse trains became a major traffic artery with a small stone built town established at the point where road, rail and canal met. By virtue of its location on the Lancashire-Yorkshire border Littleborough has traditionally been connected with both cotton and wool, although as a result of 19th century developments in communications Littleborough's local industry was quickly diversified by the introduction of engineering and other heavy manufacturing.

The transport heritage to be discovered in the area around Littleborough is both fascinating and unique, a fitting conclusion to the story of a county which owes so much of its life and culture to the communications initiatives of earlier generations. Within just a few square miles here one can find prehistoric trade routes, a Roman road, a complex network of packhorse trails, several turnpike roads with their characteristic tollhouses, the first canal and railway to conquer the Pennines, the M62 Trans-Pennine motorway, and even part of the Pennine Way long distance footpath!

The earliest tracks across the moors were certainly prehistoric, and from them developed a network of packhorse routes which for hundreds of years were the only means of travel between the towns of the plains. In between these times came the Roman road over Blackstone Edge, still to be seen high on the moors to the east of Littleborough where the paved section emerges suddenly just below the 1,000-foot contour and climbs steeply to the crest of a ridge. The paving here is made up of stone

outcrops was quarried and used as a building material and the valley slopes fed the sheep which yielded wool for the woollen industry. Yet the most important asset of the valley was its plentiful and vigorous supply of water, channelled into the Higher Slack and Wardle Brooks and used as a drinking supply, for generating power and for washing wool — but as the villagers were to discover, this plentiful supply of water was to ultimately prove Watergrove's undoing.

Just to the South of Watergrove Reservoir we come to the pretty village of **Wardle,** characterised by several 18th and 19th century stone cottages standing shoulder to shoulder around the Square — which is also the location for the village pub and two other establishments where a more traditional form of worship has been carried on over the years. In earlier days Wardle was an important staging post on the Long Causeway, a packhorse road climbing over the moors to Todmorden, and in many ways the village still retains much of its rural character through a sense of being in touch with the open countryside immediately to the north.

Then less than two miles to the east of Wardle is **Littleborough,** the last settlement of any

real significance before we reach the county boundary with Yorkshire — and, like neighbouring Wardle, a place which has grown up largely because of its position as a gateway to crossing the Pennines. Initially Littleborough was significant only because it

*The Roman road descending from Blackstone Edge*

setts with a line of larger 'troughed' stones down the centre, totally unlike the paving used in later packhorse trails. Although some have raised the question as to whether the road really was built by the Romans, it was probably part of a route from Mancunium to Eboracum or Olicana (Manchester to York or Ilkley), perhaps constructed by the Sixth Legion which came to Britain with Hadrian in AD 120 and was stationed on the Northumbrian Wall, at York and at Ribchester. At the foot of Blackstone Edge the road probably turned south, or joined a north-south route, along the side of what would then have been a marshy valley.

The packhorse trails which were established in the area from earlier prehistoric tracks also tended to avoid the swampy and heavily wooded valleys, crossing them only when absolutely necessary by means of a characteristic zig-zag track. Many of these

*The Coach House in Littleborough — part of its transport heritage*

*Littleborough Parish Church*

trails became major trade routes, with a particularly important one being the Reddyshore Scout Gate ('Gate' in this context coming from the old Norse word for a road). This was part of a main route between Rochdale and the Calder Valley, running at one point 300 feet above the floor of the Summit Pass to the north of Littleborough and linked by secondary tracks to the Long Causeway between Wardle and Walsden as well as to the primary north-south route from Rochdale to Burnley and Clitheroe (which was known as the Limersgate because it was used to transport lime from the Craven area of Yorkshire). The Reddyshore Scout Gate is a fine example of its kind, and at one point its length is paved with a double line of stones (rather than the customary single line) reflecting a later 'improvement' to accommodate wheeled traffic. It also offers some spectacular views, since it clings to the high parts of the valley side.

By the 18th century the old routes were becoming increasingly recognised as inadequate for the needs of the time, and after a petition to Parliament in 1734 complaining about the 'deep and ruinous' state of the road over Blackstone Edge this particular route was turnpiked. Under the Turnpike Acts other roads were also improved or rebuilt, often replacing the old packhorse trails in stages, and the toll bars were erected to collect the tolls which were required to pay for the upkeep of the road. With the toll bars came tollhouses, and in the Littleborough area three of these still exist — at Steanor-bottom (where the Todmorden Turnpike met the old Calderbrook route), at Stormer Bar (where the old Blackstone Edge road crosses the new one) and at Littleborough (where the Halifax and Todmorden roads meet).

Then later in the 18th century came the Rochdale Canal, the first all-weather route across the Pennines. The initial proposals for this link between the Bridgewater Canal in Manchester and the Calder and Hebble Navigation in Sowerby Bridge had been made in 1766, but protracted disputes held up its construction until 1794. Then in 1798 the first stretch of the canal was opened from Sowerby Bridge to Rochdale, with completion through to Manchester being achieved by 1804. The Rochdale Canal was not only the first but also the most successful canal to cross the Pennines, being built as a 'broad' canal walk able to take barges 70 feet long by 14 feet wide (unlike the Huddersfield Narrow Canal just to the south). It was also quite remarkable in that it survived the competition from the railways, and its peak year was in 1888 when it carried 750,000 tons of freight traffic.

The Rochdale Canal was of benefit to the area in another way, in that it assisted with the drainage of the valley floor even though it also drew a supply of water from a complex of nearby reservoirs. One of these was Hollingworth Lake to the south of Littleborough, which developed into something of a pleasure resort in the mid-1800s in the days before cheap excursions to the seaside were possible. Here could be found several pubs, a number of open-air dancing stages, and a mammoth steam-driven roundabout as well as a busy steam ferryboat across to the pleasure gardens on the southern shore. Although those times have since passed the 'lake' is now enjoying a renaissance as the nucleus of a popular country park, with the opportunity for sailing and boating as well as waymarked circular walks around the water's edge .

The 19th century in Littleborough also saw proposals for a railway between Manchester and Leeds, this being first mooted in 1825 and surveyed just a few weeks after the opening of the Liverpool and Manchester Railway in September 1830. As was the case with the canal disputes initially held up construction of the line, but by July 1839 the first length was opened from Manchester to Littleborough. Then in 1841 the Summit Tunnel was completed, and the first trans-Pennine railway began running through-trains in March of that year. When built in 1841 Summit Tunnel was the longest railway tunnel in the world, and it has remained a lasting tribute to the men who built it.

Another remarkable engineering and constructional achievement in this part of Lancashire is of course the M62 Trans-Pennine motorway. Work on the Littleborough section began in May 1968, and some of the difficulties which had to be faced in taking a six-lane highway over the Pennine barrier were enormous — in many places the peat was 20-feet thick, cuttings over 100 feet deep had to be blasted through solid rock, wind speeds of up to 120 miles per hour had to be allowed for when building bridges and snow could be expected any time between November and May! The Rakewood viaduct to the south east of Hollingworth Lake is one of the most notable engineering feats of the motorway, a surprisingly elegant structure which reaches a height of 140 feet above the valley below. Severe cross-winds can be experienced on the viaduct, and at the western end joints have been incorporated to allow for the considerable expansion and contraction experienced as a result of substantial temperature variations. Between the viaduct and the crest of the Pennines at Rockingtones the motorway climbs steeply, curving along the shoulder of the moor and then into a cutting 120 feet deep which is designed to keep the roadway below the prevailing cloud level. Extra large drainage channels have also been cut on this section to take the heavy run-off of water from the moor.

In a county of superlatives the M62 Trans-Pennine motorway has been called 'The Last Superlative', by virtue of its remarkable engineering achievements. It also completes a quite unique 'collection' of transport routes in this part of Lancashire, symbols of the county's growth and development over the centuries.

*Hollingworth Lake and Rakewood Viaduct*

# INDEX OF PLACES AND PEOPLE

## PEOPLE

# SOURCES OF INFORMATION USED IN 'THE TREASURES OF LANCASHIRE'

## CHAPTER 1

### LANCASHIRE — THE LAND OF PLENTY

A History of Lancashire — J.J. Bagley
Lancashire — J.J. Bagley
Lancashire — J.D. Marshall
Lancashire's Early Industrial Heritage — John Champness
Lancashire's Villages — Jessica Lofthouse

## CHAPTER 2

### LANCASTER AND LONSDALE

The City of Lancaster — Lancaster City Museum Service
Prospect of Lancaster — Architects Journal
The City of Lancaster: Historical Sketch — T. Pape
A New Walk around Historic Lancaster — John Champness
A North Lancashire Archaeological Trail — Lancaster City Council
Churches in the Lancaster Area — Lancaster City Council
Lord Ashton and Lancaster - Lancaster City Council
HMP Lancaster: An Hisorical Outline — Directorate of Works, London
Williamson Park — Lancaster City Council
Historic Houses in the Lancaster Area — Lancaster City Council
Caton: Past and Present — Caton Village Exhibition Committee
A Pocket Guide to Hornby
Friends in Wray — Emmeline Garnett
Return to the Lune Valley — Stan and Freda Trott
Glasson Dock: A Walk Around the Village — J.D. Hayhurst
Heysham Village and Churches — Lancaster City Council
The Story of Sunderland Point — Hugh Cunliffe
The Changing Face of Morecambe — Lancaster City Council
Garnforth Official Guide
Warton: The Story of a North Lancashire Village — Anne Morley and
Muriel Smalley
Silverdale Official Guide
Silverdale: Its History, People and Places — T.E. Bolton and I.J. Fogg
Leighton Hall, Carnforth — Guide to the House
Borwick Hall — J. Rawlinson Ford

## CHAPTER 3

### THE FYLDE AND THE WYRE

The Over Wyre Historical Journal, Volumes 1, 2 3 and 4 — Pilling and
District Historical Society
Guide to Preesall and Knott End
Poulton-le-Fylde Official Guide
Poulton-le-Fylde Parish Church: A Short History and Guide
Fleetwood: A Town is Born — Bill Curtis
The Fleetwood Ferry — Wyre District Libraries
Early Buildings of Fleetwood — Wyre District Libraries
A Short History of Fleetwood — Wyre District Libraries
Fleetwood: A Town Trail — Martin Ramsbottom and Hilary Knight
The Port of Fleetwood — Wyre District Libraries
Out and About in Fleetwood and Wyre — Catherine Rothwell
History of the Marsh Mill, Thornton — R.B. Bulter, H.B. Ellwood and
J.A. Tillotson
A History of Blackpool — Blackpool Borough Council
Stanley Park Conservation Area Leaflet — Blackpool Borough Council
Lytham Town Trail — Lytham St. Annes Civic Society
Companion to the Fylde — R K Davies
Lytham Windmill — Lytham St. Annes Civic Society
Lytham St. Annes and the Sea — Lytham St. Annes Civic Society
The Story of Wrea Green Schools — Ann Berry
The Story of Wrea Green Church — Ann Berry
Kirkham Town Guide
Traditional Houses of the Fylde — Centre for
North West Regional Studies
A Brief History of Elswick Church — Roy Garlick
Churchtown Village Trail — Churchtown Society
Garstang Official Guide
Garstang and Over Wyre in Times Past — Catherine Rothwell
Shireshead 1520-1987: Picture of a Parish — E. Mary Higman
From Inglewhite Cross — D.M. Cowell

The Secret Treasure of Chaigley — J.E. Bamber
Woodplumpton: Its History in Religion, Houses and Families —
Rev. George Jackson
Broughton Roundabout — Rev. George Jackson
A Short History of Broughton Parish Church — F. Eden Wilson and
Roger D. Houghton

## CHAPTER 4

### PRESTON AND THE RIBBLE VALLEY

Ribchester: A Short History and Guide — A.C. Hodge and J.F. Ridge
Ribchester Parish Church: A Goodly Heritage — J.H. Finch
Stonyhurst Revisited — A.M. Perry
A History of Chipping — Stuart Crainer
Historic Walks Around Bleasdale — John Dixon and Jaana Järvinen
Waddington: A Village Trail — The Curriculum and Professional Centre
Blackburn
The Parish Church of St. Helen, Waddington — Nora Mary Goodchild
Clitheroe Discovery Trail — Curriculum Development Centre, Burnley
Clitheroe Castle — Curriculum Development Centre, Burnley
A Walk Through Clitheroe — Ribble Valley Borough Council
All Saints Church Pendleton — Derek Layland
A Guide to Pendleton
Exploring Bowland and the Hodder — Ron Freethy
Foulridge History Trail — Fay Oldland
The Lancashire Witches — W.R. Mitchell
A Curse on Pendle — Burnley Curriculum Development Centre
Short Walks in the Barley Area — North West Water
Newchurch-in-Pendle: Folklore, Fact and Fiction — Clifford H. Byrne
Window on Whalley — Jimmy Fell
Whalley Discovery Trail — Curriculum Development Centre, Burnley
Historic Walks in the Ribble Valley — John Dixon
A History of Lovely Hall
Mellor: A Short History — T. Counsell
Ribble Valley Guide
Samlesbury: A Short History — Alistair C. Hodge
St. Leonard the Less, Samlesbury — G. Clayton
Hoghton Tower — Frank Singleton

## CHAPTER 5

### EAST LANCASHIRE UPLANDS

A Walk through Old Blackburn — Blackburn Recreation Department
Rishton Official Guide
Walking the Paths of Great Harwood — Great Harwood Civic Society
Great Harwood Gleanings — Louie Pollard
Old Harwood — Louie Pollard and Harry E. Eaton
The Story of a Village Church — Louie Pollard
Great Harwood Official Guide
Clayton-le-Moors Official Guide
Church Official Guide
The Haworth Art Gallery — Borough of Hyndburn
Accrington Official Guide
Towneley Hall — Burnley Borough Council
Briarfield Official Guide
The History of Marsden and Nelson — W. Bennett
Colne Official Guide
Walks in a Lancashire Township — Roger Frost and Malcolm Higgin
Wycoller — John Bently
A Guide to Sheddon Clough — Lancashire County Council
The Borough of Pendle Official Guide
Worsthorne Church and the Thursbys — Leslie Chapples
A Pennine Parish: The History of Cliviger — Titus Thornber
Rural Houses of the Lancashire Pennines 1560-1760 — RCHME
All O'er t'Parish — Lancashire County Council
Burnley Official Guide
Bacup Official Handbook
Rawtenstall Official Handbook
Haslingden Town Centre Trail — Haslingden Local History Society
Rossendale Official Guide
Rossendale Rambles — Ian Goldthorpe
Darwen Official Guide
Jumbles Country Park — West Pennine Moors Area Management
Committee

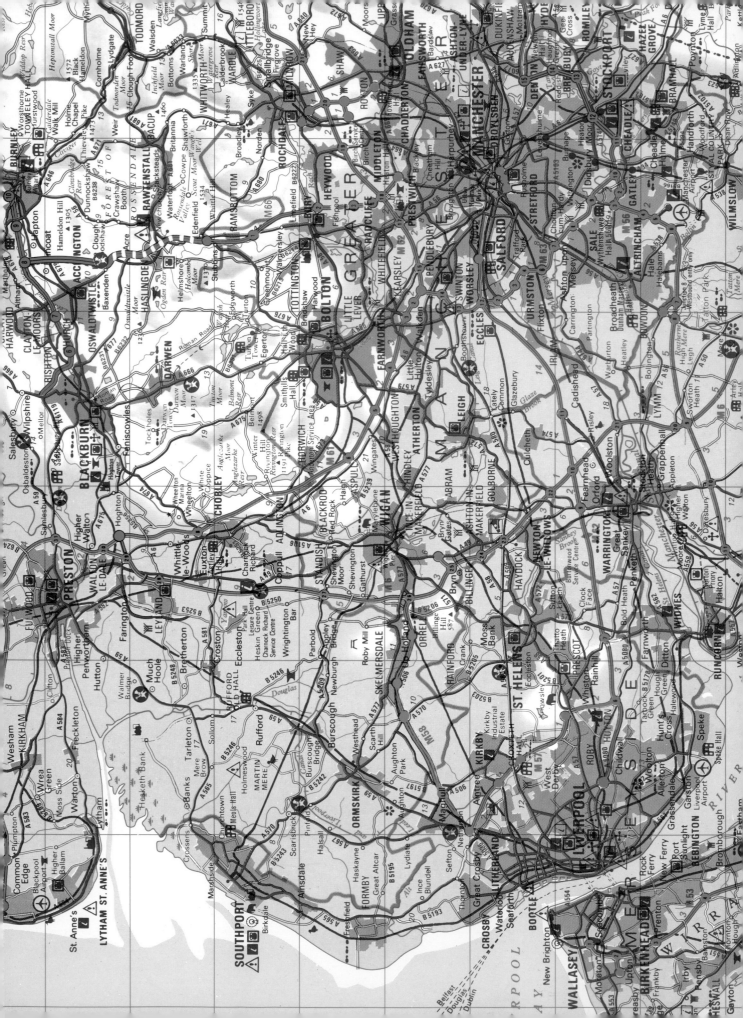

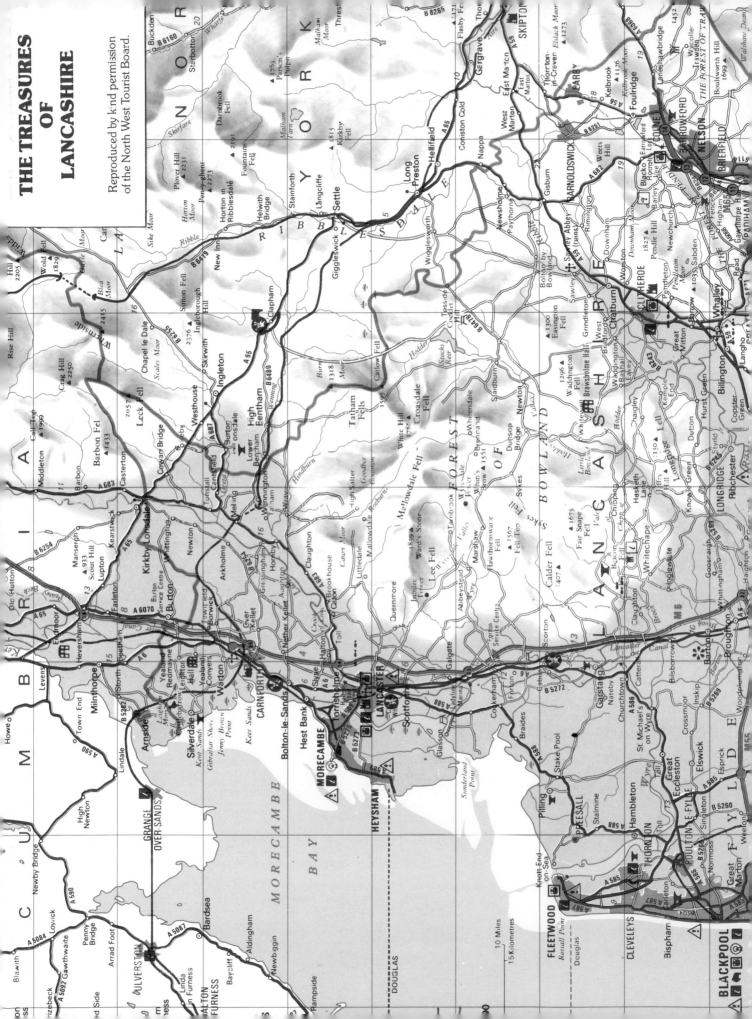

# THE TREASURES OF LANCASHIRE

Reproduced by kind permission of the North West Tourist Board.

Borough of Blackburn Official Guide
Rivington Terraced Gardens Trail — West Pennine Moors Area
Management Committee
The Enchanted Hills — George Birtill
Chorley Official Guide
Withnell Fold Village Trail — Withnell Fold Conservation Society

## CHAPTER 6

### WEST LANCASHIRE PLAIN

Over the Five Barred Gate — George Birtill
Leyland Cross Heritage Walk — South Ribble Borough Council
South Ribble Official Guide
Leyland Official Guide
Euxton Parish Guide
Astley Hall — G.A. Birtill
Astley Hall Official Guide
Eccleston and Heston in times past — Alan Marsden and
Alex Threlfall
A History of the church and parish of St. Michael and All Angels,
Croston — Gordon Earl
Bretherton in times past — Geoffrey Coxhead
125th Anniversary of Southport Pier
Southport Town Trail — Southport Civic Society
Viking Village: The Story of Formby — Edith Kelly (The Formby Society)
Maghull Official Guide
Lydiate and Maghull in times past — John K. Rowlands
Aughton Official Guide
Ormskirk Town Hall — Vivian Keyte
Ormskirk Official Guide
Ormskirk Parish Church
North Meols to South Ribble — John Cotterall
Rufford Old Hall — The National Trust
Lathom Park Chapel — A Short Illustrated History
West Lancashire Official Guide
Skelmersdale and Holland Official Guide
Rainford Official Guide
Tourist Guide to West Lancashire
A History of Rainford — Martin Rigby
Kirkby Official Guide
Melling with Cunscough — Edward E. Newton

## CHAPTER 7

### LIVERPOOL AND ITS HINTERLAND

City of Liverpool Planning Handbook
Liverpolitana — Peter Howell Williams
Jesse Hartley, Dock Engineer to the Port of Liverpool 1924-60 —
Nancy Ritchie-Oakes
Sefton Park — Sefton Park Civic Society
A Short History of Mossley Hill — Mossley Hill Residents Association
City of Liverpool Official Guide
Speke Hall — Merseyside County Museums
History of Much Woolton — The Woolton Society
Walks around Gateacre — The Gateacre Society
A History of West Derby — John Cooper and David Power
Liverpool Conservation Areas — Liverpool Heritage Bureau
Buildings of Liverpool — Liverpool Heritage Bureau
Croxteth — Merseyside County Museums
Litherland Official Guide
Bootle Official Guide
Crosby Official Guide
Horological Workshops in Prescot — Merseyside County Museums
Prescot: A Town Trail — Knowsley MBC
St. Helens Official Guide
Whiston Official Guide
The Story of Rainhill — R. Dickinson and R. Dickinson
Knowsley Official Guide
Spike Island Visitors Guide — Mersey Valley Ranger Service
West Bank Promenade Conservation Area — Halton Borough Council
Widnes Official Guide
Warrington Town Hall — Warrington Borough Council
Warrington Official Borough Handbook

## CHAPTER 8

### THE MANCHESTER METROPOLIS

Greater Manchester County Guide
Manchester: A Short History of its Development — W.H. Shercliff
Manchester Conservation, The Way Forward — Manchester Literary and
Philosophical Society
Guide Across Manchester — Philip Atkins
A Guide to Manchester Cathedral
Castlefield — City of Manchester
Castlefield — David Brumhead
Eccles Official Guide
Irlam Official Guide
Metropolitan Borough of Trafford Official Guide
Victoria Park, Manchester — Maurice Spiers
Looking Back at Rusholme and Fallowfield — Peter Helm and Gay Sussex
Didsbury's Railway — Didsbury Civic Society
Hatting in Denton — H.C. Caffrey
Droylsden Official Guide
Tameside Official Guide
Ashton-under-Lyne Official Handbook
Old Ashton — Town Trail
The Story of Mossley — Alfred Holt/Mossley Civic Society
Saddleworth Historical Society Local Interest Trails 1-9
Oldham Official Handbook
Royton Official Guide
The Cotton Mills of Oldham — Duncan Gurr and Julian Hunt
Failsworth Official Handbook
Chadderton — A Brief Historical Sketch
Early Middleton: A Centenary Celebration — Middleton Civic Association
Guide to Prestwich
City of Salford: Where to Go, What to See — Salford City Council
Worsley Official Guide
A Guide to the City of Salford
Atherton: The Official Guide
Local Interest Trails and Local History Fact Sheets — Worsley Civic Trust and
Amenities Society
Tyldesley Official Guide
Leigh Local Plan — Wigan MBC
Leigh Official Guide
Wigan Town Centre Plan — Wigan MBC
Wigan Metropolitan Borough — Wigan MBC
Wigan Town Centre Trail — Wigan MBC
Wigan Pier — Wigan MBC
Wigan — The Borough Guide
Westhoughton Official Guide
Blackrod Official Guide
Horwich: A Century of Railway History — Bolton Environmental Education
Project
The Buildings of Bolton — Bolton and District Civic Trust
The West Pennine Moors — Lancashire County Council
Bolton Survey — C.H. Saxelby
Barrow Bridge History Trail — Bolton and District Civic Trust
Smithills Hall — Bolton MBC
The Best of Bolton — Bolton MBC
Bolton Town Centre History Trail — Bolton and District Civic Trust
Little Lever Official Guide
Radcliffe Official Guide
Whitefield Guide
Bury Heritage Series, Nos. 1, 3, 5 and 6 — The Federation and
Bury Civic Societies
Bury Town Centre Conservation Area Report — Greater
Manchester Council
Bury Official Guide
History of Greenmount — C.B. Taylor
Holcombe Conservation Area Report — Greater Manchester Council
Holcombe Historic Trail — Bury MBC
Rossendale Rambles — Ian Goldthorpe
Ramsbottom Official Guide
Ramsbottom Conservation Area Report — Greater Manchester Council
Brooksbottoms, Pot Green and Summerseat Conservation Area Report —
Greater Manchester Council
Ramsbottom Historic Trail — Bury MBC
Mount Pleasant Conservation Area Report — Greater Manchester Council
Rochdale — Rochdale MBC
Toad Lane Museum — The Co-operative Union
Rochdale MB Official Handbook
Whitworth Official Guide
Littleborough — Littleborough Coach House Trust
Littleborough Heritage Trails — Littleborough Coach House Trust